T0393139

Metamorphic Imagery in Ancient Chinese Art and Religion

Metamorphic Imagery in Ancient Chinese Art and Religion demonstrates that the concept of metamorphism was central to ancient Chinese religious belief and practices from at least the late Neolithic period through the Warring States Period of the Zhou dynasty.

Central to the authors' argument is the ubiquitous motif in early Chinese figurative art, the metamorphic power mask. While the motif underwent stylistic variation over time, its formal properties remained stable, underscoring the image's ongoing religious centrality. It symbolized the metamorphosis, through the phenomenon of death, of royal personages from living humans to deceased ancestors who required worship and sacrificial offerings. Treated with deference and respect, the royal ancestors lent support to their living descendants, ratifying and upholding their rule; neglected, they became dangerous, even malevolent. Employing a multidisciplinary approach that integrates archaeologically recovered objects with literary evidence from oracle bone and bronze inscriptions to canonical texts, all situated in the appropriate historical context, the study presents detailed analyses of form and style, and of change over time, observing the importance of relationality and the dynamic between imagery, materials, and affects.

This book is a significant publication in the field of early China studies, presenting an integrated conception of ancient art and religion that surpasses any other work now available.

Elizabeth Childs-Johnson is a specialist in ancient Chinese art, archaeology, paleography, and religion. Her research focuses on a comprehensive interdisciplinary approach to identifying belief systems in early China, specifically covering the late Neolithic Jade Age through the Bronze Age, ca. 3500–3rd century BCE. She currently holds the position of Research Professor at the Institute of Asian Studies, Old Dominion University.

John S. Major taught at Dartmouth from 1971 to 1984, and since then has been an independent scholar based in New York. A leading authority on ancient Chinese religion and cosmology, he is also a highly regarded translator of classical texts. Much of his work, like the present volume, has been collaborative.

Metamorphic Imagery in Ancient Chinese Art and Religion

Elizabeth Childs-Johnson and John S. Major

Routledge
Taylor & Francis Group

LONDON AND NEW YORK

First published 2023
by Routledge
4 Park Square, Milton Park, Abingdon, Oxon OX14 4RN

and by Routledge
605 Third Avenue, New York, NY 10158

Routledge is an imprint of the Taylor & Francis Group, an informa business

© 2023 Elizabeth Childs-Johnson and John S. Major

British Library Cataloguing-in-Publication Data
A catalogue record for this book is available from the British Library

ISBN: 978-1-032-37649-3 (hbk)
ISBN: 978-1-032-37657-8 (pbk)
ISBN: 978-1-003-34124-6 (ebk)

DOI: 10.4324/9781003341246

Typeset in Times New Roman
by codeMantra

Contents

Figures

13.6 cm, width: 8 cm. (K) Red painted ceramic li tripod with the abstraction of semi-human head, Xiajiadian, Inner Mongolia. (L) Large bronze semi-human head, Sanxingdui, Sichuan. No. 1 Cache. (M) Rubbing and drawing of the semi-human head and heraldic bird on two different sides of a jade gui blade, National Museum of Asian Art, Washington, D.C. (N) Heraldic birds crowning semi-human head, Tianmen, Hubei, Longshan Period, Shijiahe Culture. (J) Tripod li and lei vessel types with painted images of cloud scrolls and humanoid with crown extensions and extended mouth, Xiajiadian, Liaoning Province. (A), (C–E), and (O) were published with the permission of the chief excavator, Sun Zhouyong as provided in the archaeological report to the Institute of Archaeology CASS 2019: 9. All drawings by Margaret Panoti. (B) After Henan 2001: colorpl 6.1 and drawing by Margaret Panoti. (D) Drawing by Margaret Panoti. (I) Zhongguo Shehui 1998: colorpls III.2 and XI.3. (J) After Qijia yuqi: no 155. (K) Photo: University of Pittsburgh, index.html pitt.edu. (L) After Sichuan 1999: colorpl 4 (K1.5). (M) After Childs-Johnson and Gu 2009: colorpls 7-06. (N) http://en.hubei.gov.cn/news/newslist/201601/t20160120_780229.shtml

four standard metamorphic tropes of Bronze Age China (deity power mask; dragon, mythic bird, and flight). Leigudun, Hubei, last phase, Springs and Autumns/early Warring States, 5th century BCE. (D) Displayed *yi* images grasping a pair of wild animals seen in compositions featuring the liminal hunt in the after, other world. (E) Shang pictograph emblem of displayed figure flanked by hunting animals and a hunting dog. (A) Hubei 1999: Figures 21–22. (B) Jingzhou Museum, Jingzhou, Hubei. (C) *Hubei meishu* 1995: colorpls 77–79 and Hubeisheng 1999: Figures 21–22. (D) Munakata 1991. (E) Henan 1999: Figure 104:3 213

8.9 Whole and abstract variations of representative metamorphic hybrid deities as a tiger with head extensions of stag horns and as part tiger with bird wings, or as a bamboo crafted image, Spring and Autumn–Warring States periods. (A) Addorsed hybrid tiger deities, lacquered wood, Xu Jialing M9, Xichuan, Henan. Henan Provincial Institute of Archaeology and Cultural Relics, Zhengzhou, Henan. (B) Squatting bronze tiger with turquoise inlay, Xu Jialing, Xichuan, Henan. Henan Provincial Institute of Archaeology and Cultural Relics, Zhengzhou, Henan (C) Opposing pair of hybrid deities supporting four sets of 32 stone chimes, Leigudun, Hubei. (D) Ground plan of burial and context of bamboo crafted hybrid metamorphic deity. (A) After Creative Commons CC0 1.0 Universal Public Domain Dedication, Daderot, exhibited Portland Art Museum Nov. 2, 2017 DSC0851.jpg. (B) S Lee 1997: colorpl 46. (C) Hubei 1989: Figures 59, 61. (D) Wang H 2003:7 216

8.10 The liminal hunt as narrative featured on various vessel types, Eastern Zhou Period. (A) Detail of bird headed and winged human archer depicted as part of a hunting narrative (B) Rubbing of body of *hu* vessel, Liulige, Henan. (C) Round bronze lidded *dou* vessel with narrative of a spirit hunt, Walters Art Gallery. (A) For this detail see related images in Fig 8B for reference. (B) *Shanbiaozhen yu Liuliko*: pl 93 and Weber 1966: Figure 43A. (C) Weber 1966; Figure 52 217

8.11 Variations of the bird person (usually a winged human in fetal position with bird head) from the Jade Age through Eastern Zhou periods, 3000–300 BCE. (A) Two views of a jade birdman from Xingan, Jiangxi, Middle Shang period. (B) Three views of bird mount plus birdman with wings in bronze, from Jingmen Tianxingguan, Hubei, Warring States period. (C) Jade birdman, Zhaolingshan, M77: 71,

Preface

This book is the product of a long-term collaboration between its two authors. Our aim has been to integrate our individual disciplinary backgrounds to achieve a new way of approaching the study of ancient Chinese art and religion. One of us (Childs-Johnson), a recognized expert in the study of ancient jades, brings to the project a comprehensive knowledge of archaeological sites in China and the perspectives of archaeology and art history. The other is a specialist in early Chinese intellectual history, with expertise in ancient Chinese cosmology. Using the methodologies and insights of these fields and others, we have been able to devise and refine a theory of the origins and development of an elite or royal-based concept of metamorphism. By approaching the development of that religion from a multidisciplinary point of view, we have been able to avoid the monofocal approach that has characterized most studies of ancient China.

As we explain in the book's Introduction (Chapter 1), the principal motif in early Chinese figurative art, the metamorphic power mask, played a central role in ancient Chinese religion. We demonstrate that this power image represented metamorphosis, through the phenomenon of death, of royal personages from living humans to deceased ancestors who required worship and sacrificial offerings. Their visages bespoke their numinous power. Treated with suitable deference and generous respect, the royal ancestors could act in support of their living descendants, ratifying and upholding their rule; neglected, they became dangerous and even malevolent. Over the long period covered by this book, the privilege of worshipping spiritually transformed ancestors expanded from a narrow ruling lineage to a wider elite, and the symbolism of the metamorphic power image evolved under the influence of changing socio-political structures.

This book has gone through many drafts over a period of many years. During that time, the manuscript, or parts of it, has been read and critiqued – sometimes vigorously – by a number of readers. We have taken advantage of these critiques to improve the book. We have worked hard to provide readers with insights into the nature and inner workings of imagery and belief systems, reviewing appropriate literary and archaeological data from the Jade and Bronze Ages. We have ourselves been enlightened by our progress in isolating appropriate metamorphic icons to solidify our arguments. It has been very rewarding to learn from one another in the course of writing this book.

There is still much work to be done, particularly in isolating terms beyond *yi* ("to become spiritually empowered") and *bin* ("to identify with and host a divinity"), and objects of worship beyond the familiar celestial deities Shang Di, Tian, and Tai Yi. Vast quantities of new evidence in the form of documents on wooden slips and visual materials in a variety of media are becoming available in contemporary China, a flood of archaeological material that threatens to overwhelm the scholarly world. The multidisciplinary path that informs this book, applied to evidentiary materials old and new, promises to yield clearer and more profound answers to questions about the religious life of ancient China. The Chinese traditional belief in nature's power(s), rooted in the remote past, appears everlasting and completely tethered to artistic expression.

Although we anticipate that this book may be controversial, it is our hope that any controversy it engenders will advance the study of early China. We are pleased to offer this book to the scholarly world.

Elizabeth Childs-Johnson
John S. Major
Norfolk and New York City, July 2022

1 Introduction

In this book, we introduce, and present evidence for, a theory about the development of ancient Chinese religion. Our thesis is that the concept of metamorphism was central to ancient Chinese religious belief and practices from at least the late Neolithic period through the Warring States Period of the Zhou dynasty, i.e. about 3500 BCE to the 4th/3rd c BCE, and remained fundamental to "Chinese" ways of thinking about the world and human interactions with that world. Central to our argument is the principal motif in early Chinese figurative art, the metamorphic image or metamorphic power mask, anachronistically known in Shang and Western Zhou studies as the *taotie* 饕餮. We show that, while that motif underwent considerable stylistic variation over time, its formal properties remained remarkably consistent, underscoring the image's ongoing religious centrality. In these pages, we demonstrate that this power image represented metamorphosis of royal personages from living humans to deceased ancestors who required worship and sacrificial offerings. Their visages bespoke their numinous power. By numinous, we mean "spiritual and awe-inspired emotion aroused by the presence of divinity." Treated with suitable deference and generous respect, the royal ancestors could act in support of their living descendants, ratifying and upholding their rule; neglected, they became dangerous and even malevolent. Over the long period covered by this book, the privilege of worshipping spiritually transformed ancestors expanded from a narrow ruling lineage to a wider elite, and the symbolism of the metamorphic power image evolved under the influence of changing socio-political structures.

Any satisfactory exploration of religion in early China and its manifestation in material form clearly demands a comprehensive and holistic approach, but extant studies of early Chinese art fall short in that respect. Some monographic studies of imagery were published as early as the 1940s. In more recent decades, some scholars have argued against any attempt to discern religious or any other content in the decorative motifs of ancient Chinese art; others, while not necessarily denying that such motifs were meaningful, were skeptical about discerning that meaning. None of those studies could be characterized as multidisciplinary or interdisciplinary.[1] Here we take a new and multidisciplinary approach, relying primarily on

DOI: 10.4324/9781003341246-1

visual material, especially archaeologically documented works of art, placed within appropriate historical context and making use of oracle bone and bronze inscriptions and literary evidence from both historically transmitted and archaeologically recovered texts. Our approach is culture-historical, drawing inferences from the development of material culture, as defined and reviewed at length by Bruce Trigger in his *History of Archaeological Thought* (2006: 211–313). We do not concern ourselves with such topics as the origins and evolution of Chinese states, the rise of urbanization, and the dynamics of relations between the center and the periphery, subjects that have been well covered by a number of recent scholarly studies that build on the pioneering earlier studies of K.C. Chang.[2] In the chapters that follow, we allude briefly to social and political matters, but always and only insofar as such topics provide context for our study of metamorphism and religion.

Our study makes detailed analyses of form and style, and of change over time; thus, we observe the importance of relationality and the dynamic between imagery, materials, and affects, as articulated by A.M. Jones and A. Cochrane in their 2018 study, *The Archaeology of Art, Materials, Practices, Affects.* That study makes the point that to elucidate style and meaning one needs to recognize the importance of effective practices such as gesture, exaggeration, assembly and disassembly, or the use of distinctions in color. The latter considerations "enable key concepts, such as style and meaning, to be re-imagined as affective practices," particularly in the field of ancient art and imagery.

In these pages, we use a few terms that are not yet fully established as part of the discourse on early China and which, therefore, require some discussion and clarification. For example, we make frequent use of the term "Jade Age." It refers to the phase at the end of the late Neolithic period, ca. 4500–2000 BCE, when the technology of jade-working reached a high point and objects of finely worked jade symbolized the apex of wealth, prestige, and cultural power.[3] After about 2000 BCE, while jade retained considerable cultural power, it became eclipsed by bronze vessels as prestige goods.

The term "East Asian Heartland Region" was coined by Victor Mair[4] as a way of avoiding the anachronism of using the word "China" to refer to the territory that became "China" in historic times but was not yet "China" in antiquity. It also invites consideration of the ethno-linguistic and cultural diversity of the region in ancient times. It encompasses the land from the northern edges of the North China Plain to the southern reaches of the middle and lower Yangzi River Valley, Sichuan, the Wei, Han, Huai, and other major river valleys, and adjacent territories. The great majority of the sites discussed in these pages are within the East Asian Heartland Region.

In using the term "metamorphic" we refer to two distinct but closely related phenomena: on the one hand, figurative imagery that can be viewed as an image that is mask-like when viewed as a whole (a deified ancestor transformed) but which may dissolve into its component parts; and on the other hand, the ability of a person – whether a living king or a dead royal ancestor – to achieve a state of metamorphic empowerment (*yi* 異) that endows the recipient with special powers and religious efficacy. Evidence for the power of metamorphic imagery is likewise of two kinds: the imagery itself, expressed through art in media including ceramics, jade, ivory, bone, bronze, and lacquer; and, with the emergence of writing in the Shang period, oracle-bone inscriptions and other divinatory texts of later eras. Physical evidence shows that metamorphic imagery in early Sinitic cultures went back to Neolithic times, reached its apogee in the Shang, and continued to exist and evolve as a cultural meme in the Western Zhou, Spring and Autumn, and Warring States periods and beyond. As we demonstrate, metamorphic imagery in art and religion was continuous from the late Neolithic Jade Age through the Warring States period.

Much ink has been devoted to metamorphosis from human to animal in western cultures of ancient and more recent times, though more often in the context of literary rather than artistic genres. What most of these studies and our own have in common is the belief in some form of transformation, whether it is labeled zoanthropy or therianthropy, or shapeshifting.[5] The Chinese context is enhanced by paleographic data, which is not the case in the Mesolithic Danube boulder art nor does the Chinese case depend on mythic associations, although the latter may be revealed in more detail with the discovery of excavated dateable texts and references. Other terms specifically relevant in the ancient China case include *yi* 異 in Shang oracle bone inscriptions. As noted above, *yi* means "metamorphic power" or "to be metamorphically empowered" (Childs-Johnson 2008). A king alone, "the one man (*you yi ren* 有一人)," maintained metamorphic empowerment and continued to exercise that power after death. The ubiquitous metamorphic power mask motif on Shang ritual sacrificial bronzes is probably a representation of the metamorphically empowered ancestor-king. The ability of the living king to *yi* is the basis for our use of the term "institutional shamanism" with reference to China's early monarchical states (see below).

Bin 賓 is another Shang oracle-bone word with special relevance to the concept of metamorphosis (Childs-Johnson 2008). It means not "to visit" as has been commonly identified, but "to spiritually accompany and identify with" a deceased royal ancestor or a deity such as Di, the High Cosmological God of Shang religion. Both *yi* and *bin* were royal prerogatives.

We use the terms "metamorphic power image" and "metamorphic power mask" to refer to the composite motif, described above, that symbolizes a royal personage transformed by death into a deified royal ancestor. That motif is almost ubiquitously, but incorrectly, known as the *taotie* 饕餮 in the literature on ancient China.[6] The inadequacy of the term has long been known, but it remains in use. As one prominent scholar rationalized, "I have therefore reluctantly opted for the traditional name, *taotie*, which was surely not used by the Shang but has the advantage, at least, of a thousand years of usage" (Allan 2016: 29). That will not do. Our objection to *taotie* has two bases: it is anachronistic, and it is misleading. The term does not appear in Shang oracle bone inscriptions, Zhou bronze inscriptions, or early literary sources. Glossed as meaning "glutton," it appears in late Warring States and Qin-Han texts as one of many monstrous beings that inhabited the imaginary world of that era. It is described as ravenously hungry but unable to swallow because (like the metamorphic power mask) it lacks a lower jaw. (It may well be that the *taotie* monster arose in the imagination of the time to provide a "back-story" for the metamorphic mask motif that was well known from highly prized heirloom antiquities such as Shang bronzes.) The term became further entrenched in the vocabulary of art history in the Song dynasty when a vogue for collecting antiquities stimulated the production of catalogs of collections in which the metamorphic power mask was described as *taotie*. This anachronism makes clear the inappropriateness of using *taotie* to discuss the religion of Jade Age and Bronze Age China. It is also misleading, because what should be seen as a motif symbolizing the immense spiritual power of the deceased royal ancestors is reduced and trivialized as a depiction of an unimportant Warring States imaginary monster with peculiar eating habits. It is time, and indeed past time, to retire the term *taotie*.

Our employment of the expression "institutional shamanism" requires some explanation. The term "shamanism" appears often in discussions of ancient religion, including that of China. Sometimes it is deployed in a restricted sense as a phenomenon of tribal societies (e.g., those of Siberia); but often it is used imprecisely in ways that drain the term of meaning. As Russell Kirkland put it, "A specific problem here is the widespread use of the term 'shamanism' for any kind of 'popular' religious activity in which humans interact with unseen personal beings. Daoists of later periods certainly did, at times, interact with unseen personal beings, but by that token Krishna in his chariot or Moses on his mountaintop would have to be explained as having 'shamanic origins'" (Kirkland 2004: 277, quoted in Michael 2015: 282 n. 29). There is little reason to doubt that shamanism in the "classical" tribal sense was widely practiced in ancient China, by numerous populations in the East Asian Heartland Region. Here, however, we are concerned with shamanic practices at the pinnacle of ancient Chinese society, that is, in some of the ritual obligations of the king himself. These involved making regular contact with the metamorphically transformed royal ancestors (Kirkland's "unseen personal beings") on behalf of the whole community. This probably involved the king's attainment of an alternate state of consciousness using the techniques of shamanism such as chanting, drumming, masked dancing, and possibly the ingestion of psychoactive substances. We refer to these practices as institutional shamanism.

We begin our study of metamorphic imagery with three chapters on the high cultures of the Jade Age rather than with pictorial representations on pottery from earlier cultures in the East Asian Heartland Region, such as the famous fish mask figures on pottery from Banpo and other Yangshao sites. That imagery might indeed be described as metamorphic, but in our view, it is difficult, and (with ongoing archaeological discoveries) increasingly so, to discern a straight line of descent from Yangshao to Jade Age to Bronze Age cultures. Everywhere in northern and central China, Yangshao sites are overlain by Longshan (late Jade Age) materials, and it seems more probable now that the Yangshao culture was displaced by, rather than evolving into, Jade Age cultures. Intriguing though they are, the Banpo fish masks are outside the purview of this study. This book is organized chronologically, with chapters reflecting well-attested phases of China's prehistory and early history. Chapters two, three, and four deal with the successive cultures of the Jade Age, namely the Hongshan, Liangzhu, and Longshan cultures. They depict the development of metamorphic imagery, particularly works of jade, and the concurrent development of rites of ancestral sacrifices as the basis of royal (or proto-royal) religion. Chapters five, six, and seven describe the effects of bronze as the new prestige medium for royal ancestral worship in the Erlitou culture (sometimes equated with the "Xia dynasty"), the Shang dynasty, and the Western Zhou phase of the Zhou dynasty. Shang cultural and political power extended widely in the East Asian Heartland Region, as artisans created magnificent versions of the metamorphic power mask in bronze, a development that extended into the Western Zhou. In these chapters, we emphasize both organic change and significant continuities with the passage of time. Chapter eight deals with the Springs and Autumns period and beyond, when the rise of territorial lords diminished the importance of the royal ancestral cult. But metamorphic imagery lived on, in the culture of the great southern state of Chu, and in various manifestations that resonate to the present day. The book ends with a brief concluding chapter.

Notes

1 See, for example, the earlier works of *Florence Waterbury 1942: Early Chinese Symbols and Literature: Vestiges and Speculations*, New York: E. Weyhe; Phyllis Ackerman 1945: Ritual Bronzes of Ancient China, New York: Dryden Press; Consten von Erdberg "A Terminology of Chinese Bronze Decoration," Monumenta Serica XVII: 208–54; XVII: 287–314; XVIII: 245–93 and in particular MS XVIII: 291–93 for a list of terms used; Kwang-chih Chang 1972: Monographs of the Institute of History and Philology, Academis Sinica, Taipei; "Preliminary Remarks on a Comprehensive Study of Form, Decoration and Inscriptions of Shang and Chou bronzes," BIE 30 (1970): 239–75 (Ch), 274–315 (Eng)); Carl Hentze 1937: Frueh-Chinesische Bronzen und Kultdarstellungen, Antwerpen: De Sikkel; 1932: Mythes et Symboles Lunaires, Anvers, De Sikkel; 1936: Objets rituels, croyances et dieux de la Chine Antique et de l'Amerique, Anvers: De Sikkel; 1941: Die Sakralbronzen und ihre Bedeutung in den Frueh-Chinesischen Kulturen, Antwerpen: De Sikkel; Hayashi Minao 林巳奈夫 1960: "The demon spirit as represented amidst artifacts of Yin and Chou eras," Tohōgaku zasshi 東方学 雜誌. More recent studies by art historian Robert Bagley, specializing in Shang period art, denies the significance of imagery, preferring to deal with vessel and imagery style, mechanics of production, and archaeological context (see e.g., Bagley 1989).

2 See e.g., Li Liu 2004; Liu and Chen 2012; Underhill 2013; Shelach-Levi 2015; Campbell 2016. The eminent anthropologist and archaeologist, the late K.C. Chang, explored and wrote extensively on what he defined as shamanism in the Shang period; see Art, Myth, and Ritual, The Path to Political Authority in Ancient China. Cambridge, MA: Harvard University Press, 1983) but his analyses were based primarily on anthropological and archaeological data and do not take into consideration contemporary paleographic materials or how style affects representation which the present study does and Childs-Johnson has carried out much earlier (see the Ph.D. dissertation, "The Relationship between Symbol and Function in the Ritual Art of Shang China: New Archeological and Bone Inscriptional Evidence," IFA, NYU, Ph.D. dissertation, 1984 and successive articles and books on the subject, e.g., 2008, 2016). Also see K.C. Chang, 1981 "The Animal in Shang and Chou Bronze Art," Harvard Journal of Asiatic Studies 41 (2), 527–54; 1990 "Shang dai de wu yu wushu 商代的巫与巫术," in Zhongguo qingtong shidai, 2nd series, pp. 39–66 (Beijing: Sanlian Press); 1993. "Shang Shamans," in Willard Peterson (ed.), Power of Culture, pp. 10–36 (Princeton: Princeton U.P); 1993. "仰韶文化的巫覡覡资料" "Yangshao Culture and Shamanic Arts," Zhongyang yanjiuyuan yuyan yanjiusuo jikan 中央研究院语研究所集刊 64 (3): 611–625; 1993 "人類歷史上 的巫教的一個初步定義 (A preliminary definition of shamanism in human anthropological history)," Guoli Taiwan Daxue kaogu renlei xuekan 49 (1993.12): 1–6.

3 For an extensive analysis of the concept and cultural application of the term Jade Age see Childs-Johnson 1998:11–20; 2009: 291–393. See also Paola Demattè, "The Jade Age: Between Antiquarianism and Archaeology," *Journal of Social Archaeology* 2006.

4 See "Worker from the West" [interview with Victor Mair], Archaeology Archive 10 July 2006, http://archive.archive.org/online/interviews/mair.html, accessed 24 May 2020.

5 See for example Chiara Thumiger's 2014 study, "Humans into Animals". An earlier study by Dušan Borić entitled "Body Metamorphosis and Animality" (2005: 35–69) traces representational and 'aniconic' stone boulders from Lepenski Vir and other Meso-Neolithic sites in the Danube Gorges. He hypothesizes through analysis of these boulders *in situ* and their imagery that the simplified therianthrophic carvings were "volatile bodies, undergoing continuous metamorphoses." Liane, in 2011, wrote a Ph.D. thesis (University of Stellenbosch), titled Hybrid Monsters in the Classical World: The Nature and Function of Hybrid Monsters in Greek Mythology, Literature and Art. Earlier Annetta Alexandridis (with Markus Wild and Lorenz Winkler-Horaček 2008) wrote about a similar subject in Mensch und Tier in der Antike: Grenzziehung und Grenzüberschreitung.

6 For a detailed analysis as to why the term is misleading and anachronistic, see Childs-Johnson 1998c: 11–20; 2009. Childs-Johnson introduced the term "metamorphic image" at that time. For various studies on Shang imagery without consideration of oracle bone data, see also Ladislav Kesner 1991, The Taotie Reconsidered: Meaning and Functions of the Shang Theriomorphic Imagery, Artibus Asiae 51, 1–2 (1991), 29–53; Sarah Allan 2016; Robert Bagley 1989. (Shang Ritual Bronzes in the Arthur M. Sackler Collections, Harvard Univ. Press) and my review of Bagley, The Art Bulletin Vol. 71, No. 1 (March 1989): 149–56. The latter studies do not offer any clear-cut understanding of underlying religious practice or belief of Shang which I have identified through analysis of relevant oracle bone inscriptions and images.

2 Hongshan Culture, the Jade Age, and the Origin of Metamorphic Imagery

The Hongshan 红山 Culture, which flourished circa 3500–2500 BCE, was the first of the classic Jade Age cultures of late Neolithic China. Its archaeological remains give striking evidence of sacred edifices linked to rites of veneration of deceased powerful elite figures who were interred in rich and elaborate graves.[1] Hongshan grave goods strongly suggest that elite members of that culture possessed the power of metamorphic transformation and that those powers persisted after death, requiring rites of veneration and ongoing sacrificial rituals. Two types of Hongshan material production with clear ties to belief and ritual are well known to scholars of early China: the monumental clay sculpture of female figures in the so-called "Mother Goddess" temple at Niuheliang, and the finely worked jade pendants known as "pig-dragons." Both are associated with distinctive Hongshan burial practices that include stone-lined graves and above-ground stone altars.

Numerous Hongshan cultural sites, dating from about 3500–2500 BCE, have been surveyed, but few of the known sites have been fully excavated. Hongshan cultural remains have been identified as far east as Shenyang, as far south as Chengde in northern Hebei, and as far north as the Gulf of Bohai. Thus far, no unambiguously royal center featuring burials of Hongshan rulers has been discovered. The most important Hongshan site to have been excavated thus far is a ritual center at Niuheliang 牛河梁 in Liaoning province (Guo and Sun 1997). Elaborately constructed stone altars associated with deep cist burials evidently celebrate powerful elite figures, who were buried with rich grave goods consisting of finely worked jade artifacts. Several large-scale Hongshan settlements have been surveyed, and preliminary excavations of some of them have been carried out.[2] Present evidence suggests that Hongshan residential areas are geographically separate from sacred centers containing altars and elite burials. (Guo 1997b; Liu Guoxiang 2005.3: 7–20). Settlements are concentrated in the Laoha river valley, whereas sacred centers are concentrated in the Daling and Xiaoling 小凌 river valleys (see Figure 2.1).

DOI: 10.4324/9781003341246-2

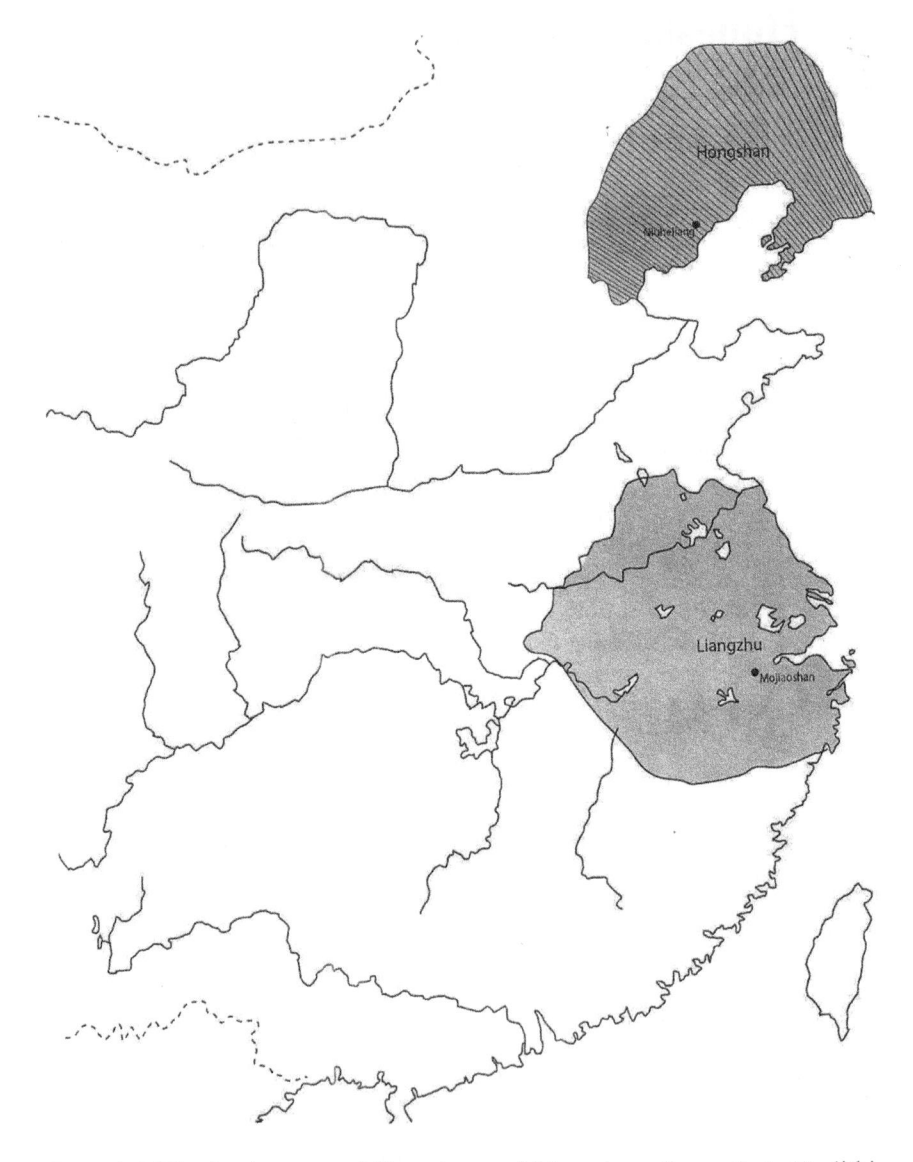

Figure 2.1 Distribution map of Hongshan and Liangzhu cultures, Late Neolithic Jade Age, ca. 3200–2100 BCE.

Niuheliang

The principal Hongshan sacred sites known to date comprise a center at Niuheliang, south of Zhushan 猪山 ("Pig Mountain"), with eight additional sites lying mostly to the northeast and south of Niuheliang (Map 2.1). The so-called (on dubious grounds) "Mother Goddess" temple (Niuheliang

1), incompletely excavated, is located to the northeast of the burial altars at Niuheliang (Chaoyang 2004: 53). All of the Hongshan elite burial sites are located on mountain terraces, are constructed of stone (both local and imported), and combine large-scale single cist burials with raised outdoor altars and accompanying rows of secondary burials. Reflecting a high degree of cultural uniformity, each usually includes a centralized deep cist burial, in one case clearly identified with a male corpse (from the burial at Niuheliang 5), surrounded by stone walls that are usually south-north in orientation and open at the south, forming an inverted squared U in shape. In addition, these deep cist single burials are flanked by three-tiered circular stone-lined altars, and at their southern open side are filled with middle- and small-scale stone-lined burials located in east-west oriented rows. The deep single centralized cist burials are typically defined by their own raised ground-level altars that are sometimes square (Niuheliang 2Z2) or rectangular (Niuheliang 16), or sometimes circular in shape. Hutougou 胡头沟 and Niuheliang 3 are circular stone altars with centralized cist burials. Hutougou is the smallest, measuring approximately 12 meters in diameter. Niuheliang 3 measures 15 meters in diameter; Niuheliang 5 is the largest rectangular cist burial, measuring 35 meters in diameter (Guo and Sun 1997). The social ranking of the deceased can probably be inferred to a certain extent by the size of the burial chamber and the quantity of burial goods (Figure 2.2).

Three major categories of elite burial types stand out: large-scale, centralized shaft burials oriented mostly north to south (the head faces slightly northwest), with stone coffins, stone chambers, above-ground-level stone-paved altars, and surrounding stone boundary wall open at the south; medium-size rectangular shaft burials oriented west to east with stone coffins, earthen (sometimes stone-lined) pits, without above-ground-level altars; and small, subsidiary burials, half-above, and half-below ground level. These three apparently reflect different levels of elite status within Hongshan society. Some burials are characterized by a second-time burial, indicating that these cemetery sites were used by more than one generation, probably of kin.

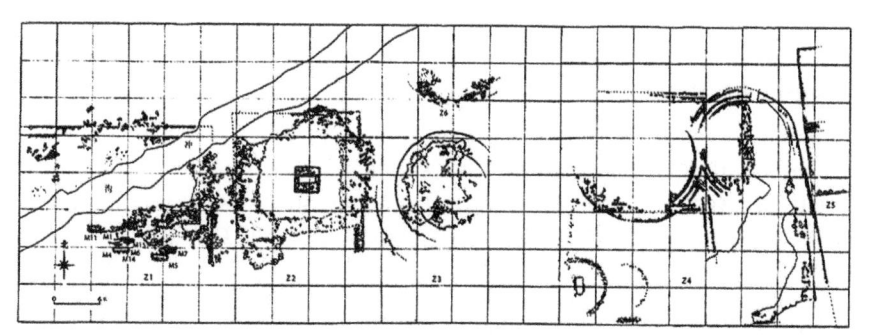

Figure 2.2 Overview and ground plan of raised burial sites at Niu 2 (Z1-5), Niuheliang, Liaoning. After Liaoning 1997:74 colorpl 50 and Luan 2006: 552, Figure 2.

Burial goods within the three classes of burials in most cases consist entirely of jades (Childs-Johnson 1991). Currently, available data suggest that the number of jades represented in the three burial types (large, medium, and small) belonging to the Hongshan elite range from 0 to 3 for the smallest burial type, to approximately 4–10 or more for middle-size burials, to over 20 for the largest burials. This distribution of jades is, however, to some extent speculative because the largest burial was robbed, a problem which may explain the irregular distribution of jades in other elite sites.

The "Mother Goddess" temple is part of the Niuheliang ritual complex. It consists of a subterranean room, with a stone floor and plastered walls that show traces of having been covered with mural paintings. A stone altar faced several naked female human or humanoid clay statues of monumental proportions, ranging from approximately human life-size to as much as three times human size. In addition to the statues was a life-size clay painted mask with jade eyes, projecting as a relief sculpture that was originally attached to the wall, and probably was once part of a larger image of a pregnant female as can be inferred from other finds, including fallen parts of a bulging belly and breasts. Breast and pregnant belly parts of equally large size were found in the same deposit as the head with inlaid jade eyes, which suggests that the head was also intended to represent a female. These figures have no parallel in Neolithic or later Chinese sacred art. The Hongshan culture was pre-literate and left no written clues as to the identity of these figures. The identification of these figures as a "mother goddess" and her retinue is entirely speculative. Whether they were intended to depict a mother goddess, or several goddesses of unknown identity, or female ancestors, or something else entirely can only be guessed at. Although these painted clay female figure types are unknown elsewhere in the East Asian Heartland Region, in one respect, Hongshan may be considered a contributor to the complex of cultural streams that evolved into Chinese civilization: jade, the most prevalent artistic medium associated with Hongshan culture, became one of the most distinctive artistic markers of Sinitic culture throughout the Heartland Region.

Hongshan Society

Politically, the Hongshan culture probably was a form of advanced chieftainship, with a ruling elite but not a stable dynastic line of royal descent. Chieftains were powerful but chieftainship was unstable; ruling authority might have been hereditary for a few generations but ruling families did not have a firm hold on power (Peterson 2015; Peterson *et al* 2017). (There is no evidence, for example, of a royal cemetery organized on lines of kinship.) It is likely that the known Hongshan culture area was divided into several regional chieftainships, which might have been, at various times, rivals, enemies, or allies (Peterson *et al* 2010). Chieftains probably lacked the authority, and the techniques of rulership, to unite the entire culture area under a single person's, or lineage's, rule. We may surmise that chieftains relied on a combination of personal charisma, military success, and claims of spiritual potency to be acknowledged as leaders. Despite limitations, however, the Hongshan chieftains exercised considerable power, including the power to extract wealth (for example, in the form of grain and other agricultural products) from the laboring classes, to organize labor on a large scale to build walls, structures, and tombs, to command the production of expensive, labor-intensive jades, and to devote considerable amounts of jade wealth as grave goods for the post-mortem benefit of dead elites.

The presence of altars constructed out of local stone in close proximity to Hongshan elite burials suggests that ongoing rites of some kind were performed at the tombs of the dead. It is uncertain, however, whether or not this amounted to ancestor worship as that term is generally understood, involving regular rites of specified kinds and at specified times devoted to deceased members of a lineage extending over several generations. But the altars themselves give evidence of sacrificial rites conducted at elite tombs, whether or not such rites were performed on an ongoing basis. Animal bones, especially those of pigs, together with burned human and animal remains, and along with ceramic and jade images, signify some form of sacrifice and ceremonial use at these outdoor sites. For example, one human bone and several pig and ox bones were found on the altar surface of the big square cist burial at Niu 2Z2. Three human skeletons were found in the debris within the three-tiered circular altar of Niu 2Z3. Hongshan clay figurines were collected from the surface of the tiered mounds flanking the large-scale cist burial with a rectangular paved altar at Niu 5 and at Dongshanzui 東山罪, another stone altar site distant from Niuheliang. Precisely how these sacred structures were used, together or individually, is not yet clear. It is probable that the ceremonial sites remained in use over a sustained period of time, judging from the number of burials spread over a wide geographical area. The abundance of Hongshan sites with large-scale stone cist burials, stone altars, and surrounding U-shaped stone walls supports the impression of a thriving and sophisticated culture with a large labor force and some form of centralized control, and with a powerful commitment to extensive mortuary rituals for the benefit of the elite dead.

Hongshan Jades

In addition to painted clay sculptures of naked and apparently pregnant women within "temple" compounds and on outdoor altars, abundant jade objects, distinctive in shape and subject, have been found in Hongshan sites (mainly in tombs) (Figure 2.3).

They are instantly recognizable as products of the Hongshan culture and belong to the evolutionary line of descent of Sinitic metamorphic imagery. "Dragon" and "cloud" shaped jades are two of the most distinctive types of mythic images in the Hongshan jade repertoire that persisted as important elements in later Chinese art.[3] The "dragon" jades take a curling fetal form – an incomplete circle in the shape of a capital letter "C" (Figure 2.4).

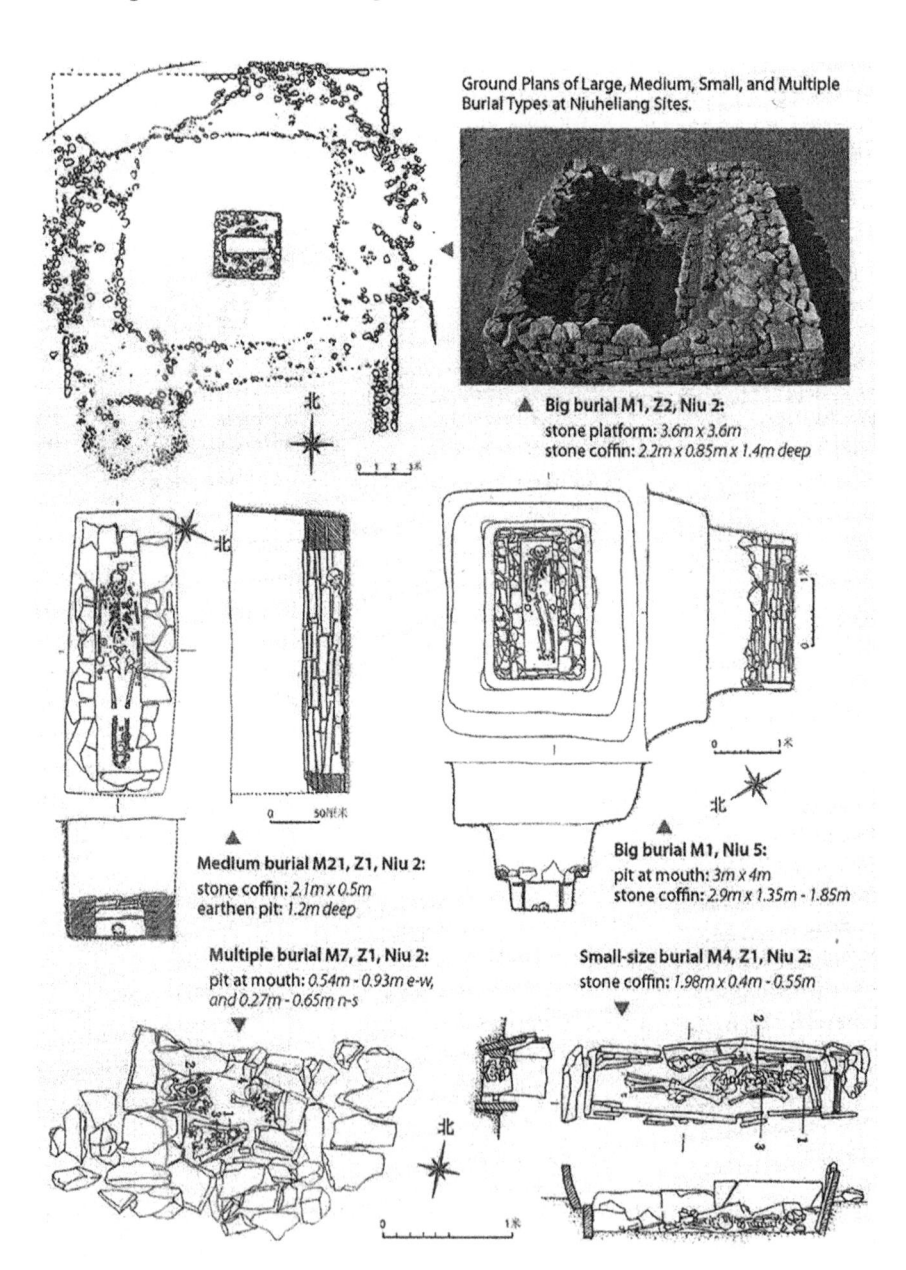

Ground Plans of Large, Medium, Small, and Multiple Burial Types at Niuheliang Sites.

▲ **Big burial M1, Z2, Niu 2:**
stone platform: *3.6m x 3.6m*
stone coffin: *2.2m x 0.85m x 1.4m deep*

▲ **Medium burial M21, Z1, Niu 2:**
stone coffin: *2.1m x 0.5m*
earthen pit: *1.2m deep*

▲ **Big burial M1, Niu 5:**
pit at mouth: *3m x 4m*
stone coffin: *2.9m x 1.35m - 1.85m*

Multiple burial M7, Z1, Niu 2:
pit at mouth: *0.54m - 0.93m e-w,*
and 0.27m - 0.65m n-s
▼

Small-size burial M4, Z1, Niu 2:
stone coffin: *1.98m x 0.4m - 0.55m*
▼

Figure 2.3 Multiple burial types from Niuheliang sites, Liaoning. After Chaoyang 2004:30, colorpl 31 and Liaoning 1997, 20-21, Figure 18 (M1, Z2, Niu 2); Chaoyang 2004: 59, Figure 73 (M1, Niu 5); Liaoning 1997: 23, Figure 20 (M21, Z1, Niu2), 18-19, Figures 14-15 (M4, Z1, Niu 2), and 22, Figure 19 (M7 Niu1 Z2).

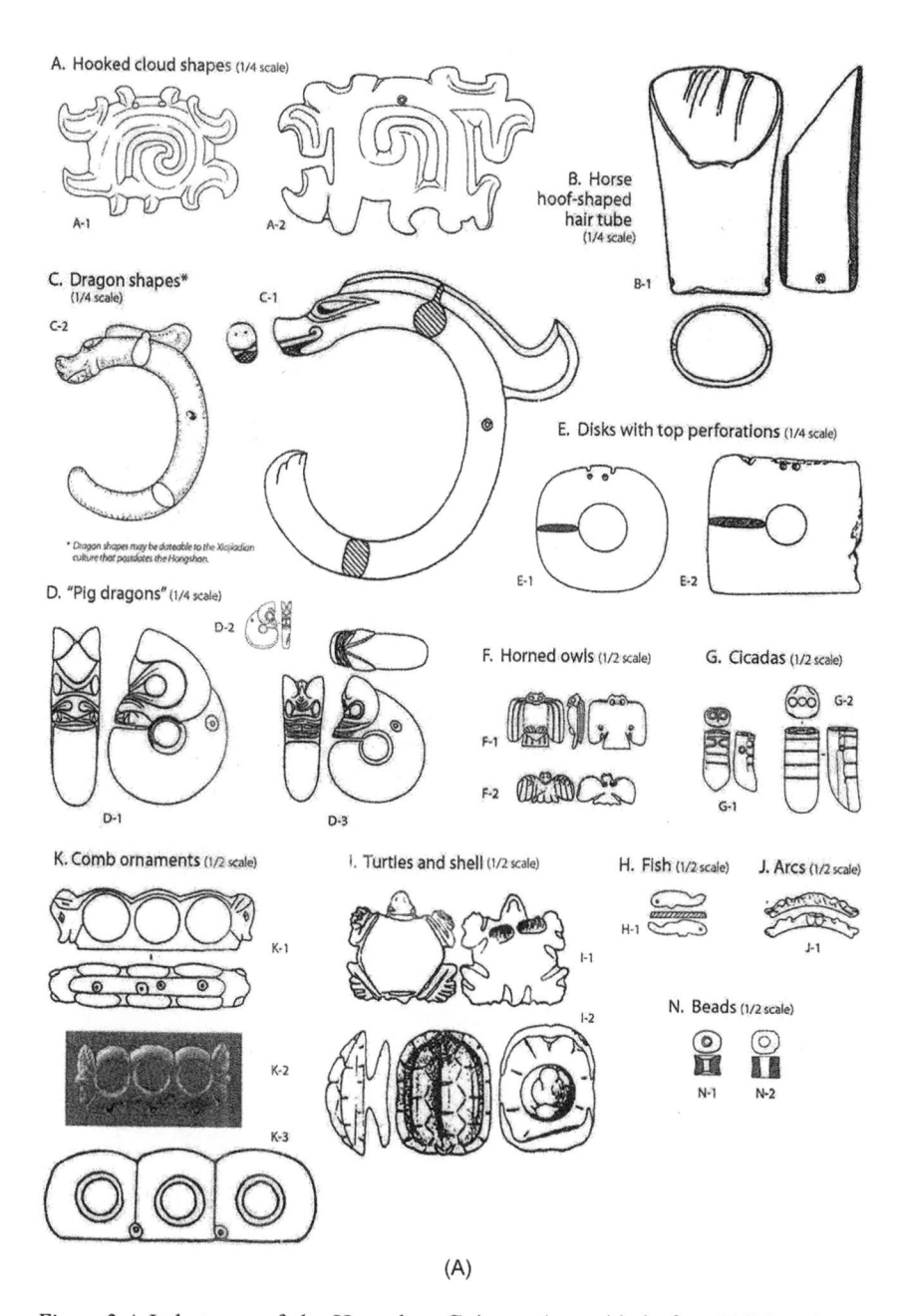

Figure 2.4 Jade types of the Hongshan Culture. Assembled after Childs-Johnson 2009: Figure 8C.

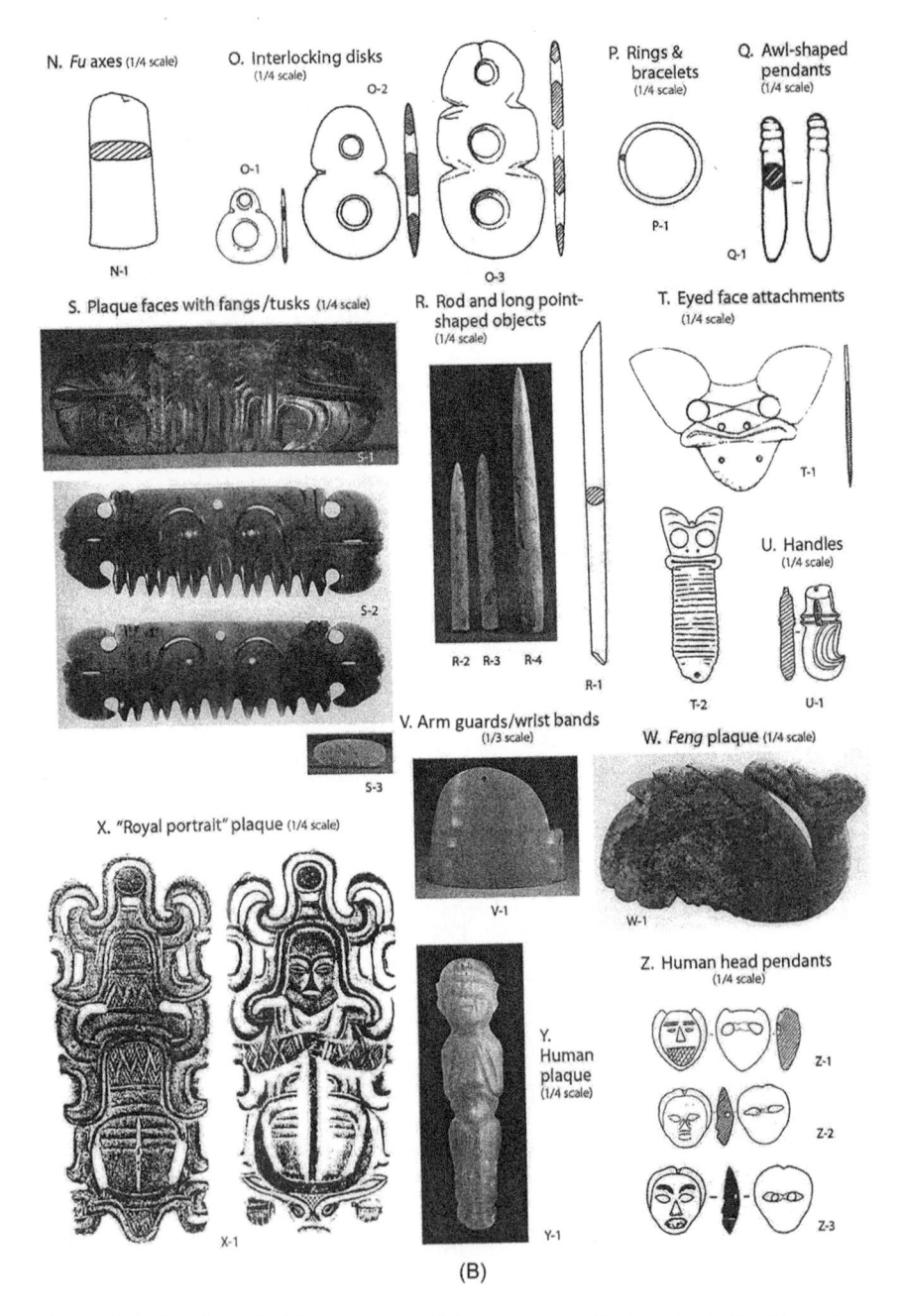

Figure 2.4 (Continued)   The two open C dragon types C3–4 postdate the Hongshan cultural period in dating to the Xiajiadian culture (see text below). Assembled after Childs-Johnson 2009: figure 8C.

They range in size (measured at the widest point of the curl) from 5 to 21 cm. One end is carved in the shape of a zoomorphic head; the other is unadorned, although sometimes this end is left connected at the inside of an otherwise open slit. These jades are commonly known by the generic term "pig-dragons" from a fancied resemblance of the carved head to that of a pig (boar). They are not anatomically accurate depictions of any type of real animal, although the pair of tusks, wrinkled snout, wide ear flap, and short snout defining the head strongly suggest inspiration from the most common product of Late Neolithic animal husbandry, the domesticated pig (derived from wild swine) (Figure 2.5).

Pigs became the predominant meat component of the Hongshan and other Jade Age cuisines, as deduced from bones and other archaeological traces of cooking. The rest of the jade body is a thick sausage-like curl powerfully reflective of a fetal form and suggestive of the earliest written rendering for the word dragon, *qiu* 虬 (Childs-Johnson 1991: 93, Figure 23). These are early examples of what we term metamorphic images, probably worn to enlist animal powers to protect and benefit their human wearers. The jades are intimately connected with the human body (see Childs-Johnson 1991). Most were amulet types, worn as talismanic pendants suspended on a cord strung through a drilled hole. Most of these thick C-shaped jades have been found in tombs, on or near the chest of the tomb's occupant. Tombs rarely include more than one or two of these C-shaped jades.

Other Hongshan jade objects include plaques, some with comparable zoomorphic imagery to those mentioned above (Figure 2.4). The latter type jades appear to have been sewn onto a person's clothing as indicated by the tear-shaped eyelets drilled on their reverse face for attachment.

A variation of the metamorphic thick serpentine C-shaped dragon form is known by several examples from the Lower Xiajiadian culture (dating after the Hongshan, ca.2200–1600 BCE), represented by two pieces from Wengniute in Inner Mongolia (one excavated, the other collected, see Figure 2.4:E4). The latter conform more readily to the type of dragon that is replicated and popularized in Sinitic lore and imagery. The shape and subject are identical but certain features differ: in these later examples, the snout is elongated; two nostrils are prominent; eyes are elongated as tear-drop shapes; projecting ears are eliminated in favor of a long curling ribbon-like extension behind the head; and the C-shaped body is more sinuous and thin. Both northern Late Neolithic jade types are represented elsewhere in the East Asian Heartland Region, south within excavated finds of other Late Neolithic cultures, such as Lingjiatan in Anhui (Chapter 3:3.1 top row, third from left) and the Longshan period site of Shijiahe in Hubei (Chapter 4:4.6D), and even later in historic Shang cultural remains, such as Fu Zi's tomb at Anyang (Childs-Johnson 1991:92, Figure 4). Although other variations of the dragon appear painted on Late Yangshao ceramics in the

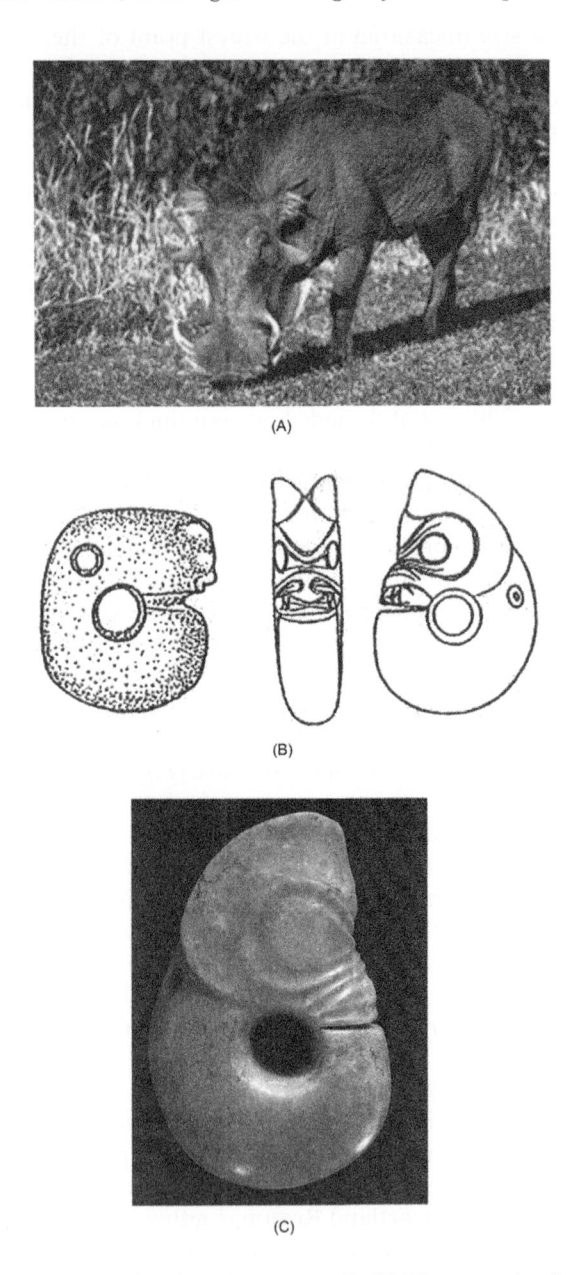

(A)

(B)

(C)

Figure 2.5 Wild Boar and Jade "Pig-Dragons". (A) Photograph of a Chinese wild boar exposing upward and downward turning tusks. https://animals. net/wild-boar/ (Wild Boar Foraging). (B) Drawings of a crudely worked (stone version) and a refined nephrite version of the so-called "pig-dragon," from Nasitai, Inner Mongolia (after Chifeng 2004: 377, Figure 1.1 and Liaoning 1997: 19, Figure 16.1 partial); (C) Nephrite jade "pig-dragon" from the Lowe Art Museum.

northwest Heartland Region and resemble the same theme and composition of dragon represented in the Taosi Culture, in the northwest Heartland Region, the curling form of zoomorphic head with C-shaped sinuous body is distinctive and probably originated with the jade creations of the Hongshan culture that influenced later Sinitic culture.

Other distinctive jade shapes and subjects also were part of the vocabulary of Hongshan metamorphic and mythic images. It is likely that the large flat horizontally oriented plaque (Figure 2.4S) and the smaller plaques (Figure 2.1T) excavated from Hongshan burials are also images related to the C-shaped dragon. The flat plaque has a central suspension hole as do the C-shaped jades but features a flattened, spread-out facial image consisting of two perforated pupils and slits for eyes, no nostrils, and several pairs of upper and lower tusks. The upper edge is flat, while the four corners are worked into four cusps simulating clouds. The smaller versions with flat handle-shaped ends may also be related to this dragon image, although other features are emphasized. Floppy-shaped ears are emphasized on a face with circular pupils. Small dots define nostrils, and the mouth is represented by an oval form, like a stretched rubber band. Mouth, ears, and eyes duplicate in one-dimensional form what is represented in two dimensions in the C-shaped jade dragons. Even the profile head turned backward on what Chinese scholars and archaeologists have labeled a large-scale *"feng"* 鳳 bird plaque because of the presence of a bird body in profile (Figure 2.1W) has features of the dragon head, including projecting ear, circular eye, and prominent snout. The designation of this bird as a *feng* is, of course, anachronistic; no one knows what the Hongshan people called the bird motif, or what meaning it had for them.

Two additional images, both plaques, add to the metamorphic repertoire of Hongshan jade imagery. Each is a flat plaque with images on both sides, although the two sides are clearly front and back; the backside is not worked in relief but left flat since it is the side that faces inward on the body. A double-worked suspension hole or two, or eyelets, are worked at on the back of the hooked cloud shape with a bird head. This abstract design, which we identify as cloud scrolls and profile bird head, corresponds with the earliest pictographic word for cloud in early Chinese script) (Childs-Johnson 1991: 84, Figure 5). Shirakawa, on the other hand, long ago pointed out that this cloud spirit was none other than a dragon head curling out of and hidden by clouds (Shirakawa 1977: 37). As with the dragon in later lore, the bird and cloud are commonly associated with rain and fertility, although whether the bird motif already had that meaning in Hongshan culture is unknown.

A large flat plaque in the shape of a seated human with a cylindrical hair spool in the Palace Museum in Beijing is another surprising find of Hongshan jade-working (Figure 2.6).

What Hongshan jade experts call a "royal portrait" (Sun 2001: 19–29) – a leader such as a chieftain – is depicted as a human seated on a "throne"

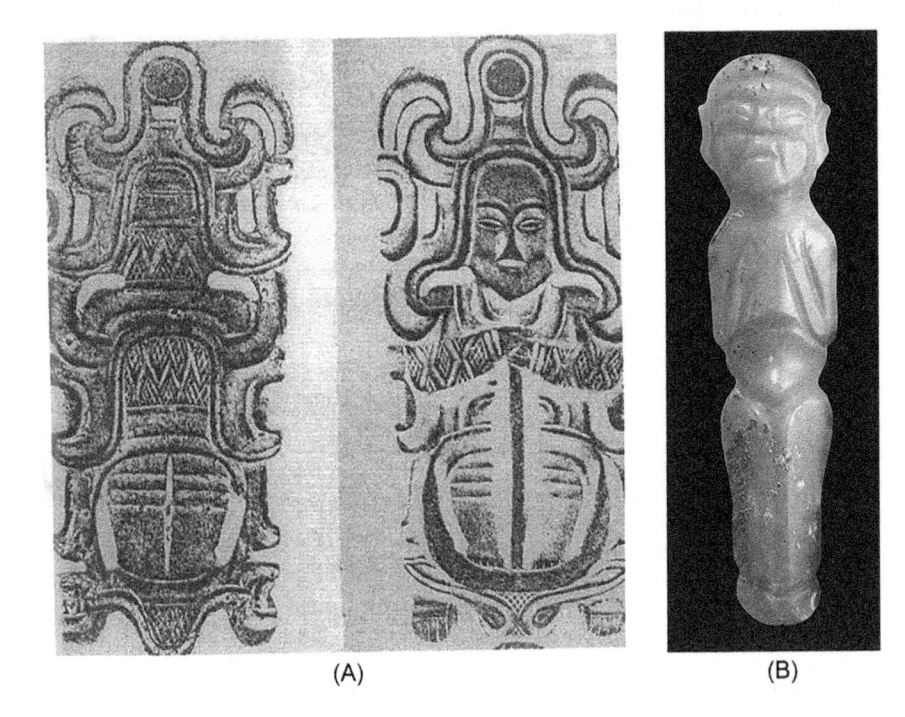

(A)   (B)

Figure 2.6 Human figural images of the Hongshan culture (A) front and reverse
faces of a flat jade plaque featuring a "royal portrait", Hongshan style,
probably post-Hongshan period, Palace Museum, Beijing. (B) Naked
human jade figure with raised arms from M4, Niuheliang No.16.
Childs-Johnson 2009: Fig 8: X, Y.

that takes the shape of the zoomorphic Hongshan cloud scroll design. The
image is crowned by the same cloud formation created by the other type
of jade plaque, the hooked cloud shape with a profile bird head. Clearly,
the attributes of this "portrait" are consistent with the Hongshan and post-
Hongshan Xijiadian tradition in the northern reaches of the Extended East
Asian Heartland Region.

The other plaque type seems to depict an unclothed human with arms
raised to chest level (Figure 2.6B). The form is a closed one-dimensional
image of what we speculate may be the prototype for the historic version of
metamorphosis represented by the graph *yi* 異 in Shang bone inscriptions
and by the ubiquitous metamorphic power mask in ritual Shang art (see
Chapter 5). The bodily features of the seemingly naked human comprise a
head with ears and facial parts; a neck; an upper body and a belly; it has bent
legs and a nub for feet. Small-scale human heads have also appeared in the
repertoire of Hongshan jades from excavated tomb finds (Figure 2.1). Evidently, Hongshan jade workers were skilled in portraying both naturalistic

and imaginary metamorphic subjects. The Hongshan culture can be credited with playing a foundational role in the development of metamorphic imagery that played such a pivotal role in the politico-religious life in later Jade Age and Bronze Age cultures.

Notes

1 For a detailed review of Hongshan sites, and their jades, see Childs-Johnson 1991: 82–95 and 2009: 295–310).
2 For a review of these settlements, see Childs-Johnson 1991; 1995: 295–309; 2001; Liu Gx 2005: 7–20; Guo 1997: 11–16.
3 For the identification of these motifs, see Childs-Johnson 1991: 82–95; 1995: 306, 309.

3 Metamorphic Images and the Beginning of Royal Ancestor Worship in the Liangzhu Culture

Liangzhu, the second great jade-working culture in the East Asian Heartland Region, dominated a large area centered on Lake Tai, the lower Yangzi River Plain, and the Yangzi Delta (Figure 3.1). The type-site of the culture was discovered as early as 1936, near the town of Liangzhu, in the northern outskirts of the present city of Hangzhou. Since that time the Liangzhu culture became famous for the distinctive jade *cong* 琮 (prismatic cylinder) and *bi* 璧 (perforated disk) artifacts associated with burials[1] (see Figure 3.2). (Also see Liu, B. 2009: 19–22; Sun, Zx 1983: 1–40.)

Subsequent archaeological investigations in the vicinity of Lake Tai in the late 20th and early 21st centuries have cumulatively produced a picture of Liangzhu culture as the product of a large and thriving polity, which, with every new discovery, reinforces the impression that Liangzhu may have been ancient China's first full-fledged chiefdom merging into a state, or at least a highly advanced chiefdom.[2]

Background of the Liangzhu Culture and Metamorphic Belief during the Jade Age

Liangzhu culture built upon earlier Neolithic cultures of Hemudu and Songze (ca. 5000–3500 BCE) in present-day Zhejiang province and Shanghai and flourished for roughly one thousand years, ca. 3200–2300 BCE (Huang Xp 2000: 125–33). Archaeologists identify four phases (P): PI-II encompass circa 3200–3100 and 3100–2850 BCE, and PIII-IV encompass circa 2850–2500 and 2500–2350 BCE (Qin L. 2013; Zhang X. *et al.* 2015). An additional PV (called Maqiao 馬橋), circa 2350–2200 BCE, witnessed the relatively rapid disappearance of Liangzhu cultural characteristics and overlaps with the emerging jade-working cultures of Longshan date in Shandong and Hubei, circa 2600–2000 BCE (Song J 1996.2: 197–236; Long and Taylor 2015). The height of the Liangzhu culture, distinguished by its elite funerary architecture, covers Phases III–IV when large-scale ritual complexes centered on pyramidal platform cemeteries reached their peak of sophistication.[3] Jade objects matured as formalized types and sets, and imagery evolved into a standardized iconographical program (Childs-Johnson 2009: 327–53).

DOI: 10.4324/9781003341246-3

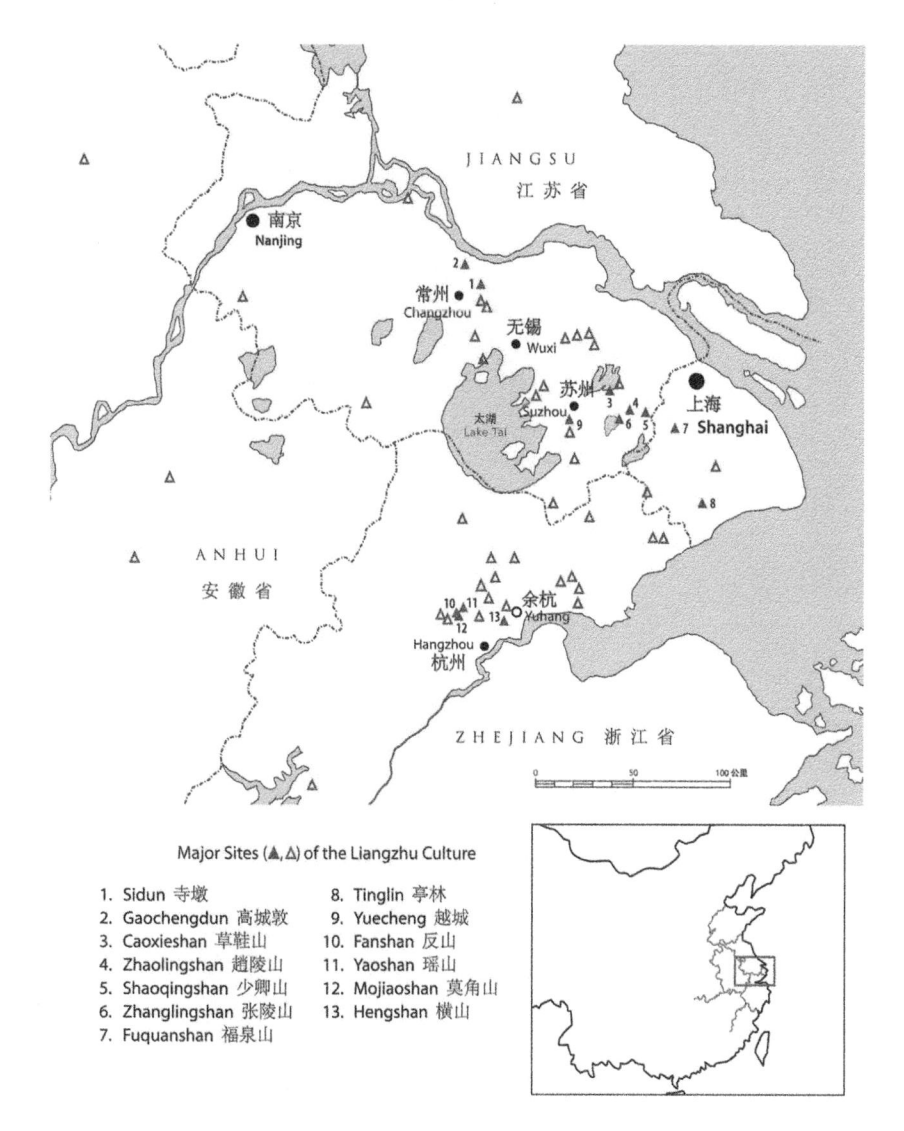

Figure 3.1 Major sites of the Liangzhu culture.

Some 200–300 Liangzhu sites have been identified as far east as Shang-hai and the Eastern Sea, extending to just north of the Yangzi River val-ley, south as far as Hangzhou, and west as far as the mountain ranges of Maoshan and Ningzhen.[4] In terms of present-day geography, these areas belong to the southeastern part of Jiangsu, southern Shandong, northern Zhejiang, and Shanghai municipality, and cover an area of about 180,000 sq. km. (Chen and Wu 1996: 306–18; Liu B 2020: 115). Mojiaoshan in Yuhang

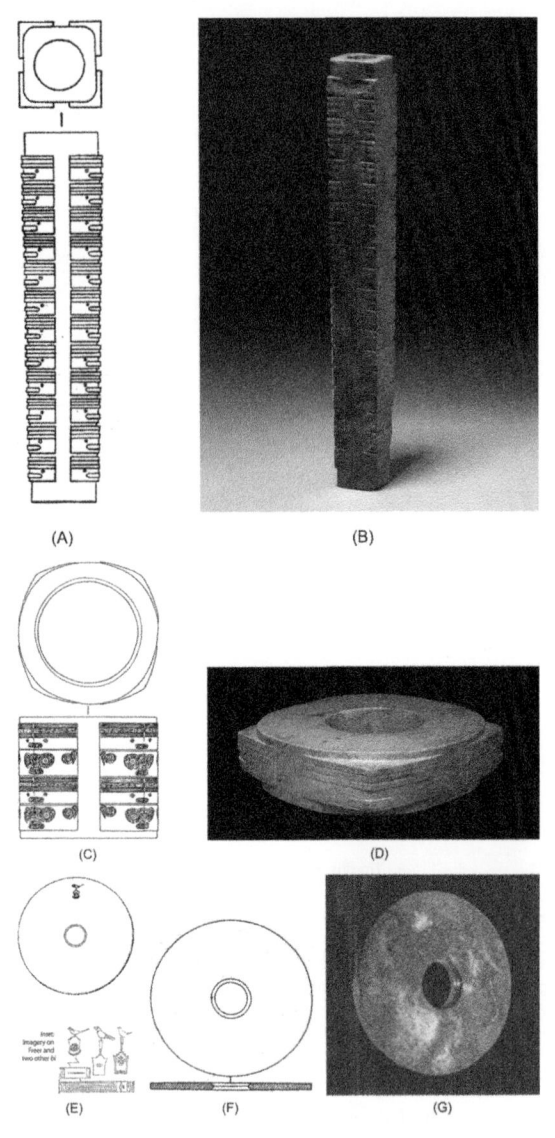

Figure 3.2 Jade *cong* and *bi* of the Liangzhu culture. (A) Jade *cong* from M3:16 Sidun. (B) Jade *cong*, ca. 2500 BCE 49 cm high, China © private collection © Trustees of the British Museum, Khan Academy, London. (C) Jade *cong* from M20:122 Fanshan. (D) Jade *cong*, ca. 2500BCE, 3.4 × 12.7 cm, China © 2003 private collection © Trustees of the British Museum, Khan Academy, London. (E) Jade *bi*, Asian Art Museums, Washington D.C. 1917.348, public domain. (F) Jade *cong* from M198:11–10, Caoxieshan, Jiangsu. (G) Jade *bi*, ca. 2500 BCE, 18 cm in diam.© private collection, © Trustees of the British Museum, Khan Academy, London. Jpeg 3.3A 33.33.3. (A), (B), (C), (D), (E), (G) images are in the public domain. (F) After Childs-Johnson 2009: 340, Figure 15:A2.

county, Zhejiang appears, based on its size and complexity, to have been the Liangzhu people's sacred center and politico-cultural focal point (Liu B. 2020: 115–38).

The principal Liangzhu city, Mojiaoshan, had massive dirt walls and ditches as well as dikes and levees that were intended primarily for flood control (Zhejiang 2016; Liu, B *et al* 2017; Zhong Y *et al* 2017, Liu B 2020: 112–25). The Director of Archaeology at Mojiaoshan, Liu Bin, estimates that the city may have had a population of as many as 30,000 people, and contained large buildings (possibly a palatial center) on pounded-earth platforms as well as neighborhoods for ordinary inhabitants. The culture's wealth was based on the cultivation of rice, a type of agriculture that lends itself to the formation of large-scale administrative arrangements to regulate the plowing, flooding, planting, draining, and harvesting of networks of paddy fields (Liu L *et al* 2007; Zhang and Hung 2008: 299–329). Recent DNA studies of skeletal remains in Liangzhu graves suggest that the Liangzhu people were genetically related to Austronesian peoples known to have been the principal inhabitants of the southeastern coast of the Heartland Region including today's Fujian Province and the island of Taiwan (Li Hui *et al* 2015: 383–88). This accords with the growing realization among scholars of early China that the Heartland was ethnolinguistically diverse and that the peoples of the central and south-central coastal area of the East Asian Heartland made major contributions to the development of Chinese civilization. This increasingly casts doubt on the older view that assigned the development of Chinese civilization primarily to a putative "North China Nuclear Region" and emphasizes the widespread and ethnically diverse origins of that civilization.

Lingjiatan and the Roots of Liangzhu Culture and Metamorphic Belief

With the gradual disappearance of the Hongshan culture and its replacement by the Xiajiadian culture in the northeast, Liangzhu in the southeast emerged as ancient China's premier jade-working culture. Evidence that these two cultures may have had contact despite the fact that their urban and sacred centers were hundreds of miles apart and direct overland contact may have been hindered by the Yellow River and the mountainous terrain of Shandong, comes from plentiful data excavated from a pre-Liangzhu southern site at Lingjiatan 凌家灘 in Anhui, and in particular from burial No. 23 (Figure 3.3A–D). Jades from Lingjiatan burials have often been typologically compared to those of Liangzhu and, in this respect, serve as a prototype for those of the Liangzhu period (Zhang Jg 2008). The prominence of stone and jade weapons from Lingjiatan tombs is southern in type and origin. Yet, Lingjiatan's importance is singular in its role as an intersection point of Hongshan and southern jade-working cultures (Wang Wj 2017: 39–41). As illustrated in Figure 3.4, a whole set of Hongshan-inspired jade types dramatically testify to the strong connection between northern

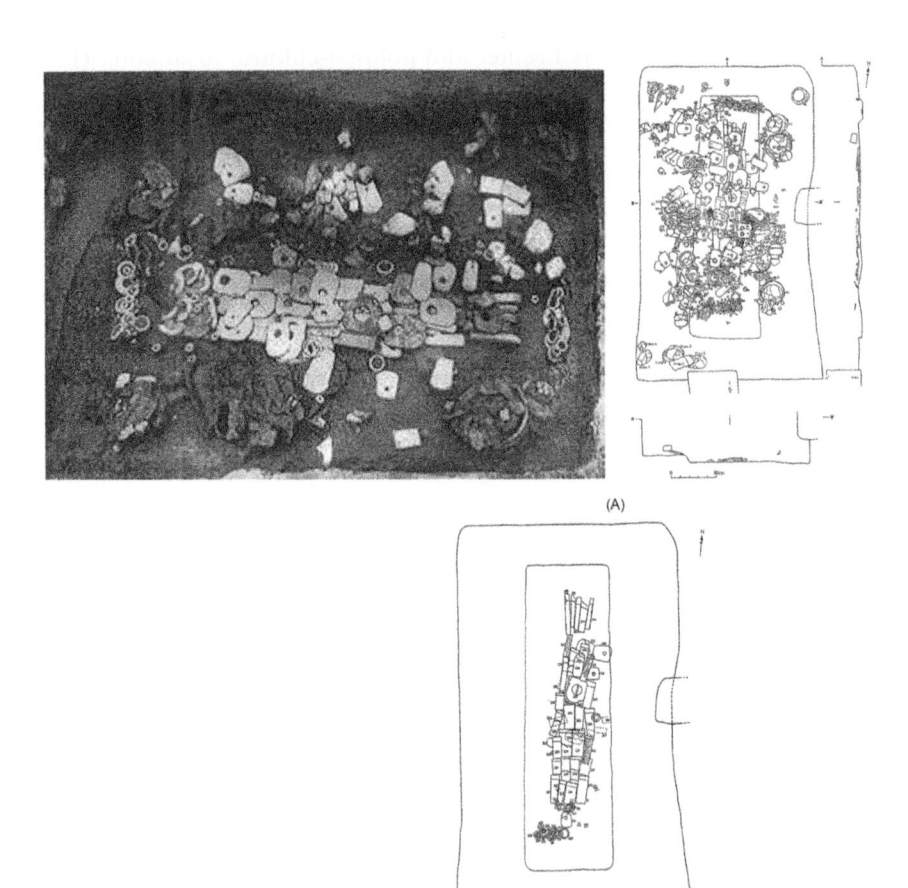

Figure 3.3 Lingjiatan Burial M23, Anhui, late Neolithic Jade Age. (A1–2) Layout of artifacts, mostly jade but also some stone, upper level. (B) Second Level.

and southern jade-working cultures. Lingjiatan is located in Anhui east of the Yangzi on the Hou River in Ma'anshan County. Lingjiatan jade images which show Hongshan inspiration and prototypes include not only a raptor with boar-headed wings; a pig-dragon; a crown to a hair comb; wrist guards (see e.g., Zhang Jg 2008 (tr): Figures 11–15); a turtle carapace and plastron with emphasis on axial directionality; but what will become ubiquitous as a metamorphic icon, human figurines with raised arms. All the latter find direct comparison with Hongshan jade types (see Chapter 2 Figure 2.5) and may be defined as Hongshan in influence, and likely are the result of trade or gifting, a friendly and probably robust interaction. The richness of burial

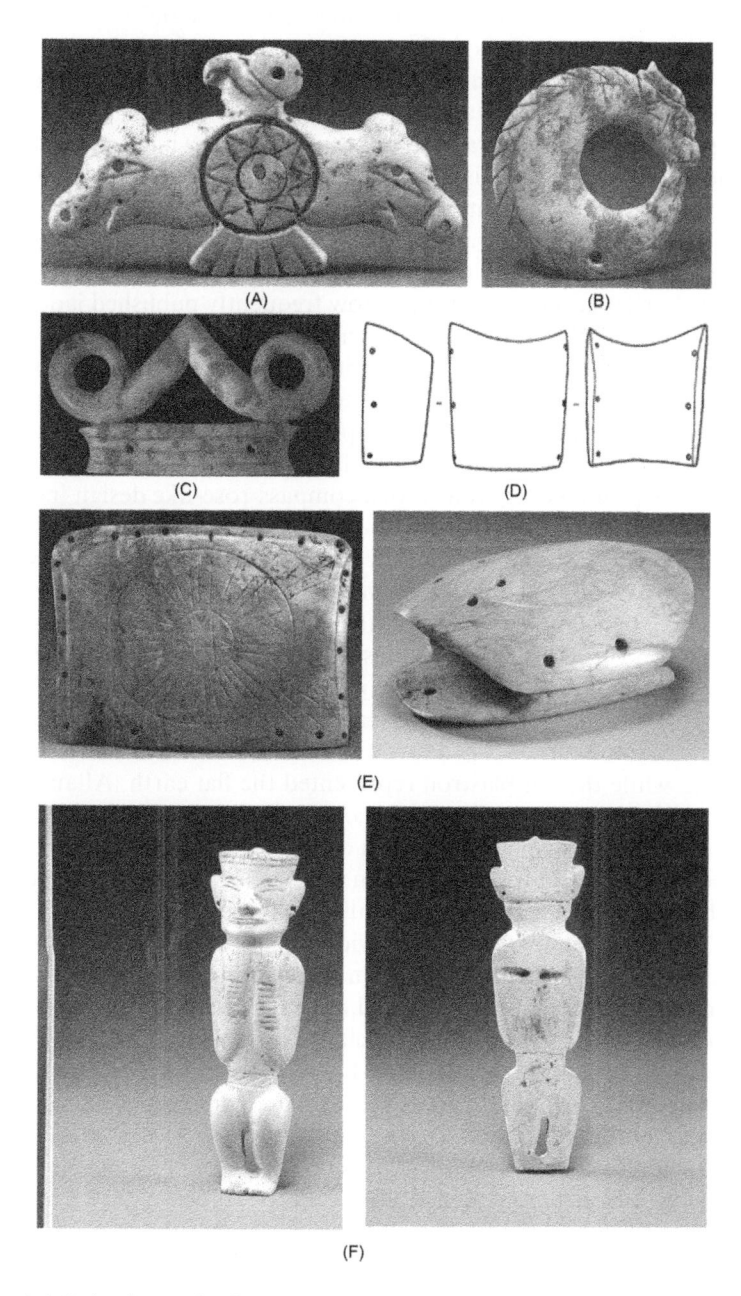

Figure 3.4 Jades from Lingjiatan, Anhui showing Hongshan influence. Representative are the following images: (A1–2) Raptor with boar-headed wings.
(B) "Pig-dragon." (C) Crown to a hair comb. (D) Wrist guard. (E) Turtle
carapace and plastron. (F) Human figurine with raised arms. Based on
images assembled in Childs-Johnson 2009: Figures 26 A, B, C10, E, F,
N2, and 16 E–F.

no. M23, with some 330 artifacts, includes 200 jades and 97 stone implements, 31 pottery pieces, a bone fragment, and piece of turquoise. The burial was uncovered overlapping a stone circular altar and pit in the center of
the cemetery area at Lingjiatan.

Complementing the celebrated Liangzhu jades and what we will define as
their metamorphic imagery is the culture's conspicuous emphasis on directional symbolism, as if in anticipation of later cosmological belief systems.
As noted below, the step-pyramid altars, and the burials within them, show
attention to orientation. But the strongest evidence for a cultural interest in
directional orientation comes from a now frequently published jade plaque
discovered at the same pre-Liangzhu period Lingjiatan site in Anhui province (Figure 3.4E). Rectangular and slightly convex, it has holes at its corners
that suggest that it was originally sewn to a cloth or leather backing. It was
found inside a jade container in the shape of a turtle, with its characteristic
domed carapace (upper shell) and flat plastron (lower shell). Spectacularly,
its convex surface was engraved with a compass-rose-like design indicating
the four cardinal and four secondary directions, with arrow-like markers
radiating from its center and pointing to the eight directions. Whoever carried or wore this object likely was seen as having power over the directions
(for example, by using it to establish the correct orientation for some rite),
just as, many centuries later, the kings of Shang saw themselves as lords of
the Four Quarters (*sifang* 四方). The jade turtle shell in which the plaque
was found is also likely to have been significant; much later in Chinese intellectual history, the carapace of a turtle was taken to be a symbol of the dome
of heaven, while the flat plastron represented the flat earth (Allan 1991). It
seems that the same symbolism was recognized and employed by the Liangzhu people, as will become apparent in our analyses below.

While both Hongshan and Liangzhu were expert jade-working cultures,
Liangzhu jade products are aesthetically distinctive and are more diverse
in type and plentiful in number. It is evident that the early Liangzhu people
were in contact with their neighbors in Lingjiatan and possibly indirectly
with Hongshan and may have learned advanced jade-working techniques
from one of them, adapting those techniques to their own religious and
ritual needs. Yet, the type of jade stone found in Liangzhu contexts (see Gan
et al. 2010) differs from the type well-known and still used today at Xiuyan
mines in Liaoning, the mineralogical source for Hongshan jade production
(see e.g., Zhang J 2002).

Ritual burials of powerful chieftains, and possible ongoing post-funerary worship of those elite figures by descendants in their lineage, are represented by some 30 archaeologically excavated Liangzhu sacred sites (see
Figure 3.5) (Renfrew and Liu 2018: 17; Liu 2020). Although the ritual center
of the Liangzhu people identified at Mojiaoshan has not yet been completely
excavated, the "walls" of the site have been, indicating that Mojiashan was
a major urban center, ten times the size of the Forbidden City, and the largest city known in Late Neolithic China. It measures 1,700 meters in width

from west to east and approximately 1,900 meters from north to south, or a total area of over 3,000,000 square meters/300 hectares (see Figure 3.6). (Renfrew and Liu 2018: 10, 2020; Zhao Y 2001). It is rectangular in plan and its central axis points due north and south (Liu B 2018: 10). The site is surrounded by an outer city rammed earth "wall" augmented by inner and outer ditches (moats?), one of which measures some 45m wide (Renfrew and Liu 2018: 11). These ditch-like moats intersected with natural water systems (Figure 3.6). They served primarily as advanced hydrological units to defend against flooding and probably were also used as reservoirs for irrigation and other economic purposes. The remains of a dock have been traced in the southeastern corner of the outer wall. Other remnants of a dirt wall, found at a distance north of the northern wall, suggest to the excavators that an additional outer "city wall" existed, thus anticipating the double walls that surrounded Shang cities (Renfrew and Liu 2018: 12, 2020).

The interior of the city site is marked at the center by a man-made raised platform, roughly rectangular in form (300,000 sqm in area), and roughly 1/10th the size of the surrounding wall (Renfrew and Liu B 2018: 12, 2020). Three additional different-sized elevated platforms occupy the same elevated part, suggesting a potential location for what the excavators theorize may be "palace remains," although no post holes have yet been published as existing from these areas.

Figure 3.5 Liangzhu culture sites in Yuhang County, Zhejiang. After Childs-Johnson 2009.

Figure 3.6 Digital elevation model (DEM) of citadel structure outside the ancient city of Mojiaoshan. After Liu B 2020: Figure 5.

The celebrated platform cemetery site of Fanshan lies northwest of this center, though still within the city walls, indicating its direct connection with this site (see Figure 3.5). Other raised cemetery altars of ca. 2800–2300 BCE are similar in form and style to Fanshan (see Figure 3.6). Unfortunately, most of these platform cemetery sites (Zhejiang 2005: 364) are either incompletely published or only partially excavated. Yaoshan 瑤山 and Fanshan 反山 mounds in Yuhang county, Zhejiang, and Fuquanshan, Sidun, and Zhaolingshan mounds in Jiangsu are representative of presently known Liangzhu sites. For Fuquanshan and Zhaolingshan platform burial sites in Jiangsu see Figure 3.7 and for Yaoshan mound see Figure 3.8. (For extensive coverage of these sites and their finds, see Childs-Johnson 2009: Table 3.)

The earthen mounds with burials of the Liangzhu elite are described in archaeological reports as "altar cemeteries" [*jitan mudi* 祭坛墓地] and are known locally as *tuzhu jinzita* 土筑金字塔, "earthen pyramids." They share special distinctive features: a stepped rectangular or square shape with usually three pounded earthen layers, leveled at the top and reinforced by stones; rows of aligned burials intruding into east, west, and south sides of the mound; burials of roughly the same size; and a north-south orientation.

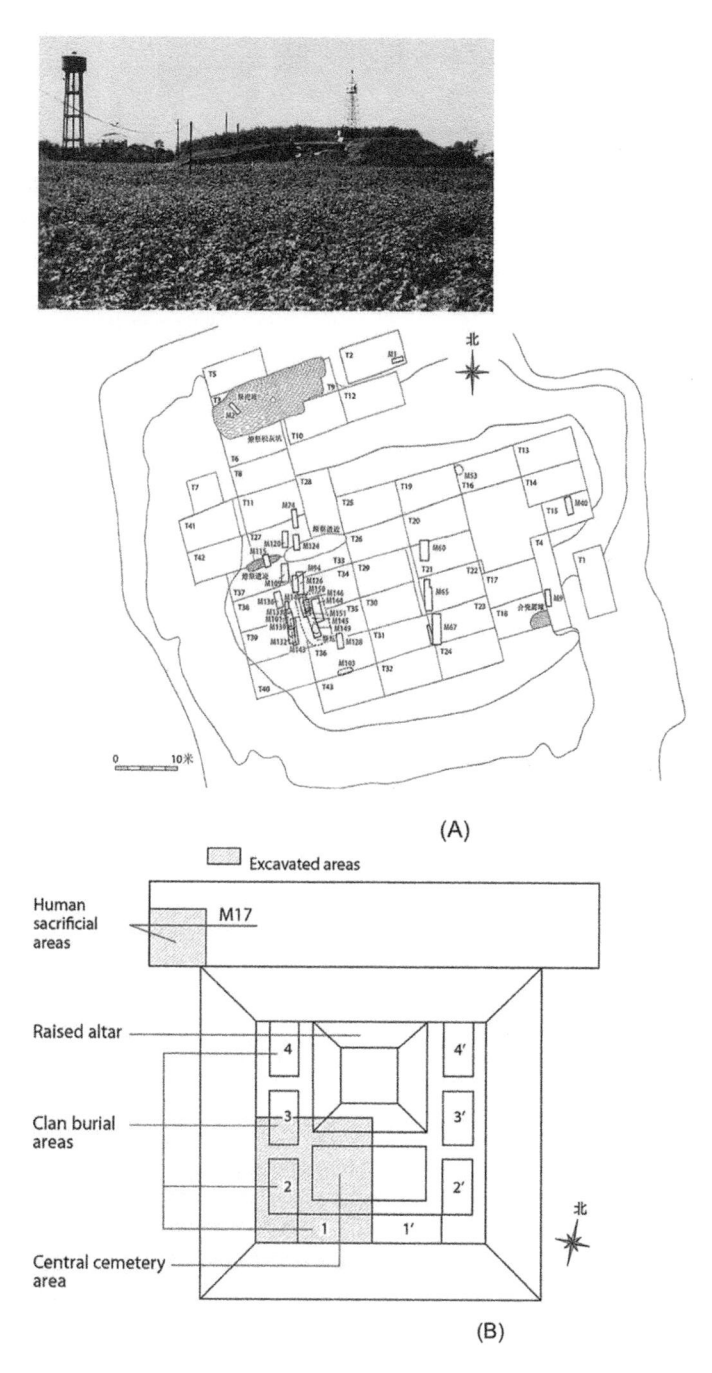

Figure 3.7 Platform burials at Fuquanshan (A) and Zhaolingshan. (B) After Childs-Johnson 2009: Figure 10DE.

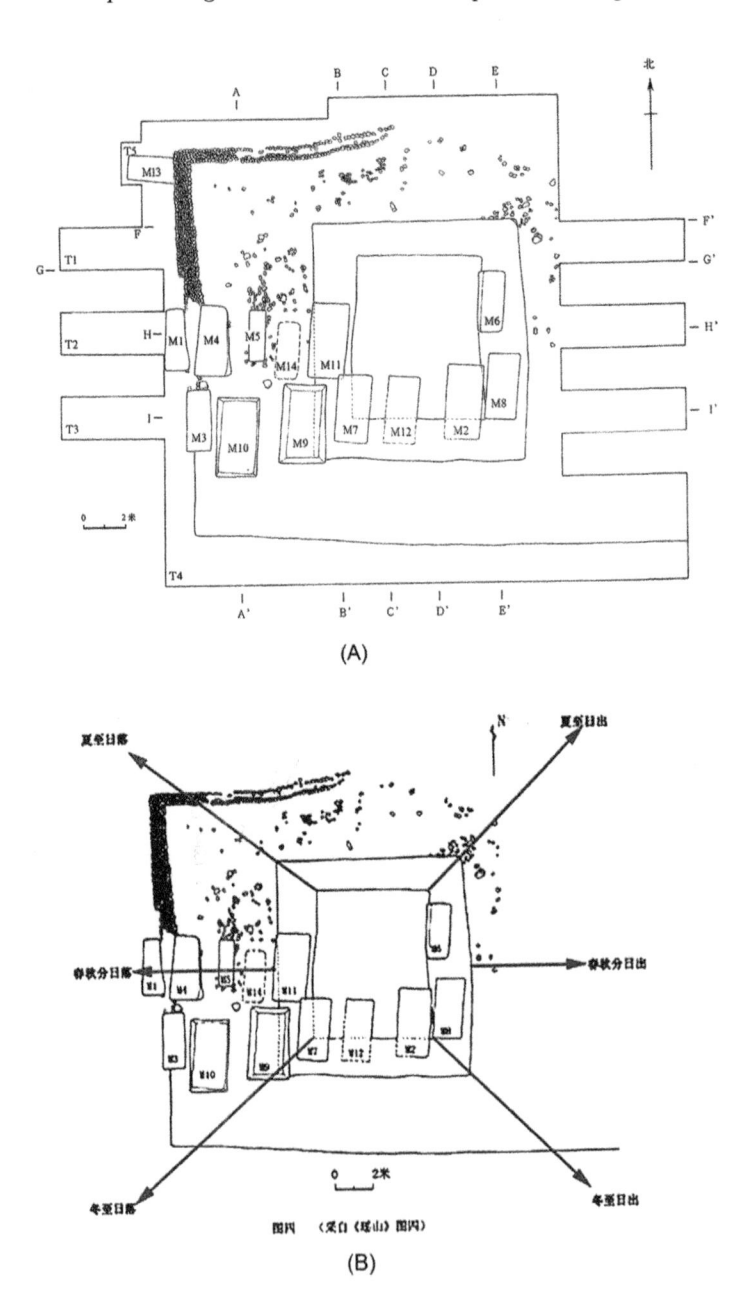

Figure 3.8 AB Yaoshan platform cemetery and diagrammatic view of the altar's orientation as a solar observatory, as postulated by Liu Bin. After Liu B 2020: Figure 7.

The layers of the mounds were frequently made of different earthen colors, as preserved at Yaoshan, with red at the core, gray in the surrounding layer, and yellow speckled with black in the outermost layer (Zhejiang 2003b: 7). Liu Bin theorizes that the orientation of these platform cemeteries suggests they were used as solar observatories (see Figure 3.6), an orientation and disposition also theorized as existing at the Hongshan site of Niuheliang (Nelson *et al.* 1995). As will become apparent below, the same orientation characterizes the shape of the jade *cong* cylinder and the layout of Liangzhu city centers, as seen for example in remains at Sidun in Jiangsu (see Figure 3.9), as reconstructed by Che Guangjun (Che Gj 1995: 31–33)

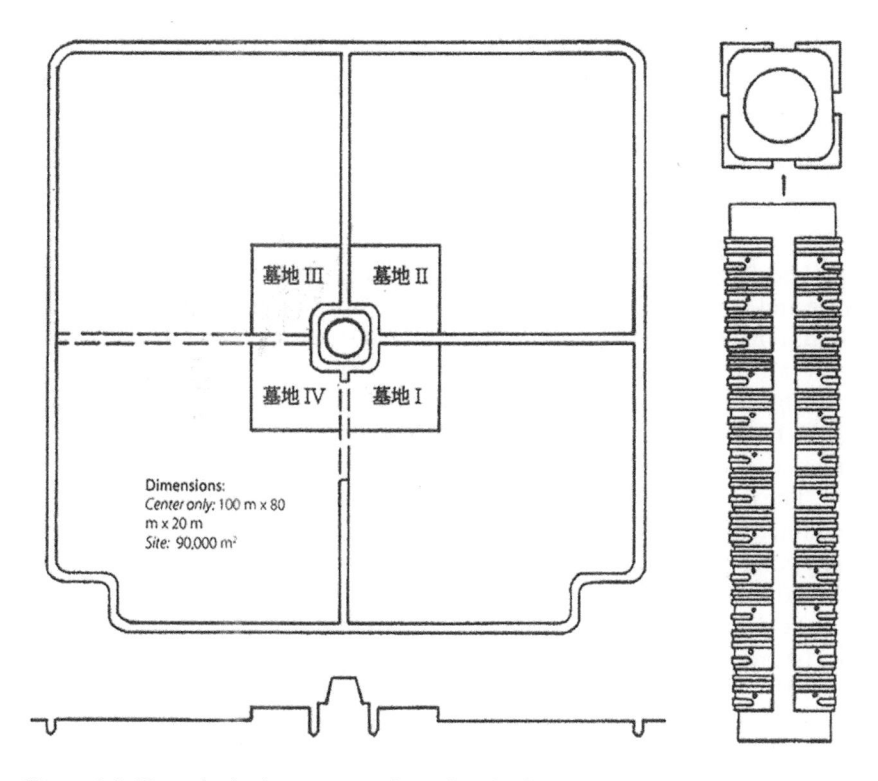

墓地 III 墓地 II

墓地 IV 墓地 I

Dimensions:
Center only: 100 m x 80
m x 20 m
Site: 90,000 m²

Figure 3.9 Hypothetical reconstruction of a platform cemetery as a simulation of the ritual jade *cong* tube. (A) Hypothetical reconstruction of ground and elevation plans of the platform cemetery at Sidun, in Wujiang, Jiangsu by Che Guangjun. (B) Drawing of a 12 tier *cong* and its open cylindrical mouth descending into a hollow tube. (A) After Che G 1995:31. (B) After Childs-Johnson 2009: Figure 11.

Liangzhu Jades and Metamorphic Imagery

Both Hongshan and Liangzhu people gave allegiance to rulers who exercised power with the support of an elite class; the ruling elite in turn dominated their societies economically, politically, and spiritually. Yet Liangzhu was a much more fully mature chieftainship, with, for example, the ability to muster military forces armed with *yue* ax weapons (which also evolved as an elite jade power symbol; (see the analysis in Childs-Johnson 2009: 310–38, esp. pages 325–28, and Figure 14). By comparison with Hongshan, Liangzhu verges on the development of an actual state, as recently proposed by Renfrew and Liu 2018 and Liu B 2020. In both cultures, but especially in Liangzhu, the power and authority of the chieftain is richly displayed by the overwhelming number of post-mortem jades deposited in burials. Specific sets of jades distinguished Liangzhu elite from lesser ranks. The three highest social tiers of elite were buried in the pyramidal cemeteries that served as sacred centers for worship (see Childs-Johnson 2009: 325–27). As deceased members, these elites were buried in alignment with the axial orientation of the cosmos, with heads located in the east to north and corpses supine. Fourth tier Liangzhu sites, such as Maqiao, Miaoqian, and Longnan, lack platform cemeteries; instead, burials were located in or near residences (Lu Jf 1996: 265–66).

Elite graves were dug into the lower parts of these altar cemeteries where ritual performances associated with the burial of the deceased person took place and, evidently, in accordance with a proper cosmological orientation. Liu Bin in 2018 maintained that these sacred structures functioned as solar observatories due primarily to their axial orientation (Figure 3.10) (see Liu B 2020). Burned remains of sacrificial offerings show that sacrifices were conducted on top of these flat platforms, consisting mostly of animals but with occasional human victims as well (Huang Xp 2000: 43, 135; Lu J 1996: 191). The pit labeled M13 at the southwestern corner of the Fanshan mound contained remains of "animals and foodstuffs" (Zhejiang 2005: 12). Scattered pottery shards and charred animal bones are also in evidence at most other altar cemeteries, which strongly suggests that post-interment rituals were held, perhaps at regular intervals, to honor and placate the powerful elite figures entombed in those graves (see data provided in Childs-Johnson 2009: 316–18).

Residential settlements are associated with most of the sacred altar sites and may be characterized as large-, middle-, and small-scale chiefdoms or city-states. Differences in size of the residential areas, together with the layout and furnishing of burials, appear to describe a hierarchical, patriarchal structure of Liangzhu society (see e.g., Lu Jf 1996; Childs-Johnson 2009: 311–29) in which case the most richly furnished burials would represent members of a ruling lineage in a direct line of descent. Somewhat less elaborate burials represent members of branch lineages that were closely or

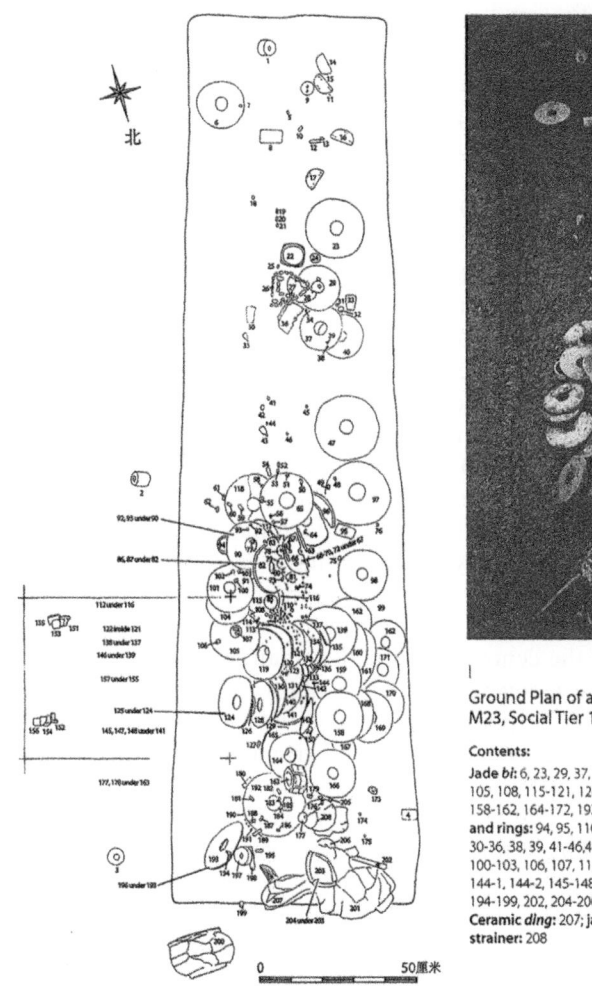

Ground Plan of a Liangzhu Burial:
M23, Social Tier 1, Fanshan, Yuhang, Zhejiang

Contents:

Jade *bi*: 6, 23, 29, 37, 40, 47, 65, 82, 90, 96-98, 101, 104,
105, 108, 115-121, 124, 128-134, 136, 137, 139-143,
158-162, 164-172, 192, 193; *cong*: 22, 126, 163; **bracelets
and rings**: 94, 95, 110; **ornaments**: 1-5, 7-21, 24-28,
30-36, 38, 39, 41-46,48-64, 66-81, 83, 85-87, 91-95, 99,
100-103, 106, 107, 112-114, 122, 123, 125, 127, 135, 138,
144-1, 144-2, 145-148-3, 150-157, 173-190, 191-1-2,
194-199, 202, 204-206
Ceramic *ding*: 207; jars: 200-201; **steamer *ding*: 203;
strainer**: 208

Figure 3.10 AB Ground plan and photograph of Fanshan burial M23, Social Tier 1,
Yuhang, Zhejiang. After Childs-Johnson 2009: Figure 15B8.

distantly related to the main lineage. Beneath these elite groups was a large
population of commoners, including artisans, farmers, slaves, and others.

The number and type of jades interred with the deceased, as well as
details of burial size, structure, and location, distinguish social rank and the
above hypothesized patriarchal structure of Liangzhu society. At the top
of the social pyramid (variously identified as a clan patriarch, paramount
chieftain, or ruler), burials are strikingly rich. Gradations of elite status
can also be inferred from the percentage of jade (as opposed to stone or

ceramic) objects among the funerary goods. For example, of the total goods recovered from tomb M3 at Sidun, 114 are jades and 13 are other goods, including ceramic vessels and stone tools, for a total of approximately 89 percent jades. At Yaoshan and Fanshan, jades occupy 97 percent of the burial goods. The percentage of jades per burial decreases as status decreases. Fewer jade artifacts and more numerous stone tools and more ceramics appear as status subsides. The percentage of jades per burial at Fuquanshan is slightly lower, averaging 79 percent. The same decreasing percentage applies to third tier platform cemetery sites, such as Zhaolingshan and Zhanglingshan (Childs-Johnson 2009: Figures 13 and 14).

The occupants of the principal tombs at Fanshan and Yaoshan, two of the highest-ranking platform cemetery sites thus far excavated, may be identified as high-ranking leaders based on both the burials' location and by the type and quantity of burial goods. The highest-ranking burial has the following characteristics: (1) a central location in the second southern row, a site associated with males as opposed to females in the northern row; (2) the richest number of jades; (3) the highest quality of jade material; (4) the most sophisticated and high-ranking jade sets identified as hair and headdress ornaments; (5) ritual jade types, including *cong* cylinders and *yue* broad axes; and (6) distinctive royal imagery. Senior burials at both Fanshan and Yaoshan occupy the central grave amidst a total of 12 or 13 total burials. Unfortunately, the central grave at Yaoshan was seriously looted and only 347 jades were recovered when the site was excavated scientifically. The largest number of jades is associated with the senior burial at Fanshan, totaling 647 pieces, in contrast to other male burials at Fanshan varying between 300 and 500 jades. The set of jades identifying a ruler or paramount chieftain includes: (1) a high-quality jade *yue* with chape and pommel fittings, as well as suspended toggles and pieces of jade inlay for the staff; (2) various *cong*; (3) *bi* disks; (4) and hair or headdress ornaments comprising D-shaped jades, one three-prong C-shaped ornament, one crown ornament for a comb, and a group of awl-shaped ornaments. Other small-scale fittings and attachments, in top-ranking burials, include small-scale plaques, *huang* pendants, belt buckles, bracelets, and elaborate beaded necklaces (see Figure 3.11).

The jade pieces from the central burial are distinguished not only by their quantity, but also by their size, fineness of their workmanship, and distinctive imagery. The central tomb at Fanshan contained the singularly large and impressive *cong* prismatic cylinder that has been dubbed by archaeologists the *cong wang*, "the king of *cong*" (Figure 3.12), and the singularly high-quality *yue* ax, similarly known as the *yue wang*, "the king of *yue*" (Figure 3.10C top). (Childs-Johnson 2009: Figure 15C3).

The standardization of form and imagery of the *cong* prismatic cylinder underscores its probable ritual and religious significance. As a rule, the

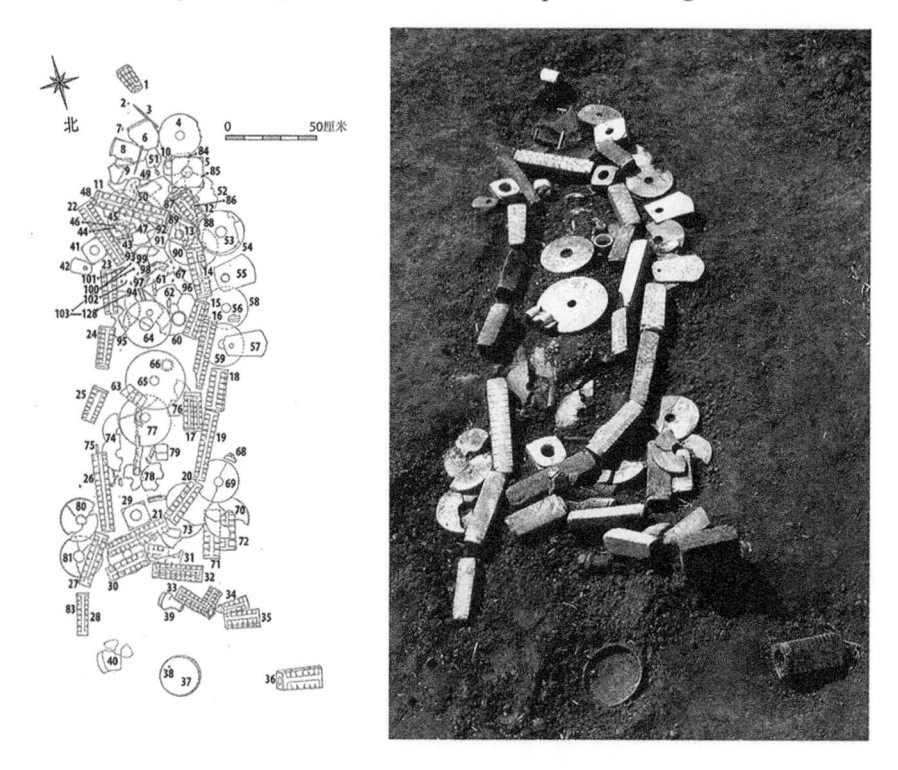

Figure 3.11 Ground plan and photograph of Sidun burial M3, social tier 2, Wujing, Jiangsu. After Childs-Johnson 2009: Figure A1.0, A3.

shape conforms to a prismatic cylinder: open and circular inside and square outside, with differentiated base and top rims (Figures 3.2AB and 3.13A). Diameters are consistently larger at the top and smaller at the base and vary in size from approximately 5–19 cm tall. The square exterior is described as prismatic because the four outer corners form triangular prisms. Exterior surfaces are decorated with facial images, and sometimes with both facial and body parts, dividing in half at each corner of the outer square. Images fill one or two circumscribing bands or as many as 19 bands (see Figure 3.2AB).

Standardization and significance of the main image neatly conjoin. The four external corners are always decorated with animal and human mask-like images, and sometimes with an additional pair of small-scale flanking "cosmic bird" images, identified by their symbolic composition of eye as a sun disk amidst clouds (as proposed by Hayashi 1992 and Childs-Johnson 2009: 350). Surfaces are rarely plain; yet when images are present, they

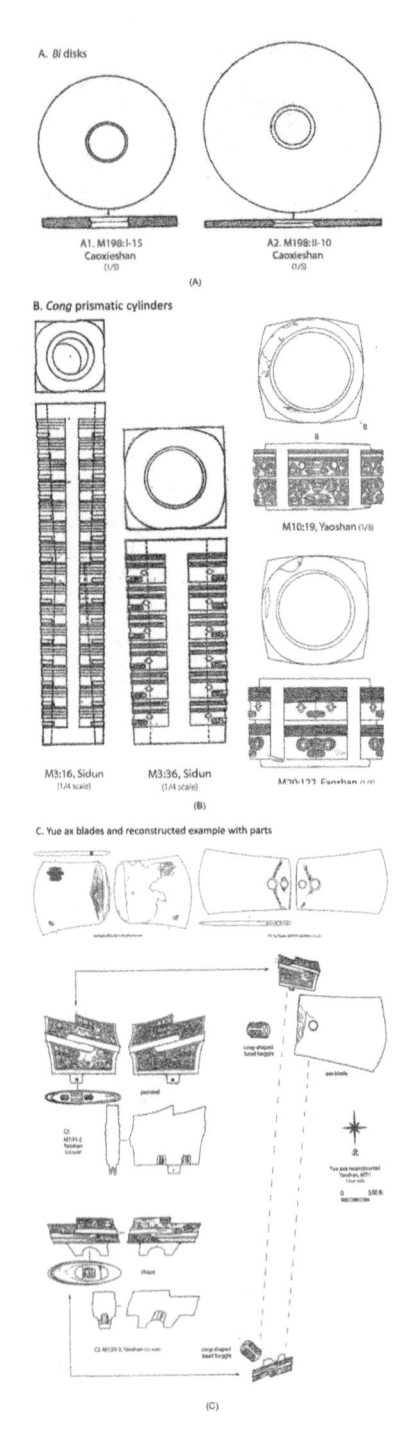

Figure 3.12 A–H Jade types of the Liangzhu culture. Based on Childs-Johnson 2009: 340–349, Figure 15A–H.

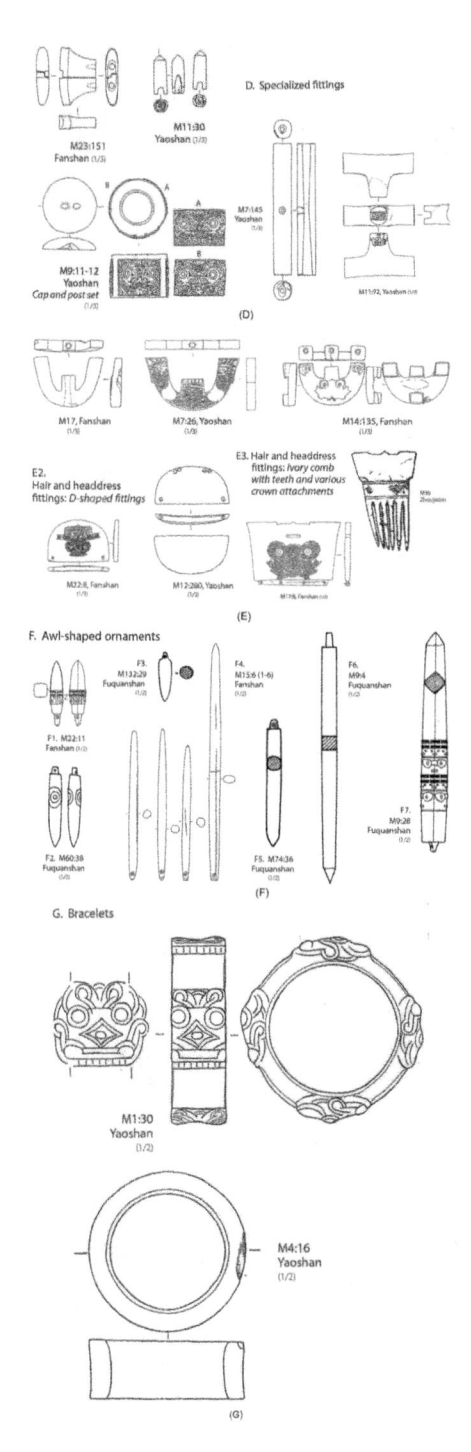

Figure 3.12 (Continued)

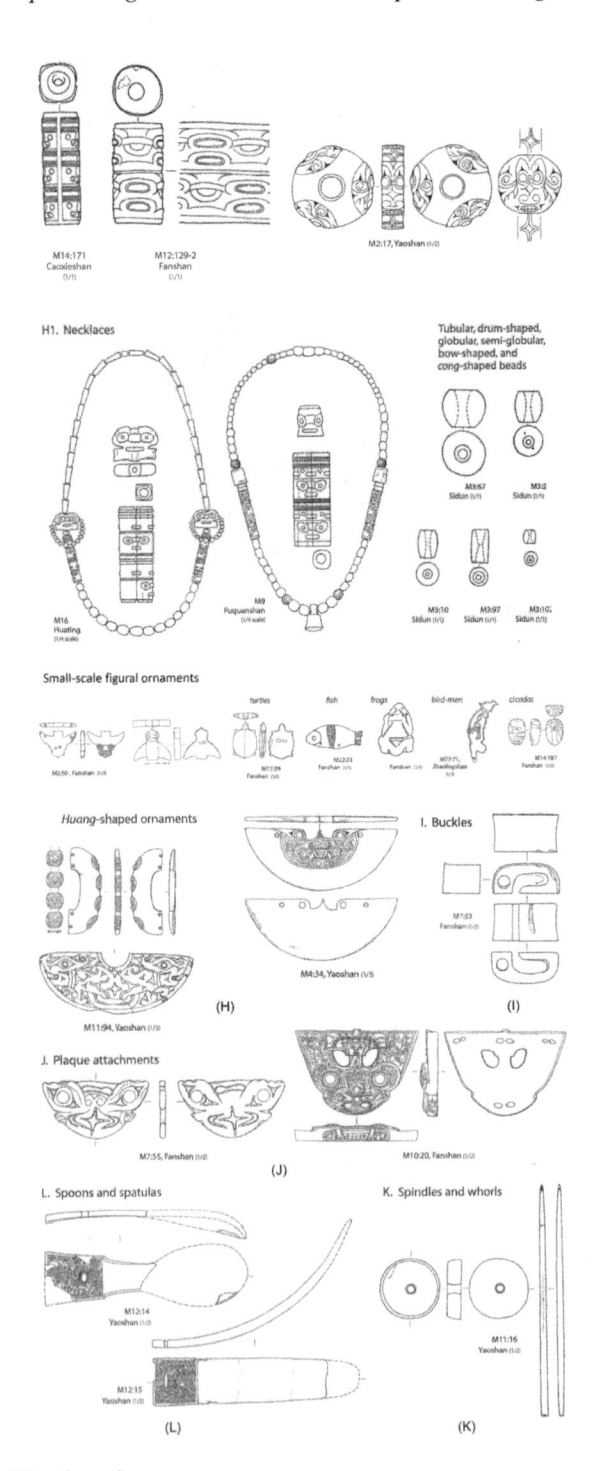

Figure 3.12 (Continued)

always number four or multiples of four (see e.g., Figure 3.13), an orientation likely connected with the jade's symbolic purpose and Liangzhu's belief in the importance of directional orientation. The assertive power of what we interpret as a literal metamorphic icon decorates the famous and often-illustrated so-called "king of *cong*" from grave M12 at Fanshan (Figure 3.14), which we will discuss momentarily.

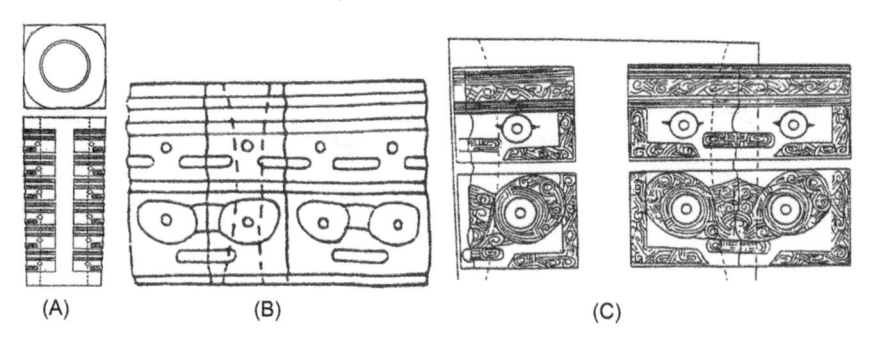

(A)   (B)   (C)

Figure 3.13 Variations on the image of the semi-human and animal deity on Liangzhu jade *cong*, exhibiting both simplified and complete versions. A Six tiers of the simplified image of the semi-human deity, M3:36 Sidun, Jiangsu. B–C Two alternating tiers of the semi-human and animal deity, M18 Sidun and M4 Sidun. After Childs-Johnson 2009: Figures 15: B8 and 16: M3A3 and A1.0.

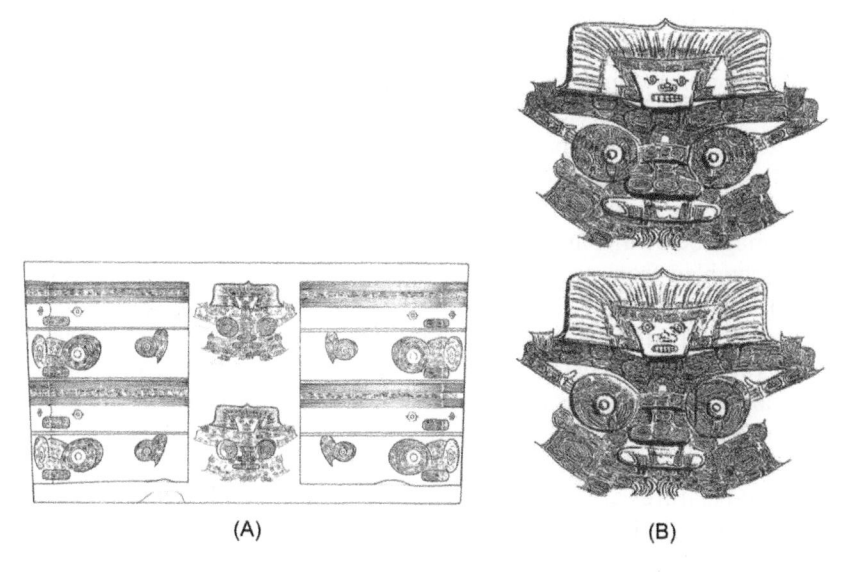

(A)   (B)

Figure 3.14 The "King of *Cong*" from M12:98, Fanshan, Yuhang, Zhejiang exhibiting two double tiers of the semi-human and animal deity flanked by cosmic birds and two images of the complete version of the semi-human and animal deity. After Childs-Johnson 2009: Figure 16B3/ Liu B 2020, Chapter 5: 129, Figure 8.

"King" in the sense of rule over a substantial area and its population appears to be appropriate for this representational interpretation of image incised on both the above *cong* and frequently the *yue* ax, another emblem of a ruler's power. This most important Liangzhu image exists in two forms, which may be termed "complete" and "schematic." There are two basic parts to the image, one humanoid and one mythic, a mask, whether represented schematically or completely. Both feature a disguise with round frontward staring eyes with round pupils. In the case of the schematic humanoid image, the ends of eyes are often elongated. The two parts of the schematic versions are often limited to (1) an upper face with circles for eyes and a long oval for the mouth with a flat band for a headdress and (2) a lower face with circles for pupils encircled by oval sockets, a nose bridge, and long oval mouth. The facial parts of simplified versions may also be filled with tiny circular scrolls extended with wing ends. These two images are often found in multiple copies on the prismatic faces of *cong* cylinders.

The complete version is a complicated image that is metamorphic in the most literal sense; a single image can be read as follows (Figure 3.13): the upper range features a humanoid with a trapezoidal face, round eyes set within open eyelids, a wide, flat nose, and a grimacing mouth full of teeth. The figure wears a large and elaborate headdress that appears to be made of a displayed bracket-shaped band of eyed peafowl feathers and an inner frame of cloud scrolls. The same cloud scrolls fill most parts of the image. Below the face, exaggeratedly long arms ending in human hands (with four fingers and opposable thumbs) are bent akimbo in a sharp angle; the fingertips touch the outer edges of a pair of prominent circles. We surmise that in this iteration of the metamorphic figure, the circles touched or grasped by the humanoid may represent *bi* jade disks that are being displayed in a ritualistic fashion. The circles also, of course, represent the large, staring eyes of the zoomorphic mask below. The *bi* as sun-disk or "cosmic eye" meshes symbolically with the all-seeing eyes that are the most prominent features of that mask.

The image below the humanoid face on the Fanshan '*cong*' is a composite mask assembled from animal and bird parts. The large ovoid pair of eyes have circular pupils and are connected by a bridge-like band surmounting a broad nose shaped like an upside-down T. Below the nose, a sausage-shaped mouth is adorned with two pairs of tusks, pointing upwards and downwards. These, along with the eyes and nose, eerily recall features of the Hongshan "dragon head," though stylistically they are very different, being linear and calligraphic rather than being sculpted in the round. Extending and framing these facial features are bent limbs set amidst cloud scrolls but readily identifiable as limbs ending in prominent claws. Cloud scrolls fill all forms of this flattened icon (with extra scrolls between eye and mouth and at the center of each folded limb); wing-like extensions at three points along the edges of the folded lower limbs apparently symbolize flight. These features are standardized in representation on a whole host of comparable jade images, for example, as at Sidun (see Figure 3.1A–C), a partially excavated Liang-zhu site in Jiangsu province. The linked concepts of metamorphosis and flight form a common theme throughout later Chinese art and find potential origin here in the southern culture of Liangzhu. The bas-relief image on Liangzhu *cong* clearly signifies a token of power; a humanoid deity riding a mythical beast made up of animal and bird parts endowed with the power of flight as symbolized by wings and cloud scrolls. (For other interpretations of the imagery, see Liu B 2013 and Liu B *et al* 2016.)

This image represents, and indeed portrays in detail, the metamorphic transformation of an elite male human into a powerful, and apparently awe-some, mask-like being that has attributes of different kinds of animals. The figure in the upper register is undoubtedly a ruler or chieftain, his rank and status indicated by his splendid feather headdress. Every physical feature of the human image has a counterpart in the lower metamorphic power mask. The human's staring eyes, with their elongated sockets, become the huge staring eyes of the mask. The human's rather lumpish nose becomes the equally bulbous nose of the mask. The human's toothy, grimacing mouth becomes the mouth of the mask, with sharper and more threatening looking teeth. The human's arms held akimbo (and which are meticulously provided with human hands) transform into the bent, bestial forelimbs of the mask figure. The limbs are furnished with long, dangerous-looking claws, which may be modeled on those of an avian raptor. The limbs of the metamorphic power mask have small wing extrusions, which together with the pervasive cloud scrolls that fill the image's surface strongly corroborate that the trans-formed figure has the spirit power of flight in a context of consuming clouds. (The mark of an immortal in Warring States and Han art similarly shows arms sprouting wings or winglets.) The message of the Liangzhu metamor-phic power mask is that a powerful human ruler has been transformed into a powerful composite beast, hungry for sacrifice, and, with imagination, ready to grasp it in fearsomely clawed limbs to devour it.

The explicitly metamorphic character of this complex image is important for its relationship to metamorphic mask images (the traditional yet errone-ously so-called *taotie*) found on Shang ritual bronzes more than a millen-nium later. The upright figure with its feather headdress and its pair of oval socketed eyes almost certainly represents a ruler or chieftain becoming a deified ancestor. The power mask into which its features are transformed is formally like the Shang metamorphic power image to a striking degree. The mask's staring eyes, shrunken arms, and claw-bearing paws likewise are directly ancestral to features of similar figures on Shang bronzes. So, too, is the engraved fretwork of cloud scrolls that fills the otherwise empty space within the mask, and the metamorphic character of some of the image's fine details – for example, the humanoid figure's arms that transform into the mask's winged forelimbs. It is difficult to escape the conclusion that the complex Liangzhu metamorphic power image represents the transforma-tion of a deceased ruler or chieftain into a post-mortem powerful being.

The inference that the Liangzhu metamorphic power image represents a deity of some kind is reinforced by the iconographic stability of the image, in both its complete and schematic forms. Multiple instantiations of these images all look alike (compare, for example, images in Figures 3.12 and 3.13). This is not mere décor, subject to modification at an artist's whim; the details are consistent and meaningful, even if we today can only guess at their meaning. The few variant details that do occur have their own standards; for example, the arm extensions of the animal mask may not be represented, although those of the human are, and vice versa. Occasionally, the complex animal mask with arm extensions is represented without the humanoid "rider," but these are exceptions to the rule. When represented alone and in repeated format, the humanoid upper part of the image may be abbreviated to two slit eyes, an oval mouth, and a crown abstracted as horizontal lines (Figure 3.13A). The part-animal, part-bird mask, when schematized, may lack limbs but is always characterized by large ovoid eye sockets, a nasal bridge, and a long flat mouth (Figure 3.13BC). When the humanoid figure and the zoomorphic mask are represented together, the humanoid is usually placed above the mask, illustrating the authority of the human over the animal-spirit world. These standardized formats reinforce the conclusion that these images represent the metamorphosis of a deceased elite male into a divine power.

We may speak of these repeated images as metamorphic power symbols for several reasons, which have to do with modes of representation (Childs-Johnson 1998a: 34–36). First and foremost, the images are flat and heraldic. Second, they combine both real and fantastic attributes. Third, sometimes cosmic birds in profile flank the semi-human figure and zoomorphic mask (Figure 3.14A), but they always are subordinate to the central power image. Fourth, the humanoid is always represented symbolically, as dominating the animal, and in the case of the king of *cong* images as riding the animal, as if the humanoid has been transformed into an immortal deity able to travel within the spirit realm. Fifth, the elongated bent arms of the humanoid and similarly those of the zoomorphic mask may be simplified as extended wings without claws or human digits. Sixth, the zoomorphic mask when represented as a complex image takes on the attributes of flight, since the limb pairs are always decorated with wing-like excrescences. Seventh, cloud scroll clusters symbolizing the sky always fill all parts of the image that would otherwise be vacant, alluding to cosmological spirit flight and transformation of the human from this world to the spirit realm. In both their complex and schematic forms, these icons of metamorphic power symbolize the ability of deceased elite males to take on attributes of flight and supernatural transformation.

The Liangzhu metamorphic power image is sometimes flanked by a pair of birds depicted in profile (as initiated during the Hemudu culture in Zhejiang, see incised masks Figure 3.15AB). These may be identified as sun symbols; the identification of the sun with a bird (often a crow or raven) is widespread in the folklore of northeastern Asia and northwestern North America and appears to be deeply rooted in early Sinitic culture as well (Erkes 1926: 32–54). Hayashi Minao (Hayashi 1992), who has formulated a comprehensive hypothesis on the interpretation of Liangzhu symbolism, sees Liangzhu bird imagery, and specifically what looks like a whorl or eye surrounded by rings, as symbolic of both the sun and the moon, richly endowed with cosmological power. Hayashi's identification of this key element of Liangzhu iconography reinforces the imagery of cosmological spirit power manifested in the metamorphic transformation of dead elite males into fearsome beings endowed with animal power. Hayashi is persuasive in his assessment that the representation of the eye filling the body of the profile bird flanking the human in flight also characterizes the eye type of the zoomorphic animal: it is significant in symbolizing the power of the sun and moon, anticipating the later cosmological concept of *qi* 氣 or "vital essence." (Hayashi 1992; also see Childs-Johnson 2012). Hayashi explores thoroughly the representation of fiery *yang qi* and the watery *yin qi* in sun and moon symbols in Han art. His most powerful evidence for the argument that the eye is cosmologically meaningful appears in the various representations of the spirit birds in Hemudu and Liangzhu period imagery (see Figure 3.15).

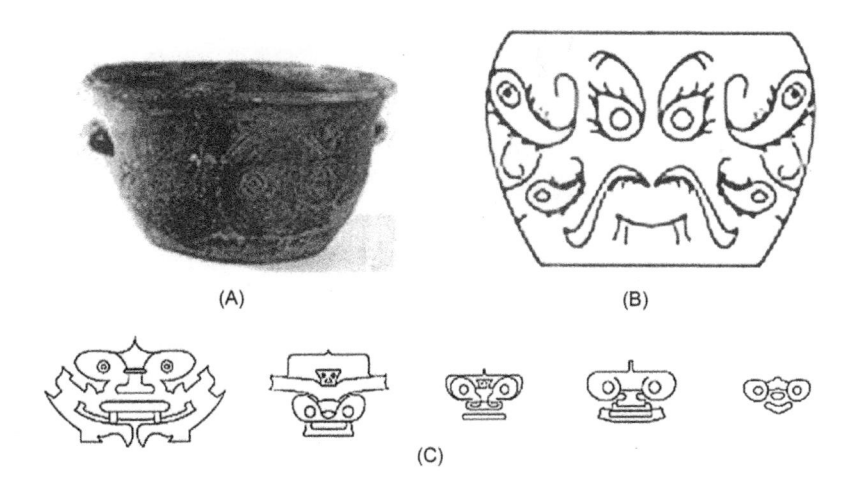

(A)   (B)

(C)

Figure 3.15 Variations on the zoomorphic mask from pre-Liangzhu and Liangzhu cultures (A–B) masks with eyes decorating two pre-Liangzhu Hemudu culture blackware basins (an incised zoomorphic mask with circular eyes and trapezoidal crown flanked by profile birds); (C) Drawings and jades with the same zoomorphic mask decorating Liangzhu jades, primarily *cong* prismatic cylindrical tubes. (AB) Based on Lin 1998:134, Figure 5–1,4,5; 373, Figure 9–1. (C) Based on Childs-Johnson 2009: 349, Figure 16B.

The pervasive presence of the eye in Hemudu and Liangzhu imagery appears to be not only a sun (and moon) symbol, as stressed by Hayashi, but also represents a vital force that endows beings (including humans metamorphically transformed after death) with life itself. The circular eye is consistently represented as surrounded by incised circular lines, sometimes with pairs of scrolls or short horizontal lines, and is extended with rays or ovoid extensions filled with cloud scrolls (Figure 3.16AB). Sometimes, as in the case of the Hemudu ivories (see Figure 3.16CD), two bird images confronting each other have bodies formed from the "empowered eye" with jutting rays (Figure 3.16C); sometimes the image is simplified to one "empowered eye" forming the body of two birds in profile (Figure 3.16D), and elsewhere on Hemudu period atlatl weapons wings flank the empowered eye depicted as a sun and moon symbol with rays (Figure 3.16B). Sometimes this "empowered eye" symbol is found on the bodies of wild boar and tiger images decorating Hemudu blackware vessels (Figure 3.16EF). What is the significance of this "eye" motif?

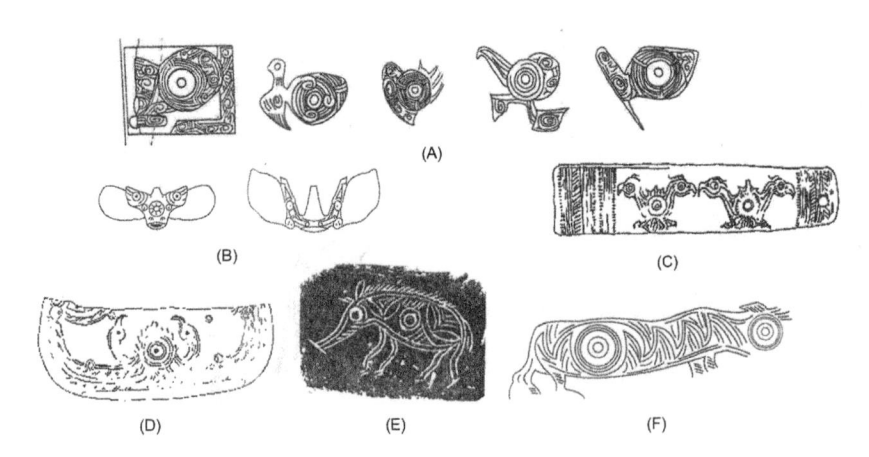

Figure 3.16 The cosmic eye symbol in pre-Liangzhu Hemudu (A) and Liangzhu culture art (B–F) (A) Detail drawing of one-half of deity mask on Liangzhu *cong* and same "cosmic eye" decorating the body of mythic birds on similar Liangzhu cong. (B) Drawing of cosmic eye and bird image of a Hemudu culture atlatl. (C–D) Two drawings of paired and addorsed mythic birds with "cosmic eye" decorating Hemudu culture bone ornaments. (E) Drawing of boar with "cosmic eye" decorating the boar's body, blackware basin, and Hemudu culture. (F) Drawing of profile tiger with "cosmic eyes" decorating body and head, blackware ceramic, and Hemudu culture. After Childs-Johnson 2009: 16B:A2 partial (A), (C1–4) and Lin 1998: Figure 7–5, 14; 268, Figure 7–3: 5,14 and 360, Figure 8–15:4 (A); 1992: 222, Figure 8–10 Є; 207, Figure 8–1 (D); 232, Figure 9–3:1,4 (B); and Hayashi tr 1997: 183 Figure 4–39(C).

We focus attention on what we call the "empowered or cosmic eye" because it is the most prominent attribute of the mythic mask of metamorphosis on Liangzhu *cong* and because it appears as the body part of the "cosmological bird" (Figures 3.16A and 3.14A) and occasionally on the body of wild beasts – wild boars and tigers (Figure 3.16EF). The fact that this eye – the most prominent feature of the power masks of Liangzhu *cong* – was standardized as an image of an empowered deity or deified ancestor underscores its significance as a symbol of cosmic power, and of the power of humans to dominate and control (presumably through ritual behavior) the power of the non-human world. Given that images of powerful wild animals – wild boars and tigers – on Hemudu pottery and the deified metamorphic image on Liangzhu jades are similarly endowed with this power symbol reinforces the hypothesis that the "empowered eye" represents a life-giving force.

It therefore is not surprising that the winged bird bearing an eye motif defines the image and shape of atlatls (spear-throwing devices) discovered at Hemudu and Liangzhu period sites in Zhejiang (Figure 3.16B; Lin 1992: 231–32). The atlatls are shaped and designed as birds in flight, with open wings framing a round or oblong eye socket, sometimes further decorated with a solar disk with eight rays or with abbreviated claws. Designed to increase the speed and force of a thrown spear, the atlatl's bird shape and eye motif would endow the spear with the power of flight and with the power to take the life of its target.

Images representing an altar, sometimes with associated motifs, are found on a number of Dawenkou and Liangzhu jades and ceramics (Figure 3.17A–D) (Liangzhu 2015). Some of these altar images include sun and moon symbols, with the placement of the sun disk and the moon crescent varying in different examples. The sun motif is variously depicted as an empty round circle, an ovoid image (that possibly anticipates the later written graph for the word sun 日), a circle filled with cloud scrolls, or a circle with interior divided into four quadrants and further decorated by winged extensions and a crown shape. The profile bird may also be included in this concatenation of symbols, perched at the top of the altar (e.g., Figure 3.17C). One isolated example of the bird plus sun and moon symbols is abstracted as an open-winged form with limbs and eyes (Figure 3.17B upper left), approximating the atlatl in the shape of a bird and eye in flight. Hayashi interprets this altar imagery as relating to agricultural fecundity controlled by cosmic forces as symbolized by the sun and moon (Hayashi 2004). In addition, the juxtaposition on some of these altar images of the sun disk and the crescent moon is an apparent reference to the recurrent physical phenomenon of the new moon, which from time immemorial in Sinitic culture has marked the beginning of a lunar month (and, via an arbitrarily designated "first month," of the new year as well). This may imply that rites proclaiming and celebrating each new month may have been conducted at such altars.

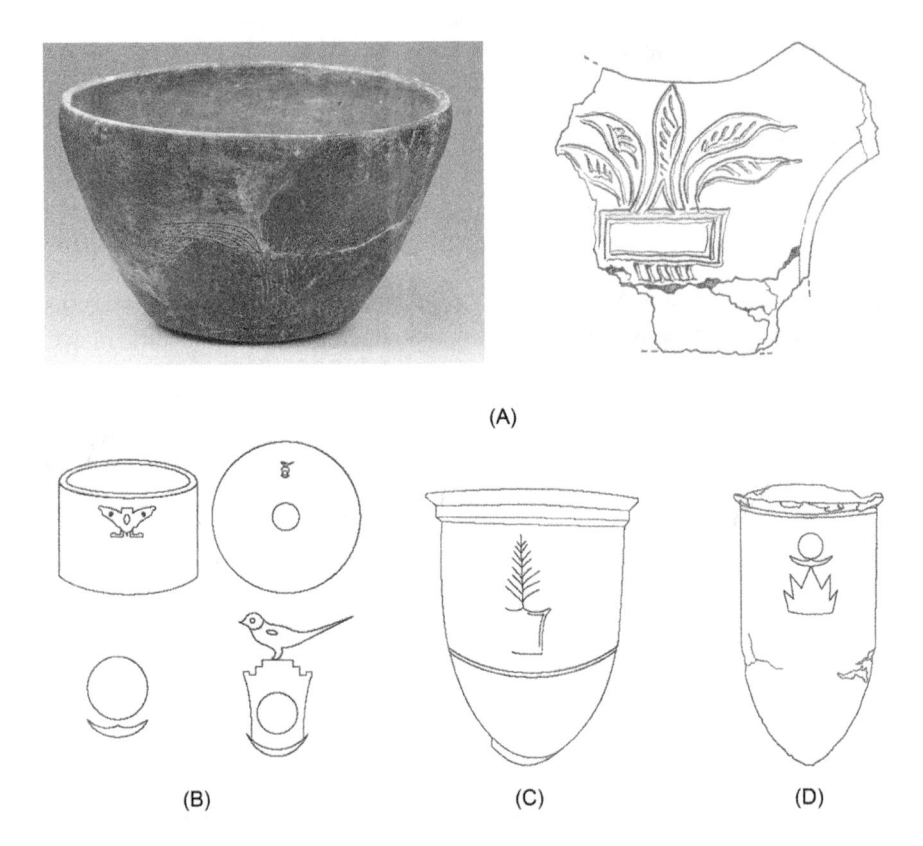

(A)

(B)   (C)   (D)

Figure 3.17 Variations of the stepped altar emblem in combination with related
cosmological symbols on jades and ceramic blackwares from southern
Hemudu and Liangzhu culture sites and northern Dawenkou, Shandong cultural sites, showing cultural interchange. (A) Blackware shard
incised with altar and sprouting growth from Hemudu. After Lin 1992:
pl.7d middle left; (B) Altar emblem in combination with the "first moon"
cosmological and bird symbols on Liangzhu jade *bi* disks and tall
ring. Childs-Johnson 2002 CAA reviews 10.3202/caa.reviews.2002.92:
Figure 8.4; (C) An altar emblem incised on large blackware zun
vessel, Dawenkou culture, Lingyanghe, Juxian, Shandong. Photo by Xu
Lin/China.org.cn/travel/201112/27/content_24223289_20.htm. (D) An
altar plus "first moon" cosmological symbol on another blackware zun,
Dawenkou culture. After Nanjing 1993: 87 Figure 49.1.

Metamorphic power, flight, and the ability of humans to dominate and
avail themselves of the power of wild beasts become associated, through
the altar image, with agricultural fecundity and the practice of sacrifice,
perhaps specifically entailing the sacrifice of harvested grain. Late Neolithic
artifacts from Hemudu, Dawenkou, Liangzhu, and Longshan cultures testify to the importance of the grain altar (perhaps an axis mundi symbol),

rendered as a platform with sprouts suggestive of grain (Figure 3.17A), as an oblong with a triad of plants (Figure 3.17A), or as a stepped pyramidal structure (Figure 3.17C) recalling the raised outdoor altars found in all elite Liangzhu cemeteries. The distinctive stepped form of these altars is thus associated with the burial rites, and hypothesized ongoing ancestral rites, associated with the graves of powerful Liangzhu chiefs and their allies.

Another emblem of cosmological significance in the repertoire of Liangzhu period imagery is a variant of the altar with bird winged disk, sometimes emphasizing a quadrant formation and sometimes including an abbreviated form of the eyed animal mask (Figure 3.17A–D). The bird-winged circular disk decorates the interior outline of the stepped altar or the same bird form and disk create a whirling extension divided quadrilaterally around a circular center as four winged parts. Sometimes the latter image is simplified to a circle surrounded by four abstract and abbreviated bird wing extensions or simply by cloud scrolls. (Figure 3.18A–C). These variations are abstract images of cosmological power: whether defined by the bird in flight, solar disk or crescent moon, the empowered eye, or scrolls of clouds, these images continued to retain their power and significance in the next era of the Jade Age, the Longshan period.

One other artistic gift of the Liangzhu people flows from the invention of thin-walled black ceramic vessels (Lu X 2013). Examples have been found not only in Liangzhu sites but also further north at Huating in northern Jiangsu and other sites in Zhejiang and Shanghai. Some of the most refined Liangzhu blackwares (similar but stylistically and technically different from

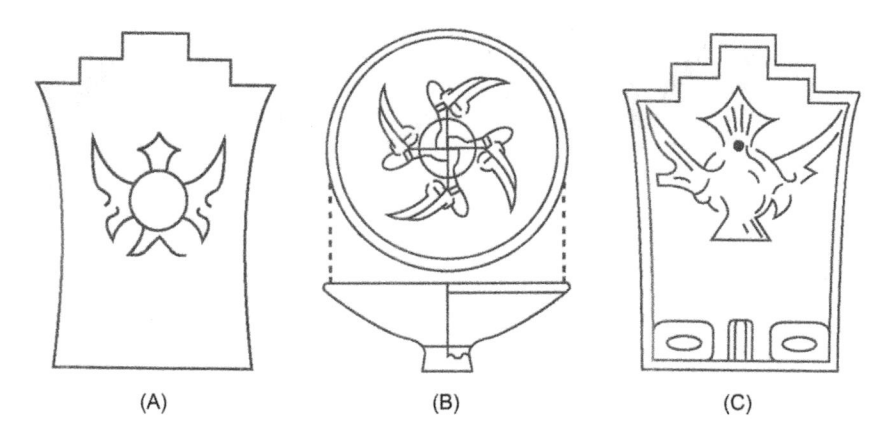

(A)   (B)   (C)

Figure 3.18 Variations of the cosmic bird symbol and eye in combination with the stepped altar symbol and semi-human mask symbol. The cosmic bird enclosed within an altar symbol worked on a Liangzhu jade *bi* disk (A); the cosmic bird disk decorating the interior of a Liangzhu blackware bowl (B); and eyed zoomorph and cosmic bird disk within a stepped altar emblem worked on a Liangzhu jade *bi* disk (C). After Lin 1992: 224, Figure 8–11.

the later Longshan *danketao* 蛋殼陶) are decorated with delicately incised images of birds and curvilinear cloud scrolls. Truly exquisite in design, these abstractions of metamorphism evenly circumscribe vessels or independently scatter on surfaces of blackware tripod *ding,* handled *he* and various jars with eccentrically shaped lids, and perforated stands.

Liangzhu's Demise

Liangzhu culture collapsed rather suddenly around 2300 BCE, possibly because of a disastrous flood, or series of floods, in the lower Yangzi River plain as theorized by Wu L (2014: 78–79) or to what geoarchaeologists describe as a crater impact that triggered the extinction of the Liangzhu culture and the creation of Lake Tai (see Xie Zd *et al* 2008). Some refugees certainly escaped south or moved to the north, becoming absorbed in the Longshan culture that had begun to establish itself in Shandong and adjacent areas around 2600 BCE. Whether mediated by refugees, or trade, or warfare, or some combination of those, elements of Liangzhu culture, including expert jade-working, did become incorporated into Longshan culture. As archaeological work in the Liangzhu culture area proceeds year by year, the Liangzhu polity appears more and more impressive. Large, powerful, wealthy, and sophisticated, Liangzhu looms ever larger as one of the key sources for an emerging Sinitic civilization and religion.

Notes

1 See, for example, Shi Xg 1938 and Liu B 2009: 19–22; Sun, Zx 1993: 1–40.
2 See, for example, Renfrew and Liu 2018; Liu B 2020; Liu, B et al. 2016; Childs-Johnson 2009: 210–392, esp. pp. 291–353; 2020; Liu, L. and Chen, X. 2003.
3 For an extensive treatment of Liangzhu site names, their location, sequence, typology, and references, see Childs-Johnson 2009: 310–53 and Liu B 2020.
4 See map in Childs-Johnson 2009: 313, Figure 9; Chen and Wu 1996: 306, Table 1.

4 Continuation of Metamorphic Imagery and Ancestor Worship in the Longshan Culture

As we shall demonstrate in this chapter, Longshan culture adhered to, modified, and passed on to its Bronze Age successors the religious rites and symbolic iconography associated with metamorphism that appeared earlier in the formal artistic expression of Liangzhu. It is not possible at present to form a well-rounded and accurate picture of Longshan culture, in part because of a dearth of scientifically reported excavations (see e.g., Sun B 2013; Liu, L 2004; Liu and Chen 2012), and also because Longshan culture spread widely and quickly in the early third millennium BCE, giving rise to local variants that complicate characterizing "Longshan culture" as a whole (see Figure 4.1) (Sun B 2013: 435, 452–53; Luan 1997). In its broadest sense, the term Longshan refers to a set of shared cultural traits that, based on currently available data, appears to have originated in Shandong and northern Henan, emerging from the earlier Dawenkou culture in those areas (Sun and Zhao 2013). The defining difference between late Dawenkou culture and early Shandong Longshan culture is the emergence in the early Longshan period of a distinctive and highly refined blackware ceramic, and of vessel sets that are related specifically to a nascent practice of worship of ancestral spirits. This newly emergent culture spread to encompass the Yellow River valley in Shaanxi, Shanxi, and even parts of Gansu and Qinghai, as well as throughout Hubei, Anhui, and Yangzi River valley sites as far west as Sichuan. The Longshan culture extended throughout most of the East Asian Heartland Region and shared a key set of cultural traits across that vast area which determined a common belief in metamorphism and ancestral cult worship.

The dating and terminology used to describe the Longshan period are confusing. As noted by Gao Guangren and Shao Wangping, well over 30 different names have been used by archaeologists to describe the time 3000–2000 BCE at different sites throughout China (Shao 1998: 41; Shao and Gao 1984; Gao and Shao 2005). Many of these terms simply use the names of excavated sites to describe variants of Longshan culture – "Shanbei Longshan," "Shijiahe Longshan," and so on. Since such emphasis impedes understanding of Longshan culture as a whole, we focus here on continuities and commonalities across the whole sphere of Longshan sites. Shao dates the

DOI: 10.4324/9781003341246-4

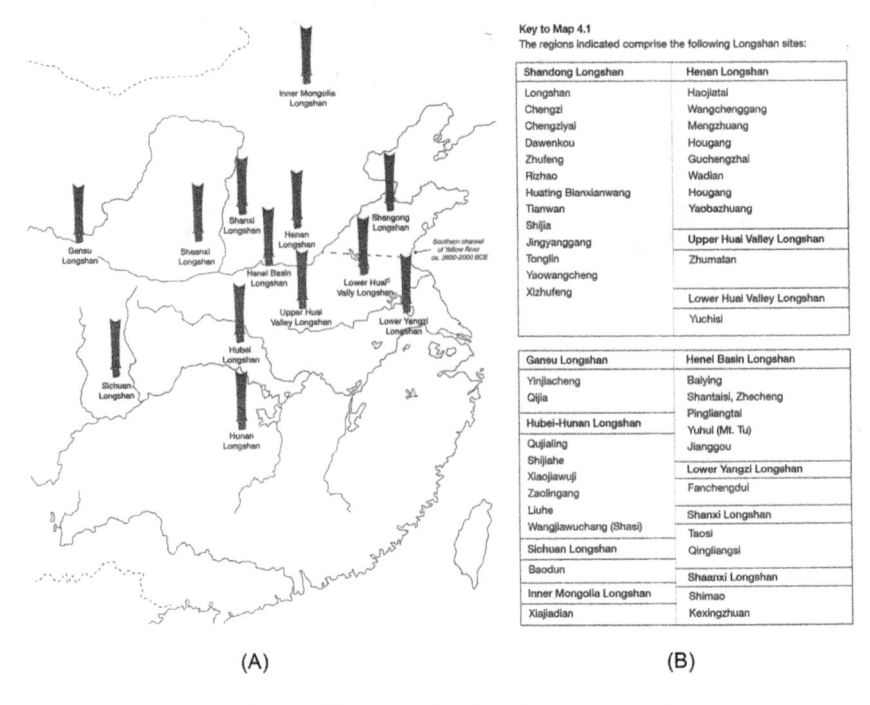

Key to Map 4.1	
The regions indicated comprise the following Longshan sites:	
Shandong Longshan	**Henan Longshan**
Longshan	Haojiatai
Chengzi	Wangchenggang
Chengziyai	Mengzhuang
Dawenkou	Hougang
Zhufeng	Guchengzhai
Rizhao	Wadian
Huating Bianxianwang	Hougang
Tianwan	Yaobazhuang
Shijia	
Jingyanggang	**Upper Huai Valley Longshan**
Tonglin	Zhumatan
Yaowangcheng	
Xizhufeng	**Lower Huai Valley Longshan**
	Yuchisi

Gansu Longshan	**Henei Basin Longshan**
Yinjiacheng	Baiying
Qijia	Shantaisi, Zhecheng
	Pingliangtai
Hubei-Hunan Longshan	Yuhui (Mt. Tu)
Qujialing	Jianggou
Shijiahe	
Xiaojiawuji	**Lower Yangzi Longshan**
Zaolingang	Fanchengdui
Liuhe	
Wangjiawuchang (Shasi)	**Shanxi Longshan**
	Taosi
Sichuan Longshan	Qingliangsi
Baodun	
	Shaanxi Longshan
Inner Mongolia Longshan	Shimao
Xiajiadian	Kexingzhuan

(A)   (B)

Figure 4.1 Longshan sites and key. Drawing by Margaret Panoti.

first phase of the Shandong Longshan culture to the end of the Dawenkou culture in Shandong, ca. 2800 BCE (see Luan 2013 and Sun B 2013).[1] The full-fledged classical Shandong Longshan period spans the period 2600–2000 BCE, comprising an early and late phase.

The Longshan culture originated in Shandong around 2800–2600 BCE, and, with many local variations, dominated the East Asian Heartland Region in the final stage of the Jade Age. It was characterized by the emergence of complex states and transitioned directly to the Bronze Age around 2000 BCE. Longshan culture is most famous for its distinctive ceramics and jades.[2] Ceremonial objects, such as goblets used in mortuary rituals and frequently found in elite burials, were made of thin-walled, wheel-thrown or hand-built blackware (Underhill 1998). Longshan artisans produced a wide variety of jade objects including some new and distinctive types, the most characteristic of which was the *zhang* 璋 blade which most likely served as a sign of rank or status in Longshan society (Childs-Johnson 1995b, 2009). Like the "pig-drag-ons" of Hongshan, the *bi* and *cong* of Liangzhu, and the eggshell-thin black-ware of Longshan, the Longshan jade *zhang* is instantly recognizable as a cultural marker (Tang *et al* 2014; Tang C 2017; Tang and Wang 2020).

The ethnicity of the people in the Longshan home territory in Shan-dong cannot be known with any certainty, but given how widely Longshan culture spread during the second half of the third millennium BCE (Sun B 2013: 435–58), and how pervasive was its influence on later cultures over a wide range of the East Asian Heartland Region, it is quite possible that the Longshan people (and their predecessors) were early speakers of a language ancestral to Chinese (see e.g., Tang L 1981b). The issue of Longshan identity is complicated, however. The Longshan population presumably included, perhaps as its major component, people identified with the middle Neolithic Dawenkou culture of Shandong (see e.g. Sun B 2007). The Longshan population also eventually probably included survivors of the Liangzhu culture, which appears to have disintegrated under the pressure of severe and prolonged flooding of the lower Yangzi River and its tributaries.[3] The refugees most likely included expert jade workers, whose skills would have been highly valued in their new homeland. Longshan culture (as expressed, for example, in mortuary rituals, ancestor veneration, and other religious manifestations) was notably different from, but influenced by, Liangzhu culture, as shown by its commitment to metamorphism as a key religious principle. Longshan culture was probably also influenced, in unknown ways and to an unknown degree, by other Neolithic cultures with which it was in contact. The Shandong Peninsula was then, and for many centuries remained, ethnically diverse (see e.g. Fang H 2013).

Stratification and Statehood

Like the Hongshan and Liangzhu cultures, but to a greater degree, Longshan was a highly stratified complex society, with at least some Longshan sites approaching or fulfilling the criteria for statehood. The emergence of highly stratified complex societies in the Longshan period has been studied in depth by Li Liu in her 2004 book, *The Chinese Neolithic*. Liu focuses her attention on northern Longshan sites, but her methods can be extrapolated for the study of southern sites as well. Longshan cities, protected by vast earthen walls and moats, exerted authority over substantial territories. The differences between the earlier Jade Age cultures and Longshan are found not only in size of cities and territories and sophistication of material culture and social complexity, but in the appearance of clear-cut social stratification, manifested in large cemeteries and burials associated with kinship lineages (see e.g., Fang *et al* 2008; Cohen and Murowchick 2014). Hongshan and Liangzhu culture sites were characterized by a centrally located "major center" exerting control over subsidiary centers comprising towns and villages, although ongoing archaeological work supports the emerging consensus that one late Liangzhu site, Mojiaoshan, approached the level of a proto-state (as maintained by Liu Bin, see Chapter 3 in this book). During the Longshan period, a pyramidal power structure comprising three and four-tier settlements (4th capital, 3rd major subsidiary cities, 2nd towns, and 1st villages) became the norm. In the most advanced of these states or proto-states, hereditary rulers (who may appropriately be referred to as kings) probably maintained their lineage positions at the peak of the social pyramid over a span of several generations. But because no clearly identifiable Longshan capital city has yet been discovered in Shandong, this picture of Longshan socio-political structure is in part theoretical and awaits validation. The only Shandong Longshan site showing characteristics of a four-tier structure is Liangchengzhen, part of Rizhao.

Unlike the Hongshan and Liangzhu well-preserved raised platform altars and cemeteries belonging to a ruling elite, no site clearly identifiable as a ritual or religious center with elite burials or an elite cemetery center dating to the Longshan era has been excavated or surveyed. Nonetheless, piecemeal data, particularly from Liangchengzhen in Rizhao, Shandong and neighboring complex city sites suggests that coastal and inland Shandong was at the center of this advanced phase of early Chinese civilization (see e.g., Underhill 2002) and spread from there to Henan, Anhui, and Hubei (see e.g., Childs-Johnson 2019). Longshan sites in the Central Plains, the middle and upper Yellow River basins, and other northern and western areas appear to have developed somewhat later. However, and somewhat ironically, the largest, best-preserved, and most completely described Longshan sites come from precisely this outlying region: Taosi in present-day Shanxi Province and Shimao in Shaanxi Province.

Despite the caveats just mentioned, there does exist excavated evidence that documents Longshan cultural innovations, as represented by often geographically separate and far-apart excavated sites in Shandong, Henan, Shaanxi, Sichuan, Shanxi, Anhui, and Hubei provinces. In architecture and urban design, these include new and specialized structures ranging from organized craft production centers for ceramic, jade, and stone objects to columned palace-like structures and large-scale sacrificial platforms (see e.g., Yan Wm 2003; Su B 2000). Elite burials, too, display characteristics that distinguish them from those of earlier cultures. Typically, Longshan burials are filled with abundant mortuary paraphernalia, including both common grayware and refined, eggshell-thin, wheel-thrown blackware. They also contain new insignia jade forms such as *zhang, gui, dao,* and *yue* blades (in sets or individually represented), unique to Longshan, that show a high degree of artistic creativity. These are based on agricultural stone tools, or, in the case of the *yue* ax, a weapon, re-configured as symbolic objects that denoted status and (probably) rank and were intended for use in ritual contexts (Childs-Johnson 1995; Shao Wp 2000, 2013). Burials also give evidence of Longshan ceramic vessel types (especially cups and beakers) designed specifically for the consumption of alcohol, especially in tomb-side feasting rituals (Underhill 1998, 2002; Underhill *et al* 2019); these vessel types are not found in Hongshan but may be related to or inspired by types (blackwares) known in the Liangzhu culture. Ritual feasting, including the sacrificial consumption of alcohol and a variety of foodstuffs, was an important step in the development of standardized worship of dead ancestors.[4]

Longshan and the Question of Civilization

In the second half of the 20th century, numerous Chinese scholars participated in a protracted debate over what constitutes civilization and when civilization arose in China. This debate eventually resulted in a view that Chinese civilization began and developed during the Longshan era (2800/2600–2000 BCE) (Shao Wp 2000; Yan and Yasuda 2000). Adapting Shao's summary of the debate, the criteria for describing a culture as having "civilization" include the following: cities protected by major defense fortifications; three- or four-tier settlement hierarchies; internecine warfare; separate building complexes for ritual use and palatial dwellings of elites; a distinction between lineage cemeteries and burial grounds for a ruling elite; marked class stratification; a large-scale labor force including conscripted commoners and slaves; advanced agriculture and animal husbandry; ritual behavior including sacrifice of humans, animals, and agricultural products; an expanded and refined suite of weapons, including the development of the *ge* dagger-ax; large-scale, sophisticated art, including textiles, ceramics, jade and other hard stones, lacquer, and wood; and the development of writing. To this list we would add a sustained interest in astronomy, cosmology, and directional orientation; the employment of divination techniques, particularly scapulimancy; the continuation of ancestor cult worship; and the development of metamorphism as a fundamental religious principle. Not all of these criteria are fulfilled at any one Longshan site. Many are already present in Liangzhu sites (evidence for regular ancestor worship is ambiguous). Some, including the development of advanced bronze weaponry and the definitive appearance of the *ge* dagger-ax, would await the early Bronze Age in the Erlitou culture. Many Chinese Neolithic cultures inscribed single signs on pottery, but these are not generally taken to qualify as "writing"; there are a few tantalizing hints that Longshan culture may have had writing in the full sense of the term (see Figure 4.2) (Li Xq 1985; Qiu Xg 2000; Luan 1994; Dematté 2010), but the evidence is viewed skeptically by many scholars. The first unambiguous written language in China dates to the Shang, a full millennium after the late Longshan period.

Many Longshan sites that have only been surveyed and remain unexcavated have formidable large-scale fortifications and evidence of large-scale architectural foundations, evidence that aids in verifying the existence of a large, well mobilized labor force. Large-scale walls were hardly unique to Longshan culture; fortified sites and stratified burial cemeteries are found all over China, from northern sites in Henan, Shaanxi, Shanxi, Gansu, Qinghai, and Shandong provinces, to southern sites in Hubei, Hunan, and Anhui (Shao Wp 2000, 2005). The building of "short" (i.e., not massive) pounded-earth fortifications was a widespread and distinctive feature of Shandong Longshan, indicating, according to Sun Bo, that cities with smaller surrounding settlements did not have to defend themselves against warfare but rather led a more stable social and economic life (see Sun

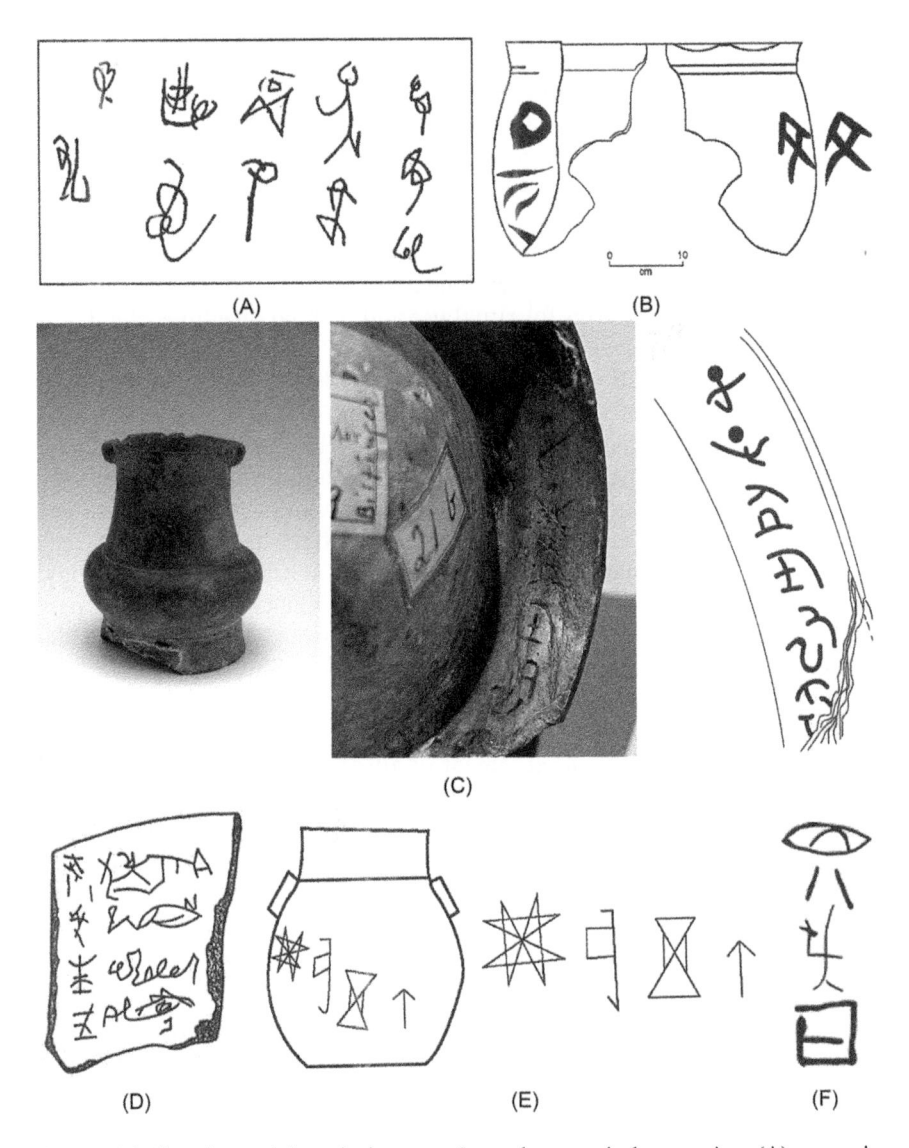

Figure 4.2 Graphs and inscriptions on Longshan period ceramics: (A) ceramic shard from Dinggong, Shandong. (B) A ceramic shard with graph *wen*文 from Taosi, Xiangfen, Shanxi. (C) *Hu* ceramic vessel with graphs *zi ru tu zhuang you* "...子入土庄又," Harvard Art Museums. (D) Ceramic shard from Longqiuzhuang, Jiangsu. (E) Writing on a black ceramic *hu* from Chenghu, Wuxian, Jiangsu. (F) Symbols (e.g., sun日 & eye 目) inscribed on turtle plastrons from Jiahu, Wuyang, Henan (ca.3600–3200 BCE).

B 2013: 435–58, esp. p. 453). Longshan culture appears to fulfill nearly all of the criteria listed above, thus it is reasonable to take the Longshan culture, in all its regional variations and its far-flung distribution, as the foundation of Chinese civilization.[5]

Divination

The quality of evidence for Longshan religious beliefs and practices is mixed. Divination by means of the shoulder bones of large animals (scapulimancy) or the bottom shells of turtles (plastromancy), for example, was in widespread use in the East Asian Heartland Region during the third millennium BCE and cannot be described as peculiar to Longshan culture. That type of divination is famously associated with the Shang dynasty, which developed techniques of carefully preparing animal scapulae and turtle plastrons for use in divination and cracking them to discern an answer to the question posed by the diviner (see e.g., Smith and Fan 2020: Ch 10). The Shang practice of inscribing the questions, and sometimes the answers, on the bones themselves, gives us the first firmly identifiable Chinese writing. In projecting backward from the Shang, one may assume that the basic idea of seeking answers from the spirit world by means of cracking bones already was current in Longshan times. Scorched sheep scapulae from a variety of sites from Shandong west to Shaanxi and Gansu demonstrate that divination was widely practiced (see e.g., Flad 2008ab). What is not clear is where this practice originated, and how and when it spread so widely in pre-Bronze Age China. Thus, although we understand divination as a form of communication with spiritual forces that probably consisted of or included deified ancestors, probably carried out by specially trained individuals acting on behalf of rulers, we have little concrete evidence for the details of this religious practice during the Longshan period. We can merely register that bone divination was ubiquitous throughout the Longshan period and continued during the historic Erlitou and Shang periods.[6] The practice of divination was not necessarily limited to the elite, but currently, only elite burials show evidence of scorched scapulae and related religious paraphernalia such as musical instruments.

Writing

The well-published ceramic sherd found at the Longshan site of Dinggong 丁公, Zouping County, northern Shandong (Figure 4.2A) is incised with 11 aligned graphs in two rows. Although the graphs are undecipherable, their composition as squared single units seems to match the style of writing seen in undoubted Chinese characters from the Shang period and beyond (Shao 2000: 106; Qiu 2000: 39; Feng S 1994). On the other hand, Demattè advises caution, noting that the "writing" is not necessarily contemporaneous with the shard itself (Demattè 2010). Other possible evidence of Longshan written language includes the character *wen*文, brushed in cinnabar red on a ceramic jar from Taosi (Figure 4.2B). Liangzhu writing on a black ceramic *hu*-type vessel, from Chenghu, Wuxian County, Jiangsu is another example of mostly undecipherable graphs arranged as squared single units incised on fired clay (Figure 4.2E). Without further evidence, the case for Jade Age written language remains unproven. The questions of whether written signs on Chinese Neolithic pottery can legitimately be described as writing, proto-writing, or something else, whether those signs were directly ancestral to Shang oracle-bone script, and whether the signs were pronounced as words (and if so, how), remain contentious (Demattè 1999a, 2010, 2018). Yet, whether they qualify as writing, those signs were meaningful.

Here, we will enlarge on a pictorial motif that we mentioned briefly in the preceding chapter, namely a sign that appears on Liangzhu jades, but also on some late Dawenkou and early Longshan vessels from the northeast, exhibiting what we identify as a Liangzhu-style stepped altar, often surmounted by a bird. This "altar" sign often also features a sun disk and a thin crescent moon. The sun-and-moon image has been seen by most Chinese scholars as an early form of the written character *ming* 明, "bright," which does indeed consist of a sun and a moon together (see Demattè 2022; Chapter 5.3). But this Liangzhu, Dawenkou, and Longshan sun-and-moon image has an obvious meaning that has nothing to do with the word "bright." The juxtaposition of the sun disk and the thin crescent moon is an "apparent reference to—or a picture of—the recurrent physical phenomenon of the new moon, which from time immemorial in Sinitic culture has marked the beginning of a lunar month (and, via an arbitrarily designated "first month," of the new year as well). This may imply that rites proclaiming and celebrating each new month may have been conducted at such altars, and perhaps the vessels bearing the new moon sign were set aside for use in those rites. The large-scale *zun* was clearly used for filtering and decanting millet ale and related alcoholic brews.[7] If this interpretation is correct (and the image seems very explicit), people in the Yangzi Valley some 3,000 years BCE were already making, and recording, astronomical observations relating to a ritual calendar.

Feasting, Sacrifice, and Burials

Li Liu cites interesting evidence for feasting and sacrifice on the household level in the Longshan era. For example, the floors of the Shandong Longshan House F204 at Yinjiacheng and the early Longshan House F33 at Yuchisi in Mengcheng, Anhui (Liu 2007), are strewn with drinking utensils and animal bones to a degree not found in earlier cultures in the East Asian Heartland Region and which imply feasting rather than ordinary household consumption. Other phenomena evident in household remains that reflect the social complexity of Longshan culture include significant numbers of human and animal remains signifying sacrifice within building and wall foundations from a wide range of Longshan sites (see e.g., L Liu 2007: 46–72, 106–8). Human and animal sacrifice was clearly common in north Chinese Longshan culture and would remain so in the Bronze Age cultures of Erlitou (Xia) and Shang date. While human and animal sacrifices were already evident in conjunction with the elite altar platform burials of the Liangzhu era, the performance of such sacrifices in architectural contexts, such as walls and building foundations, is not clearly attested for Liangzhu sites and may be a Longshan innovation.

In addition, osteological data obtained from refuse and sacrificial pits show a dramatic increase in hunted wild animals as well as in domestic ones (e.g., at Kangjia, see L Liu 2007: 53–55, 68). Liu presents data from Kangjia in Shaanxi for the domestication and herding of a new type of animal, the sheep or goat (L Liu 2007: 59). The marked increase of wild animal remains points to large-scale hunting, probably by elites, and foreshadows the "royal hunt" as a symbol of royal power during the subsequent Bronze Age. The dramatic increase in archaeologically recovered arrowheads and related hunting gear in turn corroborates evidence not only for large-scale hunting but for large-scale warfare.

Evidence for mortuary graveside feasting first appears in Shandong during the late Dawenkou phase (Underhill 1998). With the emergence of the Longshan culture in Shandong, rich burial goods were commonly placed in the graves of elites according to status, and vessels were intentionally arranged to commemorate feasting and related ritual activities (Yu Hg 2001). Although as yet no apparent burials of rulers of Longshan date have been identified, high-status elite ones have been discovered at Chengzi, Xizhufeng, and Yinjiacheng (Shandong 1990). Corpses typically lie supine within wooden coffins surrounded by a raised ledge (called an *erzengtai* 二曾台) used as an additional repository for grave goods. Some burials feature a coffin nested within a wooden coffin chamber that, along with the *erzengtai*, was used to hold grave goods. There are two types of grave goods: personal possessions of the deceased (e.g., jade ornaments or insignia), usually placed near or on the body, and vessels for preparing and serving food and alcohol arrayed along the sides and foot of the coffin or on the *erzengtai*. The latter vessels apparently represent grave-side feasting. Burial M11 at Xixiahou (Figure 4.3A), for example, contained numerous vessels for the consumption of alcohol, including *hu* and *guan* jars, along with a large *zun* incised with an emblem, plus nearly 20 thick-walled stem cups designed for food consumption.

All these vessels were carefully positioned around the coffin and corpse, presumably after engaging in graveside funeral rites (Underhill 2002: 125–27). As Underhill visualizes the ceremony, "after a feast in honor of the deceased, mourners filed by the grave and placed the cups on the body of the deceased (Underhill 1998: 125)." Such a scenario is well illustrated by another burial, M25 at Lingyanghe in Shandong, with numerous vessels (Figure 4.3B). Pig bones, scattered at the top of the coffin, corroborate this theme of mortuary feasting. Some cups on tall stems were eggshell-thin,

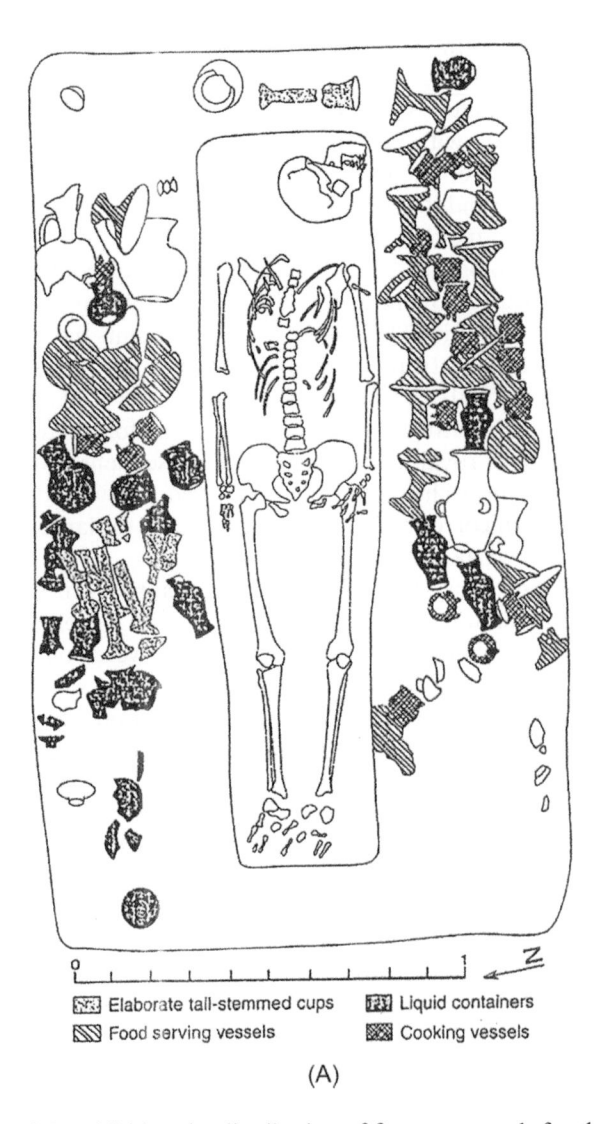

Elaborate tall-stemmed cups   Liquid containers

Food serving vessels   Cooking vessels

(A)

Figure 4.3 Burials exhibiting the distribution of funerary vessels for the ritual consumption of alcohol and foodstuffs. (A) Burial M11 at Xixiahou belonging to an old female, with numerous dou-raised basins and guan jars. (B) Burial M25, with over 30 goblets placed on the corpse, Lingyanghe, Shandong, Longshan period. Adapted from Shandong Team 1964: 64, Figure 8, and Underhill 2002: 118, Figure 5.26. 12. B After Wang Sm 1987: 71.

black, and lustrous and others were high-fired blackwares. Lesser status tombs have a higher percentage of graywares and redwares. The feasting ritual may also involve drum music, as suggested by the remains of wooden drums with drumheads of alligator skin buried in some high-status burials.[7]

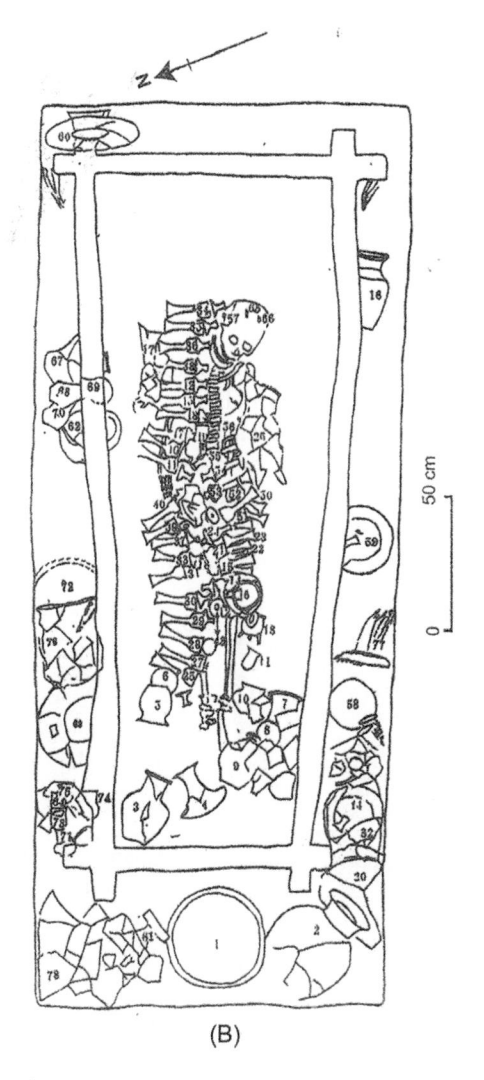

(B)

Figure 4.3 (Continued)

Several thousand burials have been discovered at distant Taosi in Shanxi, and over a thousand excavated, although only a few have been published (He N 2009, 2013, 2015, 2018). Investigators classify burials by size and inferred social status: large, medium, and small. Five of the six large burials belonged to males were in area III of the cemetery and averaged over three meters long by two and a half meters wide and lay 0.70–2.10 m deep. Forty-five medium-sized burials along with numerous small-scale burials have been identified (He N 2009: 45–46; 2015: 162–63). All large burials have the following: wooden coffins strewn with cinnabar dust; rich burial goods including 100–200 ceramic, wood, stone, bone, and jade objects; with specialized ceramics (only four include the large-scale *pan* basins with multi-colored coiling dragon motifs) (Figure 4.3A); musical instruments comprising an alligator-skin drum, earthen drum, and stone chime (in four of the five); and sacrificed whole pigs (Figure 4.4).

It is apparent, even from the sparsely reported data, that the cemetery at Taosi was partitioned into several sections, which Liu interprets as evidence of different family lineages (Liu 2007). The large burials show a clear bias in favor of males. Evidently, Taosi was a hereditary patrilineal society in full bloom, as anticipated in Longshan sites in Shandong. The type and placement of burial goods in elite Taosi burials in Shanxi reflect the cultural influence of eastern Longshan. This is contrary to the revisionist theory expressed in recent archaeological publications which regard Longshan civilization as having emerged in the northwest (see M. Li 2018). Funeral rites to the ancestors similarly included feasting and music at the time of burial. For example, in burial M2001 at Taosi, at the head of the corpse lay a small wooden table with small ceramic *jia* vessels and five wooden

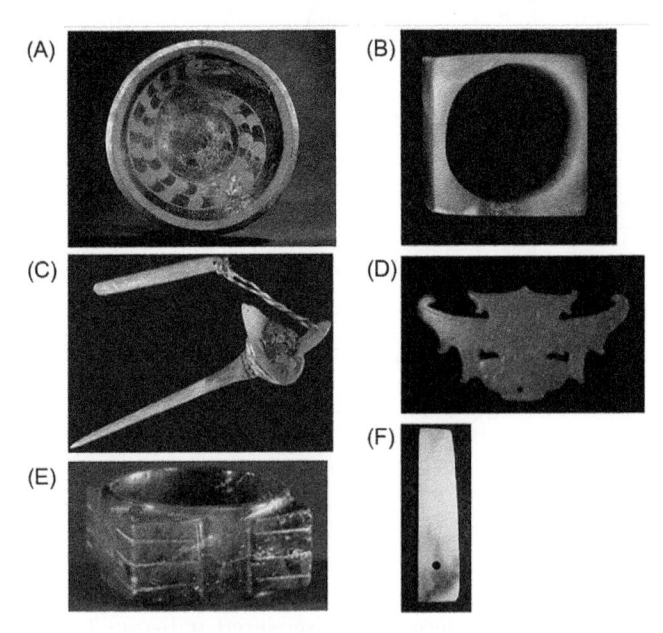

Figure 4.4 Representative grave goods from burials at Taosi and related Taosi culture sites in Shanxi, late Longshan period. (A) large blackware *pan* dish with red coiling dragon, 8.8 × 37 cm, excavated 1980, Taosi site. (B) Undecorated jade *cong* tube, 3.2 cm. tall, M3168, Taosi site. (C) Bone hairpin with turquoise inlay and jade finial, 7.9 cm long, M2023, Taosi site. (D) Small jade spirit mask, 3.4 cm tall, M22, Area II, Taosi. (E) Jade *cong*, Taosi. (F) Jade *gui* insignia blade, 17 cm tall, M1700, Taosi site. After Guojia 2002: 27; Gu 2005.6: colorpls 39, 40–41, 45, 47, 34.

granary-shaped vessels, the placement of which suggests that they were used in feasting. Nearby was a wooden granary-shaped vessel with a bone ladle, followed by a group of wooden *dou* stemmed bowls, a *zun* with a flaring mouth, various *guan* jars, with large or small mouths, and shouldered multi-colored *ping* jars. At the foot of the coffin lay the remains of whole pigs. On the right side of the coffin were a ceramic stove, a wooden chopping block, a *pan* basin with interior dragon design, along with a rectangular wooden table on which were placed seven tall wooden *dou* stem bowls with handles. This type of complex arrangement, typical of all large-scale burials at Taosi, implies that the funeral included a large grave-side feast, probably attended not only by kin of the deceased but also by elite members of his social group. It is of particular interest that these vessels were fired at low temperatures (He N 2018: 54), which would have made them unsuitable for ordinary use; they evidently were intended for one-time funerary use. The grave also contained numerous personal possessions, including a jade handle, a bracelet studded with small turquoise pieces, a waist ornament, small ornaments made of animal teeth, bone, and shell, and other items too disintegrated to identify. Unlike the other five elite burials excavated at Taosi, this grave did not contain a drum or other musical instruments.

The contents and layout of elite Longshan burials are consistent across a broad geographical area, underscoring that a shared system of religious belief and practice characterized Longshan culture throughout the extent and duration of its existence. Underhill hypothesizes that Longshan communities placed restrictions on the number and type of mortuary vessels according to the socio-political standing of the deceased. Such vessels were not simply paraphernalia of the living, but were special vessels designed for symbolic feasting at the funeral and into the afterlife of the deceased (1998; also see e.g., Demattè 1999; Sun B 2013).

Architecture

Liu documents changes in both household and community architecture in the Longshan period that testifies to a new era of social change. Residential structures were characterized by more varied and sophisticated construction. The number of rooms per household increased; floors and walls were finished with lime plaster; and houses of families became physically interconnected in suggesting kin relationships: "Public buildings become bigger in size and their function changes from communal activities at the community level to public affairs, such as ritual ceremonies and/or redistribution of goods at both local and regions [*sic*] levels (Liu 2007: 113)." Special areas in cities were set aside for craft production, such as jade working and ceramic production, implying an increased degree of control over material goods and resources, as well as symbolizing wealth and power on an individual basis. Residential segregation and linearly organized compound-like house clusters also appear. Differences in the size of burials, organized into large cemeteries, and in the number of burial goods, in turn, reflect a clear pattern of clan lineage organization and marked social stratification.

Palatial and ritual structures of late Longshan period date are documented at Taosi and Guchengzhai and are presumed to have existed also at Liangchenzhen. At Guchengzhai, a walled site with an area of 17 hectares, dating to approximately 2300 BCE (Liu 2007: 106), a "large palatial compound" measuring about 383 m^2 in area was surrounded by narrow porches on three sides and further surrounded by corridors with gates. As noted by Liu, this "closed architectural system.... is the best evidence for the emergence of residential segregation during the Longshan period, indicating that the public building became the elite residence, and the community was spatially separated by walls. More importantly, this architectural form preceded that of the palatial complex of the Erlitou state (Liu 2004: 108–9)." Large-scale palatial architecture most likely originated in Shandong and spread from there to other Longshan sites. Guchengzhai was almost certainly settled and fortified in response to the rapid population increase experienced by Liangchengzhen and its satellite settlements in Shandong (Liu 2007: 107).

*Chengzi*城子 [also Chengziya; Chengziyai]

Chengzi in Zhucheng, Shandong, has one of the most thoroughly excavated early Longshan cemeteries, with at least three related lineage sections, and a hierarchy of four classes divided amidst large, medium-sized, small, and very small tombs. The partition into three separate areas defining what archaeologists define as three different kinship lines of different status at Chengzi follows the practice at Taosi. Eighty-seven rectangular single burials were unearthed in 1976–77 at Chengzi (Chang Kc 1987: 249). Five were large graves with second-level ledges and rich burial goods, including specialized blackware ceramics, personal ornaments, and pig mandibles; eleven were medium-sized with second-level ledges; seventeen were small pits with no second-level ledge or coffin and few burial goods; and fifty-four were very narrow pits. This social stratification of burials within kinship lineage cemeteries typifies the marked social stratification of the Longshan period, which continued during the historic Erlitou ("Xia") and Shang periods. Fourteen sacrificial pits, located close to the large burials, show that the cemetery evolved over time to accommodate several generations of continued worship through sacrifice and burial. Some of the sacrificial pits were filled with ashy soil; others contained pig mandibles, pottery vessels, stone and bone implements, and abundant sherds and animal bones (Fu S 1980 rpt: 144–45; Zhu Z *et al* 2019).

Liangchengzhen 两城镇

Dating to about 2600 BCE, Liangchengzhen was a main urban center at the heart of a number of Longshan settlements near the modern town of

Rizhao, in Shandong. Based on partial archaeological investigation of the site, Liangchengzhen seems to have been the capital of a four-tier settlement complex (with capital, secondary cities, towns, and villages) that meets the criteria for a state (Liu 1996; 2004). As shown in the map originally published by Zhang Xuehai (1989), the site is surrounded by secondary fortified centers, such as Dantu (about 131 hectares), by 23 tertiary centers ranging from 10 hectares to 52 hectares; and by 184 quaternary smaller sites, averaging 8.7 hectares (Liu 1996, 2004).

If the archaeological investigation were more complete, we would expect it to reveal a city exhibiting the characteristics of a state capital, with large-scale fortifications; a ritual center possibly including an astronomical observatory; palatial residences with columned corridors; specialized craft-based residential areas; large-scale patrilineal cemeteries; royal burial grounds surrounded by pit sacrifices; rich burials filled with sets of sacrificial vessels and sophisticated jade insignia; and evidence of ancestor worship focused on burial sites, along with thriving agriculture and massive storage facilities for hunted and harvested bounty. Although excavations at Liangchengzhen and related Rizhao sites have not progressed far enough to reveal most of these characteristics, they can be inferred from other sites, such as Taosi in Shanxi and Shimao in Shaanxi.

Taosi 陶寺

Taosi in Shanxi Province and Shimao in Shaanxi Province, date from the late Longshan era (ca. 2100–2000 BCE), over 500 years later than Liangchengzhen. The two sites are currently the largest known walled Longshan sites, measuring 280 hectares in area (Shao 2000: 92) and some 350 hectares in area at Shimao (Shaanxi 2016).

Although the finds from the Taosi site are momentous, revealing rich material from a major Longshan city, a detailed excavation report has not yet been published. Nonetheless, the general layout at Taosi conforms to what we would expect, on the basis of earlier Shandong sites, of a fortified Longshan era city. Architectural features include a five-hectare palace district with an elite residential area of 1.6 hectares, a large-scale granary and storage area, a commoners' residential area, a ceramic craft and stone tool production center with a nearby quarry of raw materials, evidence of bronze-working, and a three-hectare cemetery (Figure 4.5). These features would be expected at typical Shandong Longshan and related northern Henan sites. One feature that so far is unique to Taosi, and justifiably famous, is an astronomical observatory situated on top of a three-tier pounded-earth platform (Figure 4.6). The observatory at Taosi itself is a semi-circular pounded-earth structure scored by 12 regularly spaced apertures, approximately 1.4 m apart, 25 cm wide, and 4–17 cm deep (Figure 4.6B) (He N 2018, 2020). The structure's arc "approximates the range in azimuth of sunrise along the eastern horizon at the latitude of Taosi." (Pankenier 2013: 47). The observation point of the observatory is a pounded-earth core 25 cm in diameter (Pankenier 2013: 49, Figure 3). The structure as a whole functioned as a sacrificial site and solar observatory "whose design would have permitted the establishment of a horizontal calendar" (Pankenier 2013: 48) and which "may reflect the emergence of the concept of a circular heaven" (Pankenier 2013: 52). Although modern measurements reveal many inaccuracies in the observatory's layout, "the potential use of the complex to observe and conduct sacrificial rituals at sunrise on the solstices is confirmed by the astronomical analysis" (Pankenier 2013: 55).

This solar observation platform corroborates the interest of Jade Age people of the East Asian Heartland in cosmology. Nelson *et al* posit that the Hongshan people also probably pursued astronomical interests through the construction of outdoor observatories (Nelson *et al* 2006). And Liu Bin has commented on the likelihood that Liangzhu elites paid attention to astronomical observations, in view of the directional orientation that Taosi was already a prominent feature of Liangzhu culture. Liu B (2018) has recently argued that the tiered outdoor altars at elite Liangzhu sites were designed as observatories. The three-tiered platform on which the observatory was situated might be a distant echo of the three-tiered altars characteristic of Liangzhu culture. The Taosi observatory is, to date, the only one of its kind to have been identified and excavated, but it seems highly likely that other late Longshan cities would also have had such an observatory.

Another remarkable device that testifies to the cosmological sophistication of the Taosi culture is a lacquered wooden shadow scale, intended for use with a gnomon (not present), found in royal tomb 22 at Taosi (Figure 4.6D). The shadow scale, which was discovered in slightly damaged condition, would originally have been about 1.7 meters in length and was divided into about 22 equal bands of green or black lacquer, separated

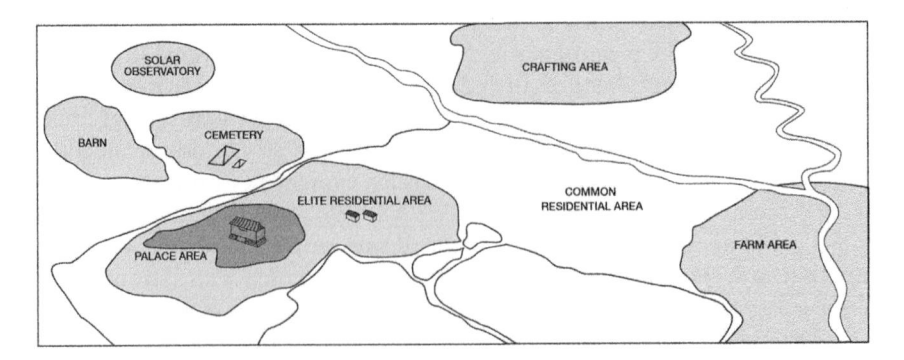

Figure 4.5 Reconstruction of city center layout, Taosi, Xiangfen, Shanxi, Longshan period, ca.2100–2000 BCE. After Liu Jue 8/29/2015, "Sunrise Before Time," The World of Chinese, digital version http://www.theworldofchinese.com/2015/08/sunrise-before time.

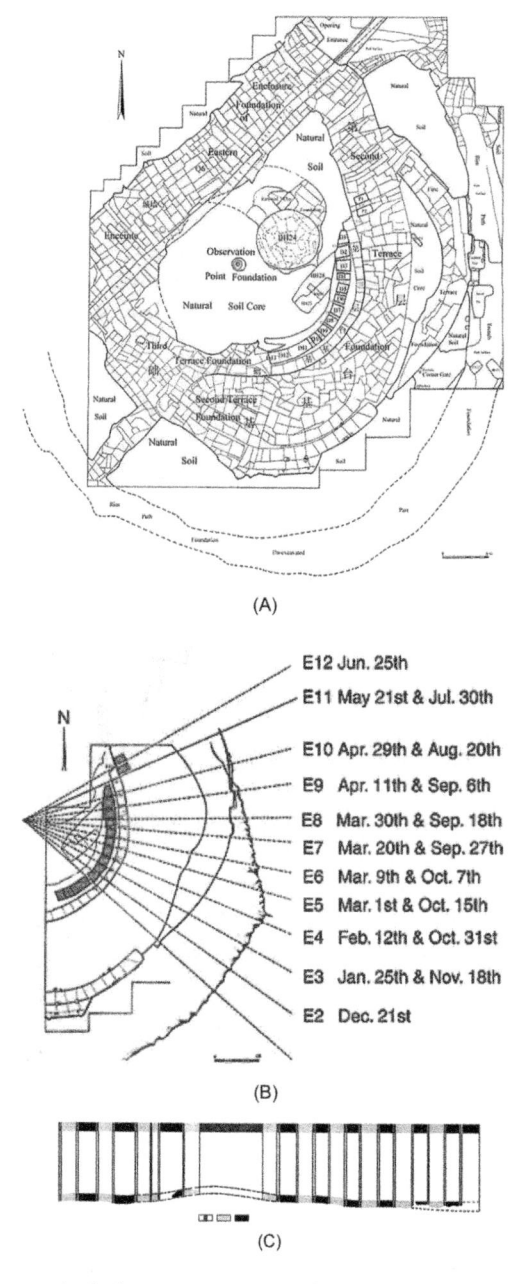

(A)

(B)

E12 Jun. 25th
E11 May 21st & Jul. 30th
E10 Apr. 29th & Aug. 20th
E9 Apr. 11th & Sep. 6th
E8 Mar. 30th & Sep. 18th
E7 Mar. 20th & Sep. 27th
E6 Mar. 9th & Oct. 7th
E5 Mar. 1st & Oct. 15th
E4 Feb. 12th & Oct. 31st
E3 Jan. 25th & Nov. 18th
E2 Dec. 21st

(C)

Figure 4.6 Astronomical observatory at Taosi, Shanxi. (A) Ground plan of observatory mound from a bird's eye point of view. (B) Ground plan of apertures for viewing the movement of the sun and moon. (C) Lacquered gnomon shadow template (IIM22:43) from Tomb IIM22 at Taosi. After He N 2018; He N and Xie X 2007; He N 2005.

by thin bands of pink lacquer. A wooden box in the same tomb contained three supplementary devices: a scale refiner, a shadow focusing device, and a plumb-bob (He N 2018b). The shadow scale would have been used with a gnomon to determine the day of the summer solstice (shortest shadow at noon) and the winter solstice (longest shadow at noon), thus providing a check on the data derived from the observatory platform. The gnomon would also have potentially been used as a surveying device, used, among other things, for fixing a true north-south line by bisecting the angle formed by the gnomon shadow at sunrise and sunset (Li G 2014). The use of gnomons in Shang times is attested by oracle bone inscriptions (see Chapter 5); this find from Taosi pushes the earliest known use of the gnomon in China back by about a millennium.

Still another Taosi cosmological device is a copper disk with 29 teeth arranged at equal intervals around its perimeter; this was found in grave number 11 in a small cemetery northwest of the city, outside the city wall (He N 2010). This almost certainly was a device for tracking the days of the lunar month. Some scholars have speculated that it is an actual gearwheel, intended for use with a solar gearwheel to calculate a soli-lunar calendar; but there is no evidence for the existence of such a solar wheel.

At Taosi, and, so far as we can tell from the limited available data, at other Longshan period sites, a clear distinction was made between the area devoted to the palaces of the elite and the area devoted to religious practices. In the case of Taosi, sacrificial rites of some kind, related to a solar calendar, were performed on a multi-level raised circular earthen platform, while palaces were rectangular buildings with roofs supported by columns. The spatial separation of palaces and religious structures, already seen in Liangzhu sites, set a precedent followed in historic eras. This innovation was an important step in the development of ancient Chinese religion.

Based on currently available information, it appears that the Taosi Longshan culture represents the final phase of the Jade Age prior to the transition to the Bronze Age at Erlitou. Wang Wei, former Director of the Institute of Archaeology, Chinese Academy of Social Sciences, has stated that the Taosi Longshan culture was directly ancestral to Erlitou culture and thus to Chinese civilization (Hc Wang 2015). More controversially, a panel of Chinese archaeologists convened by the Chinese Academy of Social Sciences (CASS) in April 2015, announced a consensus that Taosi was the capital of "emperor" Yao, one of China's pre-dynastic rulers generally regarded as legendary by most Western scholars.

Shimao

Although Taosi is the best-known and most thoroughly studied Longshan site, numerous other Longshan sites have recently been investigated and shed light on Longshan culture more broadly, especially regarding hierarchical burial practices within lineage groups and sacrificial practice (Figure 4.7).

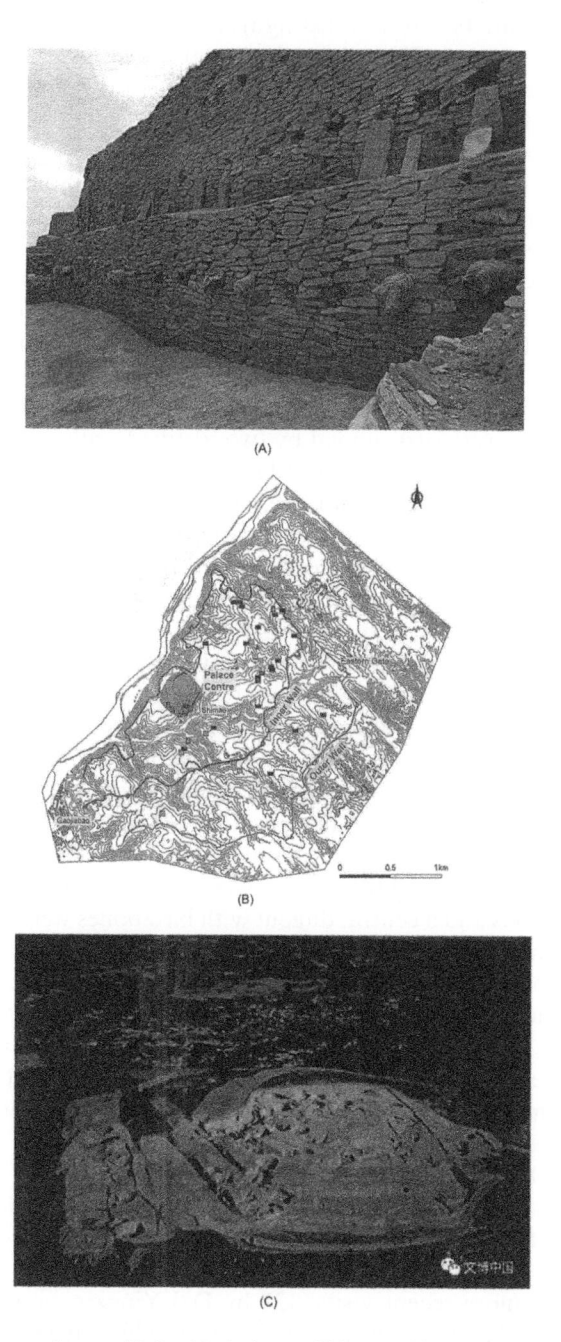

Figure 4.7 "Huangchengtai" fortified site at Shimao, Shaanxi, Longshan period. (A) Outer foundations of the "Huangchengtai" at Shimao, Shaanxi. (B) Ground plan of inner and outer parts of Shimao fortified site. (C) Bird's-eye view of the central city, Shimao, Shaanxi. (A and B) After Shaanxi *et al* 2020: 37, Figure 5. (C) After Sun and Shao 2020: 41, Figure 2.

As at Taosi, elite burials are distinguished from non-elite burials by the diversity and quantity of burial goods, in particular, jades; the use of specialized mortuary vessels rather than ordinary utensils; and special mortuary sacrifices of animals, humans, and other goods, all of which suggest the continued attention to the development of ancestor worship.

Located on the southern edge of the Ordos Desert within the great northern loop of the Yellow River and just north of the fertile Wei River valley, Shimao sits at the northern fringe of the East Asian Heartland Region (Shaanxi 2016), and dates to the late Longshan era through the beginning of the Erlitou period, ca. 2100–1900 BCE. Since 2011, major surveys and excavations at the site show that it is the largest-known fortified late-phase Longshan site, encompassing over 350 hectares in area, comprising three components: the so-called "imperial city platform," an inner city, and an outer city. These were surrounded by two fortified walls constructed using an advanced technique that combined stone with wooden beams. The highest structure at the site, the East Gate, overlooks the surrounding territory of stone cliffs and mountainous terrain. Human sacrifice is attested by six separate pits containing skulls, mostly of females, that underlie the Eastern Gate. An unusual feature of the site is the remains of multi-colored wall murals painted in abstract motifs on a lime plaster base. Vestiges of an alligator skin, possibly for a drumhead, have also been identified (Shaanxi 2016: 13). Lu Zhirong highlights the use of stone tools and implements that reflect advanced hunting skills (Lu Zr 1989: 2). The inner stone-walled "palace" area is built of nine pyramidal layers of stone revetments. Although it is unexcavated, archaeologists interpret this platform structure as a setting for palatial buildings, based on burials, finds of jade and stone implements, architectural foundations, and carved stone relief slabs with religious imagery (see e.g., Zx Sun 2019).

Thirty-six jades and a central dugout with bird bones were found in a rectangular burial pit at nearby Xinhua, just south of Shimao (Shaanxi 2016). The Xinhua burial was located in a mixed-use area that included houses, refuse pits, and burials. The blades were mostly roughly shaped *dao* knives and *yue* axes, like the types found at Shimao. Most were nephrite jade, but some were of softer stone, including serpentine and marble. All blades typify Longshan period style and typology (Childs-Johnson 2009). Additional examples have been found at contemporary Longshan period sites in Shanxi, at Licheng (Figure 4.8).

These excavated burial examples are comparable to jade blades collected on a large scale from the surface. Forty-two jade blades were picked up in 1929, initially by Alfred Salmony (see review 2016: 9) and a Beijing dealer, and after four more recent visits, 127 by Dai Yingxin, some of which he published in 1977 and later in 1988 and 1993–94 (1977, 1988, 1993, 1994, and 2013). When a formal survey began in 1976, it was discovered that an additional 100 or so jade blades had been collected over the past decade by a local farmer who passed them on to Beijing dealers (Dai 2016: 10). Clearly,

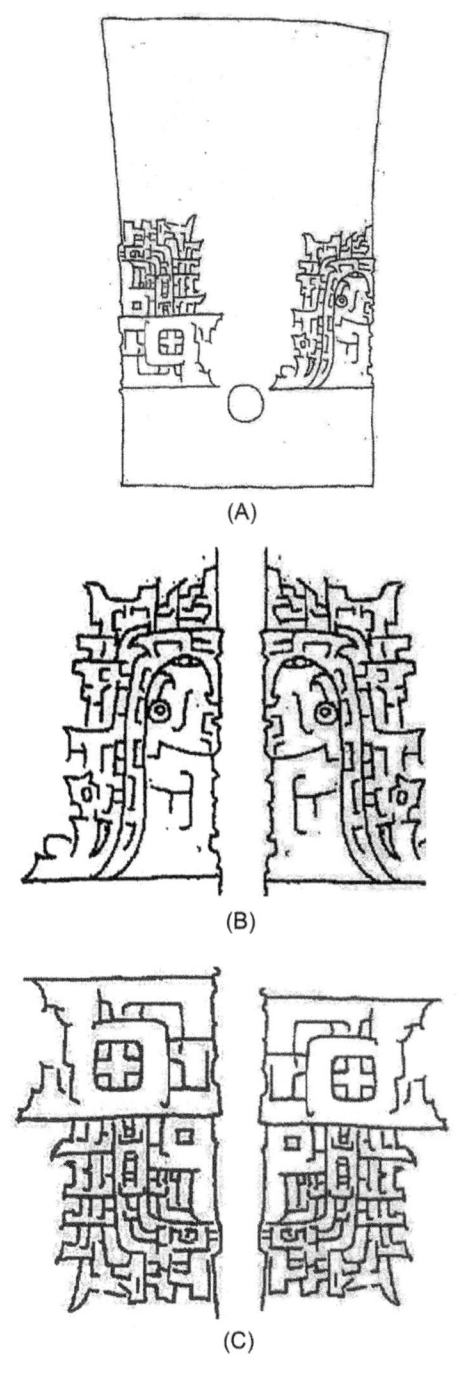

(A)

(B)

(C)

Figure 4.8 Drawing of a jade *yue* ax and its imagery reconfigured as it appears on the back and front, left, and right sides, excavated at Licheng County, 20.6 cm long, Shanxi Provincial Museum. For a colorpl of the *yue*, see Gu 2005.3 (Shanxi): colorpl 50. Drawings by Margaret Panoti.

jade *zhang* and related blades were the hallmark prestige emblem of this northwest Longshan culture. This evidence for the use of jade insignia as grave offerings confirms the use of jade in some type of ritual. The Xinhua and Shimao sites, along with satellite sites in the area, far from the mainstream territory of Sinitic culture, combine local cultural features with clear influence from Longshan cultures of the Heartland.

A set of remarkable stone sculpted relief slabs decorating reinforcing walls of the inner "palace" foundations has recently been discovered at Shimao (*Guangming ribao* 2019.1.4; Sun and Shao 2020; Sun *et al* 2020; Shaanxi *et al* 2020.4; Shaanxi 2020.4). Published illustrations reveal a semi-human masked face with inward curling horns. These recall the inward curling horns of wild sheep that are associated with Longshan iconography of metamorphosis, and possibly are intended to depict Kui, the legendary shaman-musician of Shang and later myths. (see Chapter 5: pages).

Eggshell-Thin Blackwares and Jade Insignia Blades

Two signature characteristics of the Longshan period are blackware ceramics and insignia jades. By blackware is meant the specialized highly polished black ceramic vessels found primarily in burials, but also sometimes present in elite residential areas. Most elite burials in Shandong, and to a certain extent in Longshan sites elsewhere, contain blackware vessels, and some contain the most refined examples of the type, eggshell-thin-polished blackware goblets raised on stands (Figure 4.9). Thin-walled black vessels are also known in the Liangzhu culture, as discussed in the previous chapter, yet they differ in method of production. Plentiful examples have been found not only in Liangzhu sites but also further north at Huating in northern Jiangsu and other sites in Zhejiang and Shanghai, suggesting a potential precedent for the tradition of Longshan blackware production.

Longshan blackware vessels are rarely incised with decor, although vessels are often perforated; some simulate different materials, such as rope, twisted silk, or flat leather handles, while others feature grooves, flanges, and other eccentric applied décor, as is the case in certain Liangzhu blackwares (see Chapter 3: Figure 3.17 and Figure 4.5).

Underhill proposes that the eggshell-thin Longshan blackwares found in Shandong provide evidence for social stratification, elite control of ceramic production, and symbolic mortuary sacrifice (2002: 147–99). The increasing use in the Longshan period of eggshell-thin blackware stem cups in mortuary ritual was a form of conspicuous consumption, a display of wealth and power directed both to enhancing the solidarity and self-esteem of the lineage group involved and impressing outsiders.

The vessel set of blackwares characteristic of Shandong Longshan burials includes all of the vessels required to produce the cuisine of the time. As represented by burial M32 at Chengzi and M203 at Zhufeng, refined, thin-walled blackwares ranged from flat-legged *ding* tripods with lids, *hu*-shaped

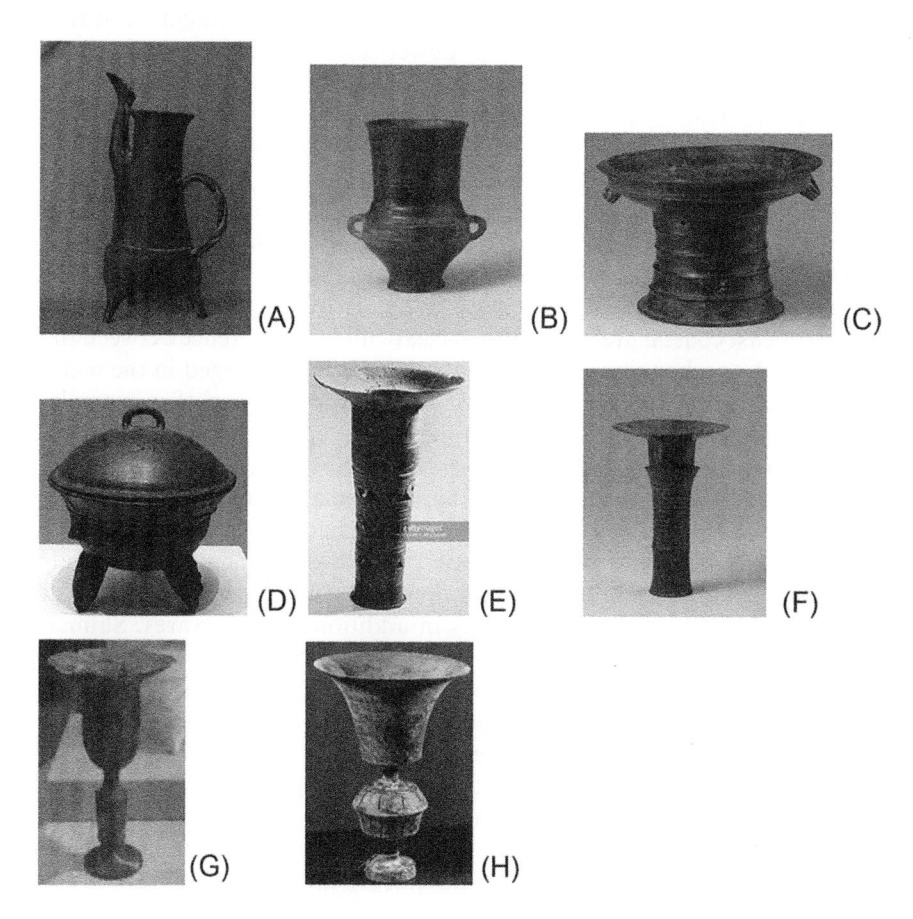

Figure 4.9 Refined eggshell-thin blackware *he* [*gui*], *hu*, *dou*, tripod *ding* and perforated and abstractly decorated variations of eccentrically shaped drink-
ing goblets with false feet (*gu*), Shandong Longshan era. (A) Eccentric
blackware gui/he. (B–D), (F), Blackware *hu, dou, ding, gu* from Yaoguan-
zhuang, Weifang, Shandong. (E) Cup/*gu* goblet with openwork stem; (G)
Cup/*gu* goblet with openwork stem. (H) Cup/*gu* goblet with eccentric stem,
Rizhao, Shandong Provincial Museum. (A), (B), (C), (D), (F) After Yf Lau
photos saved to Longshan Ceramics.flickr.com, public domain. (E) After
Photo by DEA Picture Library/De Agostini via Getty Images. (G) Asian.
allanbarker.com (RA Barker Collection). (H) Arts of Asia Flashcards/
Chegg.com.

containers with lids, *dou* stemmed dishes, *guan* storage jars, handled cups,
yan steamers, and *pen* basins (Shandong 1990). These vessels functioned to
contain alcoholic drinks, water, or grain (*hu* and *guan* jars); to serve food
(*dou* and *pen*); to cook meat or other food (*yan* and tripod *ding*)' to heat alcohol or water (*gui* and *jia*); and to drink alcohol or water (cups). All of these
typically are refined, highly polished, and delicate versions of their type that

may have been used by elites in residential contexts, although excavated data for comparison is not plentiful. Lower-status burials were filled with practical and functional wares of gray, brown, or red clay, a substitute for blackwares. Most types of Longshan blackwares were duplicated in bronze during the Erlitou ("Xia") period, affirming the cultural continuity of the Longshan era and the Bronze Age. In the late Jade Age and throughout the Bronze Age, elites showed a profound interest in honoring their dead, nurturing the spirit of the deceased through time-honored food and drink sacrifices with a specific set of vessels.

Few eggshell-thin blackwares have been discovered outside Shandong and southeast coastal areas, showing a clear cultural difference between the Shandong Longshan and the Longshan cultures that emerged in the wider East Asian Heartland Region. Blackwares found at Taosi, for example, although comparable in functional type to those from Longshan burials in Shandong, typically lack the refinement of Shandong wares. All Taosi vessels were locally made, as shown by kiln remains and plentiful sherds (He N 2015, 2018, 2020). Taosi vessels were not made on the wheel; all were hand built, unlike their refined counterparts in Shandong. Taosi burials have more wooden containers than ceramic ones, and Shandong Longshan burials have more refined blackwares in addition to whitewares. Shimao ceramics of Shaanxi in large part correspond with local grayware ceramics, particularly the *li* tripod, which is consistent with Shaanxi Kexingzhuang ceramics of the Late Neolithic period. (Sun Zy *et al* 2020: 51–52)

These observations reinforce the impression of Taosi and Shimao as regionally powerful city sites under the influence of richer and more sophisticated centers further east in Shandong and support the conclusion that Longshan beliefs and practices associated with mortuary rites and ancestor veneration originated in Shandong and quickly caught on elsewhere in the Yellow River and Yangzi River valleys.

The second hallmark of the Longshan culture is the creation of an iconic set of jade insignia blades. All originated as stylizations and reconfigurations of ordinary agricultural implements (Childs-Johnson 1995: 66, Figure 2) or *yue* axes (Figure 4.10A, B, C, D, F2–F6, F8). As badges of elite status in Longshan society, they probably were employed in rituals the details of which we can only guess at. Yet these insignia blades also exhibit worked images featuring the metamorphic power image of the heraldic *feng* bird and the metamorphic power mask.

Individual examples of jades have been uncovered at Liangchengzhen (Figure 4.10C right, 4.10B left) and elsewhere in Shandong (Figure 4.10Eab left two jade stick pins). Other jade blades have been identified at sites in Hubei (Figure 4.10E1c–h, 4.10E2 minus the jade profile *feng* excavated from Fu Zi's tomb M5 at Anyang), and a plethora of examples have been discovered in sacrificial pits at the sites of the distinctive regional cultures of Sanxingdui and Jinsha in Sichuan, and of course Shimao and Xinhua in northern Shaanxi (see Figure 4.10F1–F10). Jade insignia blades

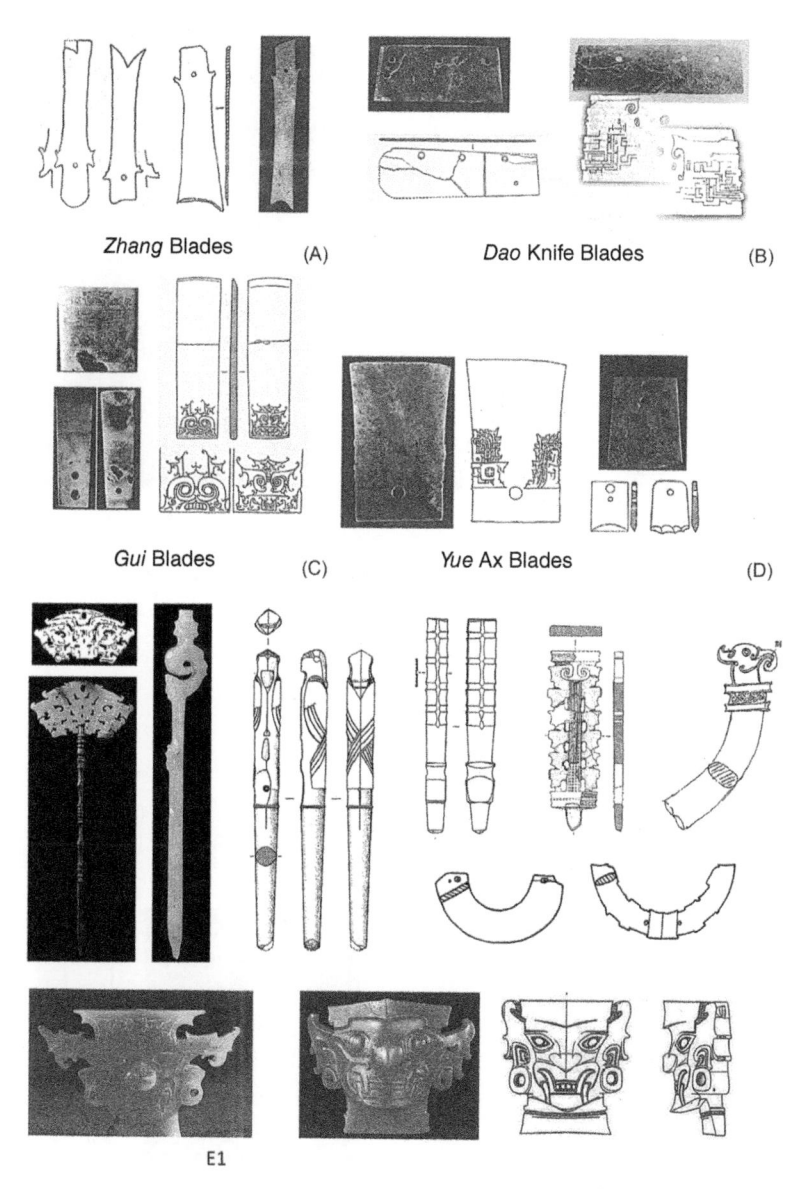

Figure 4.10 Representative jade types of the Longshan period. (A–G) Blade insignia (*zhang, dao, gui*), ax heads, and ornaments. (A1–2) from Simatai, Haiyang. (A3) from Shangwangji-agou, Wulian. (B1) from M202, Xizhufeng, Linqu. (B2) from Liangchengzhen, Rizhao. (B3) from the Paul Singer Collection. (C1) from the Palace Museum, Beijing. (C2) from Liangchengzhen, Rizhao. (D1) from Licheng, Shanxi. (D2) from 10:150, Zhufeng, Linqu. (D3) from 10:201, Zhufeng, Linqu. (E1–8) Small-scale ornaments of mostly heraldic birds of prey, feng birds, cicadas, "pig-dragons," human, tiger, deer, and sheep heads, stick pins and other ornaments, from Shijiahe Culture, Hubei. (F1–10) Representative examples of *dao, zhang, yue, huang*, rings, tri-flanged circlets, bird pommels, human heads, and tiger heads, excavated at Shimao, Shaanxi of the Longshan/early Erlitou period. (A–D) After Childs-Johnson 1995: Figure 2 and 2009: Figure 20:1, 3. (E) After Childs-Johnson 2009: Figure 21. (F1–10) After Shaanxi 2016: 159, Figure 2; 227, Figure 2:18 (8: *zhang* and *dao*), (5:ge), 229, Figures 4:21–24.

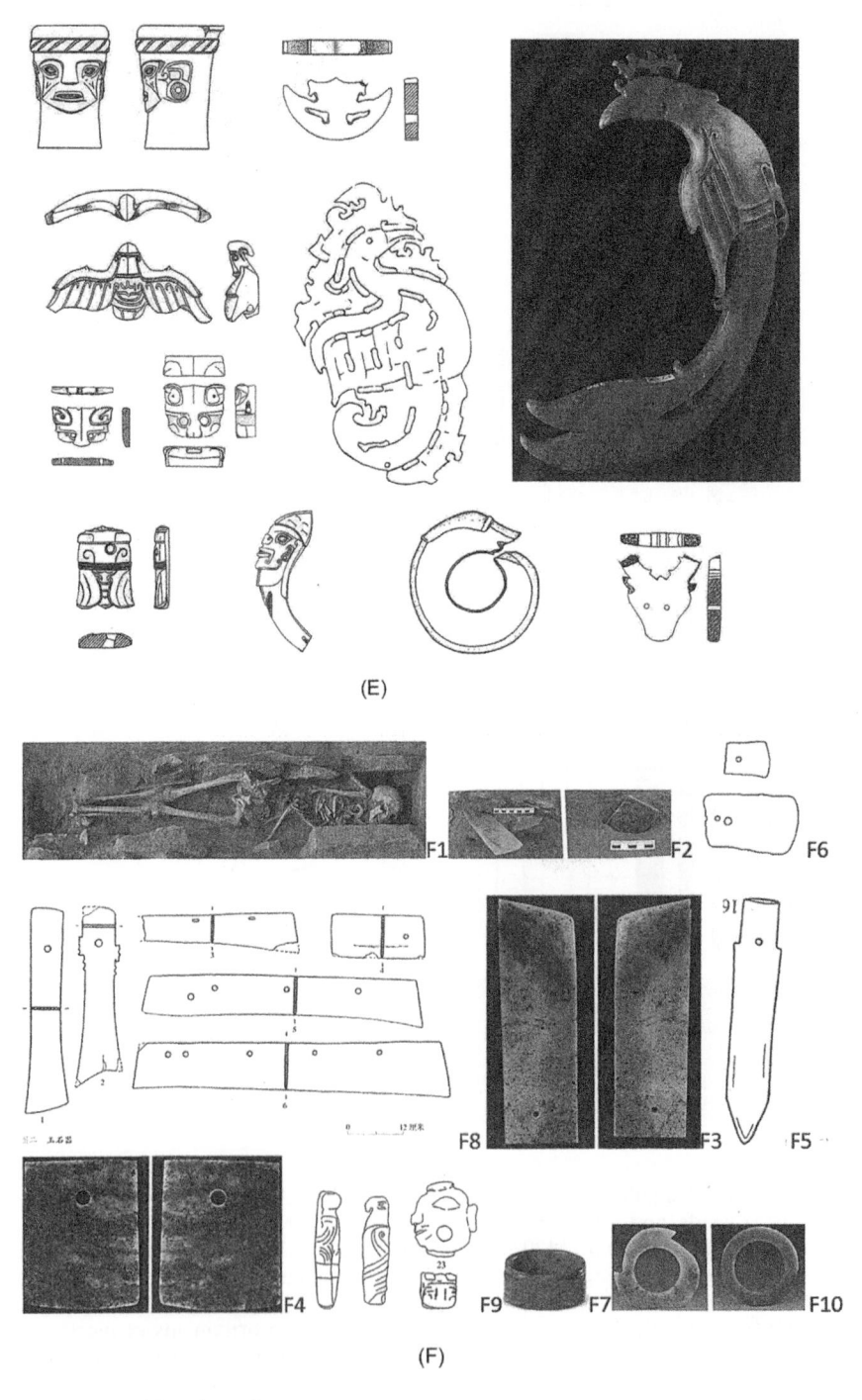

(E)

(F)

Figure 4.10 (Continued)

continue to be represented in Erlitou period finds as well as into the early Shang. Types include *gui*, *zhang*, and *dao*, along with the jade *yue* axe-head. The *ge* that appears amidst Shimao jade cache finds most likely dates to a post-Longshan period, that of Erlitou (see Figure 4.10: F5). The relative abundance of these insignia jade blades in Sichuan sacrificial pits and at Shimao in Shaanxi indicates that they were produced in significant numbers in Longshan Shandong cities and were widely traded throughout the Heartland Region, presumably as high-status elite goods. The relative paucity of excavated Longshan jade blades from Shandong, Henan, and Hubei is most likely because no large-scale Longshan "royal" burials have yet been excavated. The evidence for a major jade and stone production center at Liangchengzhen (Bennet 2007) corroborates that the jades discovered from burials and elsewhere at Longshan sites in Shandong must originally have been much more prominent as elite status symbols. The discovery of major high-quality stone and jade artworks with figural imagery and comparable jade types that come from collections or

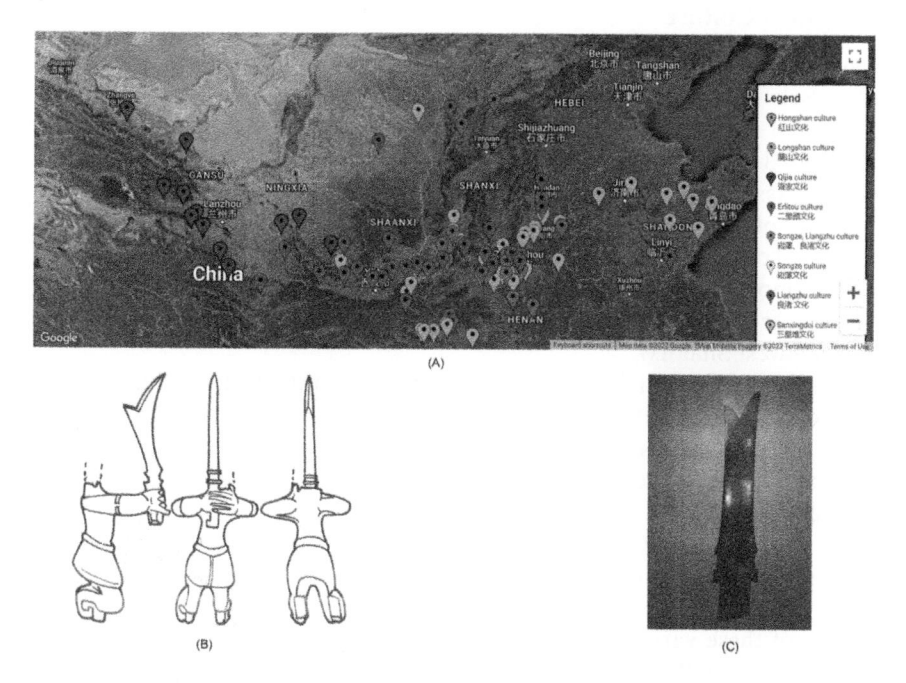

Figure 4.11 Map showing the distribution of jade *zhang* insignia blades in the East Asian Heartland and examples of *zhang* blades. (B) Kneeling devotee in bronze holding *zhang* blade, from a pit at Sanxingdui, Sichuan. (C) *Zhang* jade blade, Sanxingdui, Sichuan. (A) Map after Tang, (C) 2017: Figure 1. (B) Chen D 1994: 98, fig. 13.7.1. (C) After Childs-Johnson and Gu 2009: 11.15.

museums indicate that a thriving jade industry was centered at Liangchengzhen and probably at other major sites in Shandong. (Childs-Johnson 2009: 357–71).

Longshan jades, like refined eggshell-thin blackwares, are the artistic hallmark of this period, whether originating in Shandong or representing regional interpretations in related and distant areas. The exploitation of jade as a symbol of power seen in Longshan Period chiefdoms continued through the Erlitou period and early Shang era. All of these insignia-type blades show up either as imports or local creations in the northwestern Shanbei Longshan culture and the regional Qijia Longshan-Erlitou culture in Gansu and Qinghai provinces, in southern Shixia Longshan in Guangdong, as well as in Fujian province and southern Yuenan (Vietnam) and southwestern Sanxingdui in Sichuan (see the distribution of jade *zhang* blades in Figures 4.1 and 4.11) (Childs-Johnson 2009; Tang C 2014).

Ancestor Worship and Metamorphic Imagery in Longshan Culture

Evidence for grave-side feasting, the provision among grave goods of sets of vessels for preparing and serving food and drink, and the presence of sacrificial pits near elite burials show that ancestor worship was strongly embedded in Longshan religion and religious ritual. Longshan religion also encompassed a belief in the metamorphic transformation of a deceased member of the elite, a transformation that gave them access to the spirit realm associated with flight and the sky. Such belief is profusely reflected in metamorphic imagery on both ceramics and jades, and now recently witnessed carved stone panels within walls of the fortified complex of Shimao in northwest Shaanxi.

This prevalence of metamorphic imagery shows that the Longshan culture served as a bridge between the distinctive iconography of Liangzhu (and to a certain extent, Hongshan) and the transformation of such imagery in the new media of the Bronze Age (Figure 4.12A–D). Longshan's metamorphic imagery built on but also is distinctly different from the imagery of Liangzhu and Hongshan (Childs-Johnson 1995, 2009). The archetypal Longshan image typically depicts a bicephalic humanoid face represented frontally or in profile in either one of two guises (see e.g. Figures 4.10C and 4.13). In one of these variations, the image of the humanoid face may be shared or combined with a bird image – not the sun-bird of Liangzhu imagery, but a powerful bird, a heraldic symbol associated with supernatural power (Figure 4.13K1–K2, M). The bird lends the figure cosmological implications of flight and sky power associated with the spirit realm of the sky. Two different symbolic bird types are celebrated in jade: the heraldic bird and the *feng* mythic bird, often in combination with the semi-human spirit mask and stepped altar.

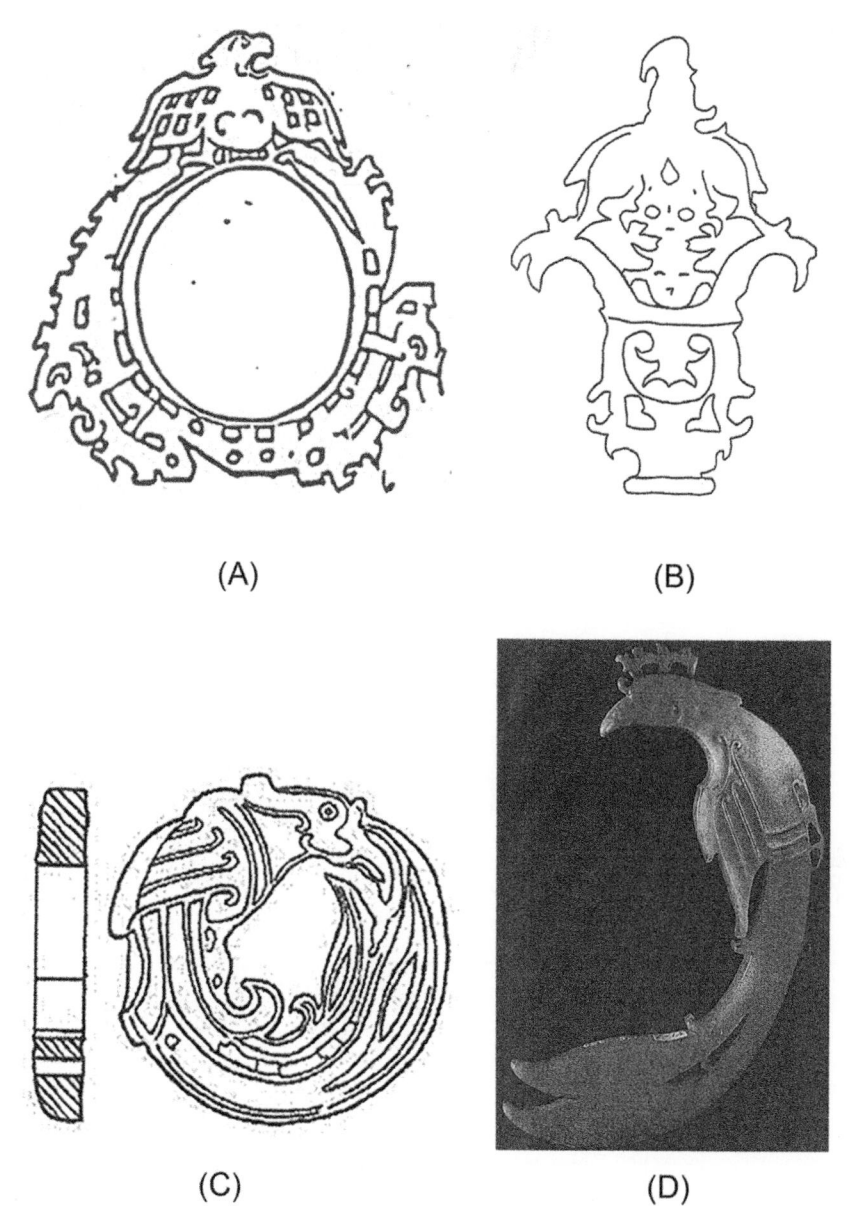

(A)   (B)

(C)   (D)

Figure 4.12 Drawings of two different symbolic bird types in jade, the heraldic bird of prey, and *feng* mythic bird, often represented in combination with the semi-human spirit mask and/or stepped altar, Longshan Period. (A) The heraldic bird of prey with accompanying cloud scrolls, Cernuschi Museum, Paris, France. Childs-Johnson 2009: Figure 20 E2–1). (B) Abstraction of the semi-human with feathered crown and heraldic bird of prey. Tianjin Art Museum. After Hayashi, tr.1991: 387, Figure 5–46; (C and D) Two jade variations of the *feng* mythic bird excavated from Tianmen, Shijiahe, Hubei. After Childs-Johnson 1995: Figure 23 D3 and from Fu Zi's tomb, M5 at Anyang, 13.6 cm long × 0.5 cm thick. Childs-Johnson 2009: Figure 24.

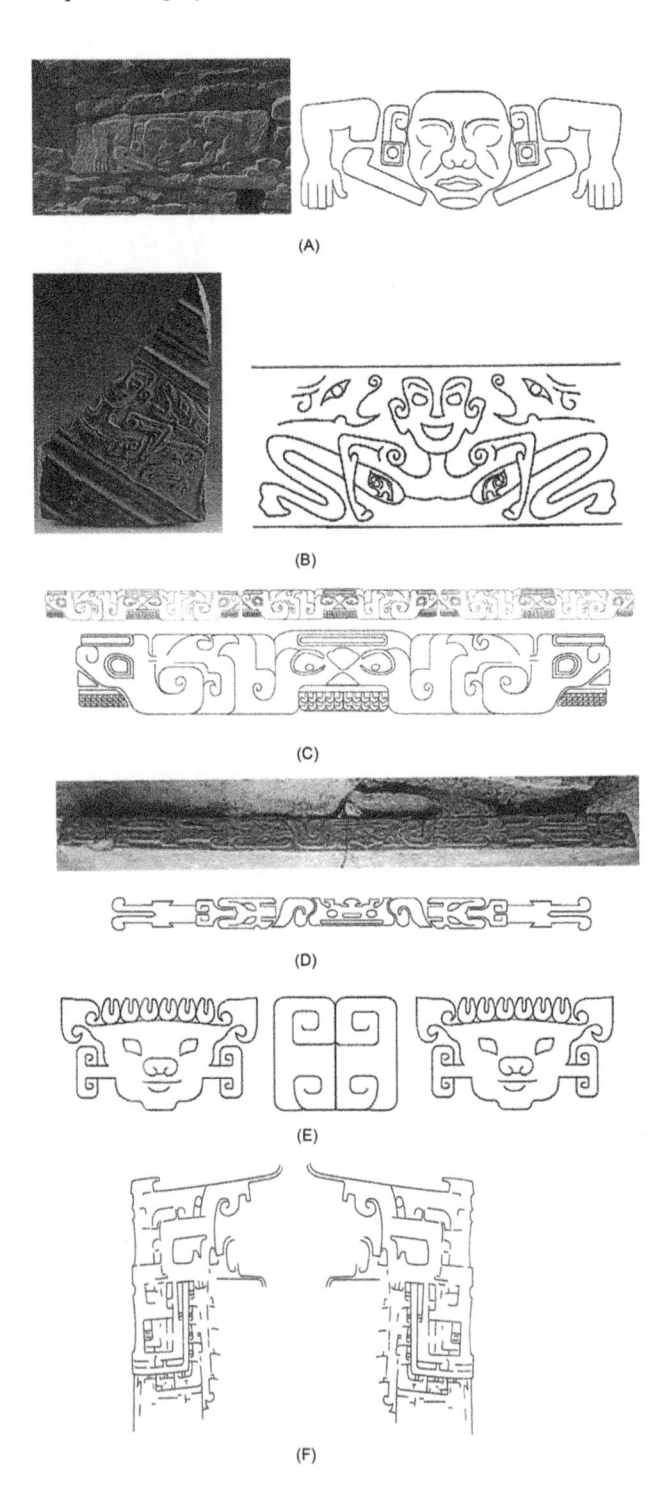

Figure 4.13 (Continued)

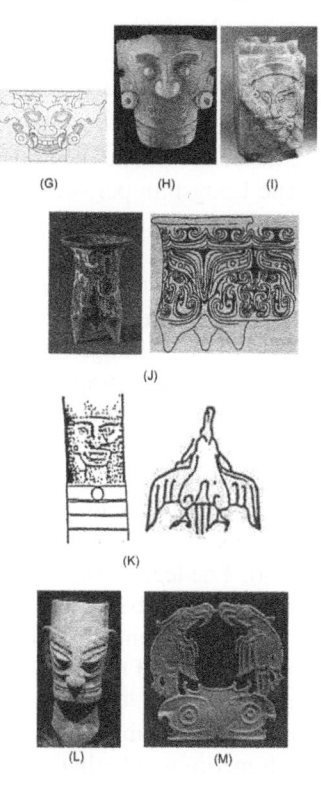

Figure 4.13 Longshan through Shang period variations of the semi-human spirit face
and spirit face combined with bird (A–N) or profile dragon (O). (A), (C–E),
and (O) are excavated stone panel relief sculptures representing primarily
the face of a semi-human, Shimao, Shaanxi. (B) Duplicated drawing of the
displayed semi-human image on a sherd found at Erligang, Early Shang
period. (F–N) Semi-human mask images, abstract and complete as types.
(F1–2) Duplicated drawing of the semi-human mask with limb extension
ending in claws worked at the two ends of a jade knife blade, National
Museum of Asian Art, Washington, D.C. (H) Drawing of the semi-human
jade mask with fangs Shijiahe, Hubei, Longshan period. (I) Semi-human
jade mask head from Shijiahe, Hubei, Longshan period; (J) Jade cong, Qijia
Culture. Height: 13.6 cm, width: 8 cm. (K) Red painted ceramic li tripod
with the abstraction of semi-human head, Xiajiadian, Inner Mongolia. (L)
Large bronze semi-human head, Sanxingdui, Sichuan. No. 1 Cache. (M)
Rubbing and drawing of the semi-human head and heraldic bird on two
different sides of a jade gui blade, National Museum of Asian Art, Washington, D.C. (N) Heraldic birds crowning semi-human head, Tianmen,
Hubei, Longshan Period, Shijiahe Culture. (J) Tripod li and lei vessel types
with painted images of cloud scrolls and humanoid with crown extensions
and extended mouth, Xiajiadian, Liaoning Province. (A), (C–E), and (O)
were published with the permission of the chief excavator, Sun Zhouyong
as provided in the archaeological report to the Institute of Archaeology
CASS 2019: 9. All drawings by Margaret Panoti. (B) After Henan 2001:
colorpl 6.1 and drawing by Margaret Panoti. (D) Drawing by Margaret
Panoti. (I) Zhongguo Shehui 1998: colorpls III.2 and XI.3. (J) After Qijia
yuqi: no 155. (K) Photo: University of Pittsburgh, index.html pitt.edu.
(L) After Sichuan 1999: colorpl 4 (K1.5). (M) After Childs-Johnson and
Gu 2009: colorpls 7-06. (N) http://en.hubei.gov.cn/news/newslist/201601/
t20160120_780229.shtml.

The Longshan image differs from the Liangzhu type in its details but its formal qualities and religious message are the same. The humanoid images were found inserted as stone-sculpted reliefs decorating the south side of the "palace" reinforcing wall foundations at Shimao, Shenmuxian, Shaanxi (Figure 4.13A, C–F). The latter are particularly rewarding in revealing the transitional character of the Longshan period, transitional between Liangzhu and Erlitou through Shang periods.

One major variation of disposition of the semi-human deity is formally identical to both Liangzhu and Early Shang representations (compare Figure 4.13A and B). The expression is seemingly threatening and dystopian, and oddly reminiscent of facial deity images from Mesoamerica: a frontal displayed image – an upper body with upper limbs and fingers frames a human face with large articulated ears punctured with spool earrings. This displayed disposition is precisely that favored during the Liangzhu period and during the Early Shang (see Figure 4.13B and Chapter 3: Figure 3). This position is "fetal" or symbolic of rebirth, used and reused throughout early Sinitic religious representations to symbolize metamorphic power (see e.g., Childs-Johnson 2002: 15–24). The legs of the Shimao image (Figure 4.13A) are awkwardly rendered as extensions below the face that move outwards in curling towards the rest of the arm extensions. The stretched elastic effect of the humanoid's mouth is also typical of this icon of metamorphosis in other Longshan period sites (see e.g., Figure 4.13) and of the same deity rendered elsewhere in carved stone relief at Shimao (Figure 4.13CD). Differences in detail have more to do with medium, whether stone, jade, or ceramic, than they do with iconography.

A second variation of the humanoid deity at Shimao is simplified to a flat facial type in relief with displayed inward curling horns and additional cloud scroll motifs. The nose is angular and prominent – an interpretation matching other Longshan period jade images of the semi-human deity, including what is a completely and uniquely southwestern local type (see accompanying bronze head mask from Sanxingdui in Figure 4.13L). Variations are clearly similarly based on a standardized type of deity who may vary in terms of more animal as opposed to human characteristics, or more elaborate delineation with headdress and extensions, ear spools, or fangs. During the Longshan era, the deity evidently was more commonly represented not riding its mount of power, as represented earlier during the Liangzhu period (Chapter 3, Figure 3.12) but with the attributes, in the form of a crown of peafowl-eyed feathers and extended horns, which in the Shimao second case appear as abstract simulations of the inward curling big horn sheep (Figure 4.13CD). Double upward and downward pairs of fangs similarly may or may not define the humanoid head and face (see accompanying Figures 4.13G, 4.13E2 top). Characteristics of the Liangzhu archetype include a display of a feathered headdress, prominent eyes, a large triangular nose, and an elastic mouth.

Stylistically, the Longshan image appears to be a curvilinear, abstracted, and simplified variation of the Liangzhu metamorphic power mask (for details see Childs-Johnson 2009). This metamorphic deity or deified ancestor may be found, for example, on *gui* jade adze insignia blades and several *dao* knife insignia blades of Longshan date and on the ends of jade handles from Shijiahe sites in Hubei and Hunan, and in the large-scale bronze heads of humanoid deities from Sanxingdui (Figure 4.13L), and now carved in stone relief decorating walls of Longshan period remains from Shimao in Shenmuxian, Shaanxi (see Figures 4.13A, C–E). Certain regional variations of this power image may be described as more representational, in that the humanoid image appears more realistically human-like (see e.g., Figure 4.13F, H, I). This remains one of the standard characteristics of early Sinitic representations of the divine. This interchange between more human-like as opposed to more abstract is, in turn, a hallmark of later Xia and Shang metamorphic imagery.

Blackware cups and vessels were frequently painted in bright colors; examples are known from Taosi, as well as from Xiajiadian, in distant northeastern Inner Mongolia (Figures 4.4A and 13J). These painted blackwares frequently feature images formally related to the image of the humanoid deity or deified ancestor discussed above in earlier Liangzhu imagery and later Bronze Age bronzes as well as contemporary Longshan jades. Features include the familiar humanoid face, sometimes highly abstracted or endowed with animal characteristics, amidst or surrounded by cloud-scroll forms (see e.g., Figure 4.13J). The paintings were executed in a wide range of colors, including white, red, yellow, black, blue, and green. At Taosi, both ceramics and wooden vessels were brightly painted with these motifs. Vessels from Xiajiadian may depict humanoid images of the type commonly found on Longshan jades: a frontal face, sometimes depicted with an open mouth bristling with teeth, with human-like eyes and eyebrows, a prominent nose, and curling lines defining an elaborate headdress. In the case of some Taosi, blackware vessels with painted designs may blur the mask so that the eyes offer the only clue that a humanoid face is represented (Figure 4.13J). Other blackware vessels are covered with curvilinear strokes of color forming a version of the ubiquitous pattern of squared or rounded clouds found earlier on Liangzhu artifacts; the cloud-scroll motif symbolizes the realm of the sky and the supernatural. Oftentimes, on Longshan ceramics, these cloud scrolls are simplified to form C-shapes or brackets with curling ends. The fact that so many blackware vessels from Xiajiadian and yet-unpublished versions from Taosi are decorated with the same motifs as found on earlier Longshan jades from Shandong indicates that during the Longshan period, archetypal imagery of the deified human, in combination with the supernatural setting of clouds symbolizing the spirit realm of the sky, shows that the metamorphic transformation of deceased elites was at the heart of Longshan religion.

Notes

1 For background details of Longshan sites, cemeteries, graves, production centers, walled compounds, etc. see e.g., Shao Wp 2000 and Childs-Johnson 2009: 353–82.
2 For the close contact between the late phase of Liangzhu and Longshan cultures see evidence for the combination of Liangzhu and pre-Longshan Dawenkou style relics excavated at Huating, in Xuzhou prefecture of Jiangsu, near Xinyi just across the border from Shandong (see Nanjing 2003: see e.g., Liangzhu style *cong* 151, Figure 149).
3 For in-depth studies of Dawenkou and Shandong Longshan cultures also see Demattè (1999).
4 For the classification of sites, see L. Liu 2005; Liu and Chen 2012.
5 For numerous studies about feasting and sacrifice in and outside ancient China, see e.g., Constance A. Cook 2005 "Moonshine and Millet: Feasting and Purification Rituals in Ancient China." Chapter One in Roel Sterckx, ed, *Of Tripod and Palate: Food and Religion in Traditional China*. 9–33. New York: Palgrave; Anne Underhill *et al* 2019, "Mortuary Ritual and Social Identities during the Late Dawenkou Period in China," *Antiquity* 93.368: 378–92. Some recent studies have questioned the relationship of grave goods to ideas of an afterlife; see Timothy Insoll, ed, 2011. *The Oxford Handbook of the Archaeology of Ritual and Religion*, 179–94, Oxford: Oxford University Press; and Michael Dietler, 2001, "Theorizing the Feast: Rituals of Consumption, Commensal Politics, and Power in African Contexts," in Michael Dietler and Brian Hayden, eds, *Feasts Archaeological and Ethnographic Perspectives on Food, Politics, and Power*, 65–114, Washington: Smithsonian Institution Press; but in the case of ancient China that relationship is not in doubt.
6 For the meaning of divination, see Jean Lefeuvre 1985: 292. For the interpretation that Shang divinations are records and not divinations see e.g., Keightley 1978: 29 note 7. Also see the recent assessment of Yongsun Back (2017: 15–22) who follows Sarah Allan's interpretation that "divinations are more like reading omens than communicating with spirits" and "not responses between ancestor spirits and the diviner" (Allan 1991: 112–14; Endnotes page 2, note 3). We believe that divinations are best understood as revelations or responses from cosmically empowered spirits.
7 For fermentation of grains, see new data from Jiahu (ca. 5000–3500 BCE), and for fermentation of a mixture of grains, including grapes, hawthorn, honey, and rice, see McGovern *et al* 2004.

5 Erlitou Culture and the Early Bronze Age: Formalized Ancestor Rites and Metamorphic Iconography

Excavations of Erlitou period burials and sites are beginning to provide data, not only to distinguish between elites and others at Erlitou and sites outside Erlitou, but to show how symbols continued to document a common tradition of belief in metamorphic power in the East Asian Heartland. The use of bronze for vessels buried with the deceased denotes a continuation of elite ancestor veneration and worship from Longshan times. The presence of similar sacrificial wares, especially *jue*, *he* plus *gu* in other high-status tombs and at sites in the Yangzi River valley, as well as northeastern Liao River valley, northwestern Qijia (Xinjiang) culture, southwestern Sanxingdui (Sichuan) culture, and southeastern Shixia (Guangdong) and Tanshishan (Fujian) cultures, illustrates that Erlitou was a commanding center with the power to inspire a set of common beliefs and practices throughout the realm. We hypothesize that the worship of ancestors became enmeshed with belief in metamorphic powers of the dead through a complex process of shared cultural influences. Erlitou's religious beliefs and practices can be inferred from material remains and their contexts, ranging from major building foundations and sacrificial altars to types of finely made jade insignia and ritual wares of bronze and hard-fired white and grey ceramics, along with artifacts of ivory, bone, lacquer, and objects inlaid with turquoise.

The theme of metamorphic power, that is, the power to transcend and transform by identifying with the spirit world, is a predominant theme in Erlitou iconography. Although Erlitou period bronze-working was still in its infancy and types of bronzes still followed the precedent of Longshan period ceramics, representational imagery appears elsewhere, mostly in connection with the art of turquoise inlay and jade insignia. Erlitou imagery grows out of what characterizes the late Longshan through late "Xia" Erlitou periods, as represented by imagery in Shandong at Chengzi and Liangchengzhen, as well as in northeast China at Xiajiadian, in Shanxi at Taosi, in Hubei at Shijiahe, and at Sanxingdui in Sichuan. Erlitou elites appear to have absorbed beliefs and images including not only the dragon icon but the archetypal semi-human and wild hunted animal icons. These probably entered Erlitou culture from various sources, as will be analyzed below.

DOI: 10.4324/9781003341246-5

Erlitou, the major successor to the Longshan culture, is named for the archaeological site, Erlitou in Yanshi City, in the fertile Yilou River valley of southern Henan province (see Figure 5.1).

Inheriting from and building upon its Longshan predecessors, the Erlitou period (ca. 1750–1500 BCE) may be described as an advanced state polity, centralized and influential well beyond what we characterize as its capital region (in following Childs-Johnson 1995; Xu H 2012; Tang and Wang 2020), surrounded by numerous smaller settlements and cities (see Figure 5.2; see Xu H 2020: ch. 7, 161–74; Xu and Li 2020: ch. 8, 179–80). We use the term Erlitou period to refer to what is known in later literary accounts as China's first dynasty, called Xia (Xu 2020: ch. 7, 161–74).[1] Xu Hong and other archaeologists maintain that Erlitou may have been a dynastic capital only in the latter part of its history since it appears to be preceded by one or more earlier capital-like cities (4th tier settlements), such as Xinzhai (near Xinmi City, Henan province), dating to ca. 1850–1750 BCE (Zhao 2006; also see Henan 2002 and Wang Lx 2006). These earlier 'capital cities' are transitional from the last phase of the Longshan culture to the first phase of the Erlitou culture (Xu H 2020; Xu and Li 2020). Xinzhai stands out due to its size and triple-wall fortifications (Beijing 2008). Recently some scholars suggested that the site of an ancient walled city at Wangchenggang, only a few kilometers from Xinzhai, also represents a pre-Xinzhai "Xia" capital-size city (Beijing 2007).

The use of bronze to create ritual and luxury items distinguishes the Erlitou culture and period from the late Jade Age Longshan culture. By the Erlitou period, the civilization of early "China" had entered what

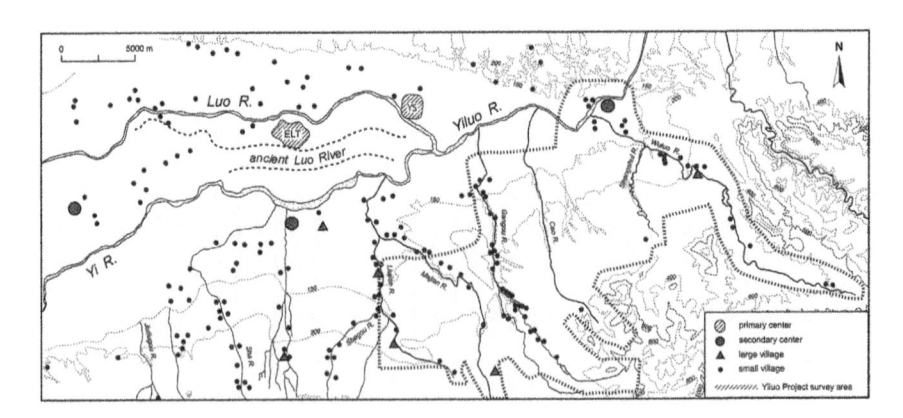

Figure 5.1 Distribution of Erlitou sites south of the Luo River and north of the Yi River in Yanshi, Henan. YS, Yanshi; ELT, Erlitou. After Liu and Chen 2004: Figure 8.3.

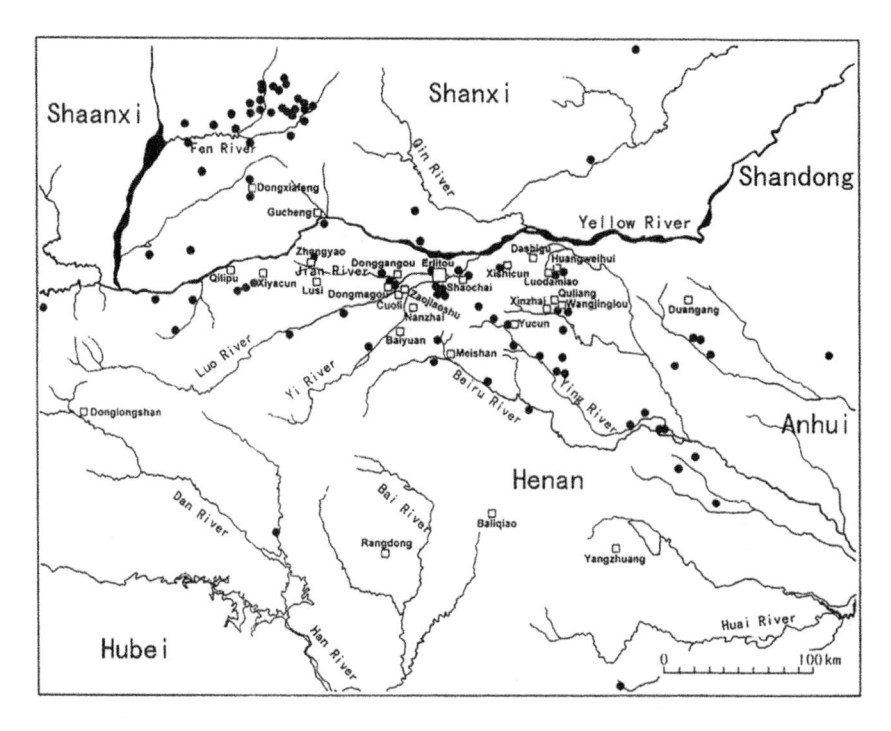

Figure 5.2 Erlitou cultural sites with ritual pottery. After Liu and Chen 2004: Figure 8.3; Xu 2013: 302, Figure 15.1.

would become an era dominated by a hereditary royal family, featuring a royal administration, royal architecture, royal imagery, and royal ritual. Precedents for centralization of power and religious practice were already present in, and emerged from, Liangzhu and Longshan complex chiefdoms and proto-states, with the momentous change that bronze, like jade earlier, came to symbolize material and religio-political wealth and power.

Although the shapes of Erlitou bronzes were largely derived from Longshan ceramic vessels, the production of ritual bronzes in sets marked a new stage in the history of Chinese sacrifice. These sets, familiar on later ancestral altars, typically included offering vessels for fermented alcoholic beverages (the *jue* 爵 libation cup, *gu* 觚 goblet, and *he* 盉 pitcher); vessels designed to hold and offer grain; and, more rarely, the meat-offering tripod *ding* 鼎 and tripod *jia* 斝. Not until the Shang and Zhou periods would these distinctive bronze vessel shapes be identified by name in inscriptions. Currently, vessels for the preparation and serving of fermented alcoholic beverages, particularly the *jue* libation cup, dominate bronze types from Erlitou sites, suggesting that alcohol, rather than meat or grain, may have played the major role in Erlitou sacrificial rituals. The development of the royal ancestor cult may be followed and identified in the evolution of these bronze vessel types and sets.

Prototypical images of Longshan date, whether painted on ceramics or worked from jade also continue to appear during the Erlitou period not only at Erlitou but also at sites showing Erlitou's cultural influence (in material goods, particularly jade insignia), extending south as far as distant Sichuan, Fujian, and Vietnam (Yuenan), as well as northwest as far as Qinghai and Gansu and northeast as far as Liaoning and Inner Mongolia (Childs-Johnson 1995; C. Tang et al 2020: Ch 10). Excavated remains at Erlitou document the emergence in the Yellow River valley of a centralized state (See Figure 5.2) (Childs-Johnson 1995; Xu and Li 2020 Ch. 7: 161–75 and C. Tang et al 2020 Ch. 10: 203–26) that by Shang times – in the same area – evolved into a flourishing Bronze Age dynastic state focused on the ritual worship of ancestor spirits in the context of "institutionalized royal shamanism" and of metamorphic imagery.

The culture of Phase I is identified as late Neolithic (Longshan), Phase II as the beginning of the "florescence of the Erlitou capital" (Xu H 2013: 306), while Phase III represents the era during which the architectural structures and city walls were finalized, reaching the apogee of the Erlitou period, and Phase IV when rebuilding took place primarily at Building Foundation No 2. Phase IV shows continued occupation and rebuilding in a context of overall decline that lasted into and overlapped with the Shang Erligang Lower Level culture (Du and Xu 2006). Although precursors of Erlitou Phase III major building forms emerged not only in the Longshan Phases I and II at Erlitou but also simultaneously at Guchengzhai, Taosi, and other late Longshan sites elsewhere in Hubei, Henan, and Shandong, the fully formed Erlitou culture, and hence the Erlitou Period, is distinctive in two important ways. Erlitou became the site of East Asia's earliest major bronze-working center, as documented by currently available archaeological data, and the Erlitou state developed as the earliest centralized power in the East Asian Heartland Region, with a cultural impact that extended throughout the north, south, east, and west areas of the Yellow and Yangzi River valleys.

The Name Xia and Xia in History

The name Xia, and the historical reality of the Xia dynasty, are highly contested subjects in the field of early Chinese history.[2] Moreover, early texts in the received tradition describe Xia as the first of the Three Dynasties (Xia, Shang, and Zhou) of Chinese antiquity and recount the story of how the Shang dynastic founder, Cheng Tang (Tang the Accomplished), overthrew the last king of Xia. Somewhat later texts in the received tradition describe the flood-tamer Yu the Great 大禹 as the founder and first king of the Xia dynasty (Lewis 2006b; Li M 2017). Western Zhou bronze inscriptions hint at the existence of a state named Xia, notably with the recent discovery, the Duke Sui *xu* (遂公盨) bronze vessel inscription of early to middle Western Zhou date (ca.10th century BCE). The inscription, which begins "Heaven commanded Yu to spread the earth, to dig the mountain, and to dredge the rivers 天令禹敷土，堕山浚川" (Li Xq 2003), shows that the legendary flood-control efforts of Yu, the supposed founder of the Xia dynasty, were known in Western Zhou times, but it is noteworthy that the inscription does not mention the word Xia. Recently, archaeologists and commentators suggested that remains from the proto-Bronze Age site of Lajia (Qijia culture) in Minhe county, Qinghai (just over the border of Shanxi in Qinghai) may be connected with the beginning of the "Xia Dynasty," via an extensive earthquake and flash flooding of the Yellow River in this area. Yet concrete data shedding light on the myth and the possibility of a large-scale deluge and the heroic feat of Great Yu are sadly lacking (Wu Q et al 2016; Normile 2016). Also still lacking is any mention in late Shang oracle bone inscriptions for an earlier state called Xia or their peoples. The only inscriptional evidence for the existence of a Xia people (or remnant of a vanished Xia state), contemporary with the late Shang period, is a pair of bone inscriptions inquiring whether the Shang general Que should take Xia captives (as forced laborers, or as sacrificial victims) (Cao D 1995):

己巳卜，雀氏夏？十二月。　己巳卜，雀不其氏夏？ Heji 8984
Crack-making on the *jisi* day it was divined: Should Que take captive Xia?
12th month. On the *jisi* day it was divined: Should Que not perhaps take captive Xia?

Extant evidence for Xia "writing" consists mostly of single graphs incised on ceramics; most scholars hold that this does not meet the criteria for written language. In any case, none of these single graphs can be read as "Xia" (Cao D 2004).

Similarly, evidence for the early use of the key term *Zhongguo* 中國 (conventionally translated as "Middle Kingdom" but better understood as "the State at the Center") is lacking or relies on texts that long post-date the Xia dynasty. The term appears first as a reference to *Zhong Shang* 中商 "Shang at the Center," in Shang oracle-bone inscriptions and as Zhongguo or "the State at the Center" in Western Zhou bronze inscriptions (e.g., He 何 *zun* vessel inscription), but there are no Xia written documents that might attest to even earlier use of the term. But a strong argument can be made for Erlitou as "the State at the Center."

Du Jinpeng deftly demonstrates through an analysis of literary and archaeological data that Erlitou may represent the earliest Sinitic example of a fully formed state which embodied the earliest concept of Zhongguo

(Du 2007:129–49). Du's argument rests on three pieces of data: (1) the reference to the area of Zhengzhou (essentially the area of Erlitou) as "Zhongguo" in the early Western Zhou He *zun* bronze vessel inscription; (2) the naturally advantageous geographical position of Erlitou; and (3) the alignment of all Erlitou site structures with the celestial north pole, implying an instrument, such as a gnomon and shadow-scale as discovered at Taosi, for locating the celestial north pole in the absence of a visible pole star, and the graph for gnomon in Shang bone inscriptions (Figure 5.3BC). A weakness in this argument is that some Erlitou (and Shang) structures were aligned quite closely (within 2°) with celestial true north, while other structures show a consistent 8° deviation, most likely because a near-polar bright star, such as Kochab, was used to approximate true north (Pankenier 2013: 114–17). However north was determined by the Erlitou astronomers, it appears highly likely that the concept of "the State at the Center," and the related concept of *Sifang* 四方, the "Four Quarters," formed the basis of Erlitou cosmology. The identification of Erlitou with the Xia dynasty is bolstered by 33 C14 dates from Phases I to IV at Erlitou. These dates extend over a period of approximately 400 years, from ca. 1900 to 1500 BCE, close to the time span inferred from data in the received texts. It is now widely accepted (by those who believe in the historicity of Xia) that the Xia dynasty had earlier capitals, for example at Xinzhai, and as a capital Erlitou lasted only for the final 200 or 300 years, spanning Phases III through IV (Du and Xu 2006: 498; Zhao Cq 2009; XiaShangZhou Duandai 2000). The recent compilation of Chinese language publications of research on and fieldwork at Erlitou as a culture and site (1959–2005) by Xu Hong and Du Jinpeng greatly facilitates understanding what is new about the Erlitou period (Du and Xu 2006; Xu H 2020) and its belief systems. Some scholars rely on received later historical works to support the theory that Erlitou represents the last capital Zhenxun under the dynasty's last three kings: Gao, Fa, and Jie (see e.g., Du and Xu 2006; Fan Ys 1965).

Although there are still many questions about the culture and site, the identification of Erlitou as a royal capital city with belief grounded in metamorphism is based on the physical evidence of the site itself, which in particular includes major art forms and their symbolic expression, as noted above and analyzed in detail below. Phases II–IV at Erlitou had a large-scale, planned city layout, north-to-south orientation, enclosing "palace" and related structures that appear to have had various functions of a royal administration (Du and Xu 2006; Du 2007). An outer wall, apparently non-defensive, as noted by Xu Hong, is the earliest paradigm of what he identifies are non-fortified primary capitals (Xu H 2013a).[3]

As illustrated in Figure 5.2, Erlitou city was nestled between two major tributaries of the Yellow River, the Luo, and the Yi, and these and the many small suburban settlements surrounding the capital would have provided some protection against attack. The non-defensive outer wall is systematically laid out as a rectangle, surrounded on its outside by interconnected,

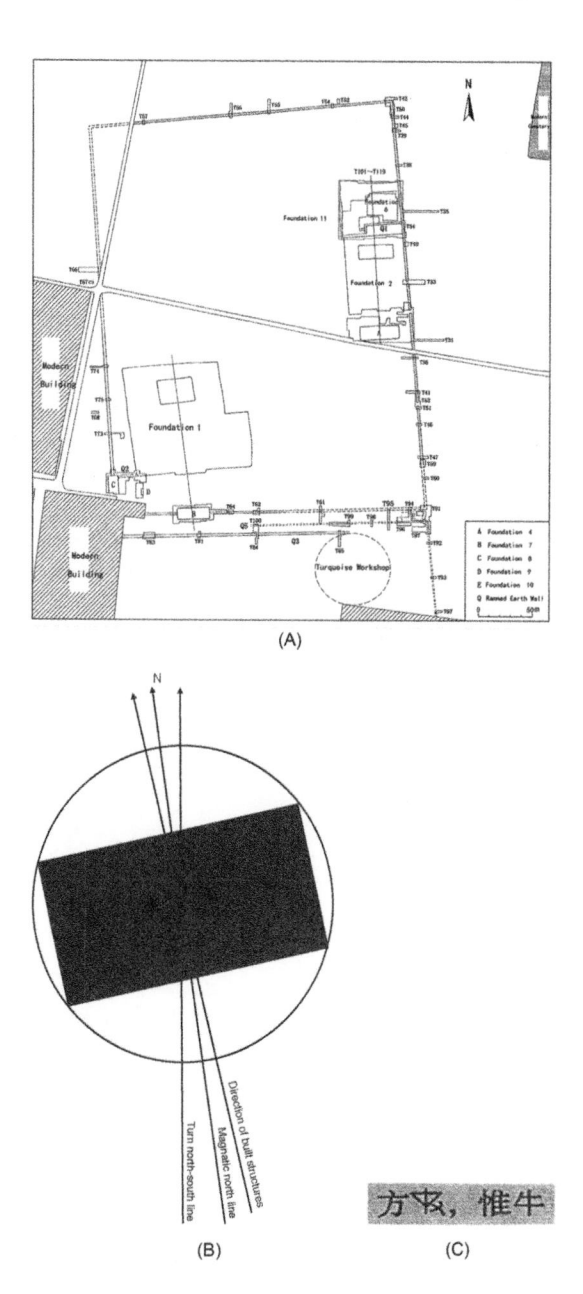

(A)

(B)   (C)

Figure 5.3 The "palatial enclosure" of the Erlitou. site. (A) Ground plan showing Nos 1–2 buildings, D3–8 structures, and Areas I–XV representing
workshops for bone, bronze, ceramics, and turquoise; a palace-temple
complex; and city enclosure wall. (B) Due north alignment of "palatial enclosure" as reconstructed by Du Jinpeng. (C) A bone inscription
reading "*fang*-directions measured with gnomon, perhaps ox [should be
offered] ? (A) After Du 2007:30, 61. (B) After Du and *Xuu* 2005; (C) As
translated by Hsu Ch 1984: An Ming 1786.

north-to-south and east-to-west roadways, the earliest documented web of intersecting roadways in the ancient Heartland of East Asia. To the south, outside of this inner-city wall is what appears to also have been a walled "work area" specializing in workshops producing high-quality goods of bone [and jade?], ceramic, turquoise, and bronze (Figure 5.4). To the north lay a sacrificial center. This large-scale walled compound with outside road-ways measured approximately 2,400 meters east to west and 1,900 north to south, encompassing an area of some 3,000,000 square meters (Figure 5.3). The walled inner "royal palace enclosure" measures approximately 292–295 meters east to west and 359–378 meters north to south, an area of 108,000 square meters (Du 2007: 107). The city wall had two gates, D7 and D8, and contained structures identified as various royal edifices: two major colon-naded rectangular buildings raised on high rammed earthen platforms along with other buildings (marked on the map as D1-2 and D 3-4, 7-8) (Figure 5.3) are described as "Foundations Nos. 1 and 2."[4]

In 2007, Du proposed that the two structures were four-cornered dou-ble-roofed halls and served as quarters for administrative (No 1) and residential (No 2) purposes, respectively (2007: 502–56; 2007: 108). This identification of Building No 1 (Figure 5.3A) as a reception hall was based

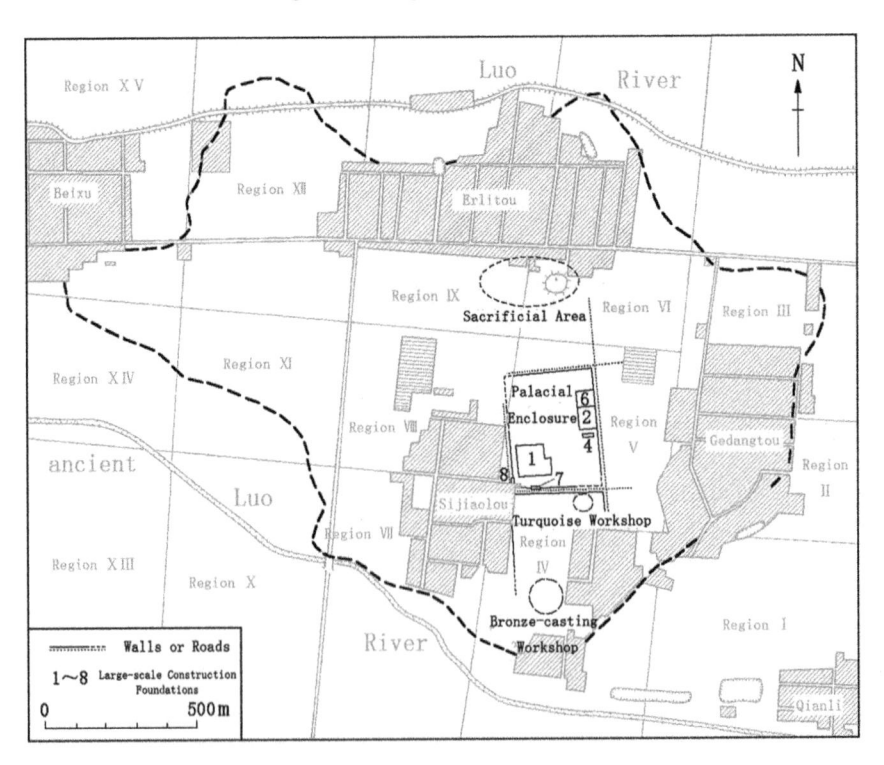

Figure 5.4 Layout of the Erlitou site showing excavated foundations and work-shops. Based on Xu 2016: 208.

on its location in the front southwestern section, and its large courtyard, double or triple the size of the columned hall. The courtyard, large enough to hold 2,000 or more people, would have been suitable for military drills or display, as well as for public gatherings (Du 2007: 508–14). Building No 2 (Figures 5.3A and 5.4), located far to the rear in the northeastern sector of the inner city, may have been a residential palace. Various burials, mostly of humans, dating to Phases II–III, in the courtyards and building foundations of Building No 1, were sacrificial (Du 2007:521–22). A large circular pit in front of Building No 2 contains abundant burnt remains, suggesting that the site was used for sacrificial rituals well known in bone inscriptions as *liao* 燎 and in historical references as *tingliao* 庭燎 (Du 2007). Offerings were burned within a worship plaza or on an altar for mounting large-scale dazzling and spiritually inspiring bonfires. These would probably have been spectacular events witnessed by a large number of high-ranking people and with the offerings consumed by the flames of a large pyre. Such rituals are distinct from rituals of human sacrifice associated with the foundations of new structures, as seen in Building No 1. It is possible that these *liao* bonfire sacrifices were held in connection with worship of the *she* 社, the altar of the earth spirit associated with a central settlement, as known in later textual references. If it were associated with the "Xia" rulership, for example, it would be identified by ruling clan and family name, thus as the Xiashe 夏社 (see Du 2007.5: 31–33). Nevertheless, excavated physical remains that would give a clearer picture of the religious, administrative, residential, and other functions of the royal buildings are still lacking.

Erlitou, the Outer City Workshops, Settlements, Burials, and a Sacrificial Center

In recognition of the site's sophistication as a capital is the outer city south of the royal center with large-scale settlements and a major site for bronze casting, one of nine centers thus far discovered for making artisanal products, including ceramics, jade, turquoise inlaid items, and articles of stone and bone (Yt Li 2022: 13–14). These areas identified on the chart as Areas IV and VII (Figure 5.4) (Du and Xu 2006: 487–88) are also known in the site literature as the "work zone," or royal government craft center. The bronze workshop is particularly large, identified as a rectangle 16m long by 6m wide (Zheng G 1985; Zhongguo nianjian 1985; Xu H 2020: Figure 2), and is replete with remains documenting various stages in the production of bronze artifacts (Du 2007: 109; L. Liu 2004: 229). There is also evidence that this "work area" was enclosed by its own surrounding wall, similar in scale and construction to the wall surrounding the royal administrative and residential city center (Du 2007:111).

What is significant about the discovery of the bronze workshop is that it is the earliest in the history of the East Asian Heartland.[5] It is a landmark change, marking one clear expression of the beginning of a Bronze Age. Bronze production requires a sophisticated technology, high management skills, and a major input of labor, and thus would reflect a control system of greater political, economic, and religious power than seen in earlier phases of the late Neolithic period (see Xu and Liu 2020; Chase 1991). The fact that most of the bronzes discovered came from tombs, as characterizes successive Bronze Age Shang and Zhou periods, corroborates their ritual use and thus the unique position of bronze as the major tool of ritual and power founded during the "first dynasty, the Xia," – assuming for the moment that Erlitou is Xia in dynastic succession – in contradistinction to any other known bronze working culture. Bronze ritual vessels became a new core element of Chinese ceremony in public and private contexts.

According to recent estimates, over 130 specimens of bronze have been published from 40 tombs (Chen Gl 2008; Lian *et al* 2011.4) and 53 bronze pieces have been tested for alloy content (Xu and Liu 2020: Ch 9). Most of the vessels, bells, and large weapons, such as *ge* dagger-axes and *yue* axes were found in tombs. Of the 17 ritual bronze vessels excavated, 13 are bronze *jue* vessels; the others include two *jia* vessels, one tripod *ding* and one *he* pitcher (see Table 1 in Xu and Liu 2020: Ch 9). Although the number of ritual bronze items uncovered thus far is small, the evolution of casting technology was fairly rapid, particularly in perfecting the ratio of alloys in what becomes less copper and more bronze. Erlitou bronze melting and casting, although experimental, was preceded by an earlier phase, which may have been associated with earlier "Xia" city centers (Xu and Liu 2020: Ch 9).[6]

In 1959, Xu Xusheng identified the area north of the royal compound as a sacrificial center (1959). Burials appear there but also elsewhere, decentralized in and outside the royal center amidst residential quarters and villages. Nothing suggests that this is a clan or lineage cemetery, leading scholars to differentiate and classify burials according to burial goods and not according to tomb site or location (Xu Xs 1959). One of the richest burials, for example, belonging to a male 30–35 years old, was covered by a shroud featuring a *long* dragon made mostly out of inlaid turquoise and some jade pieces, dating early to Erlitou Phase II. The tomb with the turquoise shroud was discovered in the courtyard of Royal Foundation No 4.

As noted, no royal cemetery has yet been securely identified at Erlitou. A likely candidate for the location of such a cemetery may be the area north and northeast of the royal city that is associated with rich burials and various large-scale circular and rectangular altars (Figure 5.4). Because small and middle size burials, as well as sacrificial remains and altars, have been found congregated together in this northern area outside the walled royal compound, it seems that this area may have been used not only to offer sacrifices to deceased ancestors but also to perform rites dedicated to other spirits, in particular the earth spirit worshipped at a *she* 社 altar (Du 2007: 531). In 1984, a circular structure with a surrounding rammed earth wall and rich burials full of bronzes, jades, lacquers, turquoise inlaid plaques, and turquoise necklaces was discovered in Area VI. So far, a total of nine circular rammed structures, described as open-air ritual platforms, *tan* 坛 have been discovered in Area VI. Area VI measures about 1,100 m^2 (Xu H 2015: 109).[7] The careful orientation of these and other structures at

Erlitou, and the rich goods found in associated graves suggests that the Erlitou elite practiced some form of ancestor worship, used astronomical observations (though no Taosi-style observatory has been found at Erlitou) in determining the layout of important buildings, and had cosmological beliefs centered around the orientation of the Four Quarters (*sifang*).

Other burials with similarly rich contents have also been found in the "royal palace compound," in the site known as M3 in Region V (Figure 5.4). Similar medium-sized burials have been found in a different area, Region III, suggesting more than one location for burial groups. Region VI appears to be the richest and most specialized area, being devoted to what are probably royal and aristocratic burials (Figure 5.4).

Although future excavations should help in identifying the function of these remains, sacrifices associated with ancestor worship may represent a continuation of Longshan practice in that sacrifices were offered at burial sites. We must await further excavations beyond surveys in order to properly identify what sacrifices and burials took place north of Erlitou.

Material Evidence for Religious Practices of the Erlitou [Xia] Period: Bronze Ritual Vessel Sets and Bronze Technology

Numbers of burial goods range widely in different burials, some containing ritual bronze vessel and weapon types and others bronze tool types or large-scale insignia jade blades (See Figure 5.5). These variations and differences in terms of burial contents might be skewed by looting, but at the present time, the burial goods do not identify a specific class or social strata that clearly refer to a cemetery belonging to aristocratic or Xia royal elite.

As was the case during the Longshan period, funeral feasting and worshipping of elite dead ancestors took place at burial sites through the offering of human and animal sacrifice and with specialized vessels containing foodstuffs or alcoholic beverages deposited on burial ledges or strategic locations next to the corpse. These rites continued during the Erlitou period but within a pyramidal and centralized system. The completely new material – bronze – was exploited for the first time in the East Asian Heartland Region to create luxury ritual vessels. Specialized hard-fired white wares, almost exclusively in the form of *he* pitchers, and nephrite jade insignia continued to be prominent in elite burials.

Although it is unclear when, where, and under what circumstances bronze technology first appeared in the Heartland Region (see e.g. L Liu 2009; Liu and Chen 2012), it is clear that the bronze workshop at Erlitou represents an already well-developed and sophisticated technology and thus a mark of the new expression characterizing a Bronze Age.[8] The bronze workers at Erlitou evidently experimented with various formulas for their bronze alloys: an analysis of slag shows not only the familiar copper + tin, but also copper + tin + lead, copper + arsenic + lead, and other combinations of metal in different proportions. The slag at the workshop is a byproduct of casting, not of smelting, indicating that the metals were smelted elsewhere, probably near where they were mined and brought to Erlitou in the form of ingots (Xu and Liu 2020: Ch 9).[9]

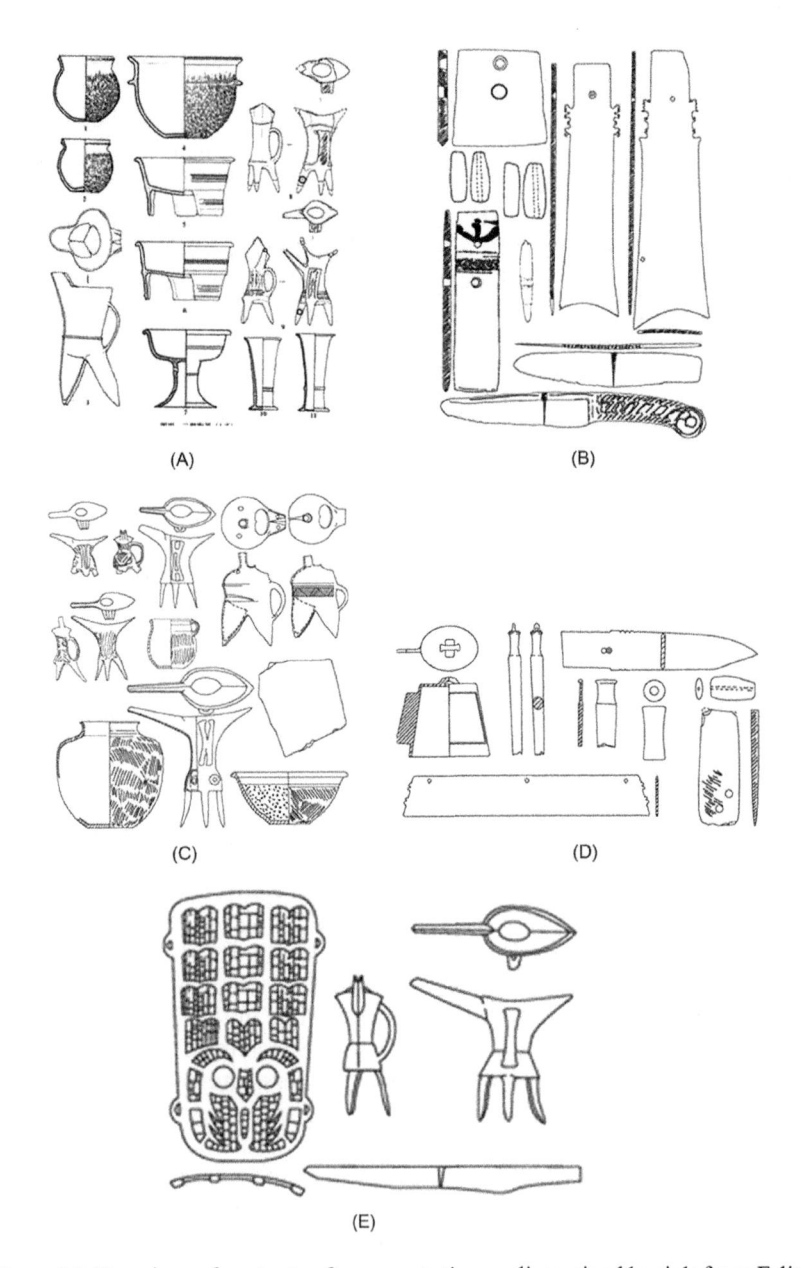

(A)　　　　　　　　　(B)

(C)　　　　　　　　　(D)

(E)

Figure 5.5 Drawings of contents of representative medium-sized burials from Erlitou Phases II–IV and Areas V and VI. (A) PII Area VI M4 with ceramics. (B) PIII, Area V M3 with two jade *zhang* (appr. 50 cm long), one jade *yue*, one jade *gui*, turquoise, jade beads, bronze *ge*, ceramic jar, cup, basin, and two *he*. (C) PIV, Area VI M57 contents: bronze bell, turquoise inlaid bronze plaque, bronze *jue*, bronze *dao* knife; jade *dao* knife, three jade handles, jade beads, and jade *ge* dagger blade; stone spade, ceramic vessels, and cowries. (A) After Du and Xu 2005: 716, Figure 4. (B) After Du and Xu 2005: 664, Figure 8. (C) After Du and Xu 2005: 714–715, Figures 2–3.

Ritual Bronzes and Other Luxury Items in Erlitou Burials

Bronze vessel types discovered so far at Erlitou belong to just a few types, and generally are small thin-walled vessels designed for individual use. These bronzes include the small-scale *jue* tripod beaker, the larger *jia* tripod, and *he* tripod pitcher for heating liquids (whose ceramic prototype of late Neolithic date is often labeled *kui* by archaeologists) (Figure 5.6A) and rarely the *ding* tripod for cooking meat.

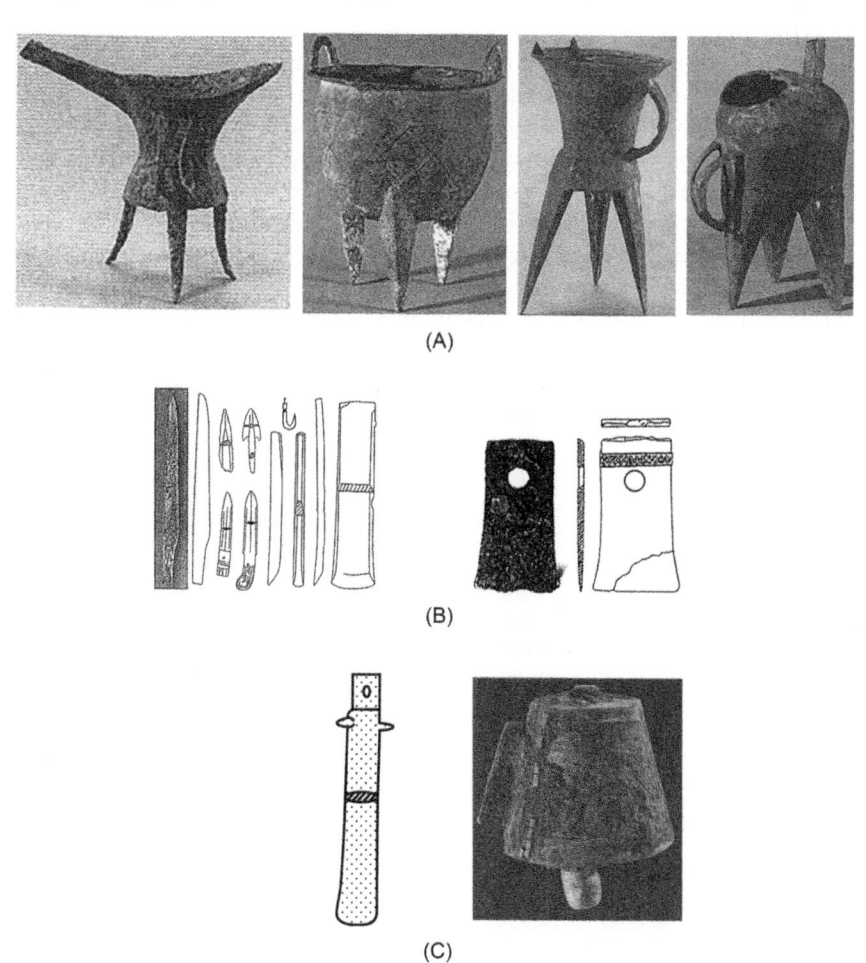

(A)

(B)

(C)

Figure 5.6 Ritual bronze and other sets from Erlitou. (A) Ritual bronze vessel set of the Erlitou Period: *jue* 13.3 cm tall (exc 1975) M8:1; tripod *ding* 20 cm tall (1987 exc); tripod *jia* 30.5 cm tall (exc.1984); tripod *he* 24.5 cm tall (exc. 1987). (B) Bronze weapon and tool sets: *yue* broad ax, arrowhead, *ge* dagger, long *dao* knife type blades, *dao* knives, *chan* spade, *ben* awl, adze, and fishhook. (C) Other bronzes: bell with jade clapper (exc.1984) and *zhang* insignia blade. (A) After Zhongguo Shehui (IA CASS) 1999: colorpl 1 VK M8 (*jue*); Zhongguo Qingtong 1996.1: colorpls 1 (*ding*); 14 (*jia*); 19 (*he*). (B) After Zhongguo Qingtong 1996.1: colorpl 23 (bell). (C) Zhao Zq 2017: 217 Figure 3:3.

Thus far, no bronze version of the *gu* goblet has been discovered, although versions in ceramic blackware and lacquer are frequently uncovered in burials. Oddly, at this point in the development of the new medium of bronze casting, no icon or image yet appeared cast onto bronze vessel surfaces although metamorphic icons appear commonly in other media of the Erlitou period.[10] The innovation of casting images on bronze ritual vessels would appear in the immediate future when a more sophisticated understanding of bronze casting mechanics took place during the second phase of the Bronze Age, the Shang period.

Many of the insignia jades inherited from the Longshan period, the last phase of the Jade Age, continued to be decorated with inherited metamorphic images. The most exquisite Longshan inherited jade set types include symbolic jade *yue* axes and insignia *gui* adze blades, *zhang* spade blades, and *dao* knife blades, often impressively large. Such aristocratic insignia jades continued to be created in the Erlitou period (Figure 5.7).

Another type of aristocratic good produced in Erlitou and often found in elite burials there is turquoise inlay (Figure 5.6, a technique well known earlier during the Jade Age, especially in association with the Qijia culture in northwest Gansu (see Qin Xl 2016).

Erlitou craft workers perfected the technique in fashioning some otherwise unknown objects including archers' arm guards (Figure 5.8), bronze

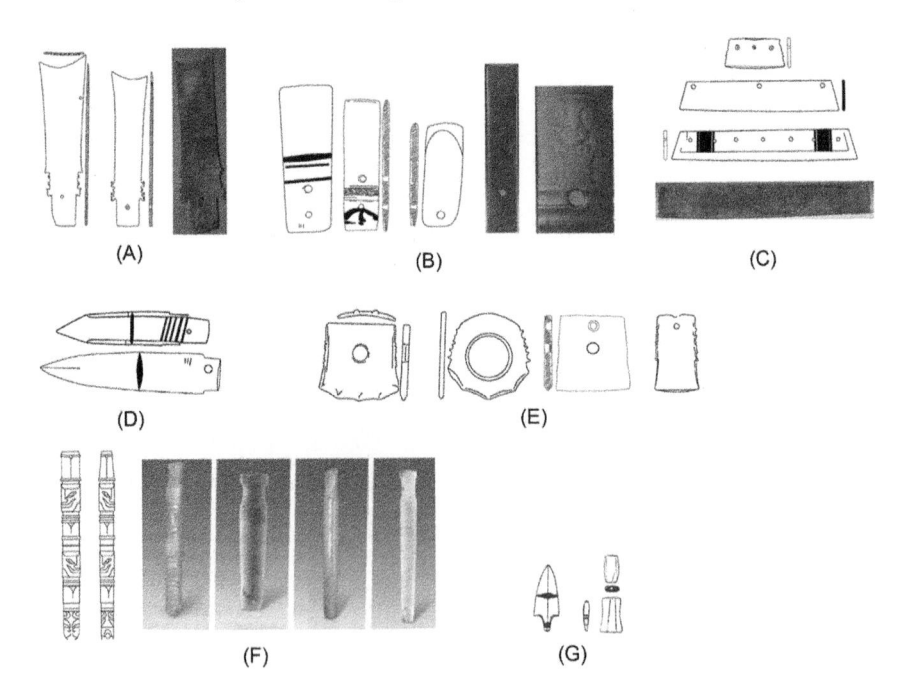

Figure 5.7 Erlitou period jade insignia and other jades. (A) *Zhang* insignia blades. (B) *Gui* adze insignia blades. (C) *Dao* insignia blades. (D) *Ge* insignia blades. (E) *Yue* insignia ax blades. (F) *Zan* handles. (G) Other jade artifacts such as arrowheads and beads. Based on figures published in Childs-Johnson 1995.

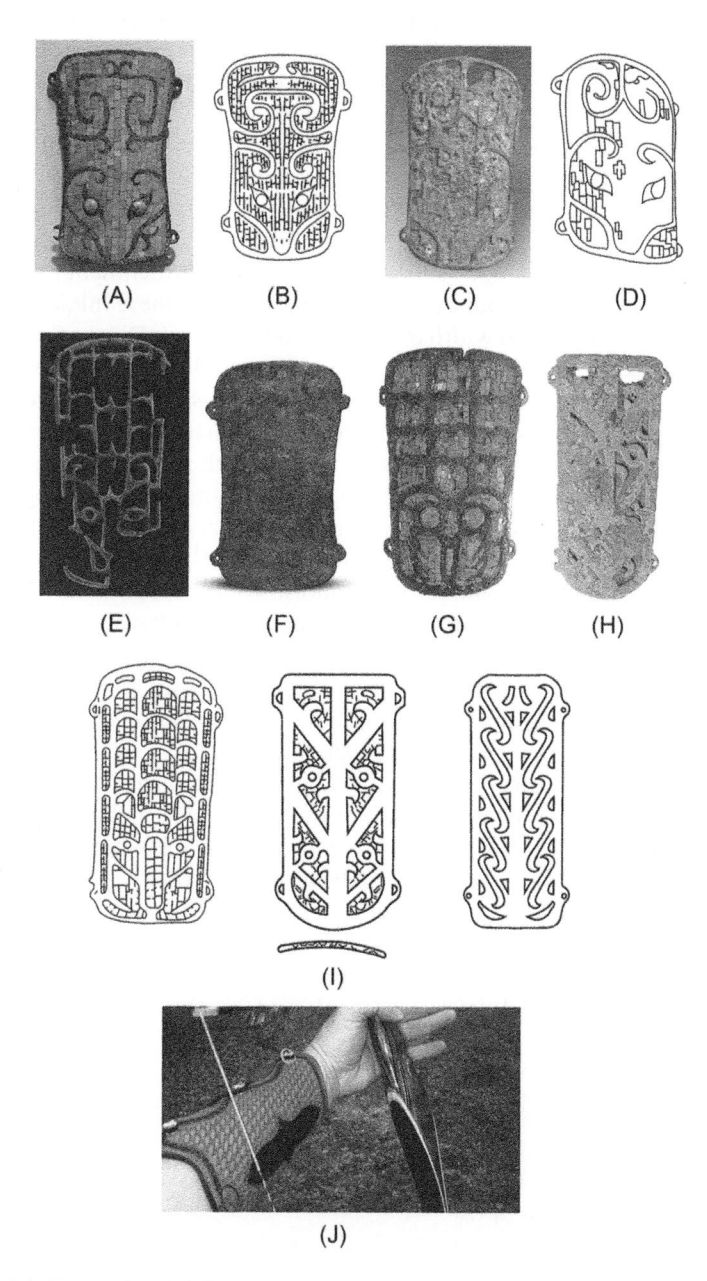

Figure 5.8 Turquoise inlaid bronze arm guards with mask imagery, Erlitou Period. (A–D) From Sanxingdui, Sichuan; Tianshui, Gansu; and Qijia-ping, Gansu. (E1–8) Small-scale ornaments mostly of heraldic birds of prey, *feng* birds, cicadas, "pig-dragons," human, tiger, deer, and sheep heads, stick pins, and other ornaments, from Shijiahe Culture, Hubei. (J) Example of arm guard used today after Buck. (A–D) After Du and Xu 2005: pls 5; 6.3–4; Du 1995; Zhang Lj 2002; Yi 2015: pl 1; Wang Q 1993: 7, Figure 1.1.11. (J) After Buck at https://outdoorwarrior.com/diy-archery-arm-guard).

mirrors and circlets, *yue* ax heads, and zoomorphic burial shrouds in the form of a sinuous long body with an oblong head (Figure 5.9). The rectangular bronze plaques inlaid with turquoise pieces forming a zoomorphic mask image are all small, averaging 7–8 inches long by 2–3 inches wide (Wang Q 2004). Burials never contain more than one of these plaques; when present, they typically lay close to the chest and arm of the deceased. The size and rectangular narrow shape strongly suggest an arm guard, worn by archers to protect the arm against abrasion from the bowstring upon releasing the arrow (Figure 5.8 last image at right). Four loops for attachment lie near the corners and the slightly rounded rectangular shape of these inlaid guards is adapted to the length and width of the left inner forearm. Due to their shape, size, and presence in elite burials, these artifacts could only have served elite archers and may have signified rank or had other symbolic connotations. Ordinary soldiers presumably used arm guards made of perishable materials such as leather. These archer arm guards with zoomorphic masks are so far unique to Erlitou culture but are known at sites under strong Erlitou cultural influence, in the far northwest amidst Qijia, and in the southwest at Sanxingdui (see examples illustrated in Figure 5.8).[11]

The most spectacular instance of turquoise art at Erlitou is the image of a dragon, extending 64.5 cm long and made of some 2,000 pieces of turquoise inlaid into what could have been lacquered wood, leather, or hemp that had largely disintegrated (Figure 5.9) (Xu *et al* 2007). This inlaid turquoise dragon-shaped body covering is extraordinary. The excavators relate that it lay on the right shoulder of the deceased, yet it is likely that it originally lay over the body proper, possibly slightly dislodged during burial. Midway along the dragon's body and near the hand of the corpse lay one bronze bell with a jade tubular-shaped clapper (Figure 5.9). Elsewhere lay hard-fired proto-porcelain objects alongside turquoise bead inlays, possibly related to head ornaments. Numerous lacquer wares, including plain *gu* and *gu* on stands and bowls, were deposited at the sides of the corpse. Ceramics included the *jue* tripod, the *he* pitcher with cap, the *he* pitcher with spout, tripod *ding*, *dou*, and *pan* (*gui*?). Shell string ornaments and 90 cowries with drilled holes

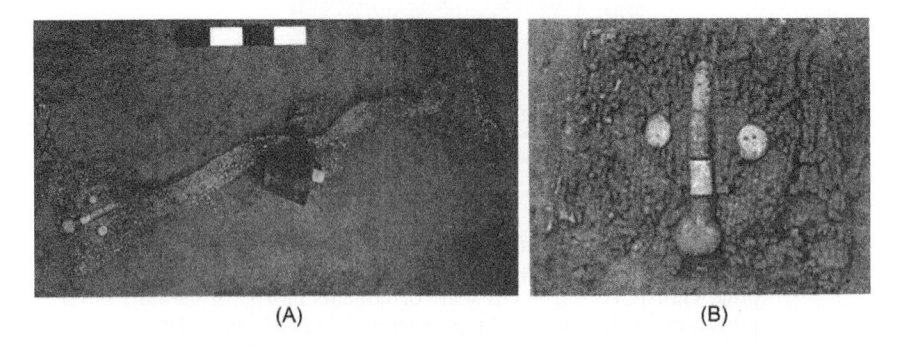

(A)   (B)

Figure 5.9 (A) *In situ* burial showing remains and inlaid turquoise dragon mosaic mantle covering the corpse (B) Detail of the "dragon" head, from the courtyard of PII Royal Building No 2, Erlitou. After Du and Xu 2006: pl 7.1.

lay in layers at neck level alongside two tubular turquoise beads. Clearly, this was a special burial. It is the earliest aristocratic burial known at the site of Erlitou, dating to Phase II, lying not outside the compound but along with others, similar in size (reportedly all destroyed) arranged in rows, in the middle of a multi-courtyard foundation, designated F3, that measured 150 m long by 50 m wide (Du and Xu 2006).

Burial artifacts, of course, aid in identifying social rank and status. The inlaid turquoise dragon shroud and bell almost certainly identify the deceased as a person of high rank and probably religious authority. What appears to be the humanoid power mask with a dragon body marks the deceased as one with spiritual power and probably spirit flight in the after-life. Since this burial shroud was probably originally laid directly over the length of the corpse, it is spiritually and intimately allied with the deceased.

The jade insignia and ritual bronzes from other tombs, lying outside the complex, and dating later to Phases III and IV are explicit symbols of aris-tocratic rank. Formalized and specialized architectural structures within the walled compound at Erlitou also clearly belonged to the ruling elite and served administrative, religious, and residential functions. Specialized craft areas, especially the turquoise and bronze workshops outside the southern gate at Erlitou and specialized sacrificial centers outside the royal com-pound at Erlitou also served the elite at the capital center. The discovery of many turquoise wasters marks a turquoise workshop occupying an area of approximately 1,000 m^2 (Du 2007; L Liu 2006).

Metamorphic Imagery in the Erlitou Culture

Metamorphic imagery during the Erlitou period may be limited in terms of available art specimens, yet it is as colorfully illuminating as it was in decorating Longshan period jades. As illustrated below in Figure 5.10A,C, in the first row are two versions of the semi-human Longshan period icon, and the same icon is portrayed in a detail drawn in black and white from a jade handle discovered at Erlitou (Figure 5.10B). This semi-human image with a wide mouth, slanting eyes, and bulbous nose, although abstracted to the shape of the tubular handle, is directly related to the Longshan period prototype. Similarly, the detail of the animal image on the same jade handle (Figure 5.10E) may identify the newly appropriated image found inlaid in turquoise on the armbands from Erlitou (e.g., Figure 5.10F) as well as the detail of a similar head etched into a ceramic fragment from another early Erlitou cultural site, Xinzhai (Figure 5.10G), nearby Erlitou in Henan.

Or this jade handle animal head may be compared with the small jade tiger head (lacking a mouth) excavated at the Longshan period site of Shiji-ahe, northern Hubei (above Figure 5.10D). Small-scale images of hunted ani-mals, including heads of stags and tigers, appear slightly earlier at Shijiahe, the large-scale Longshan period site in Hubei (see Chapter 4: Figure 5.8D). On the length of the jade handle from Erlitou, this archetypal humanoid

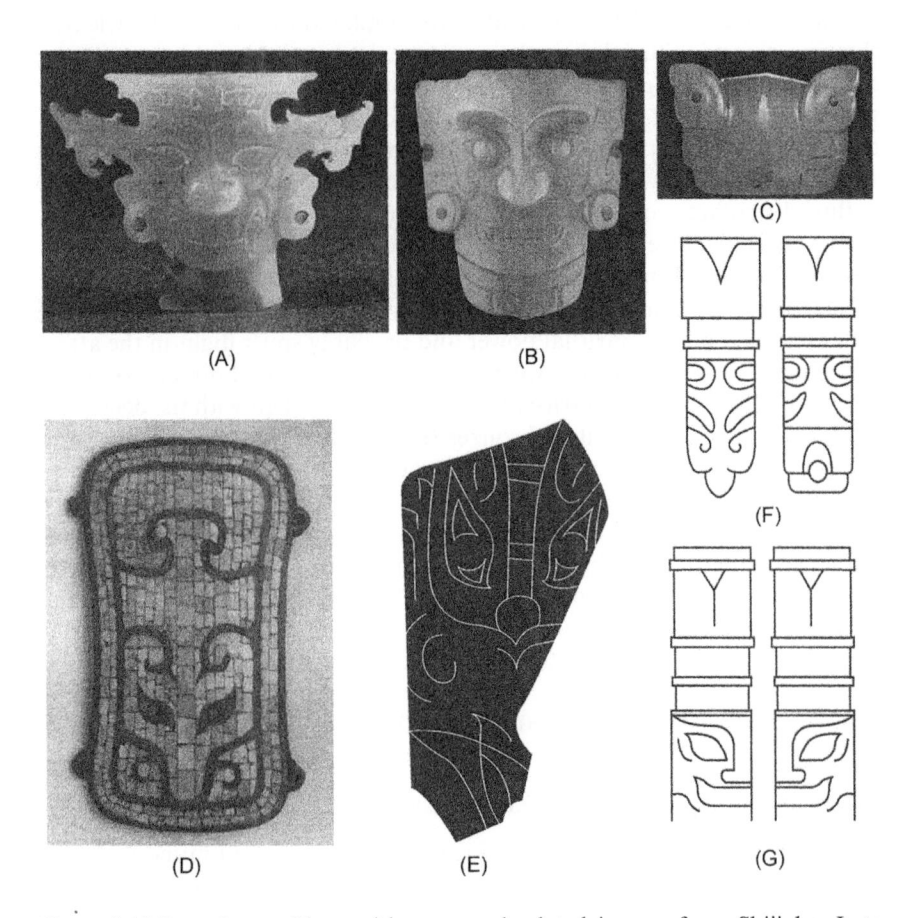

Figure 5.10 Interchangeable semi-human and related images from Shijiahe, Late Longshan, and Erlitou, "Xia" period sites. (A) Small jade head, Shijiahe. (B) Drawing of semi-human head on jade handle, Erlitou. (C) Jade semi-human head. Photo: Freer Gallery of Art. (D) Small jade tiger head, Shijiahe. (E) Drawing of tiger head on jade handle, Erlitou. (F) Turquoise inlaid bronze arm guard, Erlitou. (G) Incised ceramic shard, Xinzhai (early "Xia"). Based on Du and Xu 2006 and Childs-Johnson 1995.

image alternates with the image of a tiger head (Figure 5.10F). Evidently, the archetypal image of the semi-human icon of Longshan time and interest in wild animal types continue to predominate alongside elevation of the dragon icon, the long sinuous snake-like form, during the Erlitou period.

In these early materials, mask-like images depicting wild animal and humanoid types vary in emphasizing either human features or animal features or both in one image. Humanoid images appear in two versions, those with circular eyes and those with almond-shaped eyes. Humanoids also vary with more naturalistically representational human heads; these different versions – whether animal-like or human-like – as a rule are artistically and metamorphically interchangeable. The humanoid image persisted over the course of many centuries, evolving in its particulars but remarkably stable in its formal attributes, as will become clear in our analyses below. For this reason, these images and their variations appear to represent the metamorphic power of revered high ancestor(s), which in turn may be ascribed to the current ruler, whose authority derives from that ancestral lineage.

It is necessary to keep in mind that the Erlitou or "late Xia" phase represents a period of state control, absorbing and coalescing various cultural strains, by continuing to exploit jade as a symbolic art form as well as in developing the brand-new art form of bronze-working, and what seems to be a new height in working turquoise.

As is now well known, variations of the "dragon form" began as early as ca. 3500 BCE in the northeast with the Hongshan culture (Figure 5.11A) and occasionally appeared as a painted image on bowls from Yangshao culture sites in Henan province and Longshan (Taosi) sites in Shanxi. In those early contexts, the "dragon" already appears as a mythical creature with metamorphic attributes. The dragon image carried similar connotations during the historic Erlitou period. Although the dragon form is known from only a few Erlitou period examples, they are important. The most spectacular instance of Erlitou dragon imagery is the turquoise shroud described above (as reconstructed in Figure 5.11A).

Is it possible that this human-size dragon form was displayed at funeral rites and then deposited with the deceased? The turquoise mosaic dragon has a long, mobile serpentine body with a trapezoidal animal head. The protruding eyes and nasal ridge of the head are made of pale green jade. According to the excavators, another section of turquoise inlay lying at the end of the tail comprises a cloud-scroll or inlaid bird design, a design that suggests to some the image of a dragon flying amidst clouds. This remarkable image appears to anticipate the theme of spirits of the dead ascending to the heavens while riding on dragons, as portrayed on *feiyi* "flying wraps" or jade and textile shrouds of Western and Eastern Zhou burials (see Chapters 7 and 8: Figures 7.9a,b and 8.13).

The find is a remarkable testament to the powerful metamorphic symbol associated with elite paraphernalia. The connection with metamorphic imagery of Shang times is profound. A variation of the metamorphic image is represented on the lid and exterior of a later Shang period bronze *he* vessel as a semi-human face sprouting deer pedicels and as a body with short arms ending in claws (Figure 5.11C). A similar image but with an animal-type mask face without jaw decorates the interior of a Late Shang bronze *pan* vessel from the National Palace Museum in Taiwan (Figure 5.11D). Both serpentine bodies with rhomboid décor create circular forms and end in pointed tails. The image is almost identical typologically with the Erlitou turquoise rendering although one decorates in turquoise a human-sized long shroud and the other is cast as imagery within the interior of a bronze. Human-shaped

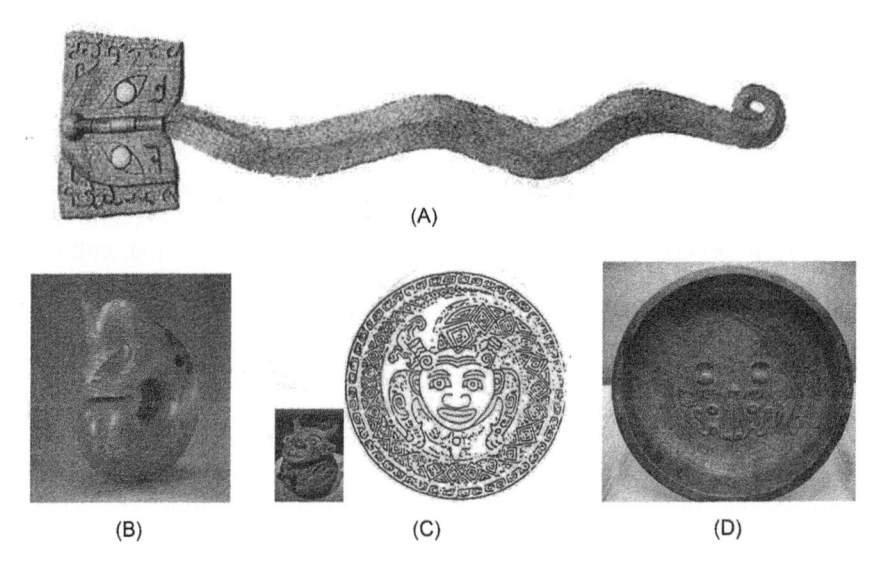

Figure 5.11 Variations of the "dragon" in Jade Age and Bronze Age art. (A) Reconstruction of the Erlitou period dragon shroud with turquoise inlay, Henan Provincial Museum. (B) Jade "pig-dragon," Hongshan Culture, Niuheliang, Liaoning Provincial Institute of Archaeology. (C) Shang bronze *he* vessel. National Museum of Asian Art, Smithsonian Institution, and flattened drawing of its dragon body with semi-human metamorphic mask. (D) Shang bronze *pan* interior with a dragon body and animal-headed metamorphic mask, National Palace Museum, Taipei, Taiwan.

ears and abstract pedicel horns define the bronze metamorphic image yet both turquoise and bronze facial types possess tear-shaped eyes and garlic bulb-shaped noses. These metamorphic icons of "Xia" and Shang are clearly directly related typologically. The dragon is a well-established symbol of metamorphic power associated with the ruling elite. It seems likely thus that the earliest and successive dynastic powers of the East Asian Heartland share common belief in the metamorphic power of the spirit realm.

The Impact of Erlitou Culture

The close relationship between the Longshan and Erlitou periods is established not only through ceramic similarities but through the emphasis on insignia jades symbolizing status and wealth. Many insignia jades of the Erlitou period have been excavated from tombs at Erlitou and one of these *zhang* (see Chapter 6) has gained fame as a symbol of the "Yazhang Culture" of East Asia, as analyzed by Tang Chung (Tang *et al* 2014; Tang C 2017). In type, they are like those known in Shandong and elsewhere where the Longshan and Erlitou cultures had a cultural impact. The Erlitou culture, including its religious manifestations, had a profound influence not only in its area of territorial control in the middle Yellow River plain but in its spread well beyond the area that earlier had been dominated by the Longshan culture, extending into what eventually would become northern and southern China (see e.g., Figures 5.12 and 5.13).

Erlitou's influences reached far-flung territories, including in the north, Qijia in Xinjiang and Gansu, and Dadianzi in Inner Mongolia; in the southwest, Sanxingdui and Jinsha in Sichuan; Yangzi River valley sites in Anhui and Hubei and still other sites as distant as Fujian, Shanghai, Hong Kong, and Vietnam.[12] What demonstrates Erlitou influence in these places is the evidence for trade in elite items, particularly jade, or the local creation

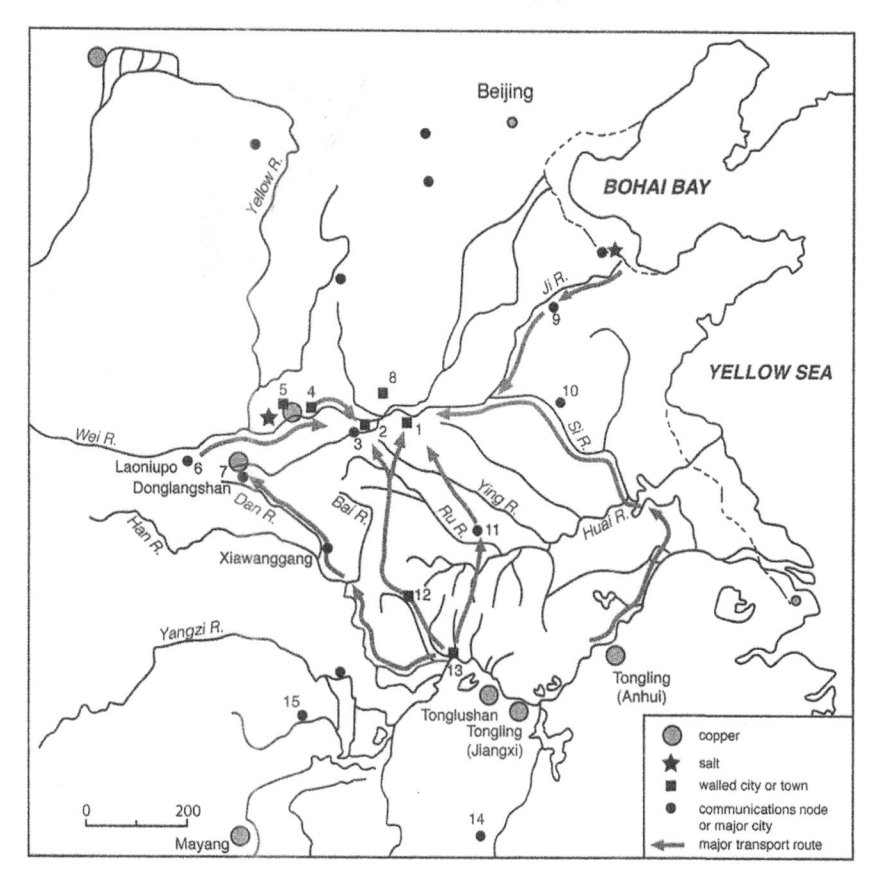

Figure 5.12 River and major trade routes between Erlitou and surrounding contacts of key natural resources (salt, copper). Key to Map 5.3: 1 Zhengzhou; 2 Yanshi; 3 Erlitou; 4 Yuanqu; 5 Dongxiafeng; 6 Laoniupo; 7 Donglongshan; 8 Fudian; 9 Daxinzhuang; 10 Qianzhangda; 11 Fangtang; 12 Wangjiashan; 13 Panlongcheng; 14 Wucheng. After Liu and Chen 2012: 289, Figure 8.13.

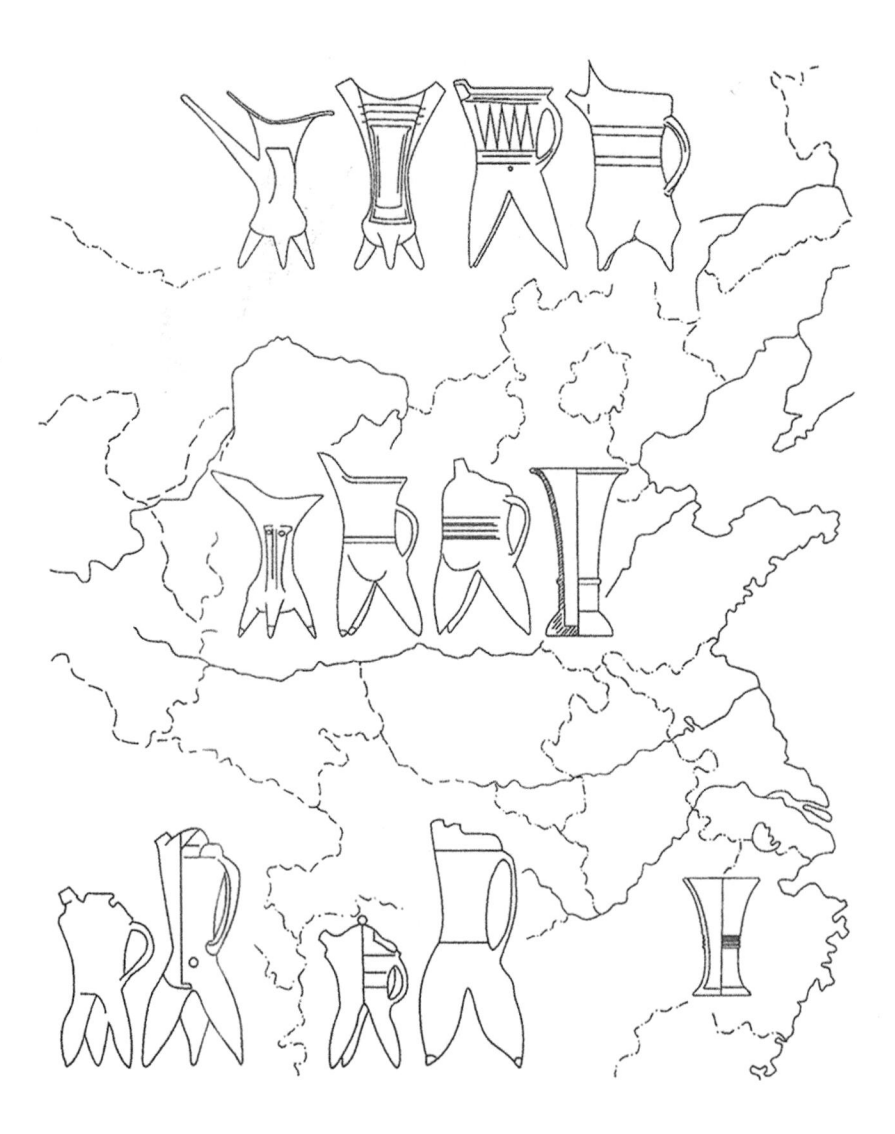

Figure 5.13 Map showing wide distribution of the ceramic tripod *he* alcohol heating
vessel of the Erlitou culture. After Tang C 2017.

of copies of elite artifacts that originated at Erlitou, as represented in
Figure 5.14A1–2. (For an extensive analysis of Erlitou jade types represented
in discoveries from Sichuan, see Childs-Johnson 2010.)

The settlement of Dadianzi in Inner Mongolia may have been a military outpost under the control of the distant but powerful Erlitou state. It
is not possible to identify the ethnolinguistic affiliations of the inhabitants
of Dadianzi and other outlying places, but it is clear that culturally they
were influenced by earlier Longshan and continued to be influenced by the

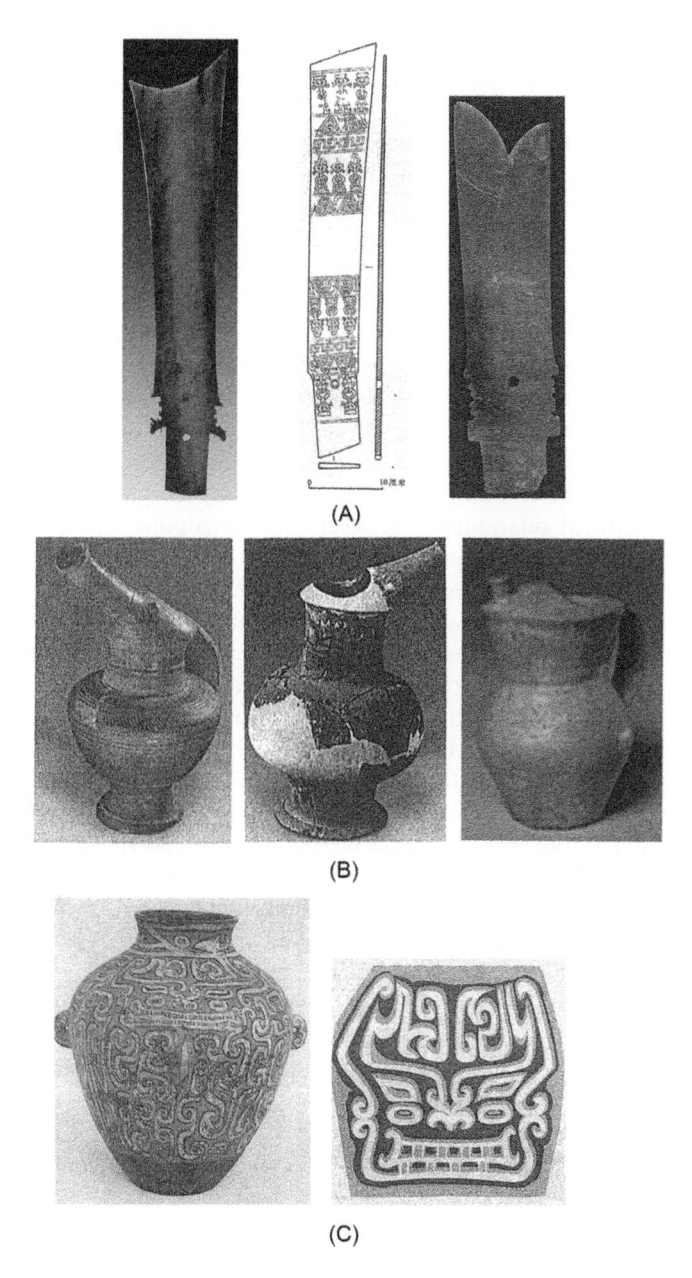

Figure 5.14 Artworks from various outlying regional cultures showing Erlitou cultural i0nfluences. (A1) Erlitou jade *zhang* from Sanxingdui. (A2–3) Sanxingdui imitation of Longshan & Erlitou period *zhang*. (B1) Ceramic he with flat base from Erlitou. (B2) Fujian. (B3) Qijiaping, Gansu, Palace Museum. (C1–3) Drawings of humanoid and cloud scroll images on Dadianzi tripod *lil̆jia* and other vessels from Dadianzi, Inner Mongolia, Lower Xiajiadian Culture.

Erlitou culture. For example, excavations at Dadianzi have revealed a cemetery of some 800 tombs loosely divided into 20 odd plots (Lavi-Shelach 2009). No bronze vessels have yet been uncovered from Dadianzi tombs, but ceramics of five types (*li/jia, gu, jue, he,* and tripod *ding*) stand out for their similarity to elite Erlitou vessel types known in bronze. These include a *gu* shape made of lacquer and ceramic *jue* and *he/gui* vessels (Figure 5.13). Two hundred pieces of turquoise inlay and 52 carved cowrie shells decorated the hair of the owner in burial M726, while turquoise beads were worn as earrings (Zhongguo Shehui 1998: 49). Vessels are typically redwares fired with an outer black skin and a brown-red interior (Figure 5.14C1–2). One of the richest tombs, M726, is representative of Erlitou period influences. Burial ceramics at Dadianzi were locally made but imitated vessel types that at Erlitou were cast in bronze as if the Dadianzi people were simulating the richest, most prestigious ritual vessels known to them, namely those used in offerings to deceased elite ancestors at the Erlitou capital center (see e.g., Figure 5.14B3). This emulation of a capital style by a regional center exemplifies the cultural relationship between the metropolis and the outlying regions within its sphere of influence.

The themes painted in red and white or black and white on Dadianzi black and redwares are idiosyncratic interpretations of metropolitan originals, in this case, of two major forms of imagery, the archetypal semi-human face and cloud scrolls. The archetypal semi-human face with elaborate feathered headdress is easily identified decorating two faces of a *guan*, and a variety of other vessels (Figure 5.14C1–2). The similarity of themes is immediately apparent in the semi-human face marked by eyes and eyebrows, a nasal ridge, and a stretched mouth with upward and downward pointing fangs, plus feathered or horned headdresses. Eyes may be round or almond-shaped. Forms curl and flow in calligraphic style, recalling the incised or raised curvilinear lines of Longshan period types. There is also a tendency towards abstraction of these facial forms, as represented by other painted interpretations, underscoring again the phenomenon of regional copying of well-known metropolitan prototypes. All of these vessels are redwares, high-fired so as to take on black skin, with images painted in bright reds and a white paste. The vessels were evidently not made for ordinary daily use but were reserved for ritual occasions.

Other discoveries of Erlitou influence are traced to the northwest Qijia and relations in Xinjiang, Qinghai, Ningxia, and Gansu. For example, at the distant northwest site of Tianshui in Gansu, archaeologists discovered an Erlitou-style turquoise-inlaid arm guard plaque, either a local copy of a metropolitan original or an import or gift from Erlitou (Yi 2015; Wang Q 1993). Erlitou influence is visible at many sites in the south as well, providing concrete evidence for Erlitou's cultural expansion, trade, and possible occupation. Luxury material and ritual remains of Erlitou period date are scattered at sites throughout the Yangzi River valley, although they are currently most profusely represented at two sites – as imports or booty at Sanxingdui in Guanghan, Sichuan, and as permanent settlement remains at the southern site of Panlongcheng, just north of Wuhan on the Fu River, a tributary of the Yangzi in Hubei province, as well as scattered in finds from Luan, Anhui province.

Metropolitan Erlitou's influence on regional cultures began during the Erlitou cultural period and remained significant through the Shang and early Western Zhou periods (Childs-Johnson 2015). Numerous jade insignia blades found in the burial caches or sacrificial pits excavated at Sanxing-dui, in Sichuan, include both local copies of metropolitan Erlitou types and authentic Erlitou pieces (Childs-Johnson 1995, 2010; Du 2007). Although people from Erlitou appear not to have settled in Sichuan, Erlitou cultural influences there are strong. Sites in Sichuan demonstrating this early Bronze Age influence include Sanxingdui and Jinsha, both near Chengdu. Specific artifacts demonstrating importation, gifts, or loot of Erlitou manufactured jades and bronze plaques with turquoise inlay stand out. For example, the jade *zhang* blades (Figure 5.14A) represent Erlitou metropolitan style and several regional interpretations of jade *zhang* (Figure 5.14BC) emanat-ing from Sanxingdui workmanship. The *zhang* blades show two extremes of craftsmanship: one, the exquisitely defined *zhang* blade with a trumpet mouth and raised and serrated handle décor representing metropolitan Erli-tou style, and two, the degraded shape of *zhang* with incised imagery of locals ceremoniously holding the same trumpet mouth jade type formulated during the Longshan period and mastered during the Erlitou period.

It has also been frequently pointed out that the *he* type ceramic vessel prevalent at Sanxingdui as well as at sites in the Yangzi River valley, and further south in Fujian, Hong Kong, and Vietnam (Figures 5.13 and 5.14B2) was fabricated locally but shows strong Erlitou influence (Tang 2007). And, as is typical of regional interpretations of metropolitan style, *he* may be exaggeratedly attenuated, again, as if to outdo the style of the culturally more sophisticated center at Erlitou (Figure 5.13). Yet ritual vessel types such as *jue* and *jia* do not appear in any of these outlying cultural excava-tions, thus demonstrating that the practice of conducting feasts and funer-ary and ancestral worship rites employing vessel types specifically designed to contain alcoholic beverages, as was done at metropolitan Erlitou, may not have been performed in the south. Equally stunning evidence in doc-umenting the pervasive Erlitou cultural influence well south of the capital include examples of Erlitou-type jade blades as far afield as Fujian, Hong Kong, Guangdong, and Vietnam (Childs-Johnson 1995). The blackware *he* from a site in Fujian province (Figure 5.14B2) is equally admirable for its distinctive Erlitou style. Erlitou period settlement remains of Phases I–III at Panlongcheng, which predate the fortification wall of the early Shang city at Erligang, and Shang city remains of Phases IV–VII at Panlongcheng (PIV–VII) (Hubei 2001:14–18, 22), are found outside the Shang walled city, at Wangjiazui and Yangjiazui. Settlement remains include ceramic work-shops and elongated "dragon" style kilns, house foundations, and exten-sive utilitarian ceramic vessels of several types, including yellow glazed stonewares. The only bronzes thus far reported from the Erlitou PII at PLC are bronze arrowheads.[13] Most illuminating in documenting well-developed elite ancestor worship at this southern settlement are M3 Yangjiawan, ritual bronze types of PIII, including *jia, jue, he,* and *li* tripods found at Yangjiazui, transitional to Early Shang, Erligang period occupation and building construction (Figure 5.15).

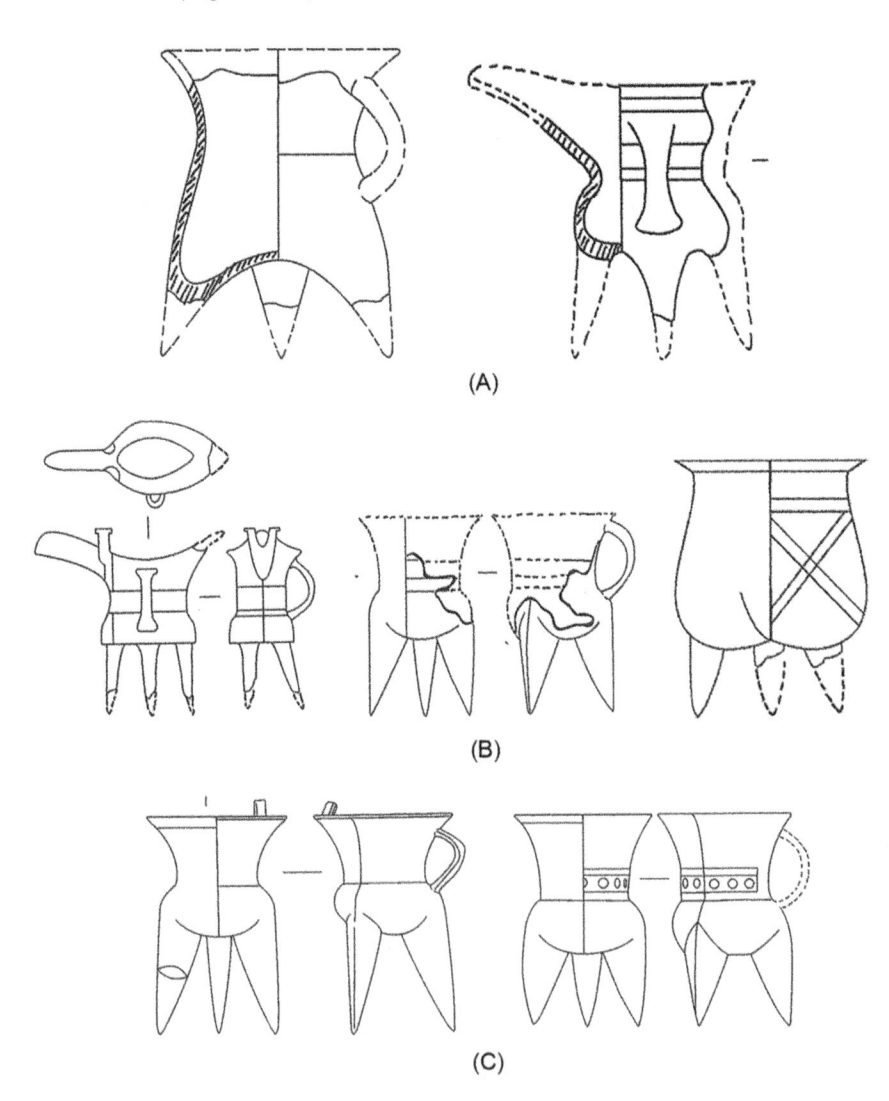

Figure 5.15 Representative ceramic and bronze vessels of the late Erlitou and early Erligang periods. (A) Ceramic *jia* and *jue* Phase 2, late Erlitou Period. (B) Bronze *jue, jia,* and *liding* from Panlongcheng, Phase 3 (Erligang first phase). (C) Bronze *jia* collected from surface Phase 3. After Hubei 2001: 222, Figure 159; 42, Figure 299; Zhongguo Shehui 2003ab.

Erlitou period bronze bells and *jia* vessel types have also been uncovered from piecemeal finds at sites in Anhui located near branches of the Yangzi River. These include two bronze *jia*, one found in 1972 at Feixi and another found at Liuan in 1965 (Anhui 2014: colorpls 2, 12; Du 2007:185–87). In style and form, these vessels belong securely to the Erlitou phase of bronze casting. The question is, where were these cast? Possibilities include the "Xia" capital at Erlitou or the "Xia" settlement at Panlongcheng in Hubei. Since Panlongcheng had its own bronze workshop, reported as dating to PII–IV, it is most likely that the bronzes were independently cast but were dependent on capital styles and models. Panlongcheng had an advanced casting facility for ceramics that was adapted for casting bronzes (see Childs-Johnson 2023). The overwhelming presence of Erlitou cultural influences, particularly metamorphic icons and vessel types clearly document again the strength of belief and its artistic complements in the East Asian Heartland. In addition to its distant influences, Erlitou also strongly influenced the rising fortified city at Erligang, which would become, on the basis of excavated finds, the origin of the Shang dynastic state.

Notes

1 See, e.g., the early accounts of Fan 1955 and Wu 1956, and Xu H 2020: Ch. 7.
2 Whether Xia as a dynasty existed or not has long been questioned and debated; why it is preferable to use Erlitou and not Xia is thoroughly discussed by Xu Hong 2020: Chs. 7–8.
3 A major mystery at Erlitou is the relative modesty of its city walls, compared with the massive fortifications that characterized cities during both the late Longshan era and the early Shang period. The inner wall of rammed earth that surrounded the royal compound appears to have been more symbolic than truly defensive, being only about three meters wide at the base and correspondingly modest in height. The outer city wall has not been systematically excavated, but it was clearly smaller than, for example, the walls of Taosi. Attempted explanations for the unexpectedly small dimensions of Erlitou's walls include speculation that the large-scale and frequent warfare between city-states of the late Longshan period, which made robust fortifications necessary, was sufficiently suppressed by the political reach of the Erlitou monarchy as to allow for much smaller walls (Xu 2013a). It is also possible that the Erlitou kings relied on a series of fortified garrison towns guarding the approaches to the city to repel any potential attackers.
4 The two are quite distant from each other in occupying the northeastern and southwestern parts of the complex. Buildings numbering 3–6 (map D3, 5, 6 predate D1–2, 4), located south and north of Foundation No 2 within the inner city, are also colonnaded structures undergoing excavation. Although details regarding the measurements of the city wall have not yet been published, the wall apparently was planned in conjunction with most of the city's internal buildings that support identifying the site as a royal center. Both the wall and foundations 1 and 2 were completed simultaneously, during Phase 3 when Erlitou became a very large settlement with an area of over one million m^2. Extensive roadways and ruts of two wheeled vehicles have also been found within and outside the compound. And although the center of the compound remains unexcavated, some 30 additional structures have so far been surveyed and identified in layout

(Du and Xu 2005: 548). The approximately similar sizes of the long horizontal columned structures with large-scale courtyards suggests that a standardized system of measurements and plans for large building construction existed. A small rectangular kitchen abuts the eastern compound wall of both buildings Nos 1 and 2 and both were divided internally into three or four rooms of equal size. A recently excavated structure No 4, fronting Building No 2 in the northeast, also consists of rammed earth foundations supporting a colonnaded rectangular structure, measuring 36m long by 12.6-13.1m wide (Du 2005: 565–75).

5 For new evidence possibly documenting early evidence for bronze working in the Yangzi River valley see Guo (Gororetskaya) 2021.

6 The bronze workshop south of the royal compound at Erlitou was in use for approximately 200 years, from Erlitou Phases 2–4. The site overlooked a river edge, occupying an area of approximately 9,600 m^2, a large rectangle some 16 m long by 6 m wide (Zheng G 1985; Xu and Jin 2005: 787). It is replete with remains documenting various stages in the creation of bronze artifacts, including melting and casting but not smelting (Liu Yx 2020; Du 2007: 109; L. Liu 2004:229). Finds from this workshop include "3 areas associated with casting, several burials, one kiln, a massive amount of cast debris incorporating ceramic molds, stone molds, cast fragments, bronze slag, copper ore, wood charcoal, and a small number of bronzes." (Zhongguo Shehui 2003: 111–12).

7 Two or three other unillustrated structures, identified as "rectangular altars" in conjunction with burials have also been identified. One of these structures is described in a 1984 report as rectangular and filled with fresh earth (Du and Xu 2006: 12–18) so that half of the platform lies below and half above ground. The surface of the rectangular structure appears to have been trampled and is dotted with burnt remains (Du 2007: 111). In a 1986–87 excavation report, sacrificial youth burials were identified lying outside the surrounding wall of the rectangular platform. Five additional burials consisting of two adults framing three youth burials were also identified as dating to Period 2 and were reported as lying in an east-to-west row under the foundations (Du 2007: 111). Nearby were rich Period 3 or 4 burials. Another report of 1994–95 describes similar remains, comprising bronzes and jade insignia, found in the eastern part of Area IX (Du 2007: 111). The careful orientation of these and other structures at Erlitou, and the rich goods found in associated graves, suggests that the Erlitou elite practiced some form of ancestor worship, used astronomical observations (though no Taosi-style observatory has been found at Erlitou) in determining the layout of important buildings, and had cosmological beliefs centered around the orientation of the Four Quarters (*sifang*)).

8 Of great significance, bronze-casting there was carried out using the indigenous piece-mold technique. Part of the reason the techniques of bronze-making were successfully developed during the Erlitou period relates to extant advanced techniques of working refined clays. The piece-mold technique used to cast bronze vessels originated in the clay molds used to create refined proto-porcelain whitewares and utilitarian grayware vessels during the late Neolithic period (see e.g., L. Liu 2009). This means that, even if the concept of bronze metallurgy was introduced into the Heartland Region via Central Asia, the technology of bronze casting employed by the earliest Sinitic metal workers was indigenous to the Heartland Region from the earliest times.

9 Where these metals were mined and smelted is slowly becoming clear. Various theories have been proposed. Li Liu and Xingcan Chen (2012) argue that metals for making bronze alloys during the Erlitou period were derived from sources in the Chongtiao mountains of Shanxi province, not far to the northwest of Erlitou. Metallurgy specialists, including Jin Zhengyao and Hua Jueming, on the other hand, have demonstrated that the lead used by bronze founders during the

Erlitou period came from more than one site, including mines in Shandong and Yunnan provinces (Jin Zy 2017; Mei 2009). Site archaeologists have also demonstrated that there were copper and tin mines in Anhui and Jiangxi provinces and smelting took place there (Hua 2008). The possibility that Erlitou acquired metals from distant sources is supported by evidence of trade relations and cultural contact between Erlitou and other contemporaneous sites to both the north (e.g., Pinggu, Hebei) and the south (e.g., Panlongcheng, Hubei), where archaeologists have discovered abundant jade insignia and ritual vessel types of Erlitou manufacture or inspiration.

10 In addition to their assumed role in rites of ancestor worship carried on at altars, it is possible that these vessels could also have been used in formalized settings such as banquets that invoked ancestor spirits since it is known that bronzes were used in various contexts during the later Shang and Zhou periods (see Chapters 6 and 7). The abundant vessels containing remains of sacrifices in Shang period tombs and the typological comparability of Longshan prototypes and Shang copies of late Erlitou period bronzes strongly supports the primary sacrificial function of specialized bronze vessel types that originated during that time.

11 As with bronze arm guards, bronze mirrors and bronze circular shapes with turquoise inlay are also found at Erlitou sites, throughout Phases 1–4 (see Qin 2016: 217 and Figure 7a1; Chen Xc 2003; Hao Y 2008) as well as in the same culturally influenced areas in the northwest in Gansu, Ningxia, Qinghai, and southwest in Sichuan (see below and see Qin 2016: 220).

12 For past analyses of this phenomenon, see Childs-Johnson 1995; Du 2007; C. Tang 2020: Ch 10.

13 Locally manufactured ceramic vessel types, matching those excavated at Erlitou, include utilitarian types (*yan* steamers, *guan* jars, *pan* basins, *ding*, and *li*) in combination with *jue*, *jia*, and *he* (Hubeisheng 2001:399, Figure 291and 401, Figure 392).

6 Institutionalized Ancestor Worship and Metamorphic Imagery in the Shang Period

Introduction

The Shang dynasty succeeded the Erlitou ("Xia dynasty") state around 1600 BCE in what was described in much later texts as a military conquest, but which may in fact have been an evolutionary and relatively peaceful transition of power. The Shang dynasty appears to have originated as a state that is now known as Erligang, after the village of that name where its remains were discovered. It is in the present-day city of Zhengzhou, on the Yellow River about 85 kilometers east of Erlitou. Its remains, in size and complexity, identify it as a capital city. The incipient state at Erligang overlapped temporally with Erlitou (whether or not the Erlitou state was called Xia) and interacted with it. The Shang city at Erligang appears to have grown and prospered as Erlitou, in Phase IV, declined.

Oracle bone inscriptions, as well as later literary sources, portray the Shang as a true dynastic state and the Shang kings as obsessively involved with their royal ancestors. They traced their lineage back to the dynastic founder Xie 偰 (or Qi 契), who was conceived by his mother, consort of the mythical figure Di Ku 帝嚳, when she swallowed the egg of a "dark bird." The rise of Shang and its emphasis on dynastic succession created a political and religious milieu in which institutionalized ancestor worship and metamorphic imagery thrived and evolved. Oracle bone inscriptions and other forms of evidence affirm the historicity of the Shang dynasty and its character as a cosmologically oriented, militarily strong, rapacious state that was religiously obsessed with displaying kingly power and royal metamorphic attributes. Below we introduce certain background elements of the Shang period which enhance the context of Shang belief systems and a complementary artistic program of metamorphic iconography.

The Shang city at Erligang served as the dynasty's capital for about 200 years during the early Shang (Song Gd 1993; Henan 2001). There is some evidence for the existence of a few of the first seven pre-dynastic kings of Shang, from Di Ku to Wang Hai; the next six pre-dynastic kings, from Shang Jia to Shi Gui are listed in scheduled royal ancestral rites and therefore were likely historical figures (Figure 6.1). The 14th king, Da Yi 大乙 (also known as

DOI: 10.4324/9781003341246-6

Cheng Tang 成湯, "Tang the Accomplished"), is said to have led an uprising that overthrew Jie 桀, the last Xia king, who had lost the support of the people through his cruelty, depravity, and impiety. Following his victory at the Battle of Mingtiao, Cheng Tang became the founder of the Shang dynasty, ruling with the reign title Da Yi. Whether or not these events took place, these early kings received sacrifices, by name, as members of the Shang ancestral line.[1]

Erligang Shang city was enclosed by a massive defensive wall, about 20 meters thick at the base and about seven extant meters high. Part of the Shang city has been extensively excavated and studied in detail; but because the archaeological remains lie beneath the heavily developed urban environment of modern Zhengzhou, it has not been possible to carry out archaeological work in most parts of the ancient site. But excavations at other sites of similar date such as Panlongcheng in Hubei, Yuanqu in Shanxi, and Wucheng and Xingan in Jiangxi have yielded rich evidence for the life and culture of the early Shang phase that complements and supplements the picture formed at Erligang (An Jh 1986; Henan 1999, 2001; Song Gd 2020: 254–86; Wang Lx 1998; Steinke and Ching 2014). Among the most significant features of this early Shang culture were more skillful and sophisticated bronze work (building on the bronze technology of Erlitou); the first

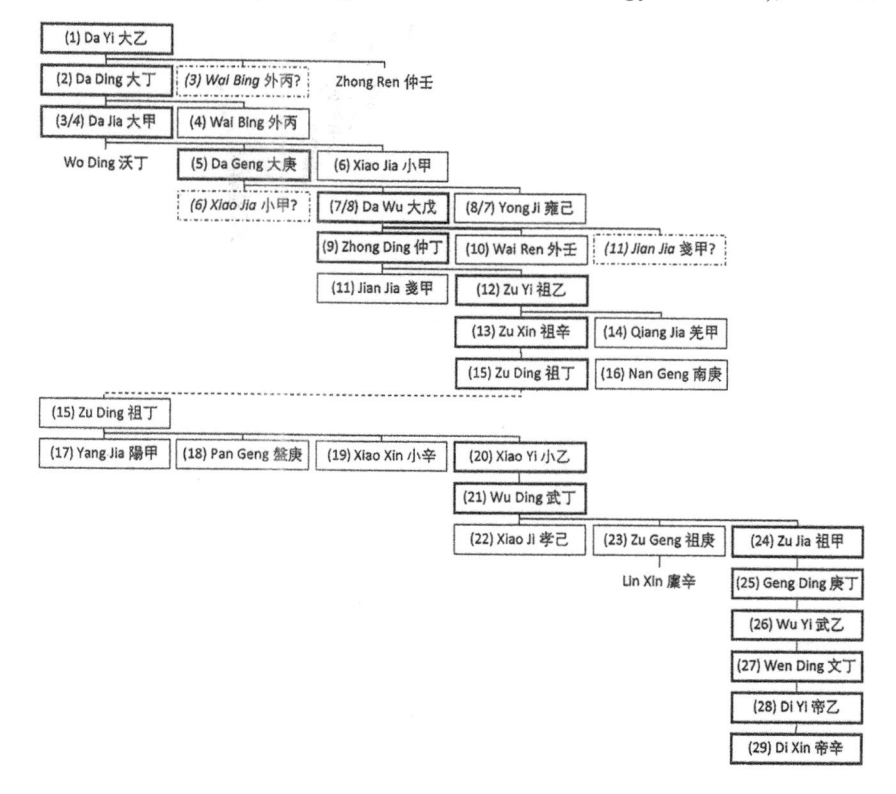

Figure 6.1 Chronological King Chart of the Shang period. After A Smith 2011.

unambiguous written language, encoding a language ancestral to Chinese; regular, codified worship by Shang kings of their deceased royal ancestors; and a belief in metamorphic power or spirit transformation (*yi* 異). All of these would remain essential elements of Shang culture and religion for the 500+ years of the dynasty's existence and into subsequent periods as well.

The Shang Kingdom

Scholars divide the Shang era into three phases: Early (ca. 1600–1400 BCE), Middle (ca. 1400–1250 BC), and Late (ca. 1250–1046 BCE).[2] The early Shang appears to have been a stable period of steady territorial growth and con-solidation of the Shang political system. Its capital, known in later texts as Bo, seems to have been for most of the period at Zhengzhou Shang City (Erligang) (Figures 6.2 and 6.3) and possibly some of the time at the cap-ital-sized Yanshi Shang City in Henan province (Yanshi Shang 2013). The middle Shang phase was marked by instability, as seen in several relocations of the capital over the course of two centuries. One of the middle Shang cap-itals was at Huanbei Shang City, adjacent to the late Shang capital at Yinxu, Anyang (Henan province) (Map 6.3). The late Shang phase begins with the move of the capital to Yinxu around 1250 BCE, where it remained for the rest of the dynasty's existence (Map 6.3).

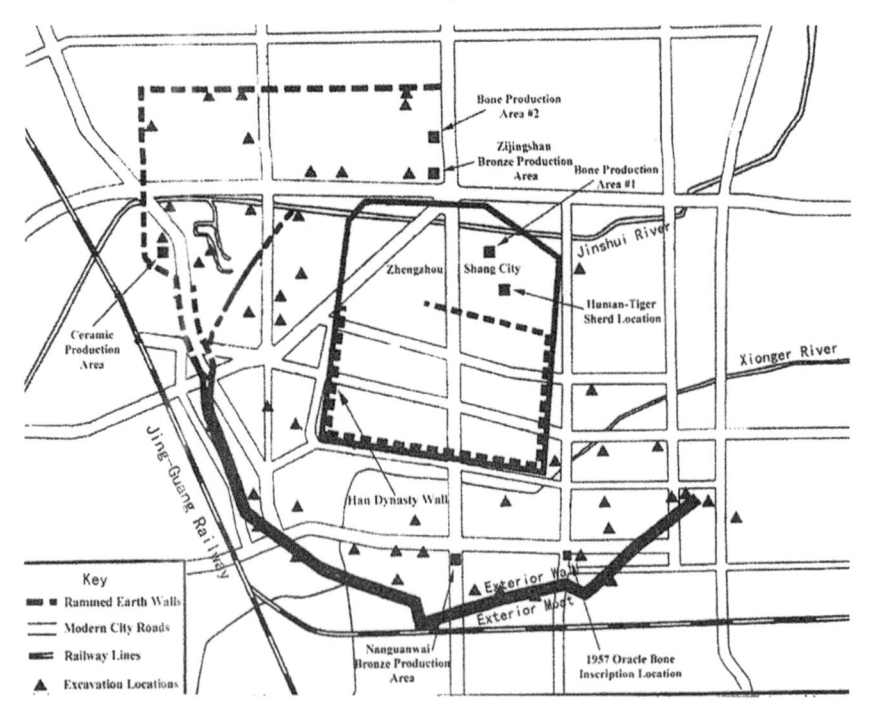

Figure 6.2 Ground plan of Zhengzhou Shang City, early Shang phase. After Liu *et al* 2010: 165.

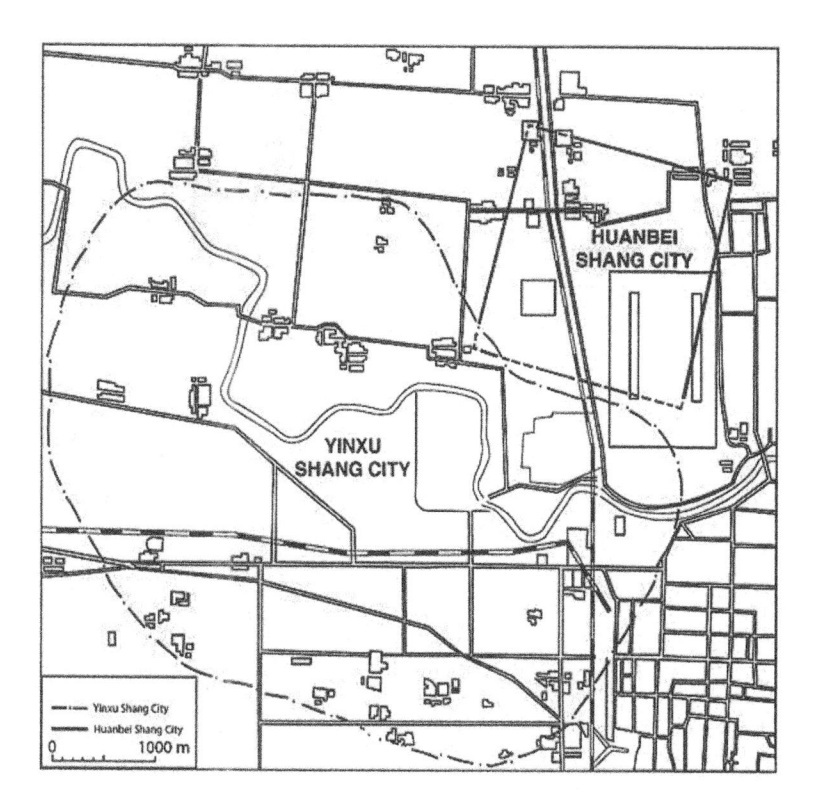

Figure 6.3 Ground plan of Huanbei Shang City, middle Shang phase (upper right
square) and Yinxu Shang City, Anyang, late Shang phase (dotted large
oblong). After IA CASS 2018.1: Figure 1, redrawn by Margaret Panoti.

Following the spectacular discovery of the late Shang capital at Yinxu
in the 1920s, and based on archaeological and inscriptional evidence found
there, it became apparent that the territory ruled by the Shang kings was not a
relatively small state in the middle reach of the Yellow River, as earlier studies
had postulated, but a much larger kingdom. The old view that the Shang kingdom was surrounded by territories known as the Four Quarters (*si fang* 四方)
whose inhabitants were primarily hostile to the Shang (see KC Chang 1980:
216, 220, 236, 248–59 and followed by Keightley 1979: 212–13; 2000: 66; Ah
Wang 2000: 29; Allan 1991) has been substantially modified in recent years.
It is now recognized that the Shang claimed control of the Four Quarters,
maintained an aggressive military policy toward them, and successfully pro-
jected power and political control far beyond the Yellow River Plain (Childs-
Johnson 2012 and cited bibliographic references; Sun and Lin 2010). Late Shang
oracle bone inscriptions speak of "receiving harvest" from one or another of
the Quarters and also of military raids against various peoples of the Quarters
for the purpose of obtaining captives for use as slaves or sacrificial victims.

Scholars are now coming to recognize that far-flung Shang-era cities such as Panlongcheng, Yuanqu, Wucheng, and Xingan represent centers of local control, probably governed by members of the Shang royal clan or its loyal aristocratic supporters (see e.g. Childs-Johnson 2013: 173–79). This is significant; it now appears that the establishment of subsidiary states or polities subservient to the royal dynasty, once considered a Western Zhou innovation, was already well established and practiced by the Shang (Childs-Johnson 2019; Song Zh 1992; Yang Sn 2005) (Figure 6.4).

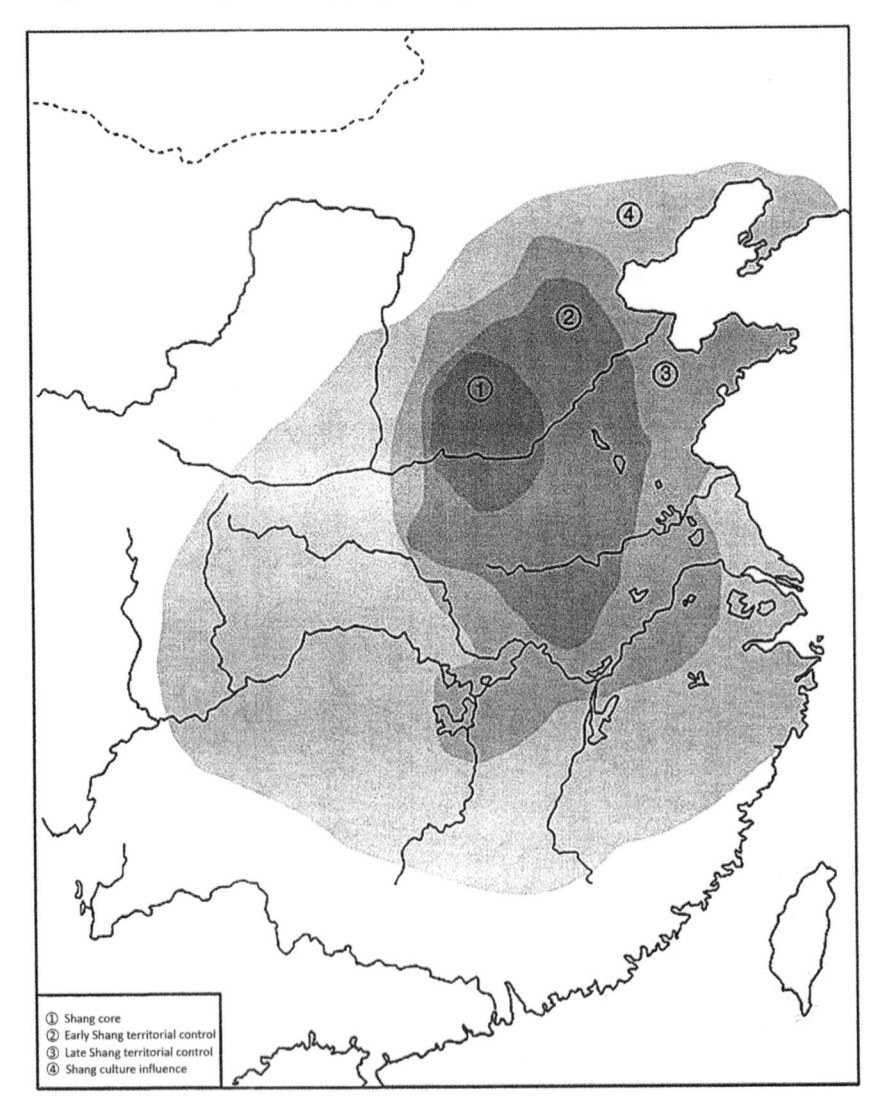

① Shang core
② Early Shang territorial control
③ Late Shang territorial control
④ Shang culture influence

Figure 6.4 Map showing distribution of Shang cultural influence. Drawing by Margaret Panoti.

Shang Cities

Although we cannot yet match any of the eight early Shang kings named in later histories with inscriptional evidence, it is likely that all of them (Da Yi (Cheng Tang), Da Ding, Da Jia, Wai Bing, Da Geng, Xiao Jia, Da Wu, Yong Ji) (see chronology Chart 6.1) ruled from the early Shang capital site of Erligang (Zhengzhou) or possibly Yanshi in the Luo river valley near Erlitou. The several inscriptions from this era briefly record divinations concerned with animal sacrifices to royal ancestral spirits, and sacrifices to the earth spirit (see e.g. Takashima 2012: 142) but none seem to date earlier than the late Shang phase.

These divination records provide uncontestable documentation that oracle-bone divination was practiced as early as the archaeologically attested beginning stages of the Shang dynasty itself. That the capital-size sites of Zhengzhou and Yanshi were commanding centers of power is demonstrated by the geographical reach of Shang cultural cities of similar date, extending as far as Panlongcheng in Hubei, Yuanqu in Shanxi, Laoniupo in Shaanxi, and both Wucheng and Xingan in Jiangxi. The disruptive middle Shang era spanned the reigns of 12 kings, and allegedly six different capitals. Tang Jigen has recently presented evidence that Huanbei Shang City may have been one of these capitals (Tang Jg 1999, 2010; Tang *et al* 2004; Wang Lx 2010) (see chronology chart Figure 6.1 and Maps 6.4–6.5). The tenth middle Shang ruler, Pan Geng, appears to have established a capital at Yinxu ("the Wastes of Yin"), today's Anyang, Henan Province, around 1250 BCE, followed by two rulers, Xiao Xin and Xiao Yi.[3] Wu Ding (Martial King Ding) – the best-known ruler from this period – and his nine late Shang successors continued to rule at Yinxu for the final 200 years of the Shang dynasty's existence (ca. 1250–1046 BCE).

The late Shang phase is comparatively well known through excavations at Anyang throughout a span of nearly a century (see e.g. Li Ji [Li Chi] 1978; Campbell 2014, 2018). King Wu Ding presided over the dynasty's longest reign, some 59 years. He was married to three successive queens, of whom the first, Honorable Queen Xin (Hou Mu Xin), also known as Royal Daughter Zi (Fu Zi, a.k.a. Fu Hao), is best known due to the discovery of her intact tomb and memorial hall at the capital site of Anyang (Zhongguo 1980, 1987; and studies on Fu Zi (Hao) by Wang Yx, *et al* 1977; Cao Dy 1993, 2020; and Childs-Johnson 1983, 2003).

Shang Geography and the Bronze Age

The Shang built on the bronze technology of Erlitou, producing more vessels of larger size bearing original, elaborate, and sophisticated images. The presence (usually in tombs) of Shang bronzes allows one to track the expansion of the Shang kingdom. Although the Shang consistently maintained capitals in the northern part of their domain, after replacing the Erlitou state in the middle Yellow River region, they consolidated their control further north, south, west, and east to create a domain that extended well beyond that of Erlitou (see e.g. the accounts of Song Zh 2005) (see Map 6.4). The Shang kings conceived their capital and the core region around it as *Zhongshang* 中國, "Shang at the Center,"[4] surrounded by outlying territories known as the *Sifang* 四方, Four Quarters, as noted above (also see Sun and Li's 2010 study of Shang geography and *fang* territories). Shang's royal relations with the Four Quarters were sometimes peaceful and sometimes hostile, but in either case, the *Sifang* absorbed Shang's cultural influence.

Shang's cultural influence in these places may be discerned through significant site remains, ceramic typology, burials, and Shang's cultural hallmark, ritual bronze vessels, as well as by an abundance of references in bone inscriptions to specific sites connected with military campaigns, hunting expeditions, administrative inspections, and a complex system of tribute and land awards (see, for example, the research of Song Zh 2005). Based on the archaeological data, the territory of the three Shang phases – early, middle, and late – included most of the Yellow River valley and the eastern and middle portions of the Yangzi River valleys but did not extend very far south of the Yangzi river. Fujian, Guangdong, Guangxi, and other peripheral provinces, although lying outside the reach of direct Shang control, were still in some cases influenced by Shang culture. But the evidence for this influence is not so strong and clear-cut as to permit characterizing these regions as participating in the Shang state religion with its attendant employment of bronze ritual vessels in sacrificial rites.

Shang Royal Government

The Shang had a well-organized and clearly defined royal system of government (Song Zh 2005; Yang Sn 1992; Wang Zz 2010; Childs-Johnson 2023). True to the concept of a dynasty, the Shang state was governed for more than 500 years of its existence by a single royal family, within which kingship normally passed from father to son but also sometimes from brother to brother and occasionally from uncle to nephew (Chart Figure 6.1) (KC Chang 1986, 1987; Smith and Fan 2020: Ch 11, 227–52; Song Zh 2005). On the basis of archaeological evidence, members of the ruling family seem to have governed territories with subordinate settlements that were hierarchically subservient to the Shang king in his capital. An important item of evidence for this is the presence in subordinate cities and settlements of sacrificial vessels, such as large *ding*, of a size and style that was limited to members of the royal family (Childs-Johnson 2013).

Much remains unknown about the structure and functions of Shang government. But it is clear (for example, from job titles mentioned in oracle bone inscriptions) that a sizeable bureaucracy assisted the king in carrying out his duties (various scholars have analyzed such data, see e.g. Song Zh 2005; Yang Sn 1992). There were officials in charge of breeding and raising sacrificial animals; maintaining the royal chariots and horses; brewing sacrificial alcoholic beverages; preparing bones and turtle plastrons for use in divination; recording and transcribing the divinatory texts; assessing and collecting the grain harvest; and many other administrative functions. As was already true during the Erlitou (Xia) period, craft workshops for bronze casting, ceramic production, jade working, and other such industries were gathered together in specialized quarters of Shang cities, where they were supervised by royal officials. Many of these officials are known to have been members or relatives of the royal family, and many positions were hereditary (especially those with the rank of *ya* 亞) (Wang C 2015:188–213), in addition to appointments conferred upon heads of neighboring states (both female and male) (Song Zh 2005).

The Powers of the King

The powers of the king derived in part from his ability to mobilize the instruments of the state to collect revenue and carry out administrative functions. He could issue orders (*ling* 令) and expect them to be obeyed. He could wage offensive and defensive warfare and had the exclusive right to organize and carry out massive hunting expeditions. But the greater and more basic source of his power came from his spiritual duties as diviner, sacrificer, and performer of rites. Royal authority was vested in, and symbolized by, ritual activities that were the exclusive prerogative of the king. He could *zhu* 祝, "invoke spirits"; *bin* 賓, "receive spirits"; and *zhan* 占, "prognosticate," i.e. perform oracle bone divination, interpret the results, and order appropriate measures to be taken in response; perform the royal ancestral sacrifices in the prescribed cycles of ten days and 60 days; and participate in and preside over other rituals as well, such as what was probably masked dance performances (see e.g. Sun Kd 1944; also see the review of the exorcistic rain dance in Chang Tt 1970: 243–47). The ability of the king to exercise these powers depended on a quality termed, in the oracle-bone inscriptions, *yi* 異, "metamorphic power" or "spirit transformation." This power enabled the king to communicate with and tap into the power of the spirit world.[5] There are many variants of the Shang graph for *yi*, but they all depict a frontally displayed human or humanoid; many versions seem to indicate that the figure is masked,[6] and some also show the figure as wearing an elaborate headpiece. As we have seen, the displayed image, in a tradition extending back to the Liangzhu jades, is a symbol of metamorphosis. It is associated with paired reciprocal values: death and rebirth, devouring and regeneration, and life-taking and life-giving. The graph straightforwardly seems to show a person, probably the king, in a state of spirit transformation in the act of conducting rituals directed at the ancestors or various divinities. Images of a displayed human, often with a headdress and sometimes associated with a cicada (symbol of rebirth), appear to depict the king in a state of spirit transformation (Figure 6.5).[7]

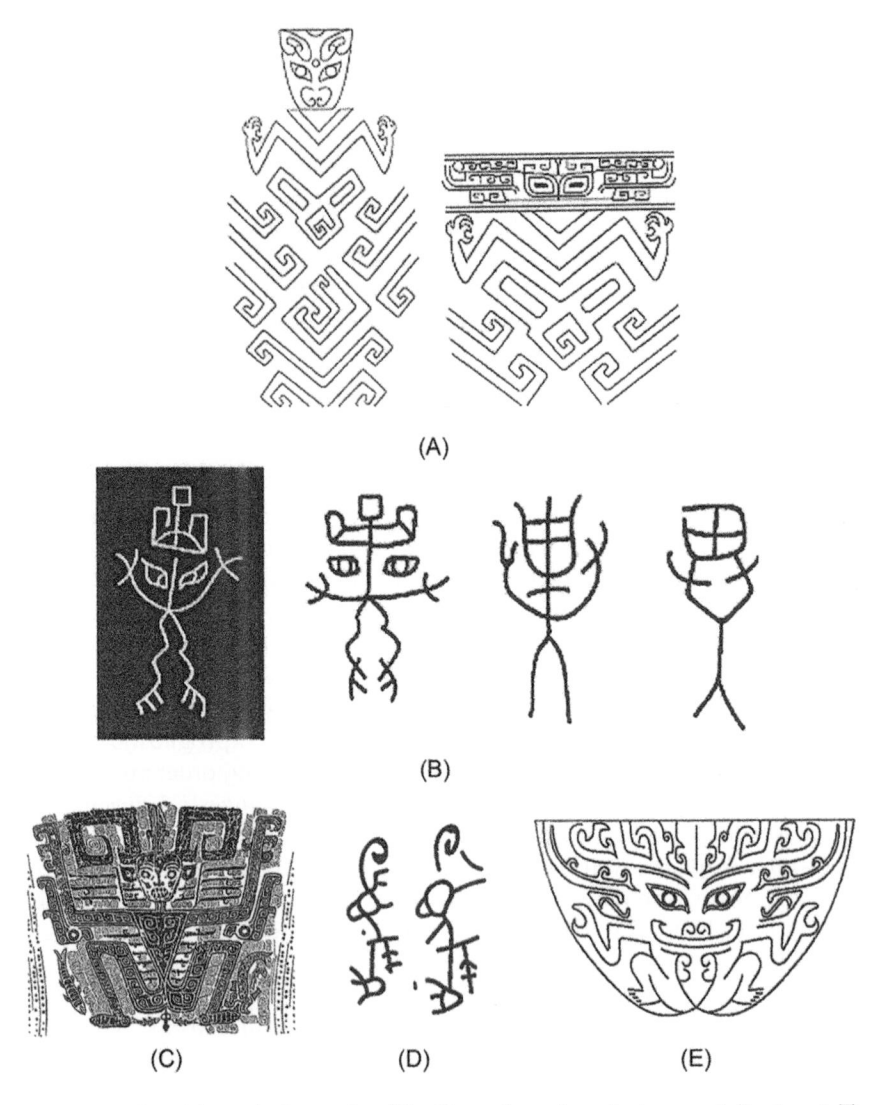

Figure 6.5 Graphic variations of *yi* 異in Shang bone inscriptions and displayed 異 *yi* images of spirit empowerment in Shang art. (A) Drawings of metamorphic imagery carved into stoneware white vases, Xibeigang M1001, Anyang. (B) Variations of the *yi* graph in bone divinatory inscriptions, Xiaotun South and Xiaotun, Anyang. (C) Rubbing of *yi* image cast on back and front faces of a bronze drum, 'Chongyang, Hubei,' Baron Sumitomo Collection. (D) Two variations of the graph Kui 夔 in oracle bone and bronze inscriptions. E *Yi* metamorphic image carved into front and reverse faces of a marble *liding*, Museum of Far Eastern Antiquities, Stockholm. (A–E) After Childs-Johnson 2008: Figure 14, including (D) after Hayashi M. 1960: Figure 60 (Kui) and Childs-Johnson 1995: 55–56 (Kui).

The Shang royal ancestors were a major focus of a regular round of divination, sacrifices, exorcisms, and other cult observances conducted by the king. In addition to rites carried out for the royal ancestors, rites were addressed to the powerful deity known as Di 帝 or Shang Di 上帝 ("Cosmological Spirit Power" or "High Cosmological Spirit Power"[8]). Di was the lineage god of the Shang kings, as seen in the incorporation of the term Di in the posthumous names of deceased kings: Di Wu Ding, Di Wen Ding, and so on (Shima K, tr: 183–84; Childs-Johnson 2008). The performance of these rites to Di rendered Shang kings supreme within the supernatural world of deceased ancestors and nature spirits. The ruler had the power to request the benevolent assistance of the royal ancestral spirits, as well as the power to identify with Di, the celestial being that controlled such natural forces as rain, wind, and disease. The cracking of oracle bones gave the kings shaman-like powers to communicate with Di, though the outcome of – i.e. Di's response to – the prognostication depended on the king. Certain scholars have misconstrued Shang belief by associating ancestral spirits with the power to mediate with Di[9] rather than having direct cosmological spirit power in association with Di.[10]

Representative oracle bone inscriptions testify to these royal prerogatives: *Yi*, as found in the bone inscriptions, is a verb "to spiritually transform" or "to be spiritually empowered" (Childs-Johnson 2008). The verb may be passive, active, or causative. The power to *yi* 異 belongs to the reigning king, past king spirits, and the High God Di. For example:

> Heji no. 11921: Crack-making on the *gengxu* day Zheng divined: If it does not rain will Di spiritually empower?
> Heji no.2274: Crack-making on the *bingzi* day Bin divined: Will Fu Yi (26th king) spiritually empower the king [his eldest son Wu Ding] with the [tetrapod] *ding* bronze vessel? Doubly auspicious. Will Fu Yi not spiritually empower the king with the [tetrapod] *ding* bronze vessel?

A long series of divination records shows how these various powers of the king were interrelated; *yi* spiritual empowerment, *bin* receiving of spirits, hunting, and intersession for fair weather are linked in this group of divinations:

> Heji no. 30439: Crack-making on the *guiyou* day it was divined: If [the king] goes hunting with nets at the He (Yellow River) should the king *bin* receive spirit(s)? Auspicious! It was divined: Should [the king] not receive spirit(s)? It was divined: Should the king go hunting with nets at Guang [near] the He? Auspicious! It was divined: [Should the king] not go hunting with nets at Guang [near] the He? It was divined: If [the king] makes invocation he indeed should make a catch. If the king on the *yi* day X-verb (makes offering?) to

the buffalo-headed spirit will he [catch] buffalo? Auspicious! It was divined: If [the king] does not make invocation [will he not make a catch]? Crack-making on the *yihai* day Quan divined: If the king enters at Yi/Yin (river?) will he not encounter danger? It was divined: If he fords [the river] at X X place will [he catch] buffalo? It was divined: If he does not ford [the river at X X place will he catch buffalo]? Crack-making on the *dingchou* day Quan divined: If [the king] uses this crack-making, undergoes spiritual empowerment, and fords [the river} at Tong will [he catch] buffalo? Auspicious! If [the king] does not [use this crack-making, undergo spiritual empowerment, and] ford [the river] at Tong will [he not catch] buffalo? Auspicious! Should the Ya (military chiefs) and Ma (horsemen) ford [the river and catch] buffalo? It was divined: Should the masses (foot soldiers) ford [the river and catch] buffalo? Crack-making on the *dingchou* day Quan divined: Should [the king] offer prayer for a grain harvest? Should [the king] use the *ding* day to invoke spirit(s)? Auspicious! It was divined: Should [the king] make invocation to Fu Jia? It was divined: If [the king] makes invocation to Zu Ding will the king receive this spirit's aid? It was divined: Will it rain on the *xin* day?

The above inscription is one of many (see e.g. Tun no 2341, Heji nos 30757, 29090, 28717, 288400, 28360, 29395) concerning the grand hunt of the Shang king and the king *yi*-ing or undergoing spirit empowerment for the purpose of making a successful catch. The divinations performed in the inscription cited here cover a period of about five days in the Shang calendar (*guiyou* (day 10) through *dingchou* (day 14)), a period of intense query intended to ensure success. This makes clear that royal hunts were great affairs of state, carefully planned and well-designed – an orchestrated royal event that required meticulous preparation, aided by the powerful mechanism of oracle-bone divination.

Since *yi* is grammatically interchangeable with *zhu* 祝, to invoke spirits (Childs-Johnson 2008), it is safe to assume that spirit empowerment involved some sort of rite, most likely one that involved wearing masks while dancing or performing mimes.[11] As documented by the large-scale hollow carved wood images of tigers and other wild and mythic spirits lying on the lids of royal burials at Xibeigang, dancing most likely took place in some sort of mimetic rite at the time of the funeral (see Childs-Johnson 2013; Sun Kd 1944). *Yi* or *zhu* rites performed in preparation for a royal hunt most likely also involved the display of wild animal masks in soliciting the aid of spirit(s) through invocation before the hunt (see e.g. Heji 30349 cited above). The likelihood that this was so is bolstered by the observation that the graph for "to hunt" in bone inscriptions incorporates a displayed mask (see e.g. Chang Tt 1970: 121, n 1). Spirit empowerment served as demonstration of the king's authority and ability to control the spirit world in various ways that included sacrificial rites to win the aid and goodwill of the spirits of dead royal ancestors, or through spirit empowerment to capture or kill wild animals in elaborate royal hunts, or to carry out sacrifices to Di to influence natural phenomena such as weather or disease, or to wage war and capture prisoners.

The 60-day Cycle and the Royal Ancestral Sacrifices

The royal ancestral cult was governed by a repeating cycle of 60 days, utilizing a day-count system that dated back at least to the Erlitou period ("Xia dynasty"). That the system was already in use by the beginning of the Shang era can be deduced from *ganzhi* conventions in the naming of Shang kings (Nivison 2009). The system combined two sets of numbers, the ten Heavenly Stems (*tian gan* 天干) and the 12 Earthly Branches (*di zhi* 地支), pairing a stem with a branch thus: Aa, Bb,... Jj, Ak, Bl, Ca,... Jl; the cycle then re-commences with Aa (see Hsü 1984; P'an 1976). It will be readily apparent that this selects exactly half of the possible 120 combinations of stems and branches, producing an endlessly repeating cycle of 60 days (The other 60 combinations are excluded; for example, the series Ab, Bc, etc. does not exist.) The day count appears conspicuously in oracle bone inscriptions, where the divination act is customarily dated by the sexagenary day on which the divination took place.[12]

Deceased Shang kings were given a ritual posthumous name that included one of the heavenly stems.[13] For example, the posthumous name, Wu Ding, means the Martial [king] who receives cult on day *ding* (the fourth Heavenly Stem). In the ten-day cycle of regular sacrifices to deceased ancestors, the days were visualized as "suns" (the word *ri* 日 means both "sun" and "day"), each of which had distinctive power, and each deceased ancestor wielded power according to the day's sun.

In addition to these regular (and thus to some extent routine) cyclical sacrifices to the royal ancestors, the king might, and often did, offer special sacrifices to the ancestors, to the High Cosmological Power [Shang] Di, and to spirits associated with various natural entities and phenomena, such as the Yellow River and other rivers, various mountains, clouds, and so on (see e.g. Chen Mj 1956; Chang Tt 1970; Shima K 1975, tr.). The king was uniquely empowered to communicate with the spirit world and perform the rites appropriate to the various spirits. Sons of the king were authorized to divine about sacrifices and various local events, but neither diviners nor the sons and daughters of the king, nor his brothers, nor his wives, could carry out sacred rituals in which the celebrant identified with the spirit to which the rites were directed. On the other hand, Di (considered also as a primordial ancestor) could *bin* "receive spirits," as could the deceased ancestors themselves, as males of the Shang royal lineage. Indeed, it is likely that the complete sets of sacrificial bronzes customarily buried with members of the Shang royal lineage were intended to permit the deceased royal ancestors to carry out the rites due to their own ancestors. (In other words, the obligation of kings to perform sacrifices to their ancestors did not terminate with death.) Thus, although the king was not the only one to address ancestral spirits with offerings in bronze vessels, he, among the living, was the only one with the right to receive and communicate with the spirits of his dead ancestors (Childs-Johnson 2008: 29). Many divination records show the king in his role as prognosticator:

> Heji 13220: Crack-making on the *gengchen* day Zheng divined: Will the sunshine on the next *xinzi* day? The King prognosticated saying: "The sun will shine."
>
> Heji 13999: Crack-making on the *dingyou* day Bin divined: If Fu Zi gives birth to a child will it be auspicious? The king prognosticated, saying: "If [the birth] is on a *jia* day there will be danger. There will be...."

There are also many examples of the king receiving spirits (*bin*):

> Tun 723 Crack-making, 10th month, in the temple of Zu Yi, Yong [divined]...If the king comes and makes flesh sacrifice hacked with the *yue* broad-ax will Di descend?
>
> Heji no.974: It was divined: Should the king offer a sow pig when carrying out the *bin* rite of receiving Fu Yi? ... Should a sow pig not be offered when carrying out the *bin* rite of receiving the spirit of Fu Yi?

The Shang king was ultimately in charge of all rites and sacrifices, whether to the spirits of deceased members of the royal house or to Di and nature spirits. In addition to scheduled cyclical royal ancestor rites, the king often presided over the spring planting *jie* [耤], the archery ceremony *she* 射, the rain-seeking dance ceremony *wu* 舞, and the *di/ti* ceremony [帝禘]. For example,

> *Wu* 舞 rain dance ceremony:
> It was divined: Should the king not perform the rain dance 舞? Should the king perform the rain dance 舞?
> Heji 11006.
> *Di*/禘禮 ceremony to Di/Shang Di:
> Crack-making on the *yiwei* day it was divined: Should [the king] carry out the *di* ceremony [to Di and] the Directions] with sacrifice of one dog, one pig, and two sheep?
> Heji 14301
> *She* archery 射禮 ceremony:
> Should the king carry out the archery rite in front of the ancestral temple?
> See Cai (Tsai) 1978: 39–58, cited as Ning 2145

Deceased kings, and to a lesser extent queens, upon dying assumed some of the powers of Di, though not Di's supreme power to *ling* 令, command from above. The King could also *ling*, but his commands while alive were understood as originating "below," that is on earth, and were directed to military commanders and other officials. Di, the royal ancestors, and secondary spirits, such as the *feng* 風 wind spirit or the 河 *he* river spirit, were each, in the appropriate degree, responsible for the fate of the Shang realm (see one of the classic citations at Heji no.14295 where the *feng* spirit(s) is envisioned as directional and in this context associated with specific names (see Hu Hx 1944 *shang*: 365–81). The royal dead apparently wielded such powers because they drew on the power of one or another of the ten day-suns. As with Di, dead royalty influenced all aspects of life. The spirits of deceased royal personages could bring benefit or inflict harm. The practice of identifying royal spirits with a name of one of the ten days of the sun probably originated with the association of that day's sun and the influence of an ancestral spirit (Chang Tt:187). Evidence for this association is consonant with the view that ancestral spirits shared some of Shang Di's powers.[14] It is tempting to think of Shang Di as having originated as a sun god due to his superior hierarchical position in relation to royal dead spirits and their direct association with the ten suns of the week. The belief that the ancestor spirit would appear simultaneously with his or her appropriate sun reinforces the possible origin of the ten suns in a sun cult. But the root of the Shang ancestral cult was the belief that deceased members of the royal lineage, both recent and distant in time, influenced a wide range of events that affected living humans, on earth, such as birth, death, health and disease, war, booty, hunts, harvest, rain, flood, and fire. It has frequently been noted that the ancestor spirits had the power to curse and harm as well as to bring good fortune. Likewise, Di could both help and harm (Kc Chang 1983: 94; Mickel 1978: 9; Keightley 1984: 3). This dualistic character of the spirit realm was a major feature of the early Chinese worldview, as such was a key to the practice of divination. Dualism remained a fundamental cosmological principle of Chinese thought, expressing the view that the universe consisted of a balance of natural possibilities that could swing either way at any time (Mickel 1978: 9; Keightley 1988: 3, 14, 17). Life was suspended in the balance, subject to natural forces; religious practices such as divination reflected, fundamentally, an attempt to regularize, tame, and make predictable this unstable and changeable dualism. Deceased royal ancestors, at death, were transformed into cosmological forces that, according to the principle of dualism, could help or harm their descendants. Since the dead ancestors were each associated with one or another of the ten suns, it was necessary to perform sacrificial rites to each deceased ancestor on the appropriate sun day. The sun power of deceased ancestors was evident in favorable or unfavorable events in the human realm. The Shang kings evidently believed the dead ancestors could be influenced, and, wary of the spirit's power, carried out various propitiatory and apotropaic sacrifices to ensure their goodwill:

> Heji 2235–2250: Crack-making on *guichou* day Que divined: Alas, is it Zu Xin who curses the king with tooth ailment? It was divined: Alas is it not Zu Xin who curses [the king] with tooth ailment?
>
> Heji 27226: Crack-making on the *jiazi* day: If [the king] carries out *Ji* rite with sacrifice of meat in the *ding* ritual vessel to Zu Yi will the king receive divine assistance (*shou you*)?

The King's Power in Relation to Di

The observation that the royal dead shared some divine powers with Shang Di reinforces the theory that the royal ancestors' connections with Di are cosmological and hereditary. The belief in the power of the spirit world to affect every aspect of human existence is an indication of the complexity and sophistication of Shang religion, built on the long-standing tradition of ancestor worship that began with burials of the Dawenkou and later Longshan cultures in Shandong and later Liangzhu culture in the coastal southeast. The cult of deceased royal ancestors reached its apogee during the Shang, remaining important thereafter as a hallmark of Chinese culture. Di (or Shang Di) appears to have originated in the Shang period or earlier as a cosmological power with whom rulers claimed identity.[15] Spirits of deceased Shang royals were his cosmological offspring. Yet, unlike ancestral spirits, Di was not addressed by a day-sun name, nor was Di the recipient of regularly scheduled ritual vessel sacrifices. Rather Di was the object of a major sacrifice and rite, *di* 禘.[16] He was a powerful cosmic deity, commanding (*ling*) the course of human events and natural phenomena from above. The Di rite often featured *liao* 燎, holocaust sacrifices, presumably in the extensive courtyards fronting raised administrative and palatial buildings, as at the Shang capitals, Shang City Yanshi, Huanbei, and Yinxu. Di was also frequently addressed in conjunction with the directional deities, the four *fang* 四方 (south, north, east, and west) in addition to nature deities, such as the *he* 河 river spirit, *tu* 土 earth spirit, or *qiu* 坵 mountain spirit.

The King's Power in Relation to Nature Spirits: Rivers, Land, Clouds, Mountains

Throughout bone inscriptions of Periods I–V, the spirits of ancestors are by far the most common objects of sacrifice. Nature spirits were never the object of ritual vessel sacrifices or of the cyclical ancestral rites, nor do they ever appear to be associated with an ancestral temple, although some, such as the He river god, had their own temples, *zong* 宗 as did royal house members. Nonetheless, sacrifices to the nature powers, frequently through *liao* sacrificial burning or *chen* 沈 sacrificial drowning, remained important in

Shang religion (see e.g. Chang Tt 1970). They were often addressed in pleas for rain, harvest, and related agricultural matters; the River God He also could influence the outcome of wars (Chang Tt 1970). By Late Shang times, sacrifices and rites to nature spirits became subordinated to those for ancestral spirits, and the once-powerful nature spirits gradually diminished to the status of local agricultural gods (see e.g. Akatsuka: 136).

Sifang Cosmology: The King at the Center

Ample paleographic and archaeological evidence attests to the king's centrality and political control. The Shang ruler played a unique cosmological role as king at the center, and therefore king of the Four Quarters (*sifang*). The conception of the Shang capital occupying a place at the center of the cosmos, with the territory of the Four Quarters extending outward in the four directions without limit, lay at the heart of the Shang religio-political system.[17] The term Zhong Shang 中商, Shang of the Center, is used in bone inscriptions to refer to the Shang and their centralized power base.[18] It is key to understanding early Chinese belief systems, as well as Shang thinking and Shang dynastic structure, the bedrock of later Chinese tradition.

Although the terms *sifang* 四方 and *situ* 四土 first appear in writing in bone inscriptions of late Shang date, the seed of this worldview originated much earlier, at least by the late Neolithic period, during the Liangzhu, Longshan, and Erlitou periods, all of which were equally and sequentially influential. We may recall the artistic symbols of the cosmos represented as a quadrant (see Chapter 3 Figure), the consistent northern orientation of burials and raised outdoor altars, and the geographically significant central location of Erlitou during the Xia era (Du 2007). We will discuss below archaeological remains of Shang date, such as large cruciform royal tombs cardinally oriented on a north-south axis. Cosmographic concepts that anticipate the geomancy of later Chinese culture are reflected in the many words in bone inscriptions referring to government lands and official titles grouped in units of four, or identified by one of the four cardinal directions. Units or titles referred to as four include *situ* 四土 (four lands), 四 *sifang* 四方 (Four Quarters), *sitian* 四田 (four fields), *sizhi* 四至 (four borderlands), *sibi* 四壁 (four suburbs), *sidan* 四壁 (four waystations), *sidian* or *sinan* 四甸/四男/ (four territorial commanders), *sige* 四戈 (four commanders of dagger-ax troops), *simu* 四牧 (four herding leaders), *siquan* 四犬 (four dog keepers), *silin* 四廩 (four government granaries), *sifeng* 四風 (four winds), *sishi* 使 (four royal emissaries), and *sichen* 四臣 (four royal officials). The same names and titles may be referred to by one, two, three, or all four cardinal directions in the same divination (Childs-Johnson 2012).

The Shang domain was large and its governing institutions were sophisticated, as reflected in the abundant numbers of officials and elaborate mechanics of keeping the territories under control. What we describe as pivotal to the belief in metamorphism is the concept of an overarching heaven surmounting lands extending in four directions. In bone inscriptions, the word *fang* conveys the abstract concept of space and limitless directional extension. As with *tu* (as in *situ*, four lands), *fang* (*sifang*, four quarters) is used generically to refer to territory, people, and polities that may be described as states. The four *fang* are specifically named by geographical direction (Childs-Johnson 2012).

The many ways in which the Shang kings referred to themselves in the bone inscriptions demonstrate their claim to axial centrality. The king may refer to himself in the plural, as we 我 (I and the realm, the ruler subsuming all of the people in his realm), as in "my/our city" *wo yi* 我邑, "my/our hunting fields and lands" *wo tian* 我田, and "my/our lands" *wo tu* 我土. The ways in which the king refers to the Shang state emphasize its centrality, for example, as "Shang at the Center," Zhong Shang 中商, as "the city-state at the center" *zhong yi*, as "the central land" *zhong tu*, or as "my/our Shang," *wo Shang*.[19] These terms underscore the concept that Shang was at the center of the four *fang* or four *tu*, the lands extending outward in cardinal directions. The term *zhongguo*, (which later became the name of China, the "country at the center" or the "Middle Kingdom," as it is often but inappropriately translated) appears earliest in Western Zhou times, as represented in the He *zun* inscription; it is not a Shang term. The following bone inscriptions are exemplary of Shang's centrality in relation to the *fang* or as *tu*:

> Heji 20650: Crack-making on the *wuyin* day the King divined: Will Zhong Shang 中商 receive harvest? 10th month.
> Heji 36975: Crack-making by the King, he divined: Will Shang 商 this year receive harvest? The king prognosticated saying: It is auspicious. Will the Eastern Lands 東土 receive harvest? Will the Southern Lands receive harvest? It is auspicious. Will the Western Lands receive harvest? It is auspicious. Will the Northern Lands receive harvest? It is auspicious.

As is evident in these inscriptions, the terms Shang and Zhong Shang are interchangeable, referring to the king's realm at the center of the Four Quarters or four lands.

The most visually provocative archaeological evidence for *sifang* cosmology and the king's centrality in this scheme is the cruciform royal burials, aligned axially and cardinally.[20] The nine royal tombs from the royal cemetery of Late Shang date were located outside the walled city, at Xibeigang. Each had four underground axial ramps or arms surrounding a deep central pit where the deceased rested within a coffin and coffin chamber. Undoubtedly, this orientation reflected the afterlife of a deceased king who continued to wield spirit power to influence events in the realm he once ruled, the cruciform shape indicating that the realm extended to all of the four directions (Figure 6.6).

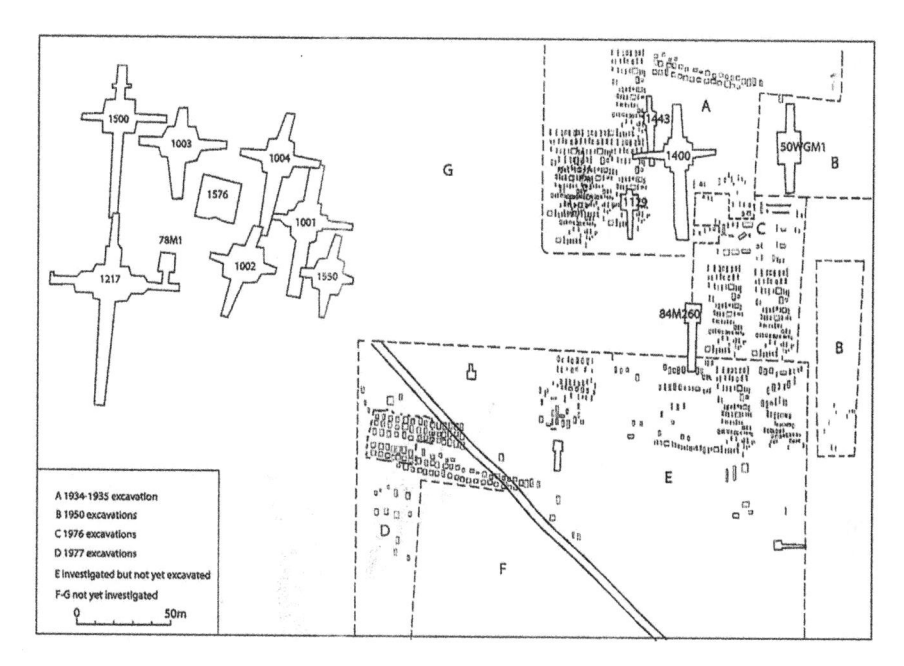

Figure 6.6 Royal cemetery with cruciform *ya*亞, *jia*甲, and *zhong*中-shaped tombs at
Xibeigang, Yinxu Shang City, Anyang, Henan. After Zhongguo 2010: 3,
Figure 2.

The King as Master of the Hunt

The most distinctive consequence of the royal hunt during Shang times was
the representation in ritual art of the metamorphic power mask incorporating physical features of hunted wild animals. Hunted animals, including
water buffalo, tigers, deer, and wild sheep, are all featured in the metamorphic power mask, which, as we will discuss further below, represents
the spiritually transformed (*yi*) deceased ancestors who have taken on the
attributes and power of the hunted beasts.

As Thomas Allsen writes in *The Royal Hunt in Eurasian History,* "while
modes of hunting changed frequently, the essential organizational features
and functions of the royal hunt were extremely stable" (2006: 275). The basic
characteristics of the royal hunt in the case of ancient Assyria, for example,
may also be used to understand the hunt in Shang China. These attributes
are as follows:

1 hunting was viewed as a test of the king's courage and skill;
2 his bag of kills is carefully tallied;
3 hunting triumphs are well publicized in royal propaganda;
4 hunting has a ritual character that was intended to legitimize authority;
5 hunting parks, which also functioned as test gardens, were built;

6   facilities created for the comfort of the royal party;
7   feasting and entertainments were integral parts of the chase;
8   hunts were well-organized, staged affairs to ensure safety and success; the hunt was equated with war, made extensive use of troops, and had a place in interstate relations (Trümpelman 1980–83: 234–38; quoted and translated by Allsen: 275);
9   To the above, we add in recognition of the special features of the Chinese case: the hunted animal is symbolically represented in art, specifically incorporated into the metamorphic mask as a symbol of royal power.

Hunting expeditions in Shang times were regularly scheduled to demonstrate the king's power over nature, his ability to tame the wild lands (*yi*), and extend the reach of civilization. By being successful as a hunter the ruler dominated nature and thereby dominated humans (Allsen). The Shang ruler traveled for various reasons, including presiding over state ceremonies and land contracts, conducting inspections, and identifying and solving problems. Traveling was a means to administer his kingdom. In his travels, the Shang king took his government, or at least a major part of it, on the road. By hunting in various parts of the realm, the ruler conspicuously asserted his royal prerogatives and reaffirmed his sovereign might. As Allsen notes, "A large-scale royal hunt conducted in the open countryside well served these ends as a dramatic and visible reenactment of the conquest/occupation/war that established the kingdom in the first place" (2006: 186).

Abundant evidence in art and in bone inscriptions documents this royal sport of Shang times (see e.g. Childs-Johnson 1995; Fiskesjö 2001) and its symbiotic relationship with the belief in metamorphism. All aspects of hunting were divined. Hunting took place at all times of the year and certain hunting fields were favored over others. Hunting was often conducted after a victory in war or as training for war. Similar to the choice of some day-names over others in naming deceased kings and queens, there is evidence that some days were preferred over others as being lucky or auspicious for hunting. Divinations addressed to Di and dead kings queried over the day to hunt, the weather, the place, what technique of hunting to use, what animal species should be caught, whether to hold a victory feast, to what deceased royal house member the hunted catch should be offered, who should accompany the king on the hunt, or whether hunting dogs and horses would be safe (Childs-Johnson 2018; Fiskesjö 2001).

The Ruler as Hunter-Warrior as Revealed by the Wild Animal Metamorphic Power Mask

Since the king was envisioned as a master of the hunt, lord of the center, and supreme transcendent, it comes as no surprise that the major image decorating ritual and related artifacts is directly connected with royal power and the hunted wild animal. The major image decorating ritual artifacts is symbolic, in particular as a royal power symbol of metamorphosis gained through human identification with the hunted animal – or human transformation into the animal whose power the human assumes to communicate with spirits. The human here refers specifically to the Shang king who had the singular power to communicate with the spirit world, as recorded in bone inscriptions (Childs-Johnson 2008: 57).

The metamorphic power mask is dominated by the semi-human image with wild animal attributes. The animals in question comprise species most often hunted by the Shang king, including buffalo, wild sheep (several species), tiger, and deer (Muntjak, Sika, Mi, Water), although, during the Wu Ding era, owls and other species of birds were added to the image repertoire. Mammals are identifiable by ear or horn type, and by the occasional representation of the entire wild animal (e.g. the tiger or wild buffalo). The tiger mask, for example, is identified by the C-shaped ear, an abstraction of the actual small, rounded ear. Wild water buffalo, wild sheep, and deer are represented by their distinctive horns. (It is not always visually obvious that wild, rather than domesticated, water buffalo and sheep are portrayed in the power mask, but the abundant evidence for the distinction between domestic and wild species in Shang bone inscriptions clarifies this distinction. The graphic and artistic evidence confirms that these animal attributes represent wild species.) By the end of the Shang, this decor deteriorated and lost many of its symbolic attributes; this is particularly true of vessels made in outlying regional sites under Shang influence.

The Art of the Metamorphic Power Mask and Demonic Imagery

Shang bronze smiths built upon and greatly extended the achievements of the Erlitou culture, eventually developing the ability to produce decorated bronze vessels of unprecedented (and, in the view of many scholars, still unsurpassed) beauty, sophistication, and technical excellence. Once the technique of casting bronze vessels and vessel imagery had been achieved and compositional variations of religious icons mapped out and designed, the creativity of artists and patrons flourished. Imagery reflected royal power, which was based on the ruler's ability to undergo spirit transformation or metamorphosis. Thus, imagery on bronze vessels was focused on the royal power of metamorphosis. The image of a semi-human or humanoid figure with abbreviated or fully realized attributes, with subordinate flanking spirit powers of *long* dragons and *feng* birds, was standardized against a dense background of cloud scrolls symbolizing the celestial realm. Some vessels also featured alternating or repeated motifs in a band circumscribing the vessel, as reflected in *lei* thunderstorm symbols and sun symbols, sometimes substituting for dragons and bird symbols.

Shang art, as seen on ritual utensils, primarily of bronze, but also on objects made of ivory, bone, horn, stone, wood, shell, lacquer, and ceramic material, is defined by specific rules of representation. Eight of these rules are enumerated below (based on Childs-Johnson 2016: 8–11):

1   *The Style of Representation Is Primarily Two-Dimensional.* Shang imagery is primarily frontal and in profile, with details that may be defined by bas-relief, or by flush, sunken, or raised line relief (Figure 6.7). Appendages, knobs, and flanges also are frequently incorporated into this imagery.

2   *The Mask Image Varies from Simple to More Complex, and in Type of Human and Animal Attributes.* Representative cast images on ritual bronzes, dating to Early through Middle and Late Shang times, are consistently composed of two eyes, ears, a headdress extension, and an abbreviated body extending to left and right of the face (see Figure 6.8). Eyes may be rendered as ovals or as circles within sockets. Sometimes the image has human features, such as eyebrows, or a complete human head, but it is always part of a larger composition featuring a wild animal, whether identified through the ears of a tiger or the inward curling horns of a bighorn sheep or flanking profile renderings of the actual animal. In the latter case, the animal is usually a tiger, although bighorn sheep, stags, and buffalo are also known to be represented in this displayed position (Figure 6.8)

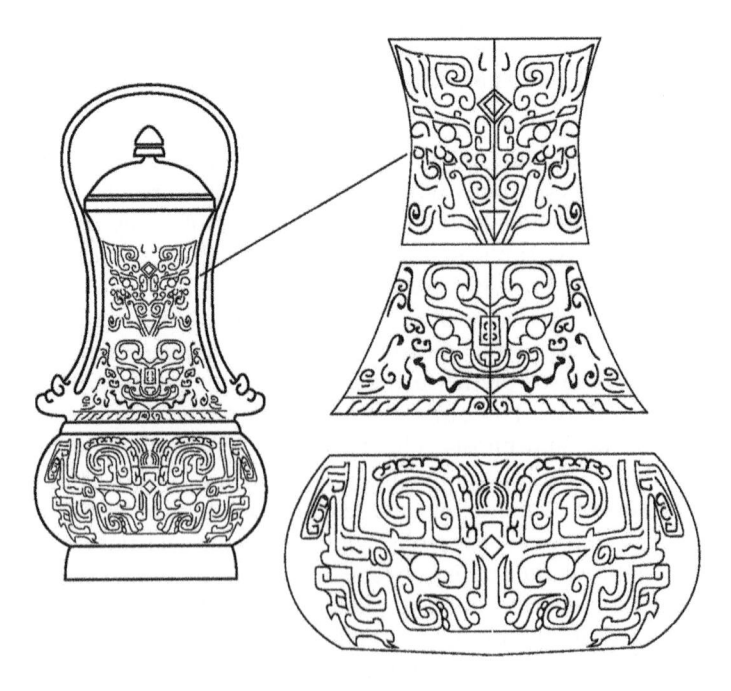

Figure 6.7 Drawing of a ritual you vessel with three tiers of metamorphic imagery, Middle-Late Shang period, M331, Xiaotun, Anyang. After Li C, ed. 1972, pls. XLII and LVII.2.

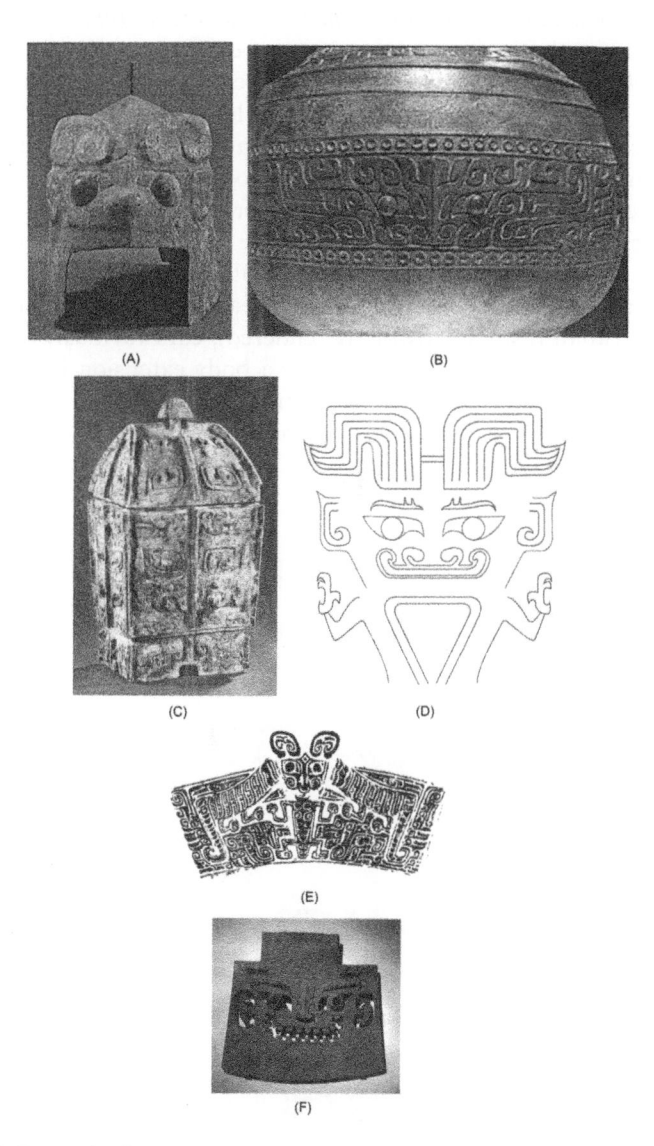

Figure 6.8 Examples in bronze art of the *yi* mask image that may be represented simply as a frontal mask (A–C) or in a complex frontal composition, with human and/or animal attributes (D–F). From top left to bottom right: (A) Bronze helmet showing a frontal tiger mask, M1004, Xibei-gang, Anyang. (B) Detail of bronze *zun* with Early Shang style big horn sheep mask, Chenggu, Shaanxi. (C) Bronze *fangyi* with Early Shang style big horn sheep mask, M663, Dasikongcun, Anyang. (D1–2) Detail of ivory beaker with Late Shang style stag horned mask and extended body in shape of a cicada with claws, M1001, Xibeigang. Drawing by M. Panoti. (E) Rubbing detail of Anhui zun bronze showing profile tigers surmounting a displayed human as if to devour. (F) Detail of Fu Zi bronze ax with profile tigers metamorphically devouring a human head. (All figures are referenced in Childs-Johnson 1998; also 2018: Figure 1.)

3   *The Animal Part of the Mask Image is Usually a Hunted Animal.* The
animal type is signified by the shape of ear, horn, or antler, referenc-
ing tigers, buffalo, bighorn sheep, and deer. As represented in the chart
below, the most common mask types include hunted wild animals (see
Figure 6.9), all of which are known in faunal remains at Anyang and
in bone inscriptions as objects of the royal hunt. These wild animal
features are usually limited to ear or horn types, although, as will be
clear below, the whole animal may also be represented. The mask image
might also include variations of the oval, round, or human-type eye,
headdress excrescences identifiable as peafowl plumage along the central meridian (usually abstractly rendered), ears variously rendered, a
nasal ridge, a mouth, and frequently a body extension in the form of
displayed flanking arms ending in bird claws opposite the upper jaw
and a headdress display at ear or horn level. These formal properties

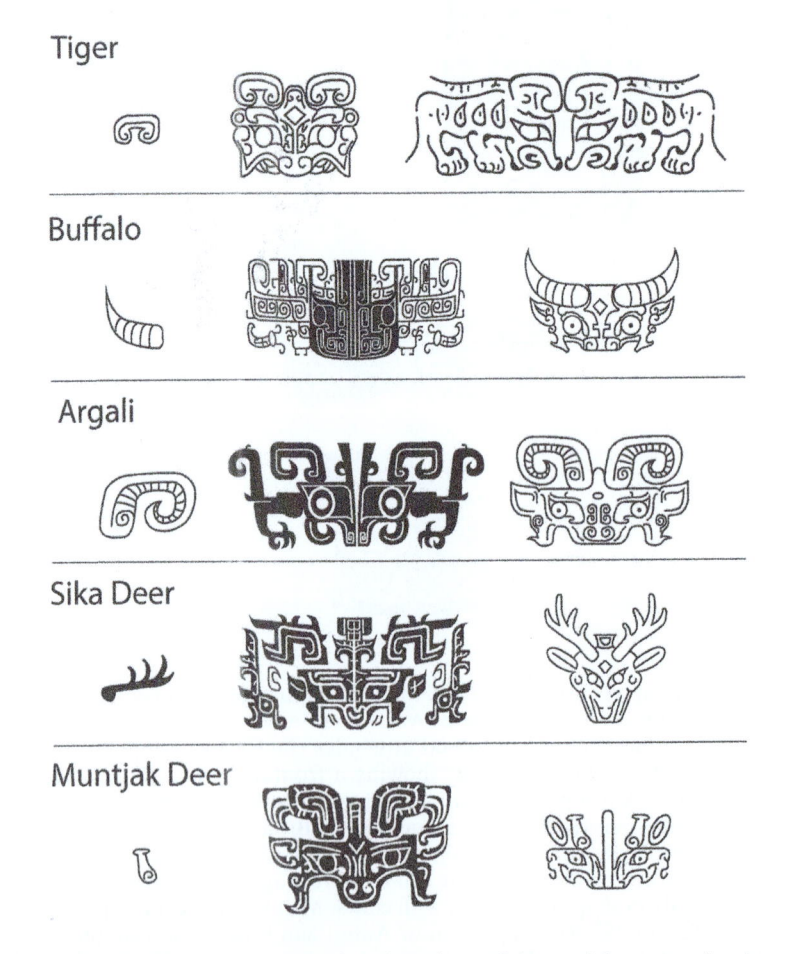

Figure 6.9 Abstract and representational versions of the semi-human animal mask.
(All figures are referenced in Childs-Johnson 1998.)

first appeared in images on Liangzhu *cong* jades and were retained, with stylistic variations, in the Longshan and Erlitou eras. The iconography of metamorphism thus was conserved throughout the Jade Age and onward into the High Bronze Age.

4 *Hieratic and Hierarchical Properties of Composition Predominate.* The ubiquitous image formed by hunted animal features combined with a depiction of a semi-human form is dominant, with subsidiary symbols usually flanking the mask in subordinate positions. The mask, when part of a larger composition of flanking images of dragons or birds in profile, is consistently larger than the flanking images (Figure 6.10). This hierarchical position of supplementary images is also characteristic of subordinate images in circumscribing bands flanking the upper or lower edges of the frontal mask. Flanking subordinate images are consistently *long* dragons or *feng* birds, both imaginary beings. Symbolic images in other contexts, such as bands, may include cicadas, snakes, and additional bird and dragon types.

5 *Semi-Human and Animal Attributes are Interchangeable.* The mask, when rendered more elaborately, is oftentimes characterized by more clear-cut human than animal attributes. Human attributes may appear in facial details, such as human-shaped eyes, mouth, nose, ears, and limbs, yet these consistently appear in the context of a frontal face of a mask with animal ears or horns, a central bird feather plume, and flanking body limbs ending in bird claws (see Figure 6.11A). The image on the upper left is drawn from an ivory carving excavated from the royal tomb M1001 at Xibeigang: the human attributes of mouth, eyes, and ears are obvious, and the central meridian plume ends in "literal" abstractions of the eyed peafowl feather; the limbs are abstracted as inward curving forms. Decorating the turquoise inlaid ivory *gu*-shaped beaker from Fu Zi's tomb, M5 (upper right), similar human attributes of the face are identifiable, yet the horns identifying the animal attribute turn inwards as abstractions of the buffalo horn; limbs end in bird claws; the headdress and central feather plumes extend upwards as a frame of the mask; the triangular body extension alludes to the cicada.

6 *Representational or Abstract, and Whole Animal or Abbreviated Animal Power Masks are Interchangeable.* As represented in the four levels of imagery below (Figure 6.12), it is apparent that there are two modes of representing the features of wild hunted animals: one that is abstract and another that is more representational. In the case of the buffalo (bottom level), the horn may represent the wrinkled upward-curving horn, as interpreted on the royal tetrapod ding from M1004 on the left, or may represent the same horn abstracted as an inward-curling horn, as represented on the lidless *lei* bronze container on the right. Moving upwards, the same treatment is witnessed with the bighorn sheep horn that turns in the opposite direction from the buffalo horn; it turns inward as simply and abstractly represented on the Zhengzhou tripod *ding* band of décor or more representationally on the bighorn

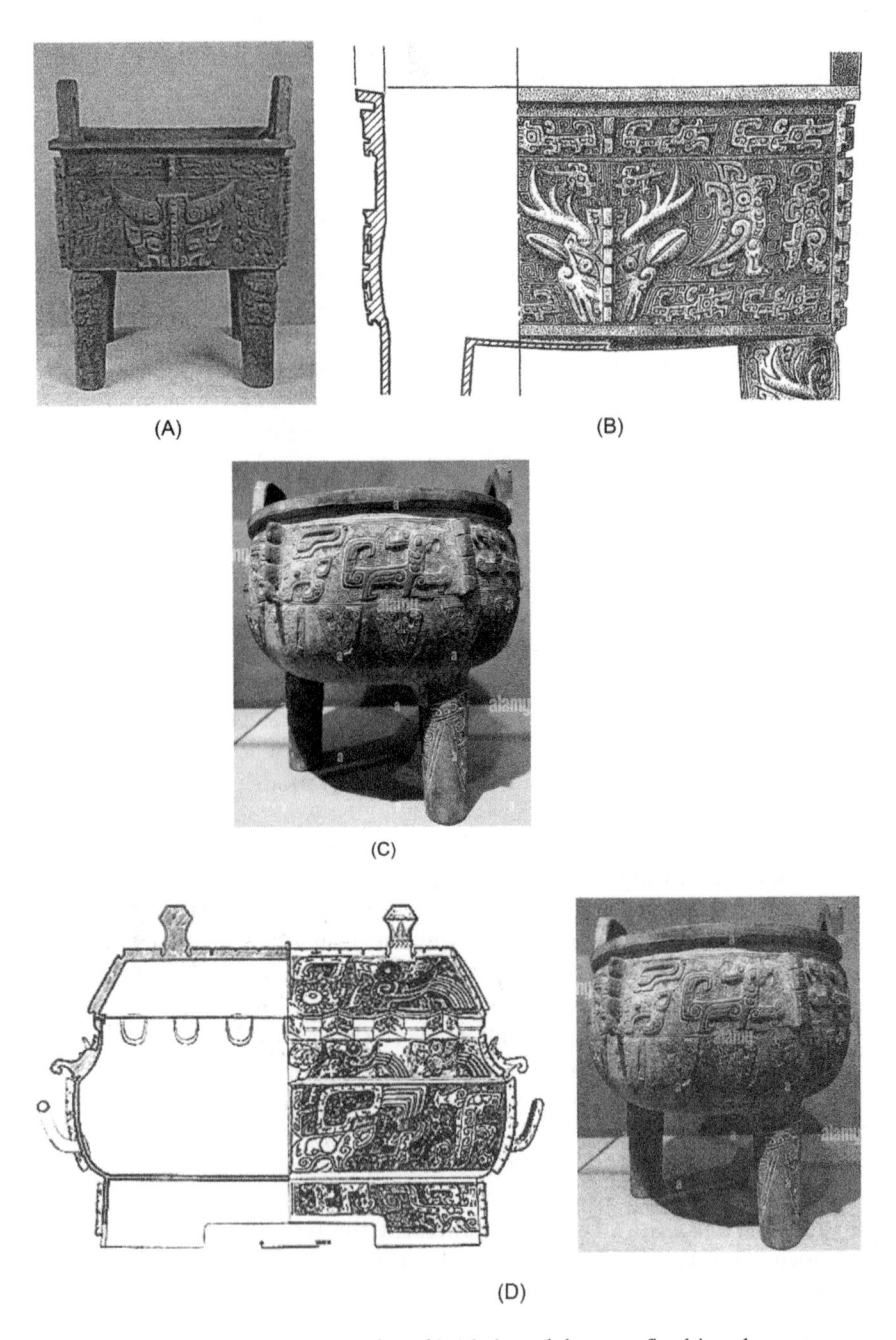

(A)   (B)

(C)

(D)

Figure 6.10 Subordinate images of profile birds and dragons flanking the metamorphic power mask. From top left to bottom right: (A) Detail and drawing of large-scale bronze tetrapod ding and (B) Detail of large-scale 'buffalo' tetrapod *ding*, M1004, Xibeigang, Anyang. (C-D) Fu Zi tripod ding. (All figures are referenced in Childs-Johnson 1998.)

Figure 6.11 Images showing varying, interchangeable human and animal features of the metamorphic power mask. From top left to bottom right, (A–D) Drawings and rubbings of bone and ivory utensils, M1001, Xibeigang, Anyang. (All figures are referenced in Childs-Johnson 1998.)

tomb at Xiaotun. Tigers' ears may be rendered abstractly as C-shapes; tigers also sometimes appear in a representational version in which a full-bodied profile tiger squats in a human-like manner. The stag horn is similarly treated as an abstract extension with a sheep-shaped alcohol container from Fu Zi's M5. Tines flowing outwards in length on the small tetrapod *ding* (middle example) or flowing outward representationally, as on the royal tetrapod *ding* from M1004 (top left level). The significant point here is that the wild animal, when represented, may be abstract or complete in the form of a ritual bronze vessel. Abstract and representational renderings and simple and more full-bodied renderings are interchangeable.

7 *Images Borrowed from Nature are Conventions Symbolizing Metamorphosis.* The latter include easily understood ones, such as the cicada, or sometimes a snake, as a body extension of the mask. The cicada is a well-known symbol of natural metamorphosis and is used to symbolize spirit metamorphosis in Shang art. The cicada symbol may appear in

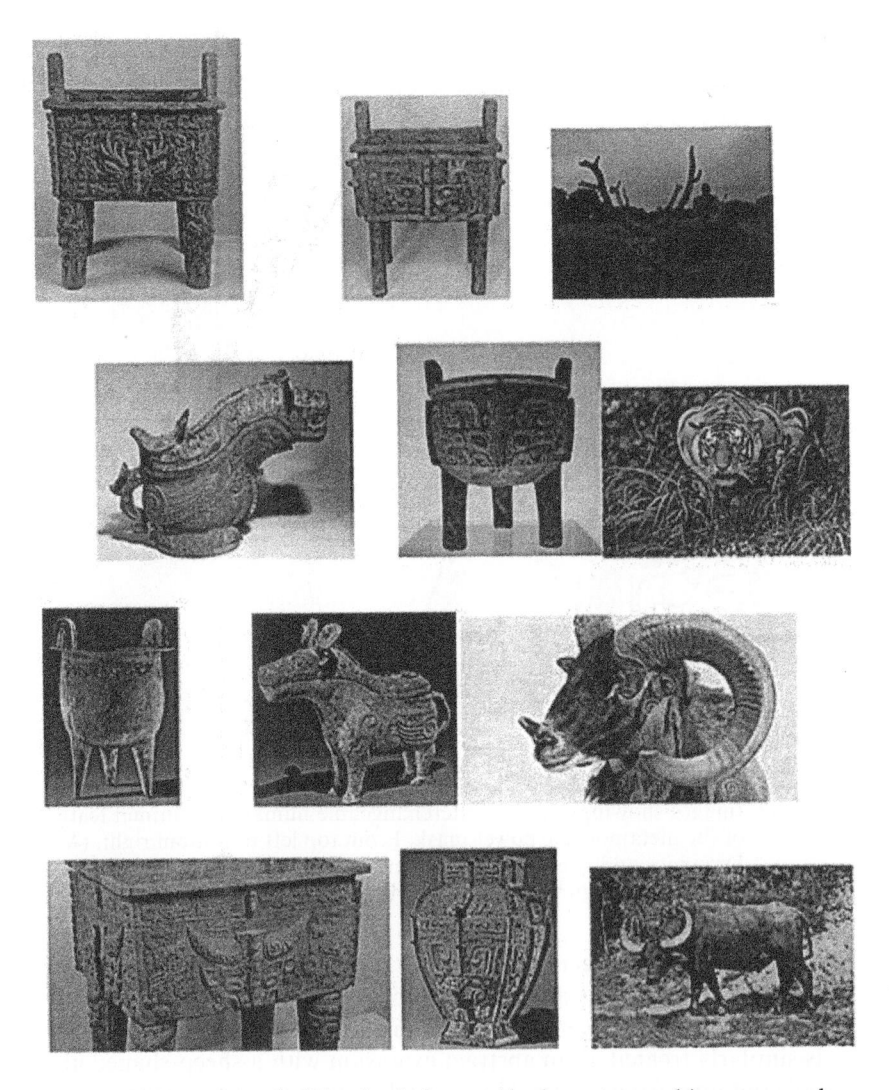

Figure 6.12 Four types of wild animals featured in the metamorphic power mask are based on the horn, ear, or antler type. (A) Variations of the stag mask and living stag; (B) Variations of the tiger mask and living tiger; (C) Variations of the bighorn sheep mask and living bighorn sheep; (D) Variations of the buffalo mask and living wild buffalo. Living examples of tiger, stag, bighorn sheep, and wild buffalo are based on images available at the National Geographic website: www.nationalgeographic.com/animals. (All figures are referenced in Childs-Johnson 1998.)

various ways in Shang ritual art, as a body symbol or extension, or as a small-scale symbol on its own decorating a bronze vessel or related ritual utensil. As shown in the illustrations below, the cicada may be represented abstractly or more representationally (see Figure 6.13). As is

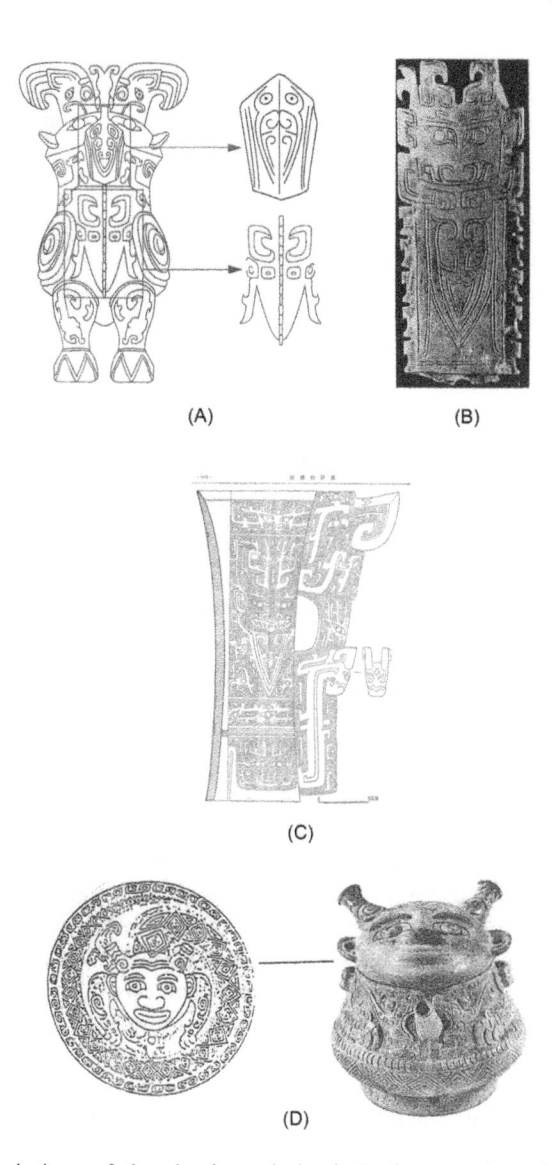

Figure 6.13 Variations of the cicada and cicada body extension of the metamorphic power mask and of the snake-dragon-like body extension of the power mask with human facial features and pedicel deer horns. The owl image is not significantly present in Early and Middle Shang eras; it was created during the earliest phase of the Late Shang period as another metaphor for metamorphosis. (A) Owl-shaped zun, Fu Zi M5, Xiaotun, Anyang. (B) Rectangular jade ornament Fu Zi M5, Xiaotun, Anyang. (C) Turquoise inlaid bone beaker, Fu Zi M5, Xiaotun, Anyang. (D) Drawing of and bronze he vessel with a lid in the shape of a human head with horns and a dragon-like body, National Museum of Asian Art. (All figures are referenced in Childs-Johnson 1998.)

apparent from the drawing of the imagery on the Fu Zi owl-shaped bronze, the cicada appears in two different ways: as a small-scale representational version seen in outline from above with eyes, triangular body, and flanking legs, or as an extension of the buffalo-horned mask with marked ears and oval eyes. In the second drawing, depicting a buffalo-horned mask, the cicada body extension is abstracted as a triangular shape. On the third object, a jade, the cicada body is rendered as a representational extension of a semi-human buffalo-horned mask with limb extensions representing arms ending in claws. The fourth, to the far right, is the familiar image decorating front and back of the bronze simulating a leather drum, from the Sumitomo collection. The semi-human wears a headdress in the form of abstract wild sheep horns and has feathered arms ending in bird claws, a feathered body defined by the abstract transformational symbol of the cicada body, and a phallus. The cicada is used more prominently in Shang imagery than the snake, which in nature sheds its skin, and thus is taken as a symbol of metamorphosis. The snake, nonetheless, is also used as a body extension, with the implied symbolism of transformation and change. It is also significant that the owl shape of vessel and mask image do not appear with any regularity until the earliest phase of the Late Shang period and there serve as another metaphor of metamorphosis. The owl is not associated with hunting.

8   *Spirit Metamorphosis (from Human to Animal) is Symbolized by the Displayed Image or a Displayed Animal Devouring a Human.* As revealed in all of these images, the displayed two-dimensional one is the most common means of representation in Shang art, whether the image is the representational tiger or human or the more abstract version of the same image (Figure 6.14). As in most other early historic cultures, two-dimensional rendering is standard and may be expressed in variations of profile and frontal depictions. The displayed type is the most frequently encountered in Shang art, and typically is composed of a frontal face and profile extensions to left and right of the face. Occasionally, a more story-telling rendering appears, as is the case in the pair of tiger-shaped *zun* vessel bronzes with tiger embracing a human with head turned in profile. The latter almost certainly describe a mythical narrative close to what is represented by the Romulus and Remus legend of ancient Rome or the supernatural birth of the founders of the Shang or Zhou lineages, respectively. The tiger played a significant role in Shang metropolitan imagery and gradually was selectively emphasized in representations on southern more regional bronzes manufactured in the Shang domain.

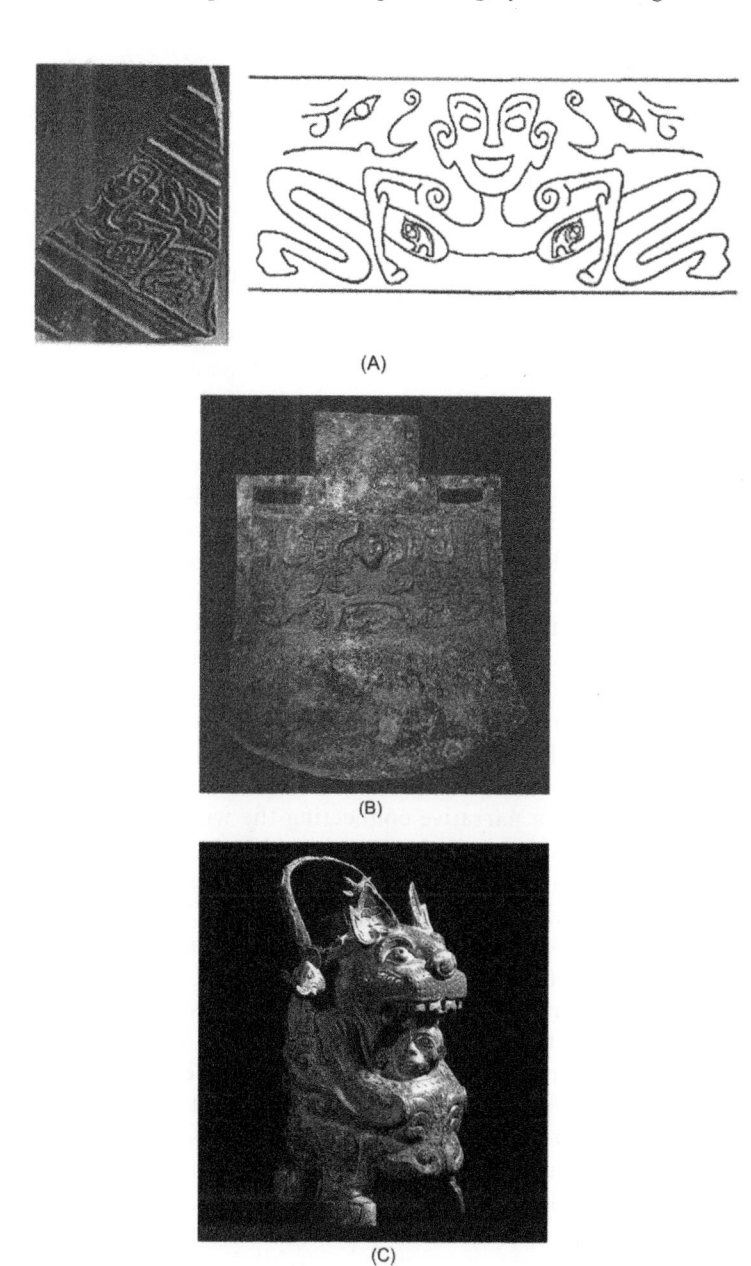

(A)

(B)

(C)

Figure 6.14 Early and Late Shang versions of the devouring or displayed image of metamorphism (A1–2) Ceramic shard from Erligang, Zhengzhou and reconstructed drawing of complete imag (B) Bronze ax from Fu Zi tomb, M5 at Xiaotun, Anyang. (C) Tiger *you* bronze vessel, Baron Sumitomo Collection, Sen-oku Hakuko Kan, Kyoto. (A1-2) After Figure 1A and Henan 2001. *zhong*: 755) (B–C) After Childs-Johnson 2018: Figure 17 and Childs-Johnson 1998.

The Meaning of the Metamorphic Power Mask

Metamorphic power masks appear to represent deceased royal ancestors, including both recently deceased personages and mythical remote ancestors. We know that deceased spirits had an afterlife and that deceased royals became assimilated into the pantheon that included Di and the spirits of the older royal ancestors. The mass of provisions buried with the deceased, and the almost daily communication by the living king and exalted members of the royal house with the spirits of the royal ancestors, make this belief in an afterlife abundantly clear. Wu Ding's pining for his dead wife, Fu Zi, in divinations asking if she would join with Di or with Da Yi, the founder of the Shang dynasty, is a concrete example of this belief in an afterlife in action.[21] The implication of this belief in a royal afterlife is that the metamorphic power mask depicted on ritual bronzes and other implements represents the transformation, at the moment of death, of a deceased royal from a living human being to a powerful ancestral spirit with the ability to affect events in the world of the living. The transformed ancestors represented by the metamorphic power mask demanded sacrifice in a regular routine of propitiatory rites. The offering of meat, grain, and millet ale in their appropriate vessels on the ancestral altar thus constituted an actual physical act of feeding the royal ancestors and not merely a symbolic performance.

By means of the metamorphic power mask, the royal ancestors take on some of the characteristics of the hunted wild animals that provide the design vocabulary of the masks. Thus, the pair of bronze *you* buckets in the shape of a squatting humanoid tiger embracing with paws and devouring a human being enacts a narrative connecting the wild animal world with the human in a transformative tale (Figure 6.14C). Versions of this tale of metamorphosis from human to tiger are repeated in the Yangzi River Valley Funan and Sanxingdui versions of Early Shang date (Childs-Johnson 2022) and by the image of transformation on the ceramic shard picked up at Erligang, Zhengzhou (Figure 6.14A, left two images).

Another pictorial image of human-to-animal transformation is almost certainly reflected in the image of Kui on front and reverse faces of the drum-shaped bronze from the Sumitomo Collection (see above Figure 6.5C). Hayashi Minao once expertly demonstrated this identification through an analysis of graphic variations of the name of the shamanic master of predynastic Shang, written in oracle bone and bronze inscriptions of Shang and early Western Zhou date (Figure 6.5D) (Hayashi 1960).

The Art of Feasting and Sacrifice

Ritual vessels had two primary purposes: for use in sacrificing and in feasting. Both purposes are well recorded in oracle bone divinations. The Shang kings used feasting as a means to placate and please friends and foes, as living individuals or as groups, and as either living or dead. Sacrificial offerings of meat, alcohol, and grain were directed to dead royal ancestors, whereas feasting was in honor of the living. By far, the most important use of ritual bronze vessels bearing the metamorphic power mask appears to have been in ritual sacrifices to the ancestors on the appropriate day-sun of the ten-day week to the spirits of the royal dead.

Alcoholic beverage containers were the primary but not only vessel types made for use in these sacrifices. Numbers of vessels in a ritual vessel set varied according to the status and rank of the ancestral spirit involved (Childs-Johnson 2020). Senior royalty such as Fu Zi, Chang Zi Kou, or Ya Qi were buried with some 200 or more bronze vessels. *Jue* and *gu* vessels for pouring libations and drinking alcoholic beverages were the most numerous, with *gu* and *jue* sets numbering five to ten each of *gu* and of *jue* per set. Tripod *jia* (and the later variant *jiao*), used to heat water or alcohol, and tripod *he* used to heat alcohol, were the third most abundant alcohol-rite-related vessels. Tripod and tetrapod *ding* for meat offerings were the fourth most frequent, and container bronze vessels, such as *you, zun* (and the variation *lei*), serving bronzes such as *gui* for grain, possibly *pou* to contain grain, *pan* to serve water, and *yan* steamer cooking vessels were less likely to be included in sets of ritual bronze vessels. Some of these vessel sets were probably used by the deceased in his or her lifetime to perform rites to the royal ancestors; others were apparently made specifically to be interred with the dead. In either case, the provision of sacrificial vessel sets in the royal tombs enabled the buried (and metamorphically transformed) personage to continue to perform the ancestral rites even after death.

The Shang period was undoubtedly the era in which the seeds of the Jade Age and Erlitou practices of metamorphism grew to inform a cogent and fully realized ancestral religion. The power images of the Liangzhu and Longshan eras, with their combined humanoid and animal elements, and dragon-related metamorphic themes found in both the Hongshan culture and the Sinitic Erlitou period, were honed into a religious vocabulary that persisted, with different stylistic emphases, during the Western and Eastern Zhou periods and later. The metamorphic image endured through the ages, from its prehistoric roots to its high point in the Shang and beyond, despite changes in religious beliefs and practices in later times.

Notes

1 For other book-length studies on other aspects concerning the Shang, see Song Zhenghao's recent editorial compendia on Shang from various disciplinary points of view 2018; Roderick Campbell 2012 and 2018; Hwang Ming-chorng's Ph.D. dissertation1996.

2 For the most recent discussion of Shang periodization, see Campbell 2018; Smith and Fan 2020; Childs-Johnson 2020.

3 For pre-Wu Ding finds at Anyang see, for example, He Yuling *et al* 2010 and Childs-Johnson 2020 Ch 15.

4 See the original study of *yi* in Childs-Johnson 1995 and the book 2008, titled *The Meaning of the Graph Yi* 異*and Its Implications for Shang Belief and Art,* East Asia Journal Monograph, London: Saffron Books.

5 For an analysis of *yi* 異, *wei* 畏, and *gui* 鬼 and their common signifier 田, see Childs-Johnson 1995. Also, see Sun Kaidi 1952 on Chinese puppets and masks in exorcistic rites.

6 For another study, see Childs-Johnson 2016.

7 See various interpretations, e.g. Eno 1990; Ruth Chang 2000; Pankenier 1995; Didier 2009; Allan 2007.

8 See e.g, Keightley 1978–79: 212–13 who maintains the king served as a mediator, followed by e.g. Wang 2000: 36, 39; Kc Chang 1983; Allan 1991.

9 As identified by Hu 1944, *shang*: 298–99: kings would *pei* 配, "accompany" Di, not mediate with Di; see Childs-Johnson 2020).

10 See the early study on the shamanic role of the *fangxiang* exorcist by Sun Kaidi.

11 Long after the Shang, the sexagenary system also came to be applied to a repeating cycle of 60 years, in which the names of the 12 Earthly Branches were used to designate a subsidiary cycle of 12 years (approximating the orbital period of Jupiter) (see e.g. the *Huainanzi* Chapter 3; Major *et al* 2010, 136–37). By the Western Han period, if not before, the 12 years were also identified by emblematic animals (rat, ox, etc.) linked to the Earthly Branches (Boodberg: 128; Needham: 405–6). Around the same time, the Branches, with their emblematic animals, also began to be used to designate the 12 double-hours of the Chinese diurnal system.

12 Interestingly, neither during the Shang nor throughout the dynastic period did the Chinese define a cumulative year-count beginning with a designated "Year One"; the establishment of a continuous year-count system came only with the introduction of the Western (Common Era) calendar after the fall of the Qing dynasty. The Gregorian calendar was formally adopted by the Republic of China in 1912; the change was implemented on January 1, 1929. In modern times, there have been several proposals for a cumulative calendar beginning with the supposed accession to the throne of the (mythical) Yellow Emperor; none of these calendars has been widely adopted. Alvin Cohen, "Brief Note: The Origin of the Yellow Emperor Era Chronology," *Asia Major* 25 part 2: 1–13 (2012).

13 Keightley 2000, 25–29 gives many examples of how this worked in practice.

14 For a reference to various studies of this deity, see Childs-Johnson 2019 and bibliographic citations.

15 Shima 1970; Chang T-t; for differing viewpoints see e.g. Keightley 1979.

16 Chen Mj 1956; Song Zh 2005; Yang Sn 2005: 99, 105; Childs-Johnson 2013.

17 See Hu 1944 *shang*:386–87; Childs-Johnson 2013: 170–71; also see Lefeuvre 1976–1978: 50–62 for a discussion of 立中; Li Zz 2008: 386–95 for a discussion of the royal flag and *zhong*; and for examples in bone inscriptions see Yao and Xiao 1989: 1123–24.

18 For a review of these terms, see Childs-Johnson 2013 and cited bibliographic references.

19 This was initially noted by Chen Mengjia in 1956 and followed by others, such as Song Zh 1996; Yang Sn 2005; and Allan 1991.

20 For other points of view see Sarah Allan, *The Shape of the Turtle: Myth, Art and Cosmos in Early China* (Albany: SUNY Press 1991–2016); Allan's study "The Taotie Motif in Early Chinese Ritual Bronzes" in J. Silbergeld and E. Y. Wang, eds., *The Zoomorphic Imagination in Chinese Art and Culture* (Honolulu: University of Hawai'i Press, 2916); Wu Hung, "Re-Thinking Meaning in Early Chinese Art: Animal, Ancestor, and Man," in Critical Inquiry 43.1: 139–90 (2016; and K. C. Chang, who in *Art, Myth, and Ritual :The Path to Political Authority in Ancient China* (New Haven: Yale University Press, 1988) and many other works identifies Shang Art as shamanistic.

21 Fu Zi, the wife of Shang King Wu Ding, was one of the most remarkable women in Chinese history, though for most of that history she was unknown. Until the

early 20th century concrete evidence for the existence of the Shang dynasty was scarce. The discovery of the Shang royal capital at Anyang and the decipherment of oracle bone inscriptions revolutionized the study of early Chinese history. King Wu Ding emerged from the fog of legend to appear as a long-lived and suc-cessful monarch. Accompanying him was his queen, Fu Zi. Wu Ding's obsessive use of divination gives us a surprisingly rich account of their lives as preserved in inscribed oracle bones. He evidently regarded her with affection and esteem. He divined on her behalf about childbirth, health issues, returns from distant lands, military affairs. death, and the afterlife. While accompanying the king on a hunting trip in the east she seems to have sustained an injury from which she later died, aged perhaps in her mid-thirties. As she failed to recover and after her death, the king made divination after divination to enquire about, for example, the rites to be performed at her passing:

> "It was divined: Should [I, i.e. Wu Ding] bin-host and identify with and ku mourn through wailing the spirit of Fu Zi? Crack-making on the day [xin] chou, Zheng divined: Will [the spirits/Di] approve?"

> (Heji 2664)

Should [I] bury [Fu]] Zi? Should [I]] bury [Fu] Zi?" Heji 17159I

The other source of information about Wu Ding and Fu Zi is her tomb (which luckily was never plundered, unlike the tombs of the Shang kings). It contained a vast wealth of bronzes, jade work, lacquer, bone, and other materials, includ-ing no doubt mountains of silk cloth long since crumbled into dust. This tomb, which must have been commissioned by the king himself, testifies to his esteem and affection for her. The rich grave goods and the oracle bone record together document Wu Ding's singular concern for her happiness in her grave as a newly transformed spirit. The profound Shang Chinese belief in the persistence of the spirit after death is seen in the sets of ritual bronzes that would enable her to continue to perform her own ritual obligations from the silence of the grave. That belief is also evident in the hope expressed by Wu Ding that she would posthumously wed Di (High Sky Power), the highest Shang divinity.

> "Crack-making on the day jimao Bin divined, Will Di 'get' [i.e. wed] Fu Zi?" Heji Fu Zi's career is without parallel in Shang and later Chinese history

7 The Zhou Mandate, The *Feng* Symbol, and Ritualized Metamorphism

Introduction

In late May 1059 BCE, the five naked-eye-visible planets (Mercury, Venus, Mars, Jupiter, and Saturn) came together in a small cluster in the night sky. This highly unusual event, with the planets gathered together in a space not much larger than the full moon, was quite naturally taken as an omen by the ancient peoples who observed it.[1] The interpretation that has come down to us in later Chinese texts (Pankenier 2013) was that promulgated by the rulers of the state of Zhou, a polity well known to the rulers of Shang, centered in the valley of the Wei River, an important tributary of the Yellow River. The Zhou king at the time, known posthumously as King Wen (the "Civil King"), took the planetary conjunction as a favorable sign. He, or his astrologer-advisors, interpreted the omen to mean that the Shang had forfeited the right to rule conferred on it, at the founding of the dynasty, by the Zhou's high deity *Tian* 天, comparable to Di or Shang Di of Shang times (Tian is commonly translated as "Heaven," but is more accurately understood as "Sky Power.") The Mandate of Tian *(Tian ming* 天命), King Wen declared, had been taken from Shang because of the decadence, profligacy, and impiety of the last Shang ruler and transferred to the virtuous rulers of Zhou. King Wen did not live to see his dynasty established, but his son, King Wu (the "Martial King," r. 1049–45), completed the high deity Tian-ordained conquest of Shang with the decisive Battle of Muye (the Wilds of Mu) in the spring of 1046. The early kings of Zhou then set about consolidating their realm and rewarding their allies, establishing a dynasty that, for the first two centuries or so of its long existence, was strong, stable, and prosperous; difficulties would arise later.[2] Yet what is seldom given sufficient weight in assessing Zhou cultural history is the importance of the spirit world, manifested as the spirit realm of dead ancestors, whether of royal or aristocratic lineage, and of nature and cosmology, encompassing celestial and terrestrial phenomena. The Western Zhou in large part inherited the Shang (and pre-Shang) belief in metamorphism but shifted certain priorities to accommodate what was new. Zhou innovations included the belief in the Mandate of the Sky Power 天命, which granted to the Zhou kings the right

DOI: 10.4324/9781003341246-7

to rule; divination by means of yarrow stalks; cult worship of dead Zhou kings (which was similar to but a modification of Shang practice), beginning with King Wen and King Wu and extending to their successors with the passage of generations; and the practice of creating historical documents in the form of inscriptions on bronze vessels. The Zhou rulers inherited the belief in metamorphism, the bedrock of Chinese religion, as revealed most vividly in the imagery of bronze vessels, jade, and other media, and as corroborated by transmitted literary records of Western Zhou origin.

The Zhou inherited from the Shang, and perpetuated in their new dynasty, certain sacrificial rituals and other rites pertaining to cosmology and divine power, indicating that Zhou religion was not a separate and independent tradition, but rather depended on Shang precedent. The fact that the Zhou never dispensed with religious imagery that originated in the Neolithic Jade Age and persisted through the Erlitou ("Xia") and Shang dynasties supports the conclusion that metamorphism was fundamental to Zhou religious belief and practice. The Zhou reinterpreted and reinvented traditional metamorphic icons and symbolic motifs, including the wild animal mask symbol, the *long* 龍 dragon, and the *feng* 鳳 mythic bird. The Zhou kings and cosmologists identified their dynasty with the direction south and the color red, and visualized the five-planet cluster of 1059 BCE as a Vermilion bird holding a jade insignia blade in its beak (Pankenier 2013: 235). The adoption by the middle phase of the Western Zhou period of the Shang mythic bird, the *feng* (or *fenghuang* 鳳凰), as a major image on their ritual paraphernalia indicates a gradual evolution of Zhou interests that absorbed their Shang roots in creating something new.

The Zhou experimented with new vessel shapes. Most conspicuously, they initially singled out the circular *gui* grain vessel and isolated it on its own square stand, seemingly in recognition of the correspondence with the cosmological symbol of the shape of square earth and circular sky. By the middle Western Zhou period, ritualists formulated rules for producing sets of bronze vessels, with size and number reflecting a person's rank. Inscriptional evidence for the Western Zhou relies on a Zhou innovation, the practice of casting texts, sometimes amounting to hundreds of characters, on the interior bodies of bronze vessels.

Zhou Divination

Zhou oracle bones are relatively rare, but the Zhou are strongly identified with another type of divination, a procedure known as stalk-casting. A sheaf of long, narrow stalks of the yarrow plant, was thrown onto a flat surface so that the sticks formed a pattern, with a result that was expressed as a number, rather than the much later solid or broken lines of the *Yijing* (or *Zhouyi*, "Zhou [Book of] Changes") (C Cook 2006b; Cook and Zhao 2017). Some numbers, including 1, 6–9, were favored and sometimes were carved into oracle bones, re-purposing that familiar medium of Shang writing.

Although numbers are usually found in groups of three or six, anticipating the trigrams and hexagrams of the *Yijing*, it is still not fully understood how some set of numbers would yield a prediction or an answer to a question. The system of stalk-casting was intricately bound up with Zhou rituals and cosmological beliefs and is a hallmark of Zhou rule. In its later *Yijing* form, stabilized in the Han dynasty, it continued to be employed by both governments and individuals throughout the imperial period and remains in use today. For the Western Zhou, the general significance of these materials is that, like the Shang kings but mostly by different means, the Zhou kings found it important to seek advice and wisdom from an external source of divine authority in making important decisions.

The Western Zhou Mandate: Di 帝, Tian 天, and Invocation 祝

In establishing their power throughout much of the East Asian Heartland Region, the Zhou rulers appealed to the authority of their high sky deity, Tian, in a manner reminiscent of the Shang kings' availing themselves of the power of Di or Shang Di. It has been suggested that Tian was simply Di by another name, but that can hardly be correct since Di did not immediately disappear with the Zhou conquest of Shang. On the contrary, Di is mentioned in many Zhou inscriptions which treat Di with respect and record sacrifices offered to Di. Like Di, Tian was specifically a Sky Power. Although the Shang kings never specifically referred to themselves as "Sons of Di," they regarded themselves as *Di*'s royal offspring since they used the prefix *di* in their posthumous titles, as in Di Wen Wu Ding, or Di Ding. The Zhou kings referred to themselves and claimed the right to be referred to by others, as *Tian zi* 天子, "Sons of Tian." The concept that Tian was responsible for conferring leadership on a dynastic founder and his dynastic descendants if they remained worthy of the right to rule was quick to develop. The king's status as the Son of *Tian*, and his possession of the *tian ming* 天命 (the "Mandate of the Sky Power"), were the ideological bases of the Zhou religio-political system. The early Western Zhou concept of Tian shared many characteristics of the Shang sky-god Di but over time Tian evolved away from *Di*, with increasing emphasis on *de* 德, the moral force conferred upon the king by Tian (Major and Cook 2017: 118–19).

Nevertheless, the Shang Sky Power Di was also sometimes associated with a *ming*, "mandate." An example of this comes from a text of the late Springs and Autumns or early Warring States period (though very likely preserving some earlier material). This is the "Cheng wu 程寤," (The Awakening at Cheng), a long-lost chapter of the *Yi Zhou shu* 逸周書 (Leftover Documents of Zhou) rediscovered among a cache of bamboo-slip texts in the possession of Qinghua University. The text, which describes a dream experienced by the wife of King Wen, says that in the dream, the king "received the Shang mandate from the august Di on high" (受商命于皇商帝). This expresses a

Zhou belief that the Shang kings had a mandate from Di, just as they themselves had a mandate from Tian (Shaughnessy 2018: 596).

The one clear-cut difference between Di and Tian is that the Shang sky-god Di does not appear to have been responsive to the virtue (or lack thereof) of the ruler. Zhou's political ideology asserted that Tian conferred a mandate to rule on the Zhou royal house and lasting for as long as these kings maintained the dynasty's virtue. This is an important distinction. The Shang kings were empowered by Di but did not serve as intermediaries between Di and the human realm; the Zhou kings were intermediaries between Tian and the human world. By employing their virtue to rule justly, they ensured that Tian would respond by prolonging their mandate to rule. Thus, the major difference between the Sky Power of Shang and Western Zhou is contained in the concept of virtue and its synonyms or applications.

Bronze Inscriptions and Zhou Ideology

Several pivotal inscriptions of the early Western Zhou period illuminate some of these basic similarities and differences between Shang and Western Zhou practice – how Zhou inherited Shang practice, and how Zhou innovated to underscore their legitimacy to rule. Although the Zhou did not continue the Five Rites of Shang addressed to dead Shang kings and queens, they continued to carry out important Shang rites addressed to their royal spirits and to the Shang deity Di. Three ritual bronze inscriptions, including that on the Tian Wang *gui* (called the Da Feng *gui* in past publications), the Li *gui*, and the He *zun,* illuminate these issues. The Tian Wang *gui* inscription (Figure 7.1), for example, is a gem of historical significance dating to the time Zhou King Wu conquered the Shang at Muye in Henan. The owner of the *gui* bronze, Tian Wang, records in detail how he assisted King Wu when he celebrated this victory in honoring the spirit world, in particular the spirit of former King Wen. The inscription reads:

> On the day *yihai,* the King [Wu Wang] held the Great Drumming (*Da Feng* 大豐) rite. The King sailed his boat on three sides [of the moat, every side but the west, the geographical location of Zhou, where King Wu resided at the time of this ceremony]. The King [then] sacrificed in the Hall of Tian [called the *mingtang* 明堂 in later texts] and (the spirits) descended. [I, Tian Wang] assisted the King [Wu Wang] in performing the Yin (Yi) rite to the King's greatly manifest and deceased Father, King Wen and in performing the Xi sacrifice to *Shang Di* [the Shang high deity]. [The spirit of] King Wen watches over us from above. May you, the greatly manifest [King Wen] illuminate King [Wu] to be supervisor [on earth] and place [or honorably accept] this King as heir, (and) enable (him) to terminate sacrifice to the Yin [i.e., Shang] kings. On the *dingchou* day King [Wu] held a *Xiang* banquet using the *Da Yi* (large meat offering hacked on a cutting board). King [Wen's spirit]

descended. (I, Tian) Wang received/obtained the *yiding* [metamorphically empowered *ding*] (and) restored X[?]. I was praised for my meritorious deeds. Respectfully, (I) extol the beneficence of the King [in making this inscribed record] on this sacrificial *gui* grain offering vessel (Revised and based on Hwang 1996a).

This inscription is significant for understanding Shang and Western Zhou rites and beliefs, especially in the reference to discontinuing the sacrifices to the Yin (i.e., Shang) kings. The Shang had lost the Mandate of Tian, and thus no longer deserved sacrifice; the Zhou sacrifices to their own royal ancestors would replace the rites to the Shang kings. Yin 殷 (衣) was the Zhou name for Shang and the name for the *yin* rite honoring the royal line of Shang and now Western Zhou ancestors.[3] The *Yin* rite is specified as being offered, not to the Shang kings but to the spirit of King Wu's father, King Wen, founder of the Zhou royal lineage and dynasty. The *Xiang* feasting rite, the *Yi* meat sacrifice, the *Xi* sacrifice, and the *Feng* drumming rite, as identified by Hwang (1996a), also demonstrate that the Zhou continued Shang rites. In addition, King Wu addresses Shang Di with the *xi* sacrifice, a demonstration that the early Zhou kings arrogated to themselves the privilege of sacrificing to the Shang High Sky Power.

Continuity of ritual practices from Shang to Zhou continues in the king's role as chief Invocator (see pages below), the power to metamorphically identify with the spirit realm. Spiritually transformed and empowered, the king causes the spirits of dead ancestors (in this case, King Wen) to descend and be honored at a *Xiang* feast that included a *Da Yi*, great offering of hacked meat.

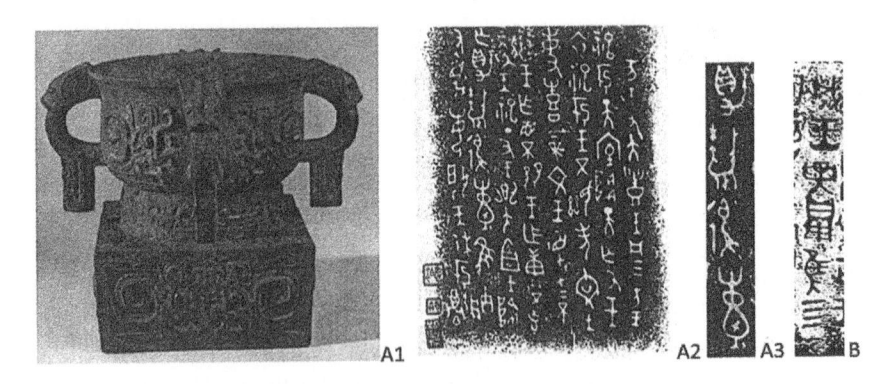

Figure 7.1 Tian Wang bronze *gui* on stand, its inscription, plus a detail of the latter citing "recovery of the *yiding* and restoration of X(?)," early Western Zhou, Licun, Qianshan, Shaanxi, National Museum of China. (B) Detail of the Zuoce Da tetrapod *ding* inscription citing *yiding*, reading "... King Cheng *yiding*, alas, 4th..." (A) Zhongguo Qingtongqi 5: colorpl. 50. (B) Childs-Johnson 2013: 197, Figure 17 second line from right in vertical succession.

Although the mask-donning rite of invocation 禓 (礻+鬼/禓) does not appear to be addressed in Western Zhou inscriptions, various related rites of invocation are, as analyzed by Hwang. *Da Feng*, the Great Drumming Rite mentioned in the Tian Wang *gui* inscription, appears to represent the first part of a grand invocation ceremony that used thunderous drumming to summon the spirits of Tian, deceased King Wen, and the Four Quarters (Hwang). Evidence from Shang bone inscriptions indicates that drumming was a major part of the *Peng* rite and other rites addressed to dead Shang royalty (Chang Yz 1987: 170–85). The *Da Feng* Great Drumming Rite mentioned in the Tian Wang *gui* inscription preceded the *Xiang* 鄉 feasting rite (for other examples of *xiang* see e.g. Yao and Xiao 1992: 139–40), [and the actual feasting] and the *Yi* and other sacrificial meat offerings (see e.g., *Heji* 28333, 31045 and *Tun* 2276), as it does in Shang bone inscriptions. The *Da Feng* ceremony is recorded elsewhere in Western Zhou bronze inscriptions on the set of Record Keeper Mai vessels (Cook and Goldin 2016: 13–15, 42–43). The king, at his capital in Zongzhou, carried out similar ceremonies connected with the *Feng* rite, including boarding a boat and hunting over a period of three days. Clearly, Zhou rites and sacrifices were based on those of Shang and testify to the continuing importance of royal possession of *yi* metamorphic power, symbolized by Tian and Tian's Mandate, and by possession of the spirit-empowered *yiding*, as related by Tian Wang in the *gui* inscription, line 7: "[Tian Wang] obtained the *yiding* and restored X(?) 得異鼎復X(?)." (see Figure 7.1 far right). The interpretation of *yi* in *yiding* ("...obtained the *yiding*...") is clarified and corroborated by the same and more complete rendering of the hewen, *yiding*, cast in the early Western Zhou inscriptions of the Zuoze Da set of small tetrapod *ding* (Childs-Johnson 2013: 197, Figure 17 second line from right in vertical succession).

Ritualist of the Right Li also records, on the inner surface of a *gui,* ceremonies connected with the conquest of Shang by the Western Zhou King Wu. Like Tian Wang, Li was a member of the Zhou royal house. Although there have been various interpretations of the two words *sui ding* 歲鼎 in the inscription (see e.g., Pankenier 2013), they most likely refer to a major Shang sacrifice of meat cut with the broad *yue* ax blade and offered in the meat *ding* vessel symbolizing royal power. The inscription reads:

Wu Wang conquered the Shang on the day *jiazi*. In the morning [of that day the King] offered *sui* sacrifice of meat in the *ding* vessel and divined that he would be able to triumphantly take Shang. On the *xinwei* day [7 days later] the King at Jian military camp awarded Ritualist of the Right Li 有事[史]李 with bronze which he used to make [the *gui* vessel] for Grand Duke Tan (pre-dynastic Zhou ruler and grandfather of King Wen, contemporary with Shang King Di Yi, the second--to-last Shang king).[4]

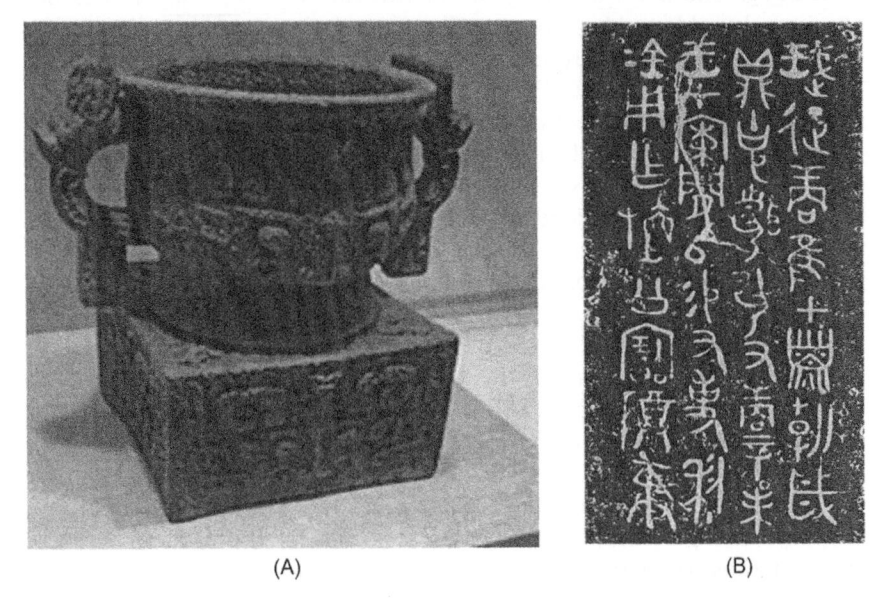

(A)   (B)

Figure 7.2 Li *gui* ritual bronze on a stand and its inscription, early Western Zhou Period, Lintong, Shaanxi. After Zhongguo Qingtongqi 5: colorpl 49.

It is significant that Ritualist of the Right Li made the propitious divination that King Wu should attack the Shang on the day *jiazi*, the first day of the 60-day cycle. For his auspicious divination, he was rewarded by King Wu several days later. Li does not use Shang terminology to address his royal relative, Duke Tan (he doesn't call him Father followed by an ancestor day-name) but invokes this dead royal ancestor by his living name through the *sui* sacrifice offered in the royal *ding* vessel. Since the *sui ding* sacrifice is well known in Shang bone inscriptions as one of the most important ancestral sacrifices (Childs-Johnson 2013), its adoption by Zhou royalty symbolizes the transfer of dynastic power from Shang to Zhou.

The inscription of the He *zun* is a further example of the nomenclature invoking dead royal ancestors using Shang rites and modified anew by Zhou. The vessel dates to the reign of King Cheng who, according to the inscription, began building the new Zhou eastern capital Chengzhou in Henan. The king is described as establishing the state at the center (*li zhong-guo*立中國), a phrase that evokes the Shang term, *lizhong* 立中 (see Chapter 5: pages XX). Moreover, the author of the inscription dates it to the fifth year of King Cheng's reign, using the Shang term *si* 祀 for years. In this "gift giving inscription," (C. Cook 1997) He, a man of royal descent, records the enactment by King Cheng of the *Feng* Drumming ceremony. A tripod *jue* 爵 alcohol libation (禄) transcribed *guan/guo* 灌/祼), a ubiquitous element of Shang sacrificial rites, was also carried out in the *Jingtang* (possibly an alternative name for the *Tiantang* Hall of Tian/Sky God) along with the *Da Feng* drumming rite. This inscription is important not only because of its reference to Tian's Mandate but also because it mentions the *feng* 鳳 bird, adopted as the symbol of Zhou royal power and cosmic authority.

The He *zun* inscription is translated as follows:

> It was the time when King Cheng began building Chengzhou (the Zhou eastern capital in Henan). King [Cheng] held the *Feng* ceremony and made a *jue* tripod libation offering of alcohol to receive *Tian*. In the fourth month, on the day *bingxu*, King Cheng in the *Jingtang* [of the *mingtang*] exhorted the young lineage descendant (*zong xiaozi* 宗小子) saying: "Formerly your late ancestor Duke Shi was able to serve King Wen. King Wen accepted the great command. It was King Wu who conquered the Great City of Shang and then announced to *Tian*: 'I must dwell at the center of the state (立中國), and from there rule the people.' [At this time] the *feng* bird sang out. You young royal person must follow the example of [your] Duke Shi so that you too may communicate (?) with *Tian*. Reverently sacrifice! Our King indeed has a virtuous character (德), compliant to *Tian*, an inspiring example to my own feeble self." When the King finished exhorting, He [the name of the vessel owner] was given 30 strings of cowries, which were used to make this vessel for sacrifices to (He's royal ancestor), Duke Shi. This happened in the King [Cheng's] fifth year.[5]

Elsewhere, the virtue of the Zhou line was confirmed by the actions of Zhou Gong 周公, (commonly known as the Duke of Zhou), a younger brother of King Wu who, on King Wu's death, became regent for the young heir, King Cheng. As regent, he defeated a rebellion and displayed his virtue by handing the throne over to the young king, though he could easily have usurped the throne for himself. This act of virtuous self-denial made Zhou Gong a model figure for Confucius and his followers in later times. As recorded in the He *zun* inscription, King Cheng had *de* virtue, compliant to Tian.

Western Zhou Cosmology

The Zhou rulers followed Shang practice in believing their capital city to be the center of the world, with outlying territories – the *sifang* or Four Quarters – radiating outwards from the center. The Zhou, employing symbolism that may have been of considerable antiquity, associated the directions with colors and symbolic animals: a blue-green dragon for the east, a vermilion bird for the south, a white tiger for the west, and black for the north (although the animal symbol of the north was not stabilized until the Han period) (Major 1978). As mentioned above, the Zhou associated themselves with the color red and the bird symbol of the south; the clustering of the five planets signifying that the Zhou had received Tian's mandate was visualized as a jade blade held in the beak of a celestial bird.

The Zhou term for the sub-celestial world, *tianxia* 天下, "All-Under-the-Sky," appears to be based on the Shang concept of *shangxia* 上下, all above and below, a reference to the Sky or spirit world of Sky Power Di and the terrestrial realm.[6] Zhou cosmography envisioned *tianxia* as being divided into nine provinces, comprising the center plus territories extending outward to the eight directions. This scheme, with its obvious similarity to Shang *sifang* cosmography, reflects a practice, possibly originating as early as the Jade Age, of matching portions of the sky with specific territories on earth for astrological purposes. The nine-provinces (or nine-continents) system was later considerably elaborated in Warring States and Han times.

The sky received its due share of attention from the Zhou rulers. Zhou astronomy, like all ancient Chinese astronomy, was polar and equatorial in orientation; and like their Shang predecessors, Zhou astronomers used a gnomon or some form of astral template to locate the celestial north pole in the absence of an easily visible polestar (Pankenier 2013: 98–108). Zhou astronomers probably also tracked the annual round of the circumpolar stars (asterisms that do not, for any given latitude, dip below the horizon at any point throughout the year) dominated by the Big Dipper (called the Northern Dipper, *beidou* 北斗, in Chinese).[7]

As is well known, written sources for Chinese mythology date almost without exception to texts no earlier than the Warring States, Qin, and Han periods. There is some evidence that one of the most important Chinese myths, the story of Yu the Great and the taming of the great flood, was already current in the Western Zhou period (Porter 1996: 143); Yu is mentioned in several early bronze inscriptions (C Cook 2017: 87–89). The Chinese great flood story is one version of a myth that was widely shared across Eurasia that may refer to the Milky Way (a "flood" of stars) by way of explaining an apparent celestial anomaly, the non-coincidence of the celestial equator (the plane of the Earth's axial rotation) and the ecliptic (the plane of the sun's path among the fixed stars). The early Zhou rulers and their astronomers/astrologers appear to have used the language of myth to explain celestial phenomena and transmit cosmological knowledge to succeeding generations (de Santillana and von Dechend 1969; Major 1973). In terms of philosophy, in the sense of drawing upon a significant body of knowledge and wisdom inherited from the past, new to Zhou around the 10th–9th centuries BCE was the concept of a past that preceded the present era (Vogelsang 2017).

The Zhou Multi-State System and the Lords of the Lands

The Zhou rulers held sway over a large territory comparable to that of the Shang that included not only the Yellow River Plain but also the Wei River valley and the loess highlands to its north, the Han River valley, part of the

Yangzi River valley, and adjacent areas (see Map in Figure 7.3). The greater part of the Zhou realm was parceled out to Zhou kinsmen and aristocratic supporters in the form of semi-autonomous states (see Map 7.1).[8] It had long been thought that the Zhou realm was much larger than that of Shang and that the system of semi-autonomous states was a Zhou innovation. As we have seen, archaeological investigation of Shang secondary cities (far from the Shang royal capital at Anyang) has shown that the Shang controlled a much larger territory than has hitherto been realized (Childs-Johnson 2019).[9] The system of establishing subsidiary states ruled by members of the royal lineage was already in place during the Shang; the Zhou kings adopted and extended an existing political system rather than inventing it themselves.

The Zhou kings quickly set up an advanced administrative system, the details of which can be reconstructed based on numerous Zhou bronze vessel inscriptions. An administrative bureaucracy was organized in pyramidal fashion, in large part following the practice of Shang. The King was on top, followed by, according to Li, the Duke, then the Armies, the Grand Secretariat, Three Ministries, and the Royal Household, and below them other functionaries (F Li 2008: Figure 30). The rapid establishment of an administrative system allowed the Zhou kings to exert control, albeit in large part indirectly, over a very large territory. As many as 100 territorial states are mentioned in bronze inscriptions and later textual sources. Shang *fang* and related states mentioned in bone inscriptions according to Sun Yabing and Lin Huan (2015) numbered some 158 (2015: 259, Ch 7, 259–473; also see Shima tr. 1970: 379–82). "Interior" states near the Zhou royal domain were small and numerous, while a few very large "outer" states protected and

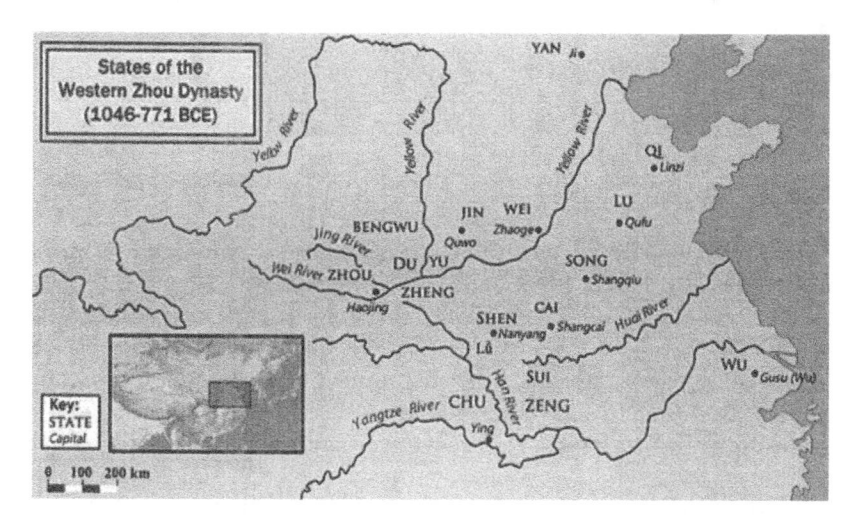

Figure 7.3 Map showing states of the Western Zhou period. Retrieved from website Philg88, accessed on January 3, 2014.

extended Zhou control in frontier areas. The rulers of territorial states had titles of nobility, *gong* 公, *hou* 侯, *bo* 伯, *zi* 子, and *nan* 男 (conventionally translated as duke, marquis, earl, viscount, and baron). Most of these terms were known already in the Shang and functioned similarly in reference to social status and position (see Yang 1992; Song 2005). During the Springs and Autumns period, these titles had clear hierarchical significance, and that was probably already true for the Shang and Western Zhou periods. Collectively, the rulers of territorial states were known as *zhuhou* 諸侯, "the many lords" or "the Lords of the Lands." Similar to Shang practice, their obligations to the Zhou kings included attending the royal court when summoned and augmenting the Zhou military force with their own troops and chariots. (The power of the territorial states during the Western Zhou was measured by the number of war chariots they could field.)

Western Zhou Cities, Buildings, and Tombs

The Western Zhou court had two capitals, one at Zongzhou in the west and the second at Chengzhou in the east near Luoyang (see Map 7.1) (Khayutina 2008, 2020; F. Li 2013). Chengzhou was not completed and occupied until the reign of King Cheng. Because the progenitors of the house of Zhou had been based in Zongzhou (Qishan) prior to the conquest of Shang, the Zhou kings kept that site as their primary capital. Chengzhou was intended to maintain control over the territorial states in the east, some of which had only recently been conquered by the Zhou and whose allegiance was uncertain. Zhou cities and towns were numerous in and around the western capital, and new settlements were founded as the Zhou presence expanded in the eastern half of the kingdom.

Buildings: Palaces, Temples, and Altars

Newly excavated remains, particularly from the Zhou homeland in the Wei River valley at sites north of the capital Zongzhou (Qishan), in Fengchu in Qishan County and Yuntang, Qizhen, and Shaochen in Fufeng County, are rich in building foundations and in cache burials of ritual bronzes and bells covering several generations. It appears that the structures at four different sites, all north of the royal center, functioned either as ritual or palatial sites belonging to aristocratic lineages or to kings and members of the Zhou royal family.

At Fengchu, for example, large-scale rammed earth foundations of a rectangular structure aligned roughly N–S and measuring 45.2 m long north to south and 32.5 m wide have been traced and plotted (Figure 7.4) (Du 2009: 435). The building's layout is symmetrical, comprising an open front courtyard with a gate screen, leading to two front gatehouses flanking a doorway leading to a large front courtyard and thence to a columned rectangular front hall behind which were built two smaller western and eastern

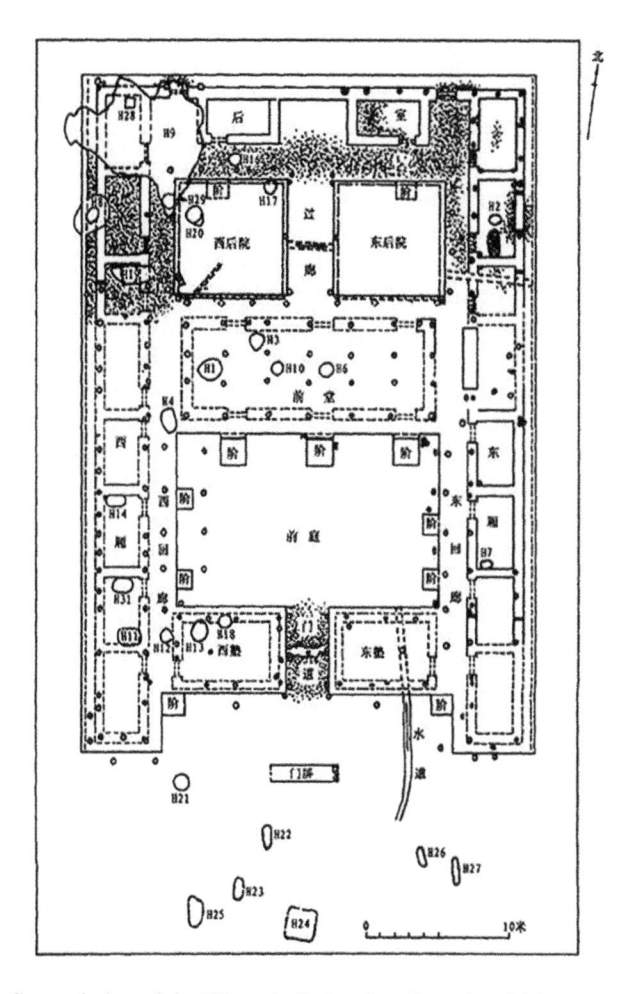

Figure 7.4 Ground plan of the "Temple-Palace" at Fengchu, Qishan, Shaanxi. Early Western Zhou period. After Du 2009: 437.

courtyards and further small rooms. Eight additional small rooms on the western and eight on the eastern side line the inner walls of the enclosed complex. This building complex resembles known Shang architectural prototypes and dates to the late Shang through Western Zhou periods. On the basis of a large number of oracle bones with inscriptions that were recovered from two storage pits in the small side rooms on the west wing (called by Du the "turtle chamber" (龜室) (Du 2009: 438–41), scholars suggest that this structure must have functioned as an ancestral temple complex. One of these oracle bone inscriptions records worship in the temple of the Shang king known posthumously as Wenwu Di Yi 文武帝乙, the second to last Shang king ruling at Anyang, indicating that this may be a temple dedicated to the worship of that Shang king. Although these inscriptions were authored by Zhou aristocrats (Cao W 2002: 1–9, reviews three theories of authorship), it is not clear whether this building, occupied throughout the Western Zhou era, was used for worship of Zhou ancestors after the rites for Shang kings were terminated.

Other columned buildings discovered at nearby sites in Yuntang (Figure 7.5A above) and Qizhen in Fufeng County (Zhouyuan 2002) are distinctly different in type from any known Shang building. The plans of two structures at Yuntang and Qizhen are, in turn, similar to the later Springs and Autumns complex at Majiazhuang (Figure 7.5B), suggesting that this architectural layout may be of Zhou origin. The complex at all three sites comprises an enclosed wall with a front gate that opens to a large open space with a pebbled walkway forming a loop with left and right paths that in turn lead to an indented large columned hall. Two smaller foundation platforms to the east and west sides flank the entrance to the large columned hall. The structures at Yuntang and Qizhen, dated to the Late Western Zhou period, differ markedly from the building compound at Fengchu. The excavators note that more roof tiles were found at the Fufeng sites than at the site of Fengchu. Water drainage and paving were handled differently. Cobblestones paving paths inside courtyards and aprons of buildings were used at Yuntang and Qizhen but not at Fengchu. The designs of these buildings were distinctly similar: rectangular and symmetrical with a central rectangular building.

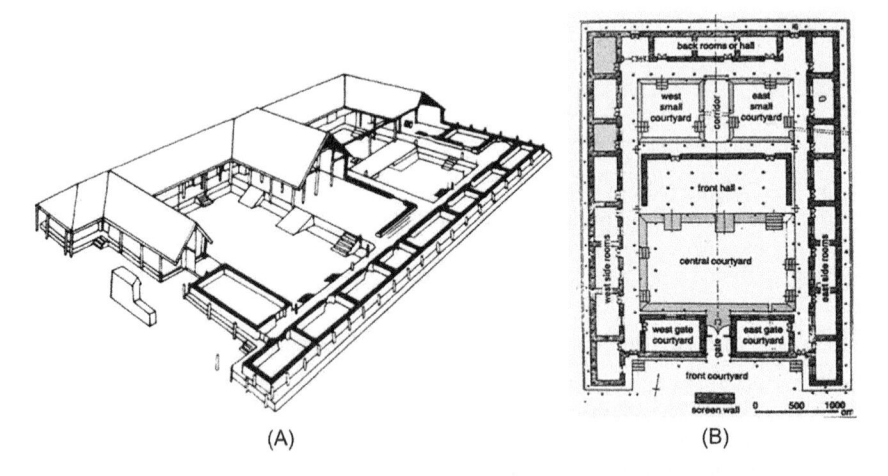

(A)   (B)

Figure 7.5 (A) Reconstruction of the ritual compound at Yuntang, Fufeng, Shaanxi, 9th–8th century BCE. (B) Ground plan of the ritual complex no.1 at Majiazhuang comprising an altar and temple, Springs and Autumns period, 7th century BCE. (A) After Li Feng 2006: 108, Figure 13. (B) After Yongcheng *et al* 1985: 14–15 with Shelach-Levy 2017: 279, Figure 190.

Tomb Layouts Continue Shang Precedents

Burial practices during the Western Zhou adopted those of Shang in com-
bining rich and not-so-rich members together in lineage cemeteries. Belief
in an afterlife continued to be a primary motive for providing the spirit of
the deceased with material goods. Although no Zhou royal tomb has yet
been excavated, surveys have uncovered a large-scale outline of a tomb in
an area of Qishan believed to contain the Western Zhou royal cemetery (see
Figure 7.6A). The tomb is in the cruciform shape characteristic of the Shang
royal tombs found at the Late Shang cemetery of Xibeigang in Anyang (see
Chapter 6: 132, Figure 6.6). Tombs with long northern and southern ramps,
ones with southern ramps, and rectangular pit burials have also been

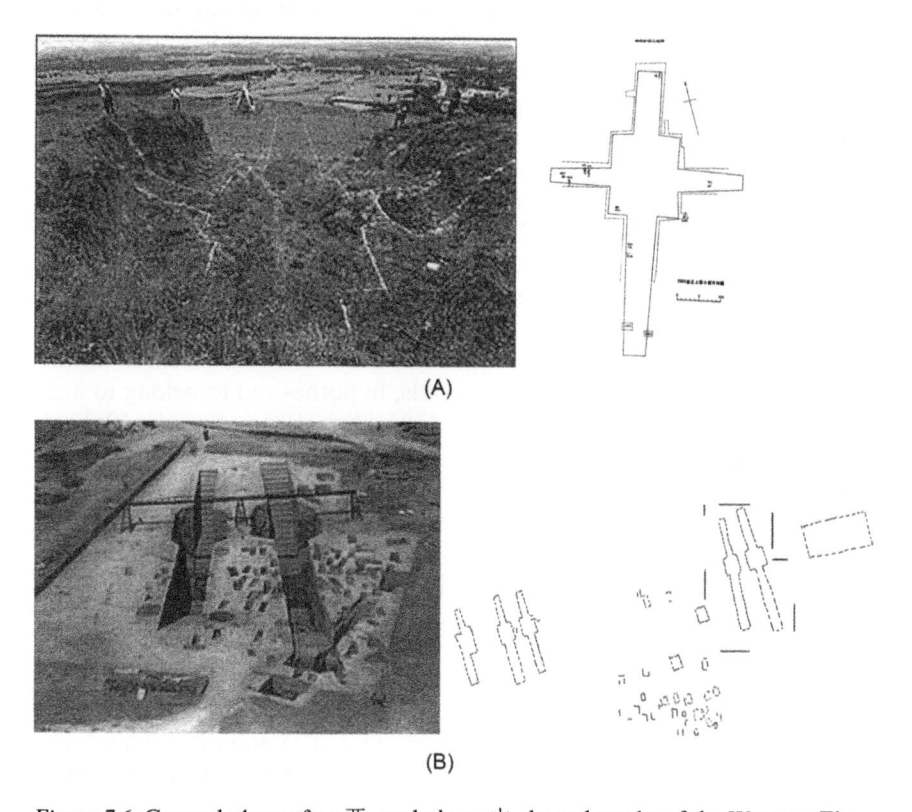

(A)

(B)

Figure 7.6 Ground plans of *ya* 亞- and *zhong* 中-shaped tombs of the Western Zhou
period. (A) White outline of a cruciform "royal Western Zhou tomb"
in Qishan County according to Wang Fankui (2004), Deputy Director
of the Shaanxi Provincial Archaeological Research Dept. (B) Ground
plan of burials belonging to Jin marquises and their spouses at Yangshe
in Quwo, Shanxi, and the excavation of burials M1 and M2 (s-n). M1
belongs to Jin Hou, and dates to the middle Western Zhou period; M2
belongs to his wife. After Ji *et al* 2009 and Zhongguo Shehui 2004: 87:
Figure 193.

excavated at various cemeteries of Western Zhou-lineage aristocrats, for example, the high-status burials in the Jin state cemetery at Beizhao, Qucun, Shaanxi (Figure 7.6B). Chariot burials, often with horses and charioteers, also frequently accompany these ranking aristocrats in lineage cemeteries.

For the moment, only a shadow line traced in white suggests that Western Zhou kings may have been buried in large-scale cruciform tombs like their Shang predecessors. Whether all Western Zhou kings were buried in the same place and with similar style burials is still unclear, but on present evidence, it is reasonable to infer that, as in Shang times, they were buried in a separate cemetery complex reserved for royalty. We await excavations to clarify this question (Wang Fk 2004; Khayutina 2008: 25–65).

The state of Jin has yielded important evidence of aristocratic burials. The state, described in later texts such as the *Shiji* as having been founded by a younger brother of King Cheng in the 11th century BCE, occupied a strategic location controlling roadways leading from the east and north to the Wei River valley and the capital Zongzhou Li (Feng 2006: 84–87). The large Jin state lineage cemetery includes two primary sites, at Yangshe and Beizhao, in the Fen River valley. The cemetery covers a total area of 12 hectares. Two recently discovered tombs at Yangshe, M1 and M2, are believed to belong to a Jin ruler with the status of marquis (*hou* 侯) and his wife (Figure 7.5B), dating to a period from the middle Western Zhou to the early Springs and Autumns period (see Shanxi 2009).

Both tombs had been looted. Comparable tombs are found at Beizhao, where 17 large tombs, 14 with ramps with a north–south orientation, are divided into nine groups of paired burials, hypothesized to belong to nine marquises and their wives (F. Li 2006: 84–86; Shanxisheng 1993: 11–30; 1994: 4–28; 1994: 22–23, 68; 1995: 4–38; 2001: 4–21; 2004: 1–21). Other burials, designated M63 and M93, similar in size to M1 and M2, were extremely rich in furnishings, as would be characteristic of all aristocratic Western Zhou burials. The corpses of the deceased were protected by jade face masks, jade gloves, and jade shoes, and large jade pectorals, jade being a material symbol of life after death.

A Royal Rite of Investiture

Li Feng has reconstructed how the Fengchu unit at Yuntang may have functioned as a temple (*gong* 宮) for making political appointments, the most common subject recorded on Western Zhou bronze ritual vessels (F. Li 2006: 145–50). Based on the well-known Song *ding* inscription, he is able to recreate the process of making the appointment. Personnel involved included the king; the appointee; the *youzhe* 右者 or "Person on the Right"; the Interior Scribe and Chief Interior Scribe; and attendants. Every detail of the costume worn by the assembled lords was specified by sumptuary rules. For example, court dress included kneepads to ease the discomfort of the kneeling aristocrats. As reviewed by Li, the rite involved six formal steps. It took place at sunrise when the king would enter first and sit on the platform in front of the Grand Chamber, facing south. He was a remote and mysterious personage, sitting motionless, his face probably hidden by the strings of jade beads that hung from the front of his elaborate headpiece. The appointee then entered the gate and stood in the center of the courtyard and faced north, toward the king. A high official, known as the Person on the Right, then took a position to the right of the appointee, the right being a superior position. The king did not speak; once the celebrants were in place, he signaled either the Interior Scribe or Chief Interior Scribe to read aloud the appointment recorded on a written document, probably consisting of bamboo strips. One of them would hold the document while the other read it aloud. The appointment and award might include a number of gifts, such as a grant of land (or a certain number of households living on a tract of land), clothing (knee pads), chariots, or a specified quantity of bronze, as well as black millet ale. In Step 4, the appointee expressed his gratitude. In Step 5, the document was handed to the appointee. In Step 6, the appointee handed

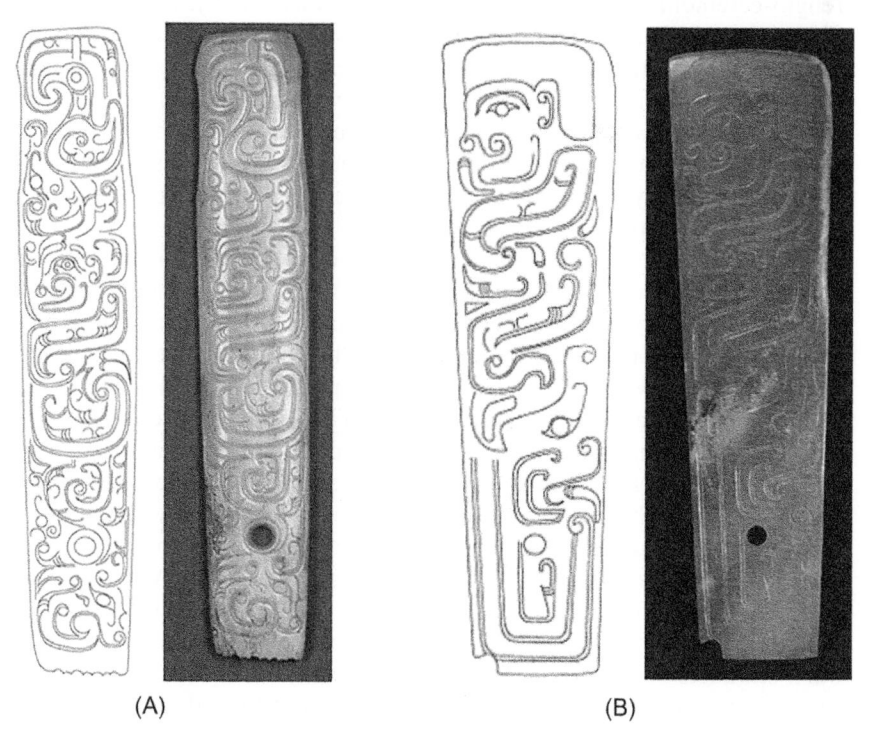

(A)   (B)

Figure 7.7 Types of jade blade insignia with the yi metamorphic power symbol of humanoid in a fetal pose with bird and dragon parts, most likely used by the appointee in the Song *gui* bronze inscription, as detailed by Li Feng (see text above). (A) Metropolitan Museum of Art 8.3 cm tall × 3.4 cm broad. (B) Palace Museum of Art, Beijing, 14.7 cm tall × 3.4 cm broad. After Zhongguo Yuqi vol. 2: colorpl 280 and pl 281.

the document to his assistants who then in return provided the appointee with a jade *gui* insignia blade authorizing him to speak in honor of the king [ruling Western Zhou king, probably King Mu, r. 956–918 BCE] (Figure 7.7), accompanied by deferential kowtowing.

In addition to the steps of royal appointments outlined by Li are numerous other inscriptions recording the proceedings of the royal court, including the granting and receiving of royal gifts.

The Religio-Ceremonial State: Producing Spirit Awe (*Wei* 畏 / 威) and Feasting

The 300-year period of Western Zhou witnessed a stage in the evolution of the symbiotic relationship of metamorphism and divine rulership. Although that relationship and its visual expressions changed over a vast stretch of time, it nevertheless preserved Jade Age, Erlitou ("Xia"), and Shang traditions manifested in religious imagery and sacrificial practice. As rulers of a "religio-ceremonial state," the Zhou used elaborate, costly, highly choreographed rituals to assert and sustain their power. The essence of this power is expressed by a term frequently found in early texts, *weiyi* 畏儀 [威儀], conventionally translated as "awe-inspiring decorum" but more accurately, "fear-provoking majesty." One of the most important ways that this royal attribute was displayed was through the holding of grand feasts *xiang* 鄉 for the spirits of the royal ancestor's realm followed by banquets for aristocrats and functionaries alike.

The Zhou term, *weiyi* 畏儀[威儀], was rooted in the Shang oracle bone inscription graph *wei* 畏[威] (Childs-Johnson 1995: 79–92). In that context, *wei* meant the fear-provoking or awesome charisma that the king acquired through his ability to identify metamorphically with the spirit world of the high deity Di. In Western Zhou bronze inscriptions, *wei* similarly refers to the king's identification with the high deity Tian. In Zhou bronze inscriptions and later transmitted texts, *wei* often appears in combination with *yi*, "decorum," in keeping with the moral air of Western Zhou ideology. In both Shang and Zhou, the metamorphic power of *wei* was probably instantiated through the donning of masks or similar paraphernalia by the king in his performance of sacred rituals (Childs-Johnson 1995: 90–91). As in the case of the *Da Feng* rite discussed above, Shang period rites continued to inform Zhou religio-political ceremonies. In addition to dawn sessions of the royal court, banquets were a prime forum for the display of the king's awe-inspiring spirit power. Conspicuous display by means of formal feasting in the form of sacrifices to the spirit world followed by banqueting flaunted kingly power. Other rites inherited from the Shang may include boarding a boat in the *piyong* lake surrounding the *Tianshi* 天室 or *Tiantongshi* 天通室, the Hall of Communicating with Tian to shoot fish with bow and arrow, or hunting in game parks established in the four cardinal directions. The royal *sheli* 射禮 or Archery Rite, again a rite inherited from Shang (Cai (Tsai) 1976), was a reenactment of a hunting exercise symbolizing cosmological power over the untamed wilderness, extending to the furthermost ends of the earth.

As many inscriptions attest, feasting typically involved meat of a hunted animal that was butchered with a royal *yue* ax blade (Childs-Johnson 2013). Various terms were employed in Shang oracle-bone inscriptions to designate different kinds of feasts (Childs-Johnson 2013: 167), and these terms remained in use in Western Zhou. The *xiang* feast apparently referred to a large-scale banquet accompanied by ceremonial events such as drumming, playing of bells, boating, archery, and martial dancing. Shang kings frequently divined about offering the *xiang* rite to dead ancestors:

> [Crack-making] on the *renzi* day He divined: On the next *guichou* day should [the King] carry out and you the *Xiang* Feast Rite to the spirit of Ancestress Xin (1st wife of Wu Ding Shang king). Heji 27456 front. (For other examples see Yao and Xiao: 139).

The same rite addressed to royal ancestors was performed by Zhou kings, as specified in the Tian Wang *gui* and other inscriptions (see above Figure 7.1).

The Wan (宛) rite is particularly interesting since it may be directly associated with the more mysterious aspects of communicating with ancestral spirits as embedded in the concept of *yi*, spirit metamorphosis. As mentioned in the Mai bronze vessel inscriptions (Cook and Goldin 2016: 42–44: no.14 *Zuoce Mai fangzun* pp 42–44), the king performed the *wan* invocation rite and sacrifice to his cosmological source of power in the Hall of Communicating with Tian (*Tiantongshi*). The Shang and Zhou graphs for *wan* depict a shaman-like stick figure bending over with a long extended forked tongue, sometimes standing under a roof, drinking from a *zun* type alcohol vessel *wan*.[10] That the figure represents an invocator is suggested by the graph's "mouth" radical (口), frequently symbolic of spirit invocation, for example, as in the graph for zhu 祝 to invoke (see Childs-Johnson 1995: 82–88), and by its long, forked tongue.

A gold belt ornament from tomb M1 of the Jin Marquis from Yangshe bears a similar image of a humanoid with a long, forked tongue (see Figure 7.8). The forked tongue is perhaps related to the extended tongue found not only on many tiger-headed wooden tomb guardian figures from the state of Chu but commonly on Western and Eastern Zhou metamorphic images on bronzes; see, for example, the image on the *zun* excavated in Anhui (Childs-Johnson 2016:6, Figure 4 second row, first drawing on left).

Both the *xiang* and the *wan* rites were performed uniquely by the Zhou kings in the Hall for Communicating with Tian. In their metamorphic guise as "Sons of Tian," the Zhou kings treated Tian as a royal ancestor and the source of the ruling house's cosmic power. The practice of invoking Tian and the royal ancestors, documented by many Western Zhou bronze inscriptions, is depicted in the poem "Thorn-bushes" of the *Shijing* (Mao Ode 209); probably of Western Zhou date.[11] The poem, in describing a royal

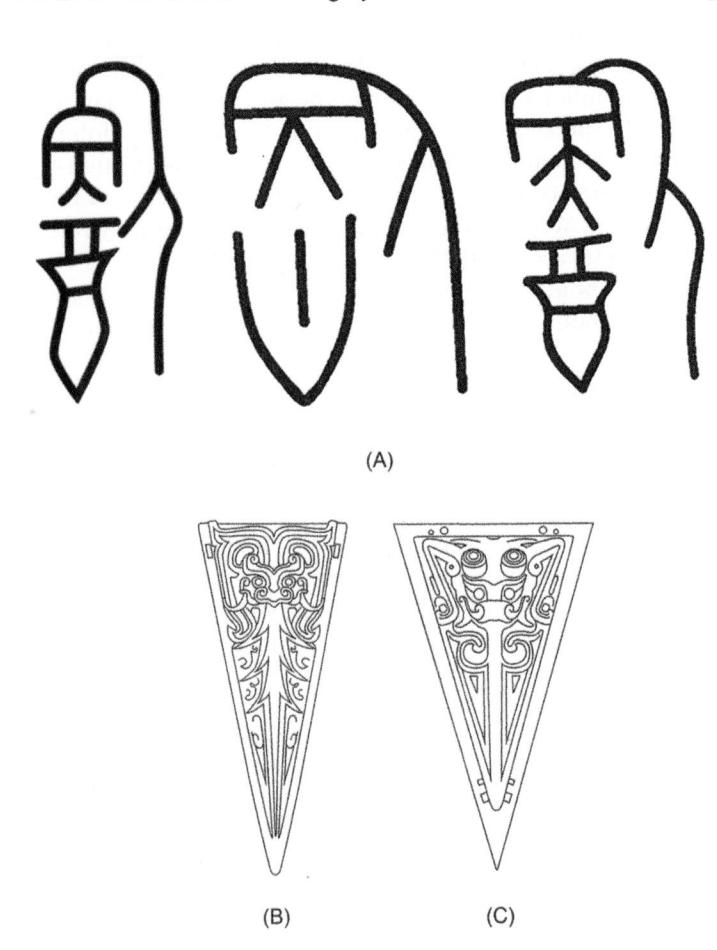

(A)

(B)   (C)

Figure 7.8 Artistic and graphic images of humanoids with forked tongues, probably referring to the Wan Feasting rite (A) Shang graph *wan* (宛) in oracle bone inscriptions. (B) and (C) Gold belt ornaments, M1:30, Jin state
cemetery, Yangshe, Shanxi and M2001, Guo state cemetery, Sanmenxia,
Henan. (A) After Yao and Xiao 1998: 281, no.0785, and 1042, nos. 2730–
731. (BC) After Ji *et al* 2009 and Henan 1999: colorpl 12.

banquet, contains elements of divination and prognostication. We translate
it as follows:

Mao Ode 209 Thorn-Bushes

Abundantly grew the thorn-bushes,
But they cleared away the thickets.
Why did they do this in olden times?
So that we might plant our brewing-millet and steaming-millet.
Our brewing-millet yields a bumper crop,

Our steaming-millet flourishes.
Our granaries are full,
Our grain-heaps are numbered by millions;
So we can prepare ale and food,
To offer prayers and sacrifices,
To make the ancestral spirits comfortable, to urge them to eat,
So that we may have bright good fortune.
Reverently and cautiously
We sanctify the oxen and sheep.
We carry out the steamed-grain harvest ritual,
Now skinning the victims, now boiling their flesh,
Now placing meat on the stands, now arranging them on the altar.
The Invocator offers sacrifices at the city gate.
All the details of the service are urgently accomplished.
The ancestors are present in their grandeur,
The Spirit Protector enjoys the offerings.
Their filial descendant is greatly joyful
And is rewarded with good fortune,
And ten thousand years of longevity without limit.
Meticulously, treading softly, we tend the stove,
We arrange the tall food-stands,
Some for roasted meat, some for boiled.
The lord's consorts, discreet and reverent,
Oversee the numerous dishes.
To guests and strangers
They offer pledge-cups all around.
Every form is ritually correct,
Every word and gesture is appropriate.
The Spirit Protector has assuredly come,
And will repay us with good fortune;
Ten thousand years' longevity will be our recompense.
We have worked very hard
To ensure that the rites were without error.
The skillful Invocator intones the Spirit's message:
And conveys it to the filial descendent:
"Fragrant and sweet were your filial offerings;
And the Spirits enjoyed your ale and meat.
They bestow on you a hundred blessings,
All in accordance with propriety and good form.
All that you have done has been proper and timely;
All was straight and as prescribed.
They will reward you with ten thousand and tens of ten thousands of
years."
The rites having thus been accomplished,
The bells and drums are made ready.
The filial descendent takes his place.

> The skillful Invocator announces:
> "Now all the spirits are drunk."
> The August Impersonator of the Dead then rises
> And withdraws to the sound of bells and drums.
> The Spirit Protector has returned to his dwelling-place.
> The numerous servants, and the lord's consorts,
> Remove the sacrificial utensils without delay.
> While the uncles and elder and younger brothers
> Head off to the secular feast.
> The musicians enter and begin to play,
> Adding informality to the after-banquet.
> The foodstuffs are set out,
> No one is dissatisfied, everyone is happy.
> They drink until they are drunk and eat until they are replete.
> Small and great all kowtow to the host:
> "The spirits enjoyed your ale and meat
> And so will grant you long life.
> They will send down blessings and favor
> Because nothing was left undone.
> May sons and grandsons forever
> Never fail to follow this example."

The poem mentions several key participants in this extended ritual. The Spirit Protector (*shen bao* 神保) is the spirit of the deceased ancestor for whom the rite is being held. The Invocator (*zhu* 祝) was likely a professional functionary whose job was to speak on behalf of the king, who displayed his "awe-inspiring decorum" by remaining silent. The *shi* 尸 Impersonator of the Dead was usually a young man, perhaps, in many cases, one of the king's sons (yet, during the Shang, it was primarily the King who carried out sacrifices, see Tt Chang 1970: 51). The ceremonial robes of Invocator and Impersonator of the Dead were undoubtedly decorated with symbols such as the *feng* bird and the *long* dragon that emphasized the metamorphic powers inherent in the spirit realm and bestowed on the ruling dynasty.

It is likely that public feasting *xiang* contrasted with the private feasting *yan* in both Shang and Western Zhou eras (Song Zh 2005 *shang*: 479–506, esp. 488). In addition to rare and luxurious foodstuffs and copious amounts of millet ale, consumed to the thunderous sound of drums, banquets also featured music for dance and entertainment of the king and his aristocratic guests. Later systematizing works on ritual such as the *Zhouli* 周禮 and the *Liji* 禮記 provide detailed descriptions of these occasions. Some of the details may be post-facto inventions, but the texts' emphasis on aristocratic hierarchy rings true. They specify, for example, that the king alone had the right to have eight lines of dancers, while a *gong* [duke] could have six, a *hou* four, and lesser aristocrats correspondingly fewer. (In *Analects* 3.1,

Confucius denounces the arrogance of the aristocratic Jisun family of Lu, who had eight rows of dancers at their feasts.) Other regulations governed the color of accessories that could be worn by various ranks. The woven silk textile recently discovered draped over the coffin of Bo Peng (Elder of Peng) was decorated with various sizes of woven *feng* bird symbols in profile with displayed ocellated feathers (Figure 7.9). The burial *gui, ding,* and bell sets from the same tomb comprised five of each, which denoted an aristocrat with the rank of *hou*, according to the Zhou formal hierarchical system. As these systematizing texts imply, the Zhou kings enjoyed unique privileges in the conduct of their ceremonial affairs, but they were not the only ones to hold court, preside over banquets, and so on. The rulers of territorial states did so as well, and regulations governing the color of clothing and accessories and the constraints on actions were applied to this third tier of Zhou aristocracy (see below, pages 176) according to rank. Throughout the nearly three centuries of Western Zhou rule, the rulers of the territorial

Figure 7.9 Coffin shroud (huangwei) with woven designs of the vermilion-colored *feng* mythic bird, Peng Bo [Peng the Elder] M1, Hengbei, Jiang County, Shanxi. Western Zhou Period, mid-9th century BCE. Drawing by Margaret Panoti. After Song Jiejun *et al* 1996: colorpl. 7 and English tr. Chinese Archaeology 20.1 (2020): 43, colorpl 6.

states increasingly expanded their roles to become mini-sovereigns replicating, on a smaller scale, the ceremonial regime of the Western Zhou kings.

Like the Shang dynasty, the Western Zhou period has been divided into three sub-periods, early, middle, and late, to facilitate the identification, dating, and analysis of bronze vessels and other physical remains. For some 100 years, encompassing the reigns of the earliest four Zhou kings – King Wu (r. c. 1049–43), King Cheng (r. c. 1043–05), King Kang (r. c. 1005–978), and King Zhao (r. c. 978–57) – bronze vessels, and presumably the rituals associated with them, closely resembled those of late Shang. Vessel types included *jia* and *jue* beakers, *gu* goblets, three-legged round *ding,* four-legged square *ding, yan* steamers, *pan* shallow water basins, and a few other familiar types. The surface decor of Zhou vessels, like Shang bronzes, included the metamorphic power mask and coiled dragon.

By the end of the early Western Zhou, some Shang vessel types had become rare or disappeared altogether and were replaced by a few new shapes; new surface treatments also appeared. Bronzes became more numerous but were less finely made; they often bore lengthy inscriptions; and they no longer found their primary use and significance in royal ancestral sacrificial rituals. Bronze vessels of the middle and late Western Zhou period underwent further adjustments, moving away from an emphasis on *jiu* (fermented millet ale) vessels 酒器 to an emphasis on food vessels 食器, particularly *ding* (meat cooking vessels) and *gui* (food serving vessels) (Guo Bj; Y. Sun) and an emphasis on the mythic *feng* bird icon instead of the metamorphic *yi* mask.

The reign of King Mu (r. 957–17 BCE) marked the transition from early to middle Western Zhou. King Mu came to the throne after a disastrous attempt by King Zhao to expand Zhou territory southwards; the Zhou army was routed and the king himself died fording a river. King Mu, in a long and largely successful reign, instituted reforms that included increasing the efficiency of the royal administration and enhancing the military readiness of the territorial lords (a reform with negative long-term consequences) (Shaughnessy 1999: 292–351, esp. 323–28). At this time and by the end of the middle Western Zhou period, bronze vessels begin to degenerate and become less robust. Vessels cast in sets of similar design and graduated size were a Zhou innovation; numbers of vessels in a set were subject to sumptuary rules (apparently loosely observed) reflecting the rank of the patrons for whom the vessels were cast. Bronze vessels of that phase often incorporate lengthy inscriptions, in some cases comprising 500 or more characters (see e.g., Figure 14E, the Mao Gong *ding*). These inscriptions attest eloquently to the primary role of bronze vessels as being made for use in ancestor worship by royalty and high-class aristocratic lineages, but with the caveat that the first concern of the inscriptions was to document the lineage history of the awardee and to specify the awards and gifts conferred on him for his service to the ruler. Inscriptions typically end with an address to the ancestral spirits that these bronze vessels and bells would be used continuously for ancestor spirit worship.

By the end of Western Zhou, the great majority of bronze vessels were not made for use in royal ancestral rituals (whether of the Zhou kings or the regional Lords of the Lands) but were cast for members of an expanding elite class that included aristocrats, military leaders, and senior functionaries. Vessels were prestige items and family heirlooms, dowry gifts, or simply gifts, often inscribed with encomiums explaining the circumstances under which the vessels were cast, frequently as a royal reward for meritorious service. This private possession of bronze vessels lies behind the gradual deterioration of the quality of bronze workmanship, and of the increasing rarity of the metamorphic power mask representing the spirit of a deceased royal and cosmologically transformed ancestor. Mythical realms, usually involving *feng* and *long* or depictions of fabled terrestrial realms with humanoids and power images, take over as the predominant subject matter. The metamorphic power mask never disappeared, yet it became subordinate in representations of the otherworldly realm. Its former prominence gave way to a growing anthropomorphism expressed in narrative interpretations of the spirit world.

Western Zhou Bronze Culture

The *Gui* 簋 cooked grain vessel.

As we have seen, Western Zhou ritualists retained most Shang dynasty bronze vessel types (and presumably the rituals in which they were used), discarded others, and developed some new ones. For example, the Zhou eventually discontinued the Shang practice of casting sets of multiple *jue* and *gu* millet ale vessels (Sun 2019–20). Instead, the Zhou showed a marked preference for grain vessel sets and related serving vessels, such as the *dou* small stem bowl, the *fu*, and the *xu* containers (see the examples in Figure 7.12). The earliest and most significant vessel form during the Western Zhou was the *gui*, forming a large bowl which, in a new gesture, was now affixed to a square stand. (The vessel's name is borrowed from the vocabulary of Shang oracle bone inscriptions, where it is a verb meaning "to eat." (Song Zh 2005: 506–08). It retains that meaning in some Zhou bronze inscriptions.) The shape of the *gui* is a concrete expression of a cosmography that described a square earth covered by a round sky dome, a belief with roots in the pre-Bronze Age East Asian Heartland Region that informed the Zhou worldview. This cosmological symbol is consistent with Shang and Western Zhou ancestor worship, and with the Western Zhou emphasis on the cosmological basis of rulership, the Mandate of Tian.

This predilection for grain vessels has traditionally been explained as reflecting a Zhou conviction that the Shang lost their mandate to rule due to their alcohol-fueled debauchery, giving rise to a consequent Zhou policy of discouraging excessive alcohol consumption and use of alcohol-related vessels. One of many extant Western Zhou inscriptions that illustrates the historical probability of Shang over-indulgence in millet ale and the Zhou kings' efforts to avoid the same problem is found on the Middle Western Zhou large-scale Da Yu tripod *ding*:

> In the ninth month, when the King was in Zongzhou he charged Yu. The King said as follows: 'Yu, Greatly Manifest King Wen received *Tian*'s aid and great Mandate. The Mandate remained with King Wu who was succeeded by King Cheng and created a nation (*bang*). [King Wu] eradicated evil and took under his protection the Four Quarters, rectifying their peoples. When it came to those in his administration to carry out the alcohol sacrifice, none dared get drunk; and as for performing [to the royal ancestral spirits] the *liao* [burning] and *cheng* 烝 grain offerings, none dared be (drunkenly) rowdy. For this reason, the awesomeness of *Tian* hovers over me [*Tian*'s] son, and the ever-protecting former Kings take under their protection the Four Quarters... Yu, pay your respects in an illuminating and radiant manner at the [*Bi*]*yong* (of the *Mingtang*). [Receive] the canon of virtue... Present memorial Feasts [to the ancestor spirits] ... and fear the awesomeness of *Tian*. The King said: ...From dawn to dusk (always) help me, the One Man, to present *cheng* grain sacrifices to the Four Quarters so that I may follow upon and oversee the peoples and lands bequeathed by the Former King...'
>
> (Cook and Goldin 2016)

Evidently, the image of excessive drinking on occasions of sacrifice and feasting that the Zhou used to characterize Yin peoples was used in Zhou propaganda to argue for their Mandate to rule. Grain sacrifices (e.g., *cheng* 烝) appear to become more common than alcohol offerings in Zhou times, with steamed grain itself perhaps being offered instead of ale made from the grain.

The Zhou emphasis on vessels for presenting sacrificial grain offerings may also reflect a belief that the Zhou lineage was founded by the mythical progenitor Hou Ji (Lord Millet), who taught agriculture and its arts to the Zhou people. Here, a caveat is needed: while it seems to be the case that the Zhou traced their origins to Hou Ji, early dateable Western Zhou references to this mythical figure are scarce. Hou Ji appears in several places in the *Shijing*, notably in Mao Ode 245, "She Who in the Beginning Gave Birth to the People," but those odes are of uncertain date. No bronze inscription other than the Shi Qiang *pan* of the middle Western Zhou period mentions Hou Ji as the progenitor of the Zhou people (Cook and Goldin 2016: no 28. 93–100). Yet this may be due to the fact no royal tombs belonging to Zhou kings who would have mentioned their heritage have been excavated.

It is not surprising that the *gui* came to be seen as a symbol of Zhou political legitimacy and that the Zhou chose to elevate the *gui* vessel – no other type (with the occasional exception of the *you* type) – by raising it onto a square hollow box (see Figures 7.1, 7.2, and 7.10 (Tian Wang *gui* and Li *gui*). The emerging early Western Zhou aesthetic featuring strong geometric shapes seems to reflect a belief in the cosmic source of political legitimacy; the realms of sky and earth are symbolized as linked square and circular bronze forms; the four prominent handles protruding from the circular upper vessel linked the upper and lower vessels visually and denoted the midpoints of the lower vessel's four sides (see Figure 7.10). Conceptually and symbolically, the *gui* was congruent with the Zhou Temple/Hall of Heaven, (later known as the *Mingtang*), with its square structure topped by a round thatched roof, emulating the square earth and circular sky. A different but not incompatible visualization of the square earth is found in the *ya* 亞 shape of Shang royal tombs, imitating the square earth extending to the Four Quarters; these tombs in some cases were surmounted by round mounds.

The same cosmography was reflected still earlier by the architectural layouts of open-air altars in circular and square shapes at Hongshan and

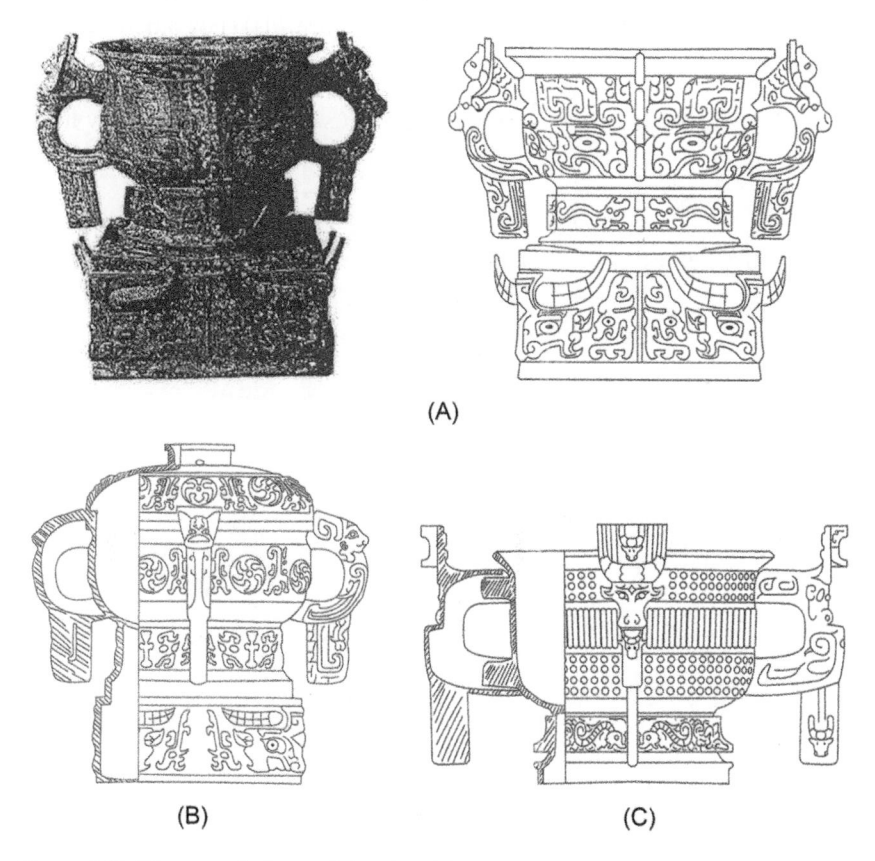

(A)

(B)   (C)

Figure 7.10 Three variations of the ritual bronze *gui*, two with a square stand and all with four prominent projecting handles, Yu Bo [Elder Yu] tomb M1, Baoji, Shaanxi, early Western Zhou Period, 11th c. BCE. After Lu and Hu 2008: pl 8:1 and Figures 17, 19, 24.

Liangzhu ritual sites. By the Western Zhou period, this design was consciously manipulated to invest the Zhou regime with the cosmic power of the Mandate, with the king, sheltered by the dome of heaven, ruling the Four Quarters from the center of the world.

The Zun and You, and Other Innovative Vessel Sets

The Zhou kings' fears about the dangers of alcohol did not mean that they did not offer alcohol in rituals. Millet ale remained important in ancestral rites, as demonstrated by the early Western Zhou invention of alcohol sets defined by similar iconography, initially the *zun* and *you* and then other vessel types, including *fangyi* and *gong* and ultimately the food serving *gui* on a stand. It is important to note that the imagery on these vessels was systematized so that the vessels formed a set that may comprise a *zun*, *you*, and *gong*, *zun* and *you*, or *fangyi*, *gong,* and *zun*. The Ge Bo set is similarly decorated with dragons sporting coiled tails (see Figure 7.11) (For others, see e.g.

(A)

蝸體獸紋

(B)

Figure 7.11 Example of early Western Zhou experimenting with look-alike décor and similar inscriptions on ritual bronze vessel sets. Ge Bo *zun, you,* and *gui* on a stand from tomb M1 at Gaojiabao, Jingyang, Shaanxi Western Zhou period, 11th–10th century BCE. After Dai 1995: pls 7–9. Drawing from Zhongguo meishu: Western Zhou I: Figure 13.

Zuoce Zhe *zun, fangyi,* and *gong* in Shaanxisheng 1980: plates14,15,16; and Bo Ju *zun* and two *you* in Shanxisheng 1980).

Zun and *you* vessel sets with identical imagery and inscriptions disappeared by the mid-9th century BCE in favor of multiple numbers of *ding* and *gui* (sometimes replaced or augmented by the new grain vessel sets of *dou* and *xu*). *Hu* alcohol containers and *jian* water basins also began to appear in sets. By the middle of the 10th century, Zhou tombs might contain a massive collection of sets of ritual bronze vessels. At the same time, sets of graduated *zhong* bells (Figure 7.12B) and *sheng* chimestones appear with similar imagery and inscriptions. Musical instruments became increasingly important by the mid-10th century. To summarize, the custom of producing individual vessel types as sets, practiced by the Shang (e.g., with sets of *gu* or *jue* or *ding*), was continued and amplified to include various types of vessels with identical imagery in the early Western Zhou. In the middle Western Zhou period, the production of vessel sets (e.g., *dou* and *hu*) was not just further systematized but was obsessively coordinated, with emphasis on quantity rather than quality, so that by the end of the Western Zhou, these sets lost interest due to their repetitive shape and numbers and lack of meaningful imagery (see all examples illustrated in Figure 7.12). The practice of using ritual bronze vessels in rites of ancestor worship waned in favor of treating them as prestige items employed in secular entertaining and gifting.

Vessel Sets

By the middle Western Zhou, the so-called "ritual *ding* system (*ding lie fa* 鼎列法" or "*ding fa* 鼎法)" was formulated as a means of exercising control over ritual bronze ownership and use (Y. Sun 2020).[12] The system was designed to limit sacrificial types and vessel numbers, as part of a larger royal program of controlling an increasingly independent-minded aristocracy. As noted earlier in this chapter, the system permitted the king to employ sets of nine *ding, gong* (dukes) were allowed seven *ding,* with correspondingly lesser numbers permitted to *hou* (marquises), *bo* (earls), *zi* (viscounts), and *nan* (barons). Sets of *gui* were allotted in even numbers: eight to the king, six to *gong,* and so on. Later ritual texts allude to this system in describing the royal "great penned animal victim sacrifice with nine ding 大牢九鼎" celebrated by the Zhou king in the *Mingtang* and the Ancestral Temple (Yu and Gao 1978–79). Archaeological evidence indicates that the system was instantiated although numbers and titles did not necessarily adhere consistently to the ideal (Falkenhausen 2006). For example, the large tomb M2001 of the Guo state and clan at Sanmenxia in Henan probably belongs to the male head of the lineage and clan, dating to ca. mid-9th century BCE (Henan 1999). Of 3,200 artifacts from his tomb, 1,700 were bronzes: seven *ding* formed a set and three *ding* were independent; six *gui* formed a set and three were independent. Other vessel sets appeared but not in such

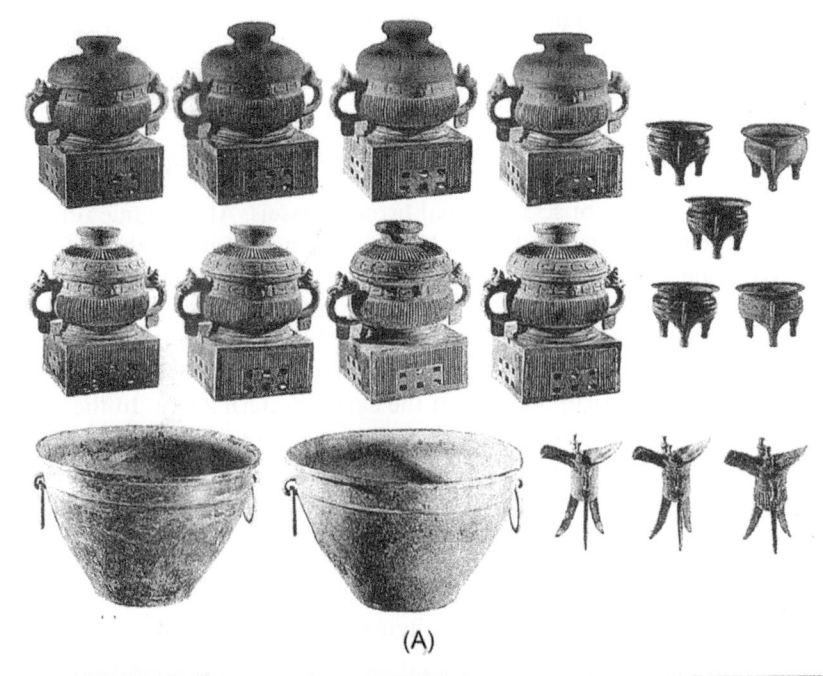

(A)

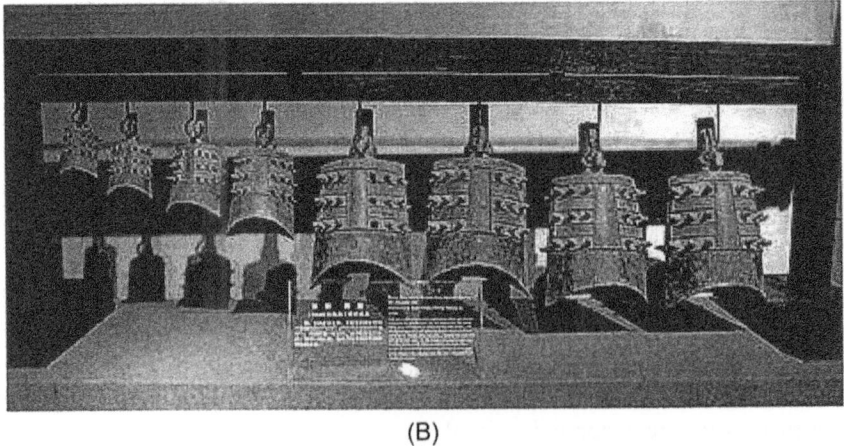

(B)

Figure 7.12 AB Late Western Zhou vessel sets with standardized imagery. (A) Eight *gui* on stands, five small tripod *ding*, two basins, three *jue*, Zhuangbai, Shaanxi cache one, third quarter of the 9th century BCE. (B) A set of suspended bronze bells, Jin Hou burial, Shanxi (A) Shaanxi 1992: 7. (B) Shanxi *et al* 2002; art-and-archaeology.com at https://in.pinter-est.com/pin/58546863897178362/

large numbers. *Ding* and *gui* vessels bear similar inscriptions identifying the owner, with the family name Li and state name Guo: "Guo Li made these precious *ding* for the purpose of ritually feasting the Li clan lineage so that for thousands and thousands of years sons and grandsons could continue to eternally honor the lineage in sacrifice" (Henansheng 1999). The *gui* inscriptions are briefer, omitting the recipient and euphemistic 'thousands and thousands of years' to read: "Guo Li made these sacrificial *gui* for use in sacrificial feasting and for eternal use by sons and grandsons." The owner may be identified as holding the rank of *hou* (marquis). Examples of other Western Zhou tombs showing interest in this practice include the Yu Bo 魚 clan cemetery at Baoji, Shaanxi (Shaanxi 1988: colorpls 6.2; 8.1 and 2; 12.1 and 2) and the Jin rulers state cemetery at Qucun, Shanxi (Shaanxisheng 2009). Some evidence from Western Zhou inscriptions corroborates the system. A range of later texts and pictorial evidence confirms a widespread belief that the spirit power of the Zhou mandate was embodied in a special set of nine *ding* (Childs-Johnson 2013).

As we shall see in the next chapter, the systematizing practice of regulating numbers and forms of ritual vessels continued during the Springs and Autumns period (see Chapter 8: Figure 8.1A–D) (sets may expand to include *dui/dou, hu, jian*), but restrictions on the number of vessels in a set were increasingly flouted. For example, the tomb of the Marquis of Zeng at Sujialong, Jingshan, Hubei, dating to the transitional period between the Western Zhou and the Springs and Autumns contained a set of nine *ding* vessels graduated in size, infringing on royal prerogative. It also contained a set of seven *gui*, just one short of the eight-*gui* set that signified the rank of king. The two largest *ding* were inscribed "Marquis of Zeng Zhongzi Youfu made these vessels for use in the *jiang* (cooked meat) sacrifice" (Hubeisheng 1999).

Funerary Jades

Sets of jade artifacts, particularly those decorating the body of the deceased, may also have been determined by rank and number, although to date sumptuary rules corroborating that assumption have not been found in Western Zhou texts. Jade face masks and body jewelry were used to cover aristocratic corpses as found in the 10th-century BCE tomb M2001 belonging to Marquis Li of the state of Guo (For a review of these finds see Feng Li 2006: 251–62). An extremely ornate set of jades not only formed a headdress and face mask, but also a pectoral made of numerous agate and nephrite pieces, probably originally bound together by a thread that is no longer extant (Figures 7.8 and 7.12). Other examples of similar mortuary jade body sets have been found in a variety of recently excavated burials associated with the Zhou aristocracy at Fufeng, Shaanxi (see e.g., *Zhongguo Yuqi Quanji* 2: colorpls 273–76). These evolved over time to become, in the Warring States and Han eras, suits that covered the entire body. The belief in the spirit power of jade to protect and preserve the physical remains of the honored dead began early with the Jade Age Liangzhu and Hongshan burials, where the highest-ranking dead were bedecked with jades (see e.g., Chapters 2–3 Figures 2.4 and 3.3). As will become evident below, the metamorphic imagery of both aristocratic jades and bronzes supported the Zhou monarchy's constant need for symbols emphasizing their divine status as Sons of *Tian* and the power they wielded as holders of *Tian*'s Mandate.

Metamorphic Imagery in Western Zhou Culture

Art, especially the art of bronze vessels, played an important propaganda role in establishing the Zhou claim to legitimacy. The Zhou kings used bronze vessels and their inscriptions, for example as manifestos addressed to the defeated Shang nobility, and rituals to emphasize the cosmic power of *Tian* and bolster their religio-political claims. The Zhou drew on metamorphic imagery developed in Shang bronze and other arts. Familiar, inherited themes of metamorphosis including the semi-human animal mask, the *feng* mythic bird and *long* mythic dragon (subordinate, in Shang bronze art, to the mask motif), abstract sun and thunder/rain symbols, cicadas, and snakes, all appear on early Western Zhou ritual artifacts. Given the Shang legacy in Zhou culture and the Zhou emphasis on continuing certain Shang sacrifices and rites for the purpose of maintaining divine control, it is safe to assume that the Zhou consciously and deliberately used metamorphic themes in art to strengthen their claim to political legitimacy. The need to decorate bronzes and jades with the numinous imagery of spirit invocation speaks loudly.

An Aggressive Style and an Awesome Aesthetic

As will be evident from the art and style of the first phase of the Western Zhou era (pre-conquest reigns and those of the first four Western Zhou kings), the Zhou were familiar with the Shang vocabulary of metamorphic imagery. Expression is characterized less by religious sentiment than by symbols of raw power and the need to flaunt their *weiyi* 畏儀, awesome majesty. The Zhou created a flamboyant and exaggerated style that was baroque, mannered, and frankly political. The sacrosanct hunted animal mask of Shang, signifying spirit communication with the deified ancestors, was intentionally exaggerated in high relief (Figure 7.13). Features of the semi-human mask appear haunting in their descriptive realism, as if physically present on earth in the personality of Zhou kings (e.g., Figure 7.13D). Tails of *long* dragons and ocellated feathers of *feng* birds are enlarged and visually eloquent: circular spirals impress by their whiplash potential; eyed plumage is ostentatiously displayed.[13] Thunder and sun symbols, decorating a band above emphatic raised and repeated lightening-like vertical bars on the Marquis of Kang *gui* (Figure 7.13B), are individually isolated

Figure 7.13 "The Awesome Style" of early Western Zhou ritual bronzes. (A) Kang
Hou *gui*, British Museum. (B) *Gui* on stand, National Asian Art Museum
31.10. (C) *You*, Poly Art Museum. (D) He *zun*, Baoji, Shaanxi. (A) After
Michaelson and Portal 2006. (B) Freer Gallery 1967: pl 66. (C) After
Poly 1999: colorpl 103, drawing 105; (D) After Zhongguo meishu 6:
colorpl 169.

as emblems of nature's relentless presence and the Zhou need to succeed
politically and spiritually in accommodating the Four Quarters and *Tian*'s
majesty. The spikes on the Freer *gui* (Figure 7.13C) similarly exuberantly
project as mighty natural forces of nature. This style of the first decades of
Western Zhou ritual art may be described as awesome and aggressive or
simply as a "Style of *Weiyi* Awesomeness."

  The imagery and style of the *you* ale bucket in the Poly Museum, Beijing,
along with the excavated Li *gui*, the Newark Art Museum *gui*, the Yu Bo *gui*,

and the Ran tetrapod *ding* in the Asian Art Museum, easily illustrate these new stylistic interests of the Western Zhou (Figure 7.13). The bucket-like *you* vessel (Figure 7.13C), although only 16.4 cm tall with a belly diameter of 19.6 cm, seems awesomely large due to the exaggeratedly prominent images of the Shang semi-human mask on its belly and lid. This is the same characteristic of supernaturally endowed *weiyi* that inflated the royal power of Zhou kings. The horn-like extensions of the belly mask image are related to the hunted deer in Shang imagery. A version of the dragon decorates the foot, and variations on the deer head and elephant head with trunk decorate the protomes of the handles, which also serve to divide the container into four strong quadrants. The plastic quality of the imagery is decidedly early Western Zhou in style, being deeply undercut and almost independent as sculpture. The semi-human attributes of the mask are indelible: ears, eyes, and nose of a human face stand out in high relief, treated as if they were modeled in clay (which indeed they were, at an early stage of creating the piece-mold for the vessel's casting). These features are disruptive and camouflage the underlying svelte ceramic-like form of the vessel.

The group of *gui* on square stands from the Earl Yu tomb in Baoji, Shaanxi may be viewed as experimental variations on the new form of the cosmologically symbolical serving vessel (Figure 7.10). On one of these *gui*, two prominently flanged handles are formed from an upright bird body crowned by the naturalistic couchant front part of a tiger; identical abstract tiger masks cover the entire surface of the front and back belly sides, while a buffalo mask with flaring horns decoratively divides the base into four quadrants (Figure 7.10C). This emphasis on cosmologically oriented geometry recalls the Jade Age *cong* prismatic jade tube with a circular interior and four outer corners forming a square and decorated at four corners with outsized demonic masks (see Chapter 3: Figure 3.2). The bell attached to the underside of the square base of the *gui* probably served to attract spirits with its sound. On another *gui,* the square base is decorated with buffalo horn masks, whereas the belly and lid of the upper vessel are decorated with alternating large-scale whirling thunder and vertical *long* dragon images (Figure 7.10AB). Savagery is again emphasized by the high relief of images, as outspoken in mood as the combination of images is direct. This daring reinterpretation that disrupts the classical expression of Shang metamorphic imagery may be criticized for its hubristic overstatement, a bombastic style of exaggeration that aims to impress and control the realm and take over the metamorphic power of the defunct Shang rulership.

Other early Western Zhou bronze vessels expressing "*weiyi*" (or simply *yi*, "spirit power") show similar characteristics of flamboyance and overstatement. The Tian Wang *gui*, He *zun,* and Li *gui*, discussed above, are three patently readable examples (see e.g., Figures 7.1 and 7.2). Flanges, handles, and masks with projecting wild sheep horns or interpretations of the spiral-tailed *long* are all large and interruptive of the vessel contour – the latter too are overstated power images aggressively asserting Zhou's victory over, and replacement of, the Shang. The upright profile *feng* birds creating four corner flanges with their hooked beaks on the Ran tetrapod *ding* similarly vehemently divide the vessel into quadrants (Figure 7.14B). The dragons with coiled tails on the *gui* vessel with square base are similarly awesome and barbaric in expression (Figure 7.11). These inherited icons of the hunted animal, semi-human masks, *feng* bird, and *long* dragons evidently represent the awe-inspiring spirit power of *Tian* and *Tian*'s sons, the kings of Zhou, rather than directly representing the royal Shang power of metamorphosis. These are perpetuated symbols of royal divinity and cosmological power.

When the Poly Museum *you* bronze bucket was first published, it was suggested that the face was an anthropomorphized image of the deity Tian or Tian Di, which would mimic the concept of earlier Shang images of anthropomorphized images of Di (Yu Wc 1999). This interpretation is generically accurate in the sense that Tian controlled the fate of the dynasty, as Di wielded power over the natural and human realms in Shang times. The semi-human mask images, although individualized initially according to combinations of attributes from the human and supernatural realms, are fundamentally reflections of the Sky Power and ancestral deities, realized in the stylistic guises invented by Shang and later Zhou specialists. The awesomeness of both takes their meanings from the awesomeness of an invoker who may be masked, or by the icon of masked imagery that symbolizes spirit power. It is the king, in his role as host and chief invocator, who possesses the spirits that descend and ascend, whether in the *Tiantang* or ancestral temple.

The Ubiquitous *Feng* Icon

In addition to the taste for a flamboyant style of representation to signify their new royal power, the Zhou also chose to exploit an inherited symbol, the mythic *feng* 鳳 or *fenghuang* 鳳凰 bird (see earlier analyses of *feng* by Childs-Johnson 1989). This new Western Zhou symbol of divine spirit power became, by the middle Western Zhou era of Kings Mu and Zhao, a signifier of mandated Zhou kingship in much the same way as the baroque style of a wild animal mask a century earlier had touted the new religio-political power source of Zhou. Corroborative literary evidence for the adoption of the bird symbol is the conception of the vermilion bird as the harbinger of Zhou power (see pages 156–157). The metamorphic power images of dragon and *yi* mask do not disappear but were sublimated to this new emphasis on flight and divinity.

The *feng* bird image, the symbol of spirit flight, is the messenger of Di in Shang divinations and imagery (see Childs-Johnson 1989). As were the *long* with coiled tail and horned or antlered *yi* mask, the early Zhou representation of *feng* was also bold and emphatic. See, for example, the pre-Conquest vessels, such as the *jia* excavated at Sucun, Chengguxian, Shaanxi province in Figure 7.14F, the King Cheng period Ran tetrapod *ding* (Figure 7.14C),

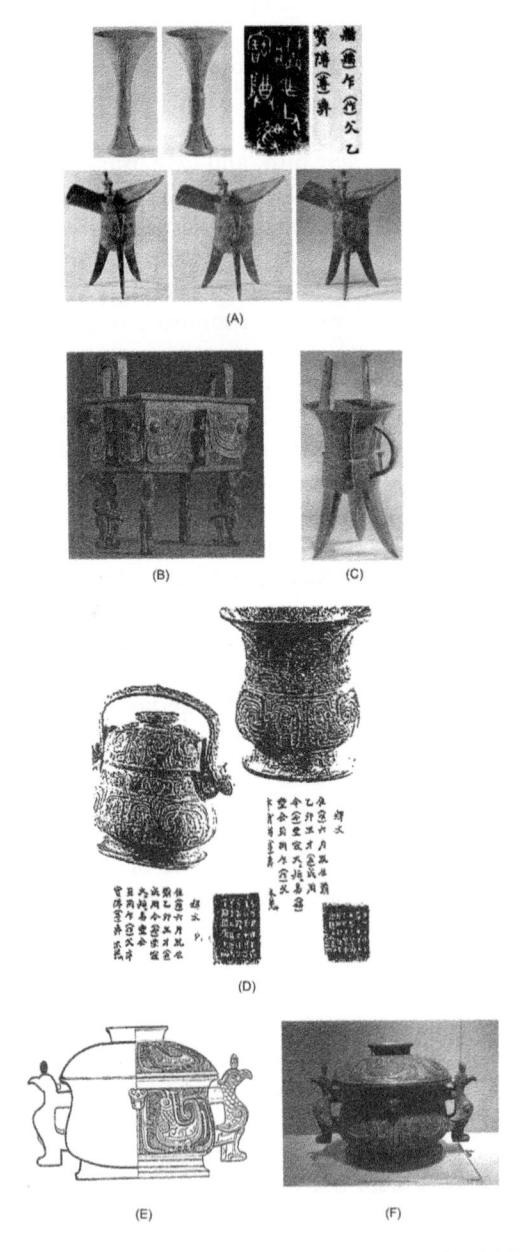

Figure 7.14 Dominant *feng* bird motif decorating early and middle Western Zhou period bronze ritual vessels. (A) Duke Tanfu *jue* and *gui* set and their inscription dedicated to the Shang ancestor Fu Yi, Fufeng, Shaanxi. (B) Ran tetrapod *ding*, Asian Art Museum. (C) Bronze *jia* with *yi* mask and bird imagery, Sucun, Chengguxian, Shaanxi. (D) Feng Bo *you* and *zu*. (E) Drawing of the Dong *gui*, Zhuangbai, Fufeng. (A) Zhongguo *qingtong* 1988.4: 85, colorpl 89; 90, colorpl 95; Shaanxi 1980:17, pl 1; 46–47, pls 25, 26. (B) Courtesy of the Asian Art Museum. (C) Shaanxi 1980: pl 113. (D) After Cao 2005: 7.

and the *jia, jue,* and *gu* alcohol vessels belonging to Feng, also probably of pre-Conquest date (Figure 7.14A). The latter three types of alcohol vessels completely disappeared by the end of the Western Zhou period, yet the fact that the bird is the only décor on them in an early context coeval with Late Shang underscores the interest of Zhou in adopting this new symbol. By the middle Western Zhou period (mid-10th–9th centuries), the stylized, imaginary bird based somewhat fancifully on the Asian peafowl became the single most prominent image on ritual artifacts, bronzes, jades, woven tomb covers, etc. The bird symbol almost never appeared alone in Shang period *gu, jue,* or *jia* and never as the only image on any Shang ritual vessel.

The Western Zhou bird type differs from the Shang type by the representationally descriptive interpretation of a crest and tail, clearly ocellated feathers, and by their new disposition on the surface of the vessel: they do not flank in profile a metamorphic mask but exist as independent symbols in profile. The two-dimensional bird takes over the entire theme of vessel imagery, including forming in profile the protruding handles of the vessel (e.g., Figure 17.14G). The Zhou unified the symbolic theme by their focus on one mythic image decorating one or a set of bronze vessels (Figure 17.14D), reinforcing the idea that this image is a standard symbol of royal divinity and supernatural power. In turn, the Zhou elaborated on the mythic *feng* symbol by reverting the head of the bird to display a calligraphic composition of swirling tail and crest feathers (Figure 17.14D). By the middle Western Zhou period, the *feng* became a major unifying image, defining one, a pair, or a set of vessels.

Some of the songs in the *Shijing*, dated to the Western Zhou period (Shaughnessy 1997, 165), specifically alluding to the mythical bird. In one ode, the "Juan a" (卷阿 "Bend in the River," Mao Ode 252), the bird acts as wings to King Cheng in unifying the Four Quarters, a term that both describes the Zhou realm and serves as a metaphor for the Zhou cosmos. Duke Shao lauds King Cheng for his success as sovereign, full of majesty (*wei* 畏(威)) as Host Invocator (主祝) of all spirits (百神), whereby the Four Quarters take him as their model. In token of his successful rule, flying *fenghuang* birds soar to the sky and sing. The relevant stanzas of this rather long poem are numbers five and seven through nine, which we translate as follows:

> 5. You have helpers and supporters,
>   they are filial and virtuous.
>   they are your vanguard and your wings.
>   O happy and courteous sovereign,
>   the Four Quarters take you as their model.
> 7. The *fenghuang* take flight,
>   Whirr, whirr go their wings.
>   They alight in their appropriate places.
>   Your Majesty's many admirable officers

Are ready to serve you,
Loving you, Son of *Tian*. The *fenghuang* take flight,
Whirr, whirr go their wings.
They soar to the sky [*Tian*].
Your Majesty's many admirable officers
Acknowledge Your Lordship's Mandate.
You are loved by the common people.
9. The *fenghuang* sing out
From their high mound
The *wutong* trees flourish there
In the morning sunlight.
How thickly grow the leaves,
How melodious the song.

The rare appearance of the *fenghuang* bird was understood as an affirmation of the dynasty's legitimacy and the king's virtue. The *fenghuang* is mentioned in many texts of the received tradition, including the *Mozi*, the *Guoyu*, and the *Shanhaijing*, a text that is clearly related to myths of Chinese antiquity (Fracasso; Birrell; Hwang 1996a). In some texts, the *feng* is defined as the male of the species, and the *huang* as the female, but there is no sign of sexual differentiation as these spirit birds are depicted on Western Zhou bronzes. In the poem quoted above, the *fenghuang* is described as singing; in some texts of the received tradition (see e.g., *Lüshi chunqiu* 5.5), music is said to have originated with the singing of the *fenghuang*. In early Zhou times, the *fenghuang* was probably understood to be a manifestation of the emblematic Vermilion Bird of the Zhou, as described in the *Bamboo Annals*:

> In the 32nd year of [Shang] King Xin [1059 BCE], five stars gathered in the Lunar Lodge "Chamber" (*Fang* 房), and the Vermilion Bird alighted on the Zhou Altar of the Soil (see Pankenier 2013: 195–97 for this and other omens connected with the Vermilion Bird).

The Deterioration of Metamorphic Imagery in the Late Western Zhou Period

By the Late Western Zhou period, the previously ubiquitous and powerful bird imagery began to deteriorate both artistically and symbolically. In form and style of expression, this deterioration is witnessed: one, by a composition that represents more a metaphysical realm of the unknown rather than royal symbolism; two, by the degeneration of the *yi* mask, the *long* dragon, and the *feng* bird into abstract undulating wave-like patterns or grooves that show only a hint of their former life as numinous symbols;

three, by *feng* or *long* as independent décor protruding as sculptures aligning the vessel exterior or vessel surface; and four, inscriptions that by the end of the period become more important than, and coincide with, the loss of vessel imagery (see bronzes illustrated in Figure 7.14).

A comparison between the forceful bird imagery of the Ran tetrapod *ding* of early Western Zhou date (Figure 7.14B) and the potpourri of animal and human images encrusted on the small, wheeled carriage from Taiyuan, Shanxi, of late Western Zhou date (Figure 7.15C) underscores the politicized religious extremes of the Western Zhou conquerors. By late in the era, ca 800 BCE, the emblem of Zhou royal divinity has lost its old splendid fierceness and appears more like a tame pheasant that one might find in a zoo. In profile relief on four miniature walls, this once heroic symbol of the Zhou Mandate is now lost amidst a menagerie of small-scale animal forms (Figure 7.15A). Conglomerate images, including the inherited Shang tiger as a pair of wheels or flanges, varied by the addition of cervid pedicel- or antler-like flanges that vertically align the six edges of the carriage, hiding the once prominent *feng* images on the vessel body almost completely from view. That mélange of motifs, including small humans, is combined more for their novel effects in representing 'greater' nature than in representing centralized kingly power. The same tendency is represented on the *zun* in the shape of a cervid (Figure 7.15C). An *yi* mask decorates the belly in flat relief, but images of dragons and birds now independently decorate the sides and tops of vessel, taking on a life of their own. This conglomerate imagery represents the degeneration of politically charged symbols. Vessels also increasingly took shapes of animals and were reduced to miniatures, a tendency reflecting preciosity and hyperbolic embellishment.

Another tendency representing the devolution of imagery is represented by abstract, undulating motifs with only a trace of the eyed peafowl feather or mask. The décor on the *hu* (Figure 7.15D left), for example, is divided into bands, the top of which exposes one ocellated feather per undulation, the middle band one dissolved *yi* mask right-side up or upside down per undulation, and third the same as the second but bigger in size. As with the vessels discussed above, the imagery lies flat across the surface of the vessel. Changes in both the decoration and the function of vessels of this sort are revealed by their inscriptions. For example, the inscription on the *hu* alcohol container reads: "…. On the *jimao* day of the tenth month of the 26th year, Fan Jusheng cast this wedding *hu* for use as a wedding present for his eldest child, Meng Feiguai. Many sons and grandsons treasure it forever" (Figure 7.15C). Clearly, the disappearance of a strictly religious use of the vessel, replaced by a more secular use as a wedding gift, accompanied the degeneration of imagery. At the same time award, inscriptions became longer and more like historical documents, as if the inscription was of primary importance at the expense of religious symbols and icons and employment in rituals.

Figure 7.15 Representative late Western Zhou (ca 9th–8th century BCE) bronzes and inscriptions. (A) Jing Shu cervid-shaped *zun*, M163:33, Zhangji-apo, Shaanxi. (B) Small wheeled bronze box, Taiyuan, Shanxi. (C) One of a pair of *hu* bronze vessels, Meixian, Shaanxi, Late Western Zhou, early 8th century BCE. (D) Zhao Ru Xing *hu* with inscription recording marriage contract. (E) Maogong *ding* and inscription with 497 characters, excavated Qishan, Shaanxi, King Xuan era (r 827/25–782 BCE). (A) After Zhongguo shehui 1999: pl 113:2. (B) After Shanxi 1996: Figure 76. (C) After Shaanxi 2003: pls 20, 21. (D) After Shaanxi 1980: pls 31–32, 29. (E) After https://warehouse-13-artifact-database.fandom.com/wiki/Mao_Gong_*Ding* (colorpl) and National Library of China at https://www.wdl.org/en/item/13542/ (inscription).

Similar degeneration of imagery and the presence of long historical inscriptions (which still mostly document awards made by the king or high aristocrats) characterize other bronze vessels. As is well known, the Duke Mao tripod *ding* inscription is the longest one preserved, totaling 497 words (Figure 7.15E). That vessel, in turn, is decorated by the final phase of degenerated imagery, a band of abstract ocellated feathers composed of double circles and elongated oblong lines. This degeneration of imagery characterizes most bronze vessels of late Western Zhou date, as illustrated in Figure 7.14.

Underlying symbols and metamorphic meaning nonetheless would soon experience a revival with a continuation of old themes of animal and mythic imagery, now designed for personal enjoyment but with a narrative thrust embracing both supernatural and human subjects. On the Meixian pair of *hu* (only one illustrated, Figure 7.15C), for example, dating to the late Western Zhou (early 8th century BCE), old and new images are combined. In the subsequent Springs and Autumns and Warring States periods, the old wave hump with an abstract ocellated feather pattern, blended with the new composition of intertwined snake-like dragon bodies and bird protomes, came into favor (Figure 7.14C).

The Metamorphic Humanoid Spirit on Western Zhou Jades and Bronzes

Small but significant jade artworks of Western Zhou date appear to be directly tied in meaning to certain of the rites with metamorphic implications carried out by Zhou kings during state ceremonies. These jades are primarily associated with the innovative jade body cover and the woven shroud (see above Figure 7.8). Multiple jade shapes with imagery decorated the face and body of the deceased, and woven shrouds with metamorphic imagery were laid on tops of coffins (see e.g. Figure 7.9). A Longshan-style jade head of a humanoid with crowning *feng* bird was excavated in one of the aristocratic Jin burials, suggesting it was a prized heirloom (see Figure 5.6 in Chapter 5).

The predominant image of the semi-human (humanoid) with partial *feng* bird and *long* dragon elements may represent the king or his speaker during the most profound, solemn, and moving invocation rites undertaken in the Hall of *Tian*. The main difference between the humanoid images of the Western Zhou era and those of the Shang era is in attributes. The semi-human form of Western Zhou date typically was associated with iconic *feng* and *long* body parts, whereas that of Shang origin decorating ritual artworks and vessels more often took on hunted wild animal attributes but also was combined with *feng* and *long* images. In cases where the entire body of the humanoid was depicted, both Shang and Zhou versions were represented in "fetal" pose, a trope for spirit rebirth, and spirit metamorphosis. See, for example, the various jades decorated with the semi-human icon illustrated in Figure 7.16. Flanking and intertwined *feng* birds and versions of the profile dragon typically encompass the humanoid *yi* personage with striated hair band and S-shaped body.

These jades mostly derive from burials and form part of a corpse's body cover (see Figure 7.17A) or were assembled into a pectoral made out of multiple pieces of jade strung together (Figure 7.17B), a forerunner of the Han period jade suit. Variations do, however, appear. For example, an excavated jade figurine from Tomb No. 8 in the necropolis of the Marquis of Jin in Quwo, Shanxi (Gu 2005.3: colorpl. 89) is flat yet depicts on front and back a human wearing a formal robe, headdress, and shoes. The face is that of a human. Yet the bifurcated headdress ends of the sleeves and two feet form dragon heads in profile. Other excavated small jade figurines depict costumed humans wearing a headdress in combination with a big-horn sheep head. mask on the back of the human head. Other versions simply represent the profile icons of *feng* and *long* without a humanoid body (see e.g., the jade handle excavated from Tomb No.31 of a Jin Marquis, Quwo, Shanxi in Gu 2005.3: colorpl. 100). Still others, and the most common in jade, show in profile the semi-human head with a fetal positioned body made of dragon and bird parts (Figure 7.16). The *long* is typically coiled in forming the arms of the humanoid. The profile *feng* may crown the head of the humanoid. Sometimes the body of the profile human takes on the body of the *feng* bird. Sometimes there are multiple small-scale humanoids attached to the back or head of a larger humanoid (Figure 7.16C and I).

Other versions of the humanoid *yi*, the icon of human metamorphosis, are represented in bronze. Two well-published examples include the bronze *yue* ax blade from burial M13 at Zhuyuangou, Baoji in Shanxi (Figure 7.16J) and the bronze *dao* knife from the Freer Gallery of Art in Washington, D.C. (Figure 7.16K). The latter two versions are intriguing for the complexity and detail of their compositions. The humanoid on the Baoji ax, for example, is distinguished by a portrait-like profile version of the male human head with Mongoloid features and a long ponytail. His upper body comprises the typical coiled dragon form, yet the lower body continues in seated fetal form with elastic legs that end in claws, just as was the case in so many of the Shang interpretations of this metamorphic icon. The complete body of the humanoid on the Freer blade is also represented in profile, with folded arms ending in fingers and toes as claws. The face is scarified on the cheek, and the jaw is open, exposing fangs. Both of these complete-bodied humanoid deities are framed by tigers.

Additional full-bodied renderings in bronze of the humanoid add variation to the metamorphic interpretation of humans. One shows a kneeling human covered by what apparently is the complete pelt of a tiger (Figure 7.16H), and another hugs the back of the humanoid (Figure 7.16G), in a version that immediately recalls the two *you* of Shang date that depict a tiger symbolically devouring a crouched human below its jaw. The human's hair is shown in one image, as are the long locks of hair in most other humanoid *yi* images. A final example from a burial at Rujiazhuang is the bronze ax featuring a human with long hair and Mongolian facial features

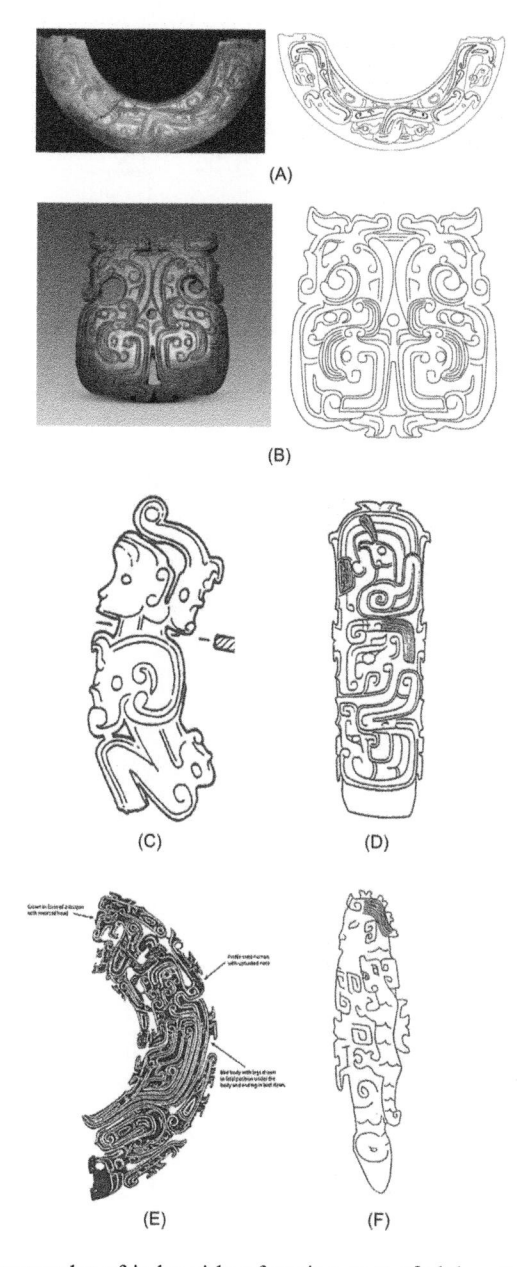

Figure 7.16 Ten examples of jades either forming part of elaborate jade necklaces and pectorals lying on the fore-body of the corpse (A–H) or forming weapon insignia (I, J). Note these figural jades feature metamorphic imagery of the mythic long dragon, *feng* bird, and semi-human spirit in fetal pose. Jades were excavated from burials belonging to Peng and Jin state rulers at Yangshe and Beizhao, Shanxi. (A) M1:30 BM1:74; (B-J) DM2158; C M1:74, M1:1; M1:75; M1:88; M1:5. Based on Childs-Johnson 2002: Figure 7,8, 9AB, 10, 14.

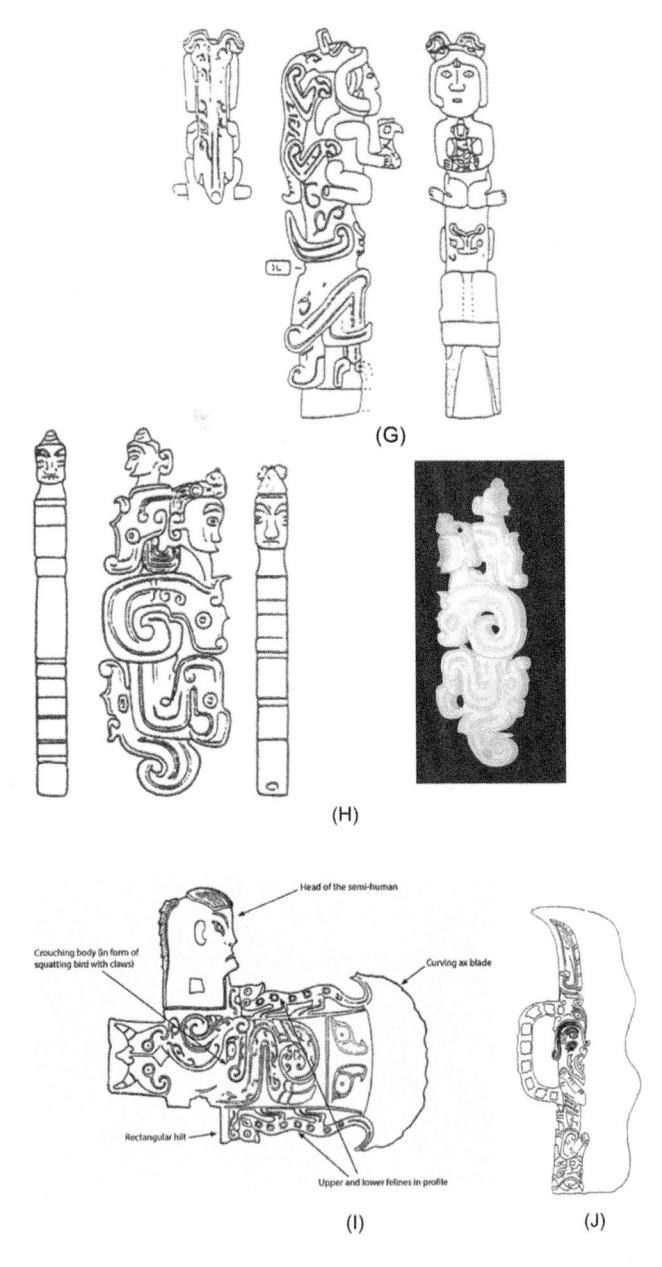

Figure 7.16 (Continued)

in a crouched position riding a wild animal symbolized in the profile head of what is probably a tiger (Figure 7.16J).

All of these images are testimony to the continued importance of the profound belief in spirit transformation that permeated the thinking of the royal lineage and the aristocracy during the Western Zhou period (Childs-Johnson 2001). Representationally, the images fit the requirements that defined metamorphic imagery in Shang times (see pp.), especially the tendency to mix real and mythic elements such as the real human body and head with the *long, feng,* or wild animal. Although the Zhou chose to emphasize the humanoid by assembling its form from dragon and bird parts, the image is still the same icon that defines belief in metamorphosis. And although clothing of Zhou aristocrats has only recently been excavated from one tomb, it is easy to imagine the type of outfit the king might wear – a tiger pelt or dragon and *feng* robe, and a carved wooden lacquered *feng* headdress. It is very possible that beyond the significance of human-to-spirit

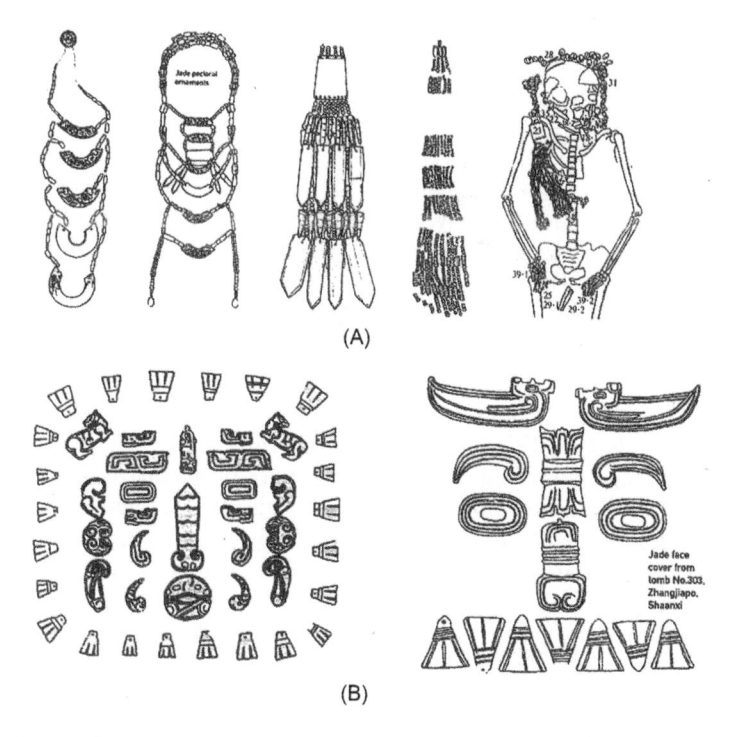

(A)

(B)

Figure 7.17 Jades serving as pectorals, necklaces, hair ornaments, slit-disk earrings, buckles, flat plaques, and face masks, Western Zhou period. (A) Jade pectoral ornaments. (B) Jade face "masks", burials Nos 62 and 92, Guo state cemetery, Shanxi. (A) After Sun Q 2008 (B) After Childs-Johnson 2010: 34, Figures 9, 16, and 43.

metamorphosis we are witnessing the experience of the filial descendant or Impersonator of the Dead who accompanied the Zhou king at the time of the Da Feng rite in the Temple of *Tian* or during other royal ceremonies. The Invocator, as related in the "Chuci" and "Shengmin" poems of the *Shijing*, is probably none other than the king, who is able to bring down the spirits of former kings, King Wu and King Wen, as well as to ascend to them in spirit himself. This ability to descend and ascend speaks to the transformative spirit as represented so prominently throughout the history of Zhou and Shang art. All of these jade and bronze parts discussed belong to aristocratic tombs and thus reflect directly religious belief of the ruling elite. Because these human-based images of Western Zhou date are standardized as a type of metamorphic image, on the other hand, they might describe a generic quasi-shamanic representation that could be either the king, possibly an elite member such as the representative of the dead, or – as is true of the image in Shang times – a manifestation of Di or Tian, the Cosmological Sky Power. Identifying the king as a type of "institutionalized invocator" helps to clarify the ruler's cosmological power as a divinity, a Son of Tian and one with the Mandate to rule the Four Quarters of the universe, not to mention his ability to invoke royal dead spirits.

The End of the Western Zhou

The long reign (957–17) of King Mu was a time of royal confidence and cultural cohesion in the middle Western Zhou period. His reign witnessed a spread of literacy, increasingly bureaucratized government in both the royal capital and in the territorial states (with many offices filled as hereditary aristocratic prerogatives), and a successful defense of the northern borderlands against invasions of non-Sinitic peoples. King Mu is remembered especially for his love of travel. He evidently made several royal progressions throughout the Zhou domain. His travels, fantastically inflated, form the subject of the *Mu tianzi zhuan* ("Tale of the Son of Tian Mu), a Warring States Period text that has been described as China's first work of narrative fiction[14] (Porter 1996). King Mu was followed by several undistinguished monarchs to round out the middle Western Zhou period. It was then that the royal court began to lose significant amounts of power to the Lords of the Lands.

The years 877–41 saw the reign of King Li, a stereotypical "bad king" who ushered in the Late Western Zhou period and who did substantial damage to his dynasty without quite forfeiting Tian's Mandate. While his faults are probably exaggerated in later texts of the received tradition, it does appear that King Li neglected his religious duties, oppressed the people, and presided over a corrupt and incompetent government that accelerated the bleeding away of power from the central government to the territorial lords. His reign was marked by natural disasters, famines, and invasions.

King Li's son, King Xuan (r. 841–782 BCE), occupied the throne for the next 46 years and managed to stave off the end of Western Zhou. Disaster ensued with the reign of King You (782–71), famous for the neglect of his duties (especially his religious duties) and his habit of indulging the whims of his favorite concubine. An invasion of northern people in 771 marked the end; the western capital was captured and sacked, and King You was killed. In an act marked mainly by self-interest, the lords of Qin and Jin rescued the remnants of the Zhou royal family and helped them restore a Zhou court in the eastern capital. But that was almost a sham; in the following Springs and Autumns period, the Zhou monarchy survived only in vestigial form, and all power flowed to the Lords of the Lands. These momentous events were accompanied by great changes in religion and its iconography.

Notes

1　In pre-modern times, the absence of artificial lighting meant that the night sky was much darker, and stars correspondingly brighter and more conspicuous, than is the case today.

2　For studies of Western Zhou history, see Shaughnessey; Li Feng 2013; Hsü and Linduff 1988; Khaytina 2020: ch.17: 367–402.

3　However, in Shang bone inscriptions, the *Yin* rite is consistently held on the day *jiazi*, the first day of the 60-day cycle and of the Five Rite cycle of sacrifices to the Shang royal lineage (see e.g., examples cited in Yao and Xiao 1992: 721–24).

4　For a related translation, see Zhang Ys 2001.

5　Based on Shirakawa 1962: 48.1, 167–80; also see translations in Li Feng 2006: 63; Cook and Goldin 2016: 16–18.

6　Hu rpt *shang*: 292–94; *Jiaguwen Zidian* 1989, 1993, Siquan Zishu Pub.: 5–6; Childs-Johnson 2008; some scholars identify the occasional use of 上下 with the former kings Shang Jia and Xiao Yi, see Chang Tt 1970: note 5, page 86.

7　The location of the sun, the moon, and the naked-eye-visible planets was expressed in terms of the 28 Lunar Lodges (*xiu*宿), constellations of unequal angular extension ranged along the celestial equator. An astral body observed to be in one or another of the Lodges would remain there even during daylight hours and so could be tracked in the daytime or when it was below the horizon. The system of Lodges appears to have been very ancient, dating back perhaps to the time of the Longshan culture's Taosi observatory. The antiquity of the *xiu* system is inferred from named asterisms that do not match up with their observed positions because of the precession of the equinoxes. (Nivison and Pang 1990).

8　See Li Feng 2006: 110–11) for an explanation of the terms fief and *feng* 封.

9　See also the map illustrated by Song Zh 2005.shang: Figure 36, which distinguishes between "actual" power and influence; Wang Zz 2013: 466–95.

10　This graph has also been translated *yin* 飲 / 酉欠 by Yao and Xiao 1998: 0785.

11　See Owen 1996: "Foreword," p. xv "The oldest poems, the temple hymns of the royal house of Zhou, may date as early as 1000 B.C....".

12　Cook and Goldin; Dobson and others cite numerous references in bronze inscriptions and received classics for Shang over-indulgence in millet ale.

13　For the original identification of this system, see Yu and Gao 1978–79. This system is not a break from Shang tradition as proposed by Rawson in 1985: 289–96 but rather a continuation of Shang vessel sets reorganized into a collective socializing system.

14　References to spirit birds in transmitted texts sometimes confuse the *feng* with the pheasant *zhi*雉, but depictions of *feng* birds on Zhou bronzes are clearly derived from the peafowl. See Childs-Johnson 1989.

8 The Springs and Autumns Period and Beyond: Revitalized Metamorphic Imagery, the Spirit Journey, and Chu as Cultural Leader

Introduction

During the Eastern Zhou Period (771–221 BCE), despite the disruption of royal power and the rapid devolution of the Zhou realm into multiple states, the polities of the Sinitic world shared a common religious-political heritage. The concept of spirit transformation, the expression of metamorphism in art, and a commitment to *sifang* cosmology continued to inform religion and dynastic ideology throughout the East Asian Heartland Region.

With the killing of King You and the sacking of the western capital at Zongzhou, the Western Zhou Period came to an end.[1] The surviving members of the Zhou royal family became refugees, escorted to the eastern capital of Chengzhou under the protection of the lords of Qin and Jin, who undoubtedly saw an opportunity to dominate the House of Zhou and profit at its expense. A young Zhou prince ascended the throne to rule as King Ping; his 52-year reign brought some badly needed stability to the newly constituted Eastern Zhou state. But compared to the Western Zhou, the Eastern Zhou monarchy was drastically weakened. The royal domain shrank to a small fraction of its former dimensions (much of the rest was absorbed into Qin and Jin); the Eastern Zhou kings no longer had any territory to award as gifts to meritorious nobles and bureaucrats. Nor did they have any independent military force of their own. Judged by the old criterion that kingship should be "fear-inspiring" (*weiyi* 威儀), the Eastern Zhou kings looked pale and weak. Their wealth, measured in palaces and temples, luxury goods, agricultural land, and dependent peasants, was far inferior to that of the Lords of the Lands (*zhuhou* 諸侯), the rulers of major states. And yet they survived as nominal holders of the Mandate of *Tian*, seemingly respected by the Lords of the Lands but covertly dominated and manipulated by them.

Against this background, belief in metamorphism continued unchallenged as the basis for political legitimacy expressed in luxurious material goods and ritual behavior, even though cultural leadership drained away from the attenuated royal house of Zhou. As the Springs and Autumns

DOI: 10.4324/9781003341246-8

Period unfolded, a new synergy of forces governing the artistic expression of the 8th through 3rd centuries BCE subtly took root, expressed not only in new bronze décor but in the other arts of jade, lacquered wood, and painting on silk. Competition amongst the Lords of the Lands was unceasing; military and political rivalry was sometimes sublimated in aesthetic competition in the creation of sumptuous and titillating works of art. Against a background of profound belief in the spirit world of metamorphism, metamorphic imagery was enlisted in the service of personal pleasure and the expression of refined taste.

The first 300 years of the Eastern Zhou era are known as the Springs and Autumns Period, taking its name from a chronicle kept by the lords of Lu, an important state in what is now southern Shandong Province. Strictly speaking, the *Springs and Autumns* (*Chunqiu* 春秋) covers only the years 722–479 BCE, but historians use the appellation to cover the entire first phase of the Eastern Zhou Period, beginning in 771 BCE. The second phase of the Eastern Zhou is the Warring States Period, 479–221 BCE. This era witnessed the end of the Bronze Age and the rise of the powerful southern state of Chu as the most important stimulant driving innovations in China's elitist art. This is the last phase in which the metamorphic religion of early China was expressed in imagery that evoked awe and fear, drawing on the power of the great realm of living nature. By the middle and late phases of the Springs and Autumns Period (632–479 BCE), the spirit world and the mundane world diverged; historical consciousness emerged, and the first examples of narrative art were created. Materials other than bronze were exploited to celebrate metamorphic belief. Distinctive forms of art associated with the expression of *sifang* 四方 cosmology and metamorphism spread throughout the Sinitic world during the Eastern Zhou period.

The Springs and Autumns Annals

The *Springs and Autumns* was compiled, presumably by professional scribes tasked with that duty, for the dukes (*gong* 公) of Lu. It presents a view of events in the first three centuries of the Eastern Zhou Period as they affected the Lu state and society. Entries in the *Springs and Autumns* are tied to the chronology of the dukes of Lu and typically are confined to a laconic recitation of facts. A typical entry reads as follows:

> Duke Xi, twenty-eighth year. In summer, in the fourth month, on the day *jisi*, the Lord of Jin, with armed forces from Qi, Song, and Qin, fought with a person from Chu at Chengpu. The Chu army was disgracefully defeated.

When multiple states are mentioned by aristocratic title in a single entry, Lu always is listed first; other states are listed in order of the rank of their ruling house. Other conventions in the recording of events are judgmental. For example, in this entry, the name of the Chu general is suppressed (he is identified anonymously and condescendingly as "a person from Chu") to indicate the duke of Lu's disapproval of his crushing defeat at Chengpu (Van Auken 2011: 577).

Other Sources of Eastern Zhou History

Transmitted texts in China's long recorded history mostly date from the Warring States Period and beyond, although some classical texts, such as the Book of Odes (*Shijing* 詩經) and the Book of Documents (*Shujing* 書 經 or *Shangshu* 尚書) probably include material dating back as far as the Western Zhou Period (Shaughnessy 1993: 376–89). Texts in the received tradition that purport to record events, beliefs, and practices of the Western Zhou and Springs and Autumns periods must be used with caution, being colored by later attitudes (Khayutina 2019: 157–80). Inscriptions on bronze vessels became conventionalized and less informative. An entirely new source of early Chinese history is texts written on bamboo slips, excavated from tombs dating mainly to the Warring States Period. Many derive from the state of Chu because of geological conditions; the water-logged soil of that region was especially conducive to the preservation of organic materials. These texts on bamboo strips belong to a new category of burial goods, ranging from slips listing an inventory of tomb goods and funerary gifts received to texts on a wide range of subjects, including texts describing and recording rituals, cosmological texts and diagrams, and texts relating to the journey of the soul in the afterlife (C Cook 2006a; Major and Cook 2017). Taken as a whole, these excavated documents provide important new information about *sifang* cosmology and spirit metamorphosis.

Bamboo texts found in burials are particularly revealing about belief in the afterlife and what practices provided safe passage to the other world. Among the earliest known tomb texts is an account of the illness (perhaps stomach cancer) and death of a Chu official, Shao Tuo, who died in 433 BCE, early in the Warring States Period (C Cook 2006a). It describes the efforts of Shao Tuo and his physicians to identify and placate, or sometimes to exorcize, the spirits that were making him ill. Those efforts were founded on a shamanic understanding of the metamorphic power of deceased human ancestors and nature spirits. This fundamental understanding of the nature of ghosts and spirits informed both Shang and Western Zhou belief systems. But whereas in the Shang, only the king and his diviners had the authority to receive the metamorphic spirits as guests and have direct dealings with them, by Shao Tuo's time divination, exorcism, and other such interventions in the spirit world were available to a much wider slice of the populace. This is the major divide between the spirit world of the pre-Eastern Zhou and the spirit world of the Eastern Zhou.

Territorial Consolidation and Continuation of Metamorphic Belief and Sifang Cosmology

One of the principal duties of the Zhou kings was to preserve and defend the lineages of rulers of the various territorial states. Aggression of one state against another was a violation of ritual norms, and the expected response of the king was to raise an army (relying on other states to supply chariots and troops) and deter the aggressor. Such military operations were referred to as "punitive expeditions." Such operations were feasible during the Western Zhou when the Zhou royal house was independently powerful and directly controlled a substantial territory (though even then, aggressors were not always deterred). They were entirely unfeasible in Eastern Zhou when the Zhou kings were not much more than figureheads. The few instances of royal punitive expeditions during the 8th century BCE were markedly unsuccessful, and none were undertaken after the end of that century. As a result, large states faced few or no barriers to preying upon small states, invading, and conquering them, extinguishing their ruling families, and incorporating their territory into the larger domains of the conquering lords. The number of territorial states decreased steadily throughout the period, with large states annexing smaller ones and thereby growing steadily larger and more powerful.

The Lords of the Lands attempted to bring some measure of order to the fraught political situation of the Springs and Autumns era (see the analysis of Hsü 1965: 53–54). Some of the most powerful of the Lords of the Lands agreed to establish a system whereby the rulers of territorial states would acknowledge one of their numbers as *ba* 霸, "hegemon," a *primus inter pares* authorized to act on behalf of the Zhou king. As described, and perhaps idealized, in later texts, the system appears to have brought to the Middle Phase II of the Springs and Autumns Period a measure of stability greater than it would otherwise have enjoyed. The *ba* system (Major and Cook 2017: 134–35) nonetheless collapsed after the reign of the fifth hegemon, and another unstable period ensued, from the mid-6th to mid-5th century BCE, amidst shifting and mutually hostile alliances of northern and southern states under the leadership of Jin and Chu. The rulers of Chu symbolically denied the special status of the Zhou monarch as Son of Tian by adopting for themselves the royal title *wang* 王, "king"; this gesture of insubordination was followed by other Lords of the Lands, who, during the Warring States Period, also began to style themselves the kings (*wang*) of their territories. These centuries of instability correspond with major cultural and artistic movements, during the Middle Phase II ca., 632–550 BCE, and the Last Phase III ca. 550–479 BCE. By the early 5th century BCE, the descent into near-chaos had resumed. Jin fractured into three separate states, Han, Wei, and Zhao. By the mid-5th century, Qin and Chu greatly expanded their territory through conquest, and apparently by outdoing each other in production of material wealth, while in the southeast, Yue conquered and absorbed the territory of the once-powerful state of Wu.

The Conformity of States, Regional Variation, and the Devolution of Power

The *Springs and Autumns Annals* records numerous conferences, convened by the (purely notional) authority of the Zhou kings supposedly exercised on their behalf by one or another of the Lords of the Lands. These conferences were attended both by leaders of ancient states such as Song, Lu, and Zheng, and by rulers of large states on the periphery of the Zhou world, such as Qin, Jin, Yan, Qi, Chu, Wu, and Yue. Those large "outer" states were thoroughly integrated into the multi-state system of the Springs and Autumns Period. They participated in multi-state and bilateral diplomacy; used the Chinese language for bronze inscriptions (and presumably other purposes); practiced funerary rites and provided grave goods for the dead that were comparable to those of the smaller "inner" ancient states; performed rites and rituals and other forms of prescribed behavior encompassed by the capacious term *li* 禮; and, in short, were participants in the Sinitic world of the Springs and Autumns Period. Burial goods from ritual bronzes to ritual jades document that conformity. The term *huaxia* 華夏 began to appear in inscriptions during the Springs and Autumns Period to designate Sinitic, or Sinicized, people who belonged to the Zhou ethno-linguistic community, the first instance of a term that could be translated as "Chinese" (see e.g., Cioffi-Revilla and Lai 1995; F Li 2006: 286). Jin, Qin, Chu, and other large outer states were part of that community. Artistic production and burial goods reflect a unified cultural expression, though with regional variations, some of which might reflect contact with non-Sinicized or partly Sinicized peoples beyond the East Asian Heartland. The state of Chu was the leader of what amounted, in this period, to an artistic revolution in setting new styles and interpretations of well-worn themes inherited from the belief systems of dynastic Shang and Western Zhou. Chu was the most precocious state representing the so-called *huaxia* during the Eastern Zhou period.

The collapse of Zhou's royal authority had important social effects. Although the various states created bureaucratic governments modeled on the Zhou regime and its rituals, administrative posts in the states came to be filled, not as sinecures for members of the high aristocracy, but from an influential ministerial class comprising the middling ranks of nobles (Hsü 1965, 1999). Bureaucrats came to be appointed from a newly prominent class called *shi* 士, members of a sort of knightly caste originally valued for their martial skills (such as chariot warfare) (Meyer 2020; Pines 2020). Then, just as power had flowed from the Zhou kings to the Lords of the Lands, so, beginning in the mid-Springs and Autumns Period, power devolved again from the Lords of the Lands to their nominally subordinate ministers. The artistic context of this period is marked by similar trends. An initial imitation of royal Zhou norms led to innovations in the casting of bronze vessel sets and the creation of extravagant jade burial shrouds, just as artistic production in the late Western Zhou had drawn upon and reinterpreted works from the earlier phase of that era.

The Continuation of Bronze Vessels Sets and Metamorphic Belief

PHASE 1: Bronze vessels and jade arts of the early Springs and Autumns Period, EarlyPhase I, closely resembled those of the final decades of the Western Zhou.[2] Abstract bands of bird, dragon, and semi-human mask parts continued to embellish graduated-size vessel sets with identical décor, which continued to appear prominently as burial goods. Bronze vessels such as *ding*, *gui*, and other types forming matched sets, as well as sets of bronze bells, from Early Phase I through Middle Phase II of the Springs and Autumns Period, continued to be cast with abstract and simplified motifs (Figure 8.1). Inscriptions remained brief and generally featured the stale and formulaic encomium proposing that the vessel should be cherished and pre-served to bring blessings to future generations:

> I, Elder Shanfu, Liang Qi has made [for] my august deceased father, Hui Chung, and august deceased mother, Hui Yi, this honored *gui* to be used in offerings of filial piety [and] in prayers for a vigorous old age without limit. May sons and grandsons forever value and use it *(gui)* for thousands of years to come. After Barnard 1996: plates 4a right, 1a; translation 25.

Presumably, the burial of such vessels with the deceased patriarch was a way of ensuring that such blessings would accrue to his descendants.

As revealed in visual media beyond bronze, including lacquer, silk, and jade, by Middle Phase II new imagery bursts on to the scene yet with con-tinued focus on the semi-human form that transposed into dragons and birds, again underscoring that spirit possession continued as the underlying pictorial theme of belief and practice. During the Middle and Late phases of the Springs and Autumns Period, metamorphic imagery informed and reflected the mainstream culture of elite classes from lords of great states to *shi* "knights," and most likely to a certain extent commoners and lower classes alike. Changes in the arts went together with social and political changes as rulers of great states vied with each other for cultural prestige as well as territorial aggrandizement.

Wu Xiaolong has shown that during the Springs and Autumns era, bronze vessels, based on shape, set arrangement, and surface treatment, may be divided into four geographical regions: the central area comprising Zhou, Guo, Zheng, and Jin; the Shandong area including Qi, Lu, Ju, and others; the Yangzi and Huai River Valleys, principally Chu and Wu; and the

Figure 8.1 Bronze vessel sets from Phases 1–2 of the Springs and Autumns Period, 8th–7th century BCE. (A) Tripod *dou* vessel set from the Ji 纪 Cemetery, Jishui, Shandong. (B) Bell set from Taiyuan, Shanxi, Jin state. (C-D) *Gui* and *ding* vessel sets and drawings of vessel decor from M2001, Guo State Cemetery, Sanmenxia, Henan BCE. (A) Shandong 2016: colorpl 17. (B) Shanxi 1996: colorpls 3.1, 4.1, 5.1, Figures 22, 30, 34. (CD) Henan 1999: pls 3, 5; for drawings see Figures 22, 30, 37:1, 54.

Guanzhong area dominated by Qin (Wu Xl 2020). The production of *ding* and *gui* vessel sets, *pan* and *fu*, *tui* and *dui*, *hu* and *dou*, bells, chimes, and other musical instruments may be represented in Figure 8.1 by sets from Jishui in Shandong (纪 Ji state) (Figure 8.1A), Taiyuan in Shanxi (Jin 晋 state) (Figure 8.1B), and Sanmenxia in Henan (Guo state) (Figure 8.1C–D). In this conservative context, innovation in the treatment of bronze did not arise from the details of sets of vessels, but rather from artistic tendencies that flourished in Chu, as will be discussed below.

The discovery in 1978, for example, of the richly furnished tomb of the Prince of Zheng (Xinzheng 1997) galvanized the study of burial goods dating to the transitional late Western Zhou and early Phase 1 Springs and Autumns Period. Wave patterns of Western Zhou were displaced by the highly esteemed pattern of intertwining bodies ending in dragon, bird, and metamorphic mask forms (see Figure 8.2). Excrescences emerged as boldly projecting feline dragons or *yi*-style images. Nothing prepares one nonetheless for the inclusion of Chu state works of art, as represented by the elegant pair of *hu* crowned by naturalistically rendered three-dimensional cranes and boldly ejecting reverted-headed dragon forms as handles (Figure 8.2A). It is as if Chu took the obvious intertwined form and gave it new life, adding natural elements to glorify the metamorphic subject.

Another Chu innovation includes the casting in bronze (and in carving and lacquer coloring of wood sculptures), and the hybrid figure in bronze holding and squatting on snakes (see Figure 8.2B). These works of art from the Prince of Zheng state tomb in Xinzheng, Henan, document the new direction taken by the arts during the Middle and Late Phases II and III of the Springs and Autumns era. Excrescences take the form of dragon-shaped handles with reverted heads and flamboyant headdresses, free-form attachments in the shape of birds, some specifically identifiable as cranes; *yi* mask appliques; and intertwining snake-like bodies transforming from dragons to birds. As the leader of this new direction in art, Chu triumphed in creating lush and texturally rich surfaces rendered through a seemingly unending complex of slithering bodies, mostly snake forms ending in feline dragon or bird heads and occasionally framing a small-scale metamorphic mask. Although the above vessels all derive from northern Jin state burials, the new forms and styles represent southern sources and imports. The life-size wood-carved hybrid holding snakes and sprouting snake horns, entwined at foot level by further reptilian forms, clearly derives from Chu.[3] Intra- and inter-state trade during this period, despite the chaos of war, was healthy and lively.

Phases II and III

The new dominance of tall *hu* alcohol container pairs of bronzes with densely worked openwork lids, handles, and appendages, dragon-like, are represented by pairs of *hu* excavated at Xiasi, Henan (Figure 8.3C); Shouxian,

Figure 8.2 New direction in ritual bronze and related arts represented by artworks
from the Prince Zheng tomb, Xinzheng, Henan, Phase 1, Springs and
Autumns Period, 8–7th century BCE. (A) One of two large bronze hu
with crane, detail of the handle image, and rubbing of body décor showing intertwined snake-like dragons, birds, and yi masks. (B) Bronze
creature grasping snake-like horns. (AB) Xinzheng 1997: colorpl 113,
plate 11 to right (rubbing of décor), colorpls 144, 146.

Anhui (Figure 8.3B); and Taiyuan, Shanxi (Figure 8.3A). Each exhibit what
became the widely used image of the feline dragon with open mouth and
extended tongue and antler or snake horns. These otherworldly creatures,
characteristic of 7th–5th century BCE art, exemplify the direction taken
by Eastern Zhou art in that period. Their extravagantly three-dimensional
decor seems to explode in a profusion of convoluted slender worm-like bodies, sometimes reduced to abstract nodules. Chu was the artistic leader in
this direction of creative expression, as is told by the numerous bronzes
unearthed from areas controlled by the Chu state (see e.g. the Zeng Hou
Yi tomb unearthed at Leigudun, Hubei, 1989 and 1996 and the Spring and
Autumn Chu tomb at Xichuan, Henan in 1991) (Figure 8.5).

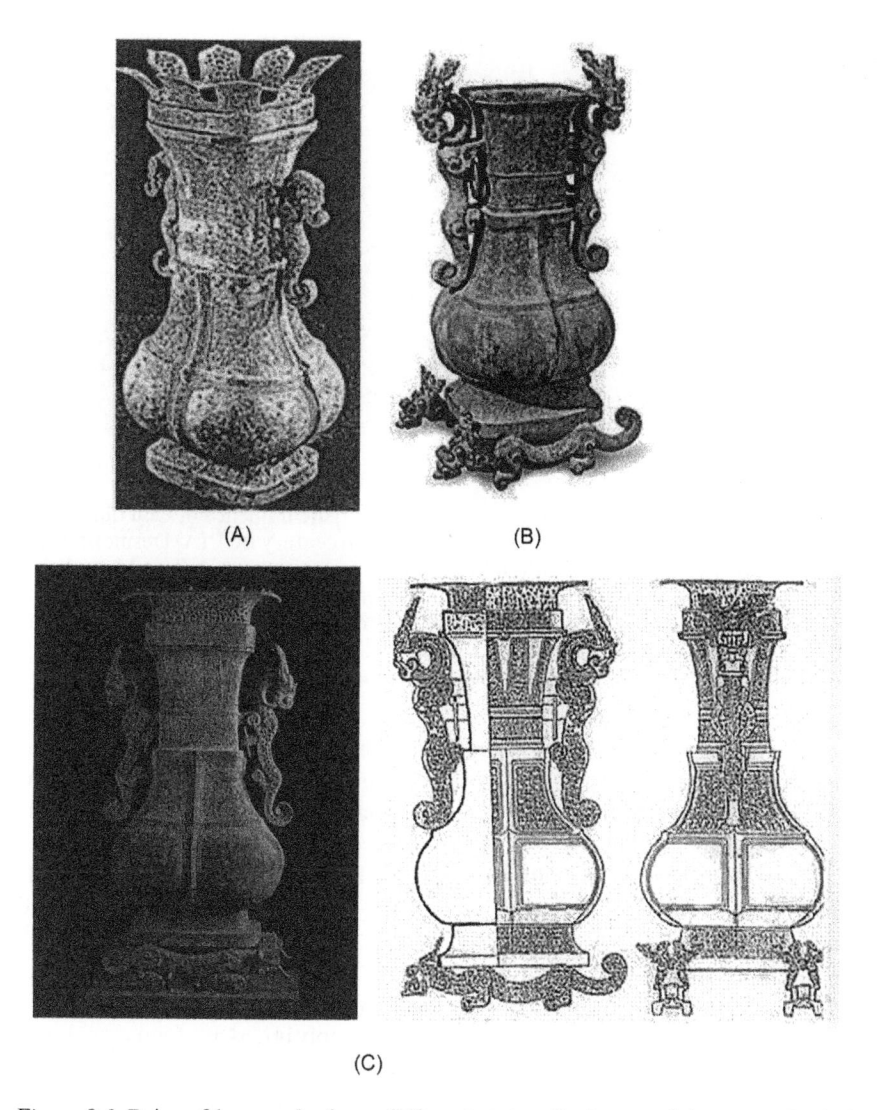

(A)   (B)

(C)

Figure 8.3 Pairs of bronze *hu* from different states, Springs and Autumns Period 7th–6th century BCE. (A) Taiyuan, Shanxi, Jin state. (B) Shouxian, Anhui. (C) Xiasi, Henan plus drawings. (A) Shanxi 1996: colorpl 3. (B) Anhui 1956: pl 7. (C) Henan 1991: colorpl 4, figs 63-64.

The set of *zun* and *pan* basin from the Marquis Yi of Zeng tomb of 5th-century BCE date (Figure 8.5A) and Xiasi serving table of the 6th-century BCE date (Figure 8.5B) are prime examples of the sort of feats in artistic expression that could be created under Chu stimulus. As an innovator, Chu was the first to experiment with lost-wax casting in producing what are the most exquisite openwork displays of dense intertwine and detail, as related

(A)   (B)   (C)

Figure 8.4 Three bronze *hu* exhibiting continued artistic influence of Chu during the late Springs and Autumns Period, 6th–5th century BCE (A) Desmond Morris Collection. (B) Lady Ji Wu Shu of Zeng state *hu*. (C) Zhao Meng X *hu*. (D) One of a pair allegedly from Huixian, Henan, British Museum, London. (A) Alamy Stock Photo DYF5HY, Desmond Morris Collection. (B) Digital Archives Program, Taiwan中铜 no 393. (C) One of a pair allegedly from Huixian, Henan, British Museum, London, Asia OA 1972.2-29.l.a.

by Zeng state bronzes (Hubei 1989) but also by those from Xichuan, Xiasi in Henan of the Late Springs and Autumns Period, 6th century BCE (Henan 1991). The Zeng state was under Chu domination and evidently Chu's artistic provenance.

By the Middle (632–550 BCE) and Late (550–479 BCE) Phases II–III, one finds an emphasis on personalized art, as the creation of art became available to a broader spectrum of the elite. Although most analyses of this trend are minimal and limited, the foresight of Munakata documented this trend in an earth-shaking exhibit in 1991 (Munakata 1991; also see Weber 1973 and Psarras 1989–99, 2015). Emphasis continued to focus on long-established *sifang* cosmology and *yi* metamorphism and themes that combined both the real and the fantastic; yet instead of the *weiyi* image of metamorphic royal power – the image of an untamed wild animal devouring a human – spirit transformation was interpreted anew as a narrative, something that could be chronicled and described, something more literal and factual. New imagery stimulated by the leadership of Chu emerged in response to the need for legitimation, seeking earlier models, as well as to the intense nature of the period – the ups and downs of war and fear of death that required an outlet in religious expression (Cook 2006a). Competition evidently took place not only on the battlefield but also in elite lineage cemeteries and the audience halls of ruling aristocrats. Competition in material culture was fueled not only by the rise of upstart ministerial families,

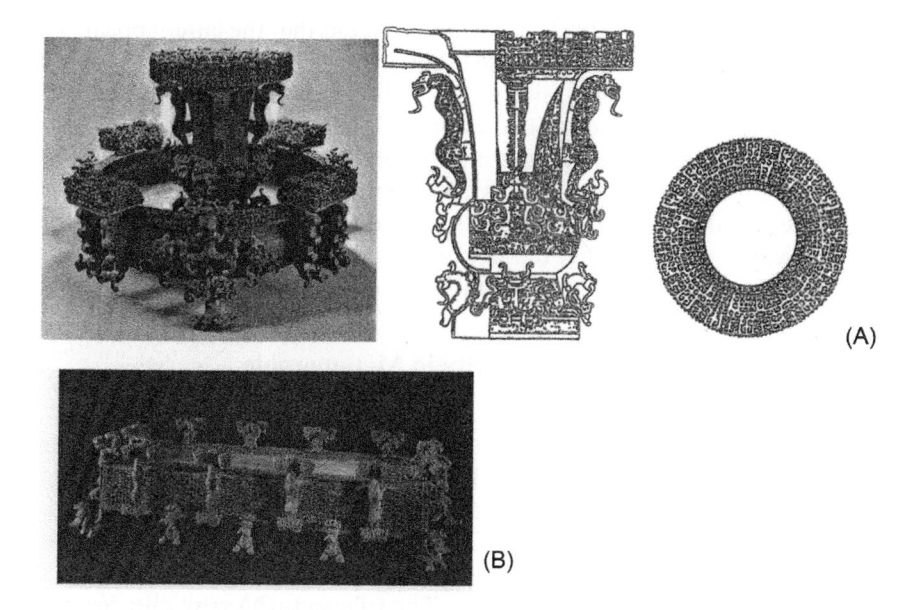

(A)

(B)

Figure 8.5 Artistic climax exhibiting the Chu aesthetic interest in small-scale intertwined imagery. (A) Drawing of the *zun* vessel and its lid. (B) The set of *zun* and *pan* basin, Marquis Yi of Zeng, Leigudun, Hubei, Late Springs and Autumns/Early Warring States Period, 5th century BCE. (B) Serving table with feline dragon supports, Xichuan, Xiasi, Henan, Late Springs and Autumns Period, 6th century BCE. (A) Hubei 1989: Figure 127 and Hubei 1995: colorpls 1–3. (B) Henan 1991: colorpl 49.

particularly in Chu, but by the same leaders who were anxious to display their wealth and good taste.

Newly styled narrative images of metamorphosis and cosmology depict the human spirit's journey after death, whether represented metaphorically by an otherworldly liminal hunt in the wild, by directional and cosmological symbols, such as trees, *feng* birds, *long* dragons, the *yi* mask, open windows, hybrid deities, displayed deities, or by painted diagrams. Tai Yi 太一, the "Great One" or "Great Unity," emerged during the Warring States Period as a new manifestation of the powerful sky deity seen in earlier iterations as Di (during the Shang) and Tian (during the Zhou and beyond) (see e.g. Li and Harper 1995; and for other interpretations see e.g., Tseng 2011: 5, 83–84,153–54). Tai Yi, who in later times would become the Sky God of religious Daoism, during the Warring States and early Han period was both a deity and a constellation, the focus of state rites of worship as a manifestation of the fundamental unity underlying the cosmology of *yin-yang* and the Five Phases. Tai Yi seems to have originated in Chu, although textual data suggest this is late, dating to the late Warring States and Han periods (Tseng

2011; Lewis 2006a). We will not engage here in an account of *yin-yang*/Five-Phase cosmology (Major 1993), except to point out that the latter appears to have been first an elaboration of, and eventually a replacement of *sifang* cosmology, placing equal emphasis on the symbolism of the center along with the four cardinal directions. The evolving symbolism of metamorphism during the Warring States Period and beyond shows how stylistic change coexists with fundamental continuity. Metamorphic imagery becomes more narrative and descriptive and appears in media beyond the old medium of bronze vessels. Social change did not overturn the basic belief systems even as the aesthetics of metamorphic symbolism evolved.

Chu Culture: Continuity and Novelty in Metamorphic Symbolism

The great southern state of Chu was an innovative fountainhead of the arts in the Springs and Autumns and Warring States Periods. Wu Xiaolong notes that some 10,000 Chu tombs, mostly from the Warring States Period, have been excavated (Wu 2017: 27). Chu originated during the Shang Period as a territorial kingdom (*fang*) centered in the middle reaches of the Han River, south of the Qinling Mountains. The rulers of Chu were also *Huaxia* relatives of the Zhou ruling clan (Cioffi-Revilla and Lai, 1995: 471–72) and were culturally similar to the Lords of the Lands of other states in the Zhou orbit. During the first half of the Springs and Autumns Period, Chu steadily expanded southward and eastward, down the Han River to the Yangzi, eventually occupying most of the middle Yangzi River Valley north of the great river itself. In this process of expansion, Chu conquered and absorbed many smaller territorial states or turned them into dependencies. As Chu grew larger and more powerful, it moved its capital six times, presumably to keep the capital city near the center of the growing state. By the mid-7th century BCE, the aggressively expansionist Chu state turned its acquisitive energy toward the states of the Yellow River Plain, probably with the aim of overthrowing the Zhou monarchy itself. The northern states took countermeasures, and at the Battle of Chengpu (632 BCE), the Chu army was annihilated by the combined forces of Qi and Jin. Settling into its final boundaries, Chu remained a powerful state until the late 4th century BCE, when inner turmoil and ineffective government sapped its strength in the decades leading up to the unification of all of China by the state of Qin. But even when it was politically weak, Chu played an important cultural role, not only within its own boundaries but throughout the Sinitic world. Chu is the primary cultural representative of Sinitic religion in the Eastern Zhou Period and into the Han. Although much of the evidence cited below dates to the Warring States and Former Han Periods rather than to the Springs and Autumns, this evidence preserves and elaborates on ideas and concepts from earlier Jade Age, Shang, and Western Zhou times. We address initially influential texts, such as the *Chuci* and *Shanhaijing* followed by characteristics of artistic imagery of this era that predominantly speaks to belief in metamorphosis, as represented, for example, by the prevalence of birdmen, cosmological trees, hybrid deities, liminal hunt, and the new image of cosmological power *yi* known anew as Tai Yi.

Influential Texts

The art of the later Springs and Autumns Period (7th–5th centuries BCE) is reflected in much later cosmological texts, such as parts of the *Huainanzi* (139 BCE), compiled under the patronage of Liu An, King of Huainan. His realm, lying mostly in present-day Anhui Province, included the eastern part of the former state of Chu, and the *Huainanzi* to some extent is reflective of Chu culture. That art expressed "embodiments of cosmological processes, the mythic landscapes of super-terrestrial fairylands, or both" (Major 1993) – the shamanic world of supernatural vehicles, *feng* birds, *long* dragons, and related mythicized animals, usually tigers and other animals of the wild, such as we have consistently met in Shang and Western Zhou art. The pre-eminent subject of Eastern Zhou art is precisely this intermediary realm where the souls of the dead journeyed and shamans summoned the spirits. The major change in art during the Eastern Zhou appears not in subject but in style and mode of expression; art becomes increasingly descriptive and narrative, though not yet so benign and tame as it would become in Qin and Han times. The fundamental pan-Sinitic belief in metamorphism powered new trends in artistic expression.

The concept of a mythical wilderness surrounding an axial mountain connecting the highest heaven with the Yellow Springs, the subterranean realm of the dead, was represented symbolically in narrative art (see e.g., Munakata 1991). Symbols of this magical wilderness comprised not only intertwining *long* dragons and *feng* birds but hunted animals (especially felines), semi-human deities depicted as hunters, or displayed images with composite bird, dragon, snake, and related body parts. Such narratives employ familiar metamorphic images put together compositionally to represent a hunt or chariot ride to an otherworldly realm (Thote 2014).

The late Warring States or early Han anthology of southern poetry known as the *Chuci* 楚辭 ("Elegies of Chu") contains two closely similar poems, the "Da zhao" 大招 ("Great Summons") and the "Zhao hun" 招魂 ("Summons of the Soul"), that exemplify these literary treatments of narrative art. Due to their narrative clarity and richness of expression, they stand out among several primary sources for understanding the continued importance of spirit metamorphism and cosmology in the art of the Eastern Zhou. These poems are among the earliest of the *Chuci* anthology, dating to the mid-to-late Warring States Period. They represent a literary treatment of what was likely an actual ritual and incantation performed throughout the culture of Eastern Zhou. In this view, the life of a human being was sustained by the presence in the body of two essences, the *po* 魄 and the *hun* 魂. The *po* was an earthly, material, *yin* soul that stayed with the corpse after death (and required appropriate grave goods and periodic sacrifices to remain benign). The *hun* was an immaterial, *yang*, ethereal soul that left the body at the moment of death; death was understood to occur when the *hun* had departed and no longer animated the physical body. The two "Summons" poems depict a ceremony in which a person (probably a son of the deceased) climbed to the ridgepole of the house of the deceased and attempted to call the departed *hun* back to re-animate the corpse. Only when that effort failed could funeral rites commence (C Cook 2006a). The salient point here is that the summons warned the departed soul of the dangers it faced in roaming bodiless in the four cardinal directions. The efficacy of the summons ritual depended on its being carried out in a properly oriented space. At the very beginning of the "Zhao hun," Di (the Shang Sky God) addresses a personage named Shaman Yang, one of ten shamans (perhaps connected to the old concept of a week of ten suns) who live on a holy mountain in the west. Di instructs him to summon the soul of a person who has just died (see the translations of Sukhu 2012, 2017). The main body of the poem thus consists of Shaman Yang's attempt to recall the dead person's *hun* soul.

Shaman Yang first tries to frighten the soul from leaving the safety of its body. Do not go to the east, he says; there are giants there, and the flames of ten suns that can melt stone. Do not go to the south, where there are savages who eat human flesh and pound the bones of their victims into paste, as well as giant snakes and a nine-headed man-eating serpent. Shaman Yang continues through the rest of the "six coordinates" (left-right, front-back, and high-low), warning the soul of the terrifying creatures that await it in the west, the north, in the Sky above, and in the land of darkness below. There is nowhere where the soul can be safe.

Having applied the stick of warning against danger, Shaman Yang next wields the carrot of enticement, describing in sumptuous detail the feast that will greet the soul if only it will return; this is a verbal description of the feasting scenes often depicted on narrative bronzes and lacquerware (see Figure 8.6), where two birdmen in costume play large *chong* bells. He paints a vivid verbal picture of the delicious dishes that will be served, the music that will be played, and the young women whose dancing leads to wild debauchery. What soul could resist such pleasures? But the poem ends in sorrow; the soul has fled and death has not, after all, been averted.

It is evident from this "Summons of the Soul" passage and the similar "Great Summons" that the *hun* soul could migrate after death to any of the four quarters of the cosmos, or upwards toward Heaven and downwards to the Land of Darkness. The intermediary area that extended in all directions was fraught with potential evil, teeming with animals of mythical dimensions and other sorts of horror that lay beyond the soul's control. The shaman, who possessed the esoteric techniques necessary to survive in this dangerous liminal landscape, made this transition in communicating with the spirit world and thereby connecting with Tian or Di above, in aiding his

(A)   (B)

Figure 8.6 Representative narrative image portraying a masked performer playing zhong bells, reflecting the imagery portrayed in the "Zhao hun" elegy from the Chuci. Lacquer painting on a side of a lacquered duck-shaped storage vessel, Leigudun, Hubei, Warring States Period, 5th century BCE. Hubei 1995: colorpls 66–67.

fellow human and his endangered soul. The author of this hymn, probably the preeminent Chu poet Qu Yuan himself (Sukhu 2012, 2017), takes on the persona of a shaman. Regardless of his exact identity, he was evidently a highly literate aristocrat comparable to the educated diviners and scribes who served the rulers of the Shang and Western Zhou eras.

In addition to the poems collected in the *Chuci,* many of which are explicitly shamanistic, other significant texts include the so-called *Chu Silk Manuscript,* the *Shanhaijing* 山海經 (*Classic of Mountains and Seas*), and two texts associated with the cosmological deity Taiyi.

The *Shanhaijing,* like many texts in China's received tradition, is an accretional work, compiled over a period of a century or more; its oldest layers appear to date from the Warring States Period. Like the "Summons" poems of the *Chuci,* it draws on the ancient cosmographical notion of the *sifang* cardinal directions. It is a gazetteer of cosmic and magical phenomena cued to the four directions, naming mountains, bodies of water, flora and fauna, extraordinary animals, and human or semi-human personages, some of whom are identified as shamans. The descriptions are in many cases reminiscent of the lands covered in the "farflight" (*zhaoyao* 招愮) cosmological journeys taken by shamans in the *Chuci* elegies. What makes the descriptions especially interesting is their mixture of real-world details with those that are totally fantastic – a combination in synchrony with the art of the era. Fantastic deities include, among a host of others, Pao Xiao (another name for Taotie, "the Glutton"), Kui (legendary founder of the Shang), and Fenghuang (the legendary spirit bird, the "phoenix") (see Birrell 1999 and Fracasso 1993, 1996). The focus of the text is on mountains, each of which is named and given an exact location by reference to direction and distance from other mountains or bodies of water. The text also names and describes the flora and fauna of each mountain, and its human or spirit-like inhabitants. The fantastic features and legendary properties of resident animals and spirits are described; some have exorcistic powers, while others are good or bad omens. The compilers of the *Classic of Mountains and Seas* envisioned a flat earth laid out in the form of three concentric rectangles: a central territory, a surrounding ocean, and a "great wilderness" stretching from the far shore of the surrounding sea and extending to an undetermined limit (Fracasso 1993).

Hwang Ming-chorng has elaborated on this idea, identifying a key chapter, the *"Dahuangjing"* 大荒經 ("Great Wilderness Classic") as not only a version of the *sifang* four directional cosmography of the Shang dynasty but as a work that originated as an oral text pictorially transcribed by shamans who served the Shang court and was handed down by their survivors (Hwang 1996b). Although this identification is not new, the corroborative evidence adduced by Hwang makes the idea convincing. The cosmic features "were the legacies of archaic shamanism and remained essentially the same from remote antiquity to the Han dynasty" (Hwang 1996b: 191). This thesis is consistent with the view, based on combined artistic and literary data, that Chinese belief in metamorphism was continuous from the late Neolithic through the Warring States Period.

A brief passage from the *Shanhaijing* (Chapter 5, "Bei shan jing" 北山經, The Classic of the Northern Mountains, Part 2) illustrates the work's characteristic blend of real and fantastical features:

> ...350 li further north [of the Duntou Mountains] is a mountain (range) called Gouwu. At its higher elevations is found nephrite, and at its lower elevations is found copper. There is a wild beast there with a ram's body and human face whose eyes are located below its armpits. It is called Paoxiao [Taotie]. It has tiger fangs and human fingernails. Its voice is like a baby's. It eats men. 300 li further north is a mountain (range) called Beixiao where there is no stone. On its sunny (south) side there is abundant *bi* green jade (jasper), and on its shady (north) side there is abundant *yu* (nephrite). There is a wild beast there called Dugu. It looks like a tiger with a white body, a dog's head, a horse's tail, and wild boar bristles. There is also a bird like a crow called Banmao. It has a human face. It flies around at night and hides during the day. If eaten it cures fever. The Cen River flows eastward from there to the Qiong Marsh.

Clearly, the *Shanhaijing* is not about ordinary landscapes; it depicts a numinous world that is the dwelling place of shamans and fabulous beasts of all kinds, and it provides a roadmap for the liminal travels of the soul.

The "Chu Silk Manuscript" in the collection of the National Museum of Asian Art in Washington, D.C. (so named when it was a unique example of its kind; today, of course, there are many other archaeologically recovered silk manuscripts from Chu) was discovered in a Chu tomb at Zidanku near Changsha, Hubei (Li Ling and C. A. Cook, 1999: 171–76). This famous document depicts the gods of the 12 months (most of which are bizarre in appearance, with multiple heads, etc.), along with four seasonal spirit trees, arranged in a square surrounding two texts in the central portion of the document. The longer text discusses, in astrological terms, the seasons, months, motions of the heavenly bodies, and the causes of various catastrophes, while the other text is devoted mainly to auspicious and inauspicious activities for 12 months (see translation by Li L and C Cook 1999). The document is both a cosmography and a cosmogony that begins with primordial chaos and continues with the birth of the four seasons, the sun and moon, the four mythical trees, and the four rebellious gods. It concludes with the restoration of cosmic order by the legendary ancestor of the Chu royal family, Zhu Rong (Invoker of Fire). The significance of the manuscript passage is multifaceted, but it is particularly important as a treasure trove of ancient Chinese mythology and cosmology, with roots stretching back at least to the Shang if not still earlier to the Erlitou culture ("Xia"). Although it is beyond the scope of this study to give a history of the correlative cosmology that in the late Warring States Period and dominated intellectual life in the Han period, it is salient to point out that Five Phase cosmology evolved from the long-lived tradition of *sifang* cosmology and metamorphism. With its depiction of the monthly gods and four trees and the mention of Kui 夔 (Jun) as one who gave birth to the suns and the moons, the Chu Silk Manuscript serves as a hinge between the ancient system and its more recent offspring. As discussed in the chapter on Shang, Kui appears to be represented as a shamanic figure on the bronze drum from the Sumitomo Collection in Japan from Chongyang, Hubei (See Chapter 7: 144, Figure 6.14C), while oracle bone inscriptions allude to his worship as the legendary founder of the Shang people (see e.g., Hu 1989–90 vol. 1; Childs-Johnson 2016). The sun and moon are familiar symbols, usually rendered in bird form during the Jade Age (Chapter 3: 47–49 and Figures 3.16 and 3.17), evolving in the Shang into a pair of symbols of transformation flanking the semi-human *yi* metamorphic power mask. Images of the sun and moon, whether portrayed as disks or as swirling birds on Liangzhu jades or Warring States silk paintings, symbolized the powerful natural forces that a shaman sought to control.

The most frequently cited literary passage documenting the prevalence of shamanic belief on a popular level during the Warring States is the 4th century BCE text, *Discourses of the States* 国语 (see e.g. Chang 1983). The discourse between a Chu king and his ministers is usually interpreted to concern a myth about the origins of shamanic practice. The key phrase reads "severing communication between Sky and Earth." This "severing" concept refers to the belief that sky and earth were once in unimpeded communication but drew apart from one another due to some cosmic disaster. The Sky Power became a transcendental realm, the dwelling place of the deities Di or Tian; it required special skills to restore that communication, at least temporarily, when shamans made their ecstatic trips to the celestial realm.

Two key passages in this text deserve special emphasis. The first is the concept that possessors of power were those into whom spirits would descend, a power like that belonging to the kings and ritualists of Western Zhou and Shang times. The second is the implied concept that earth and Sky are separate spheres that resonate with one another, so that events on earth trigger responses in heaven, and heavenly portents affect life on earth. A key role of the ruler, then, is to maintain the proper balance between sky and earth; from his place at the center of the cosmos, the ruler and his ritual assistants and diviners enable communication to be established between the two realms (Major 1993).

Two texts referring to the Chu celestial deity Taiyi (Great One) should be noted here. One is *Taiyi sheng shui* 太一生水 (The Great One Gave Birth to Water), a previously unknown text included among the many texts found at Guodian 郭店 in 1993 and dated to c. 300 BCE (Jingmen 1998; Xing 2000; S Cook 2012). It is a cosmogonic text in which Taiyi gives birth to water, which then evolves through a series of "reversions" (*fan* 反) into Heaven and Earth and the whole phenomenal world. The second Taiyi text is found on a badly damaged silk manuscript from the Han Period Tomb 3 at Mawang-dui 馬王堆 (168 BCE). The manuscript portrays seven figures,[4] including a central figure identified as Taiyi (Figure 8.7). The style of the figures recalls those featured in the Chu Silk Manuscript. Near the Taiyi figure is an incantation text intended to protect a person just setting out on a liminal journey. It reads,

> The Incantation of the Grand One (Tai Yi): Today so-and-so is about to (travel).... draw the bow. The Great Yu goes first. Red *qi* and white *qi* dare not to turn toward me. The hundred weapons dare not harm me.... is called insincere. Use the Northern Dipper as the right direction. Spit to the left and the right. Go straight, do not look back.
>
> (For another translation see Lai 2017: 131–32)

These texts show Taiyi as both a cosmogonic creator and a deity able to use magical means to avert harm to his devotees.

Revitalized Metamorphic Imagery in Art

Although textual data during the Eastern Zhou era derives mostly from the Warring States Period, the visual data for spirit possession and cosmological control is overwhelmingly consistent throughout this period and built upon earlier Western Zhou, Shang, and Jade Age foundations. The resurgence of inherited metamorphic themes is manifested in symbols of a numinous wilderness, comprising not only intertwining *long* and *feng* but also large felines and other hunted animals. Semi-human deities appear in the role of hunters or displayed images with composite bird, dragon, snake, and related body parts. Narrative art, an innovation in bronze décor, features the same images put together compositionally to represent a pell-mell hunt

(A)

(B)

Figure 8.7 Silk manuscript with Tai Yi and details showing inscribed reference to Tai Yi 太一, Mawangdui, Hunan, Western Han period. After Li and Harper (1995) 2013; Fu and Chen 1992: 35.

or chariot ride to an otherworldly realm – a mix of the naturalistic and the fantastic, as introduced by Munakata as early as 1991. The religious ideals of ancient eras again come alive under the guise of a new and more sophisticated phase of bronze making, with a richly articulated mythology narrative and a religious culture committed to "institutionalized shamanism" of pre-Eastern Zhou date.

Yi Transformative Deities

The most important trope in the vocabulary of metamorphic representation in early China, as we have shown, is the displayed image that signified spirit possession in Shang times. The image and graph as represented in bone inscriptions of Shang and bronze inscriptions of Western Zhou date, *yi* 異, is still applicable to the concept of spirit possession in terms of identity with the greater power of nature during the Eastern Zhou periods. Possession of spirit power was used in Western Zhou times to amplify the awesome power of the ruling king – his *wei yi* 畏儀 (*wei* 畏 is a cognate of *yi* 異). It is a remarkable testimony to the persistence of belief in this image of metamorphic power, a numinous power of spirit possession, and now in the Warring States Period transferred to the power expressed in the concept of Tai Yi (Grand Unity), the Chu deity who is associated with early Daoism.

The displayed image with semi-human face and horns who holds dragon and reptilian creatures and stands atop symbols of the sun and moon on the bronze *ge* from Jingmen, Hubei (Figure 8.8A) clearly represents an anthropomorphic image of a divinity with shamanic power over the animal realm. We have seen repeatedly the use of the displayed image as a trope of metamorphic representation. The fact that this displayed semi-human stands on sun and moon symbols (circle and crescent) indicates that this deity is endowed with cosmological power, a power that immediately recalls the Sky Power represented in Neolithic jade art, where sun and moon symbols conjunctively appear as attributes of the central deity (see Chapter 3: 47–49, Figures 3.16 and 3.17). The otherworldly character of this semi-human is, in turn, represented by a body covered by scales and by earrings in the form of snakes. The association of the semi-human deity with Tai Yi, the Great Unity, accorded an imperial rite of worship in the Han, and ultimately with the Di and Tian Sky Powers of Shang and Western Zhou eras cannot be mistaken. Nor can the association with the rendering of the shaman leader, the primordial religious intermediary, Kui, in Shang times (Chapter 6:125, Figure 6.5C and D) be mistaken. The question arises: are all the semi-humans represented in displayed fashion generic references to initiated spirit mediums, such as Tai Yi and Kui, or are these semi-humans both specific and general references to ecstatic enlightenment and immortality? These images are likely both generic metamorphic icons and specific metamorphic deities. Hayashi concluded that the monthly deities of the "*Chu Silk Manuscript*" may refer to deified shamans or religious leaders that stood out in

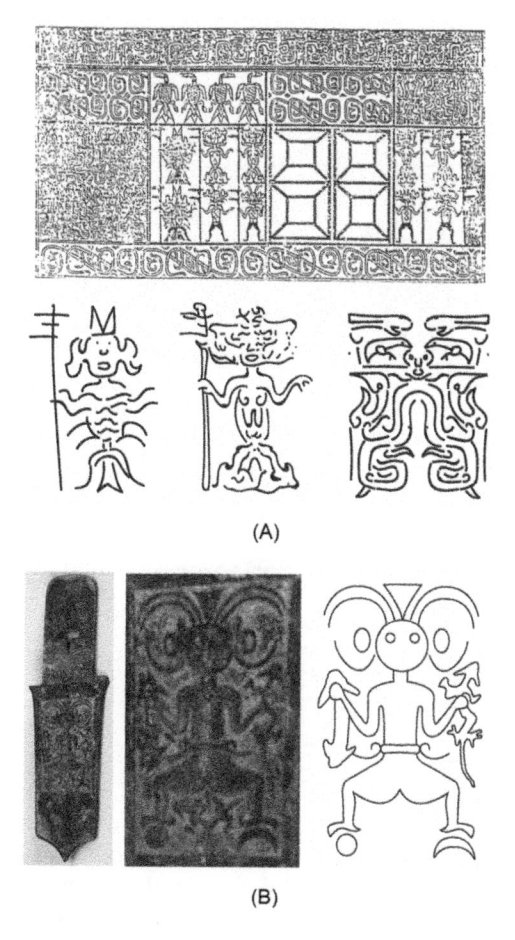

(A)

(B)

Figure 8.8   *Yi* transformative deities from Shang through Eastern Zhou Warring States date, ca. 1700–300 BCE. (A) *Yi* transformative deities decorating in lacquer the outer wooden coffin of Marquis Yi of Zeng, 5th century BCE; Hubei1999: Figures 21–22. (B) Bronze dagger with image of Tai Yi, Cheqiao dam, Jingmen, Warring States Period, 4th century BCE, Jingzhou Museum, Hubei. (C) Bronze bell depicting the *yi* spirit empowered deity riding a wild buffalo beast (as a frontal mask) and surrounded by curling feline and bird forms, representing the climax of four standard metamorphic tropes of Bronze Age China (deity power mask; dragon, mythic bird, and flight). Leigudun, Hubei, last phase, Springs and Autumns/early Warring States, 5th century BCE. (D) Displayed *yi* images grasping a pair of wild animals seen in compositions featuring the liminal hunt in the after, other world. (E) Shang pictograph emblem of displayed figure flanked by hunting animals and a hunting dog. (A) Hubei 1999: Figures 21–22. (B) Jingzhou Museum, Jingzhou, Hubei. (C) *Hubei meishu* 1995: colorpls 77–79 and Hubeisheng 1999: Figures 21–22. (D) Munakata 1991. (E) Henan 1999: Figure 104:3.

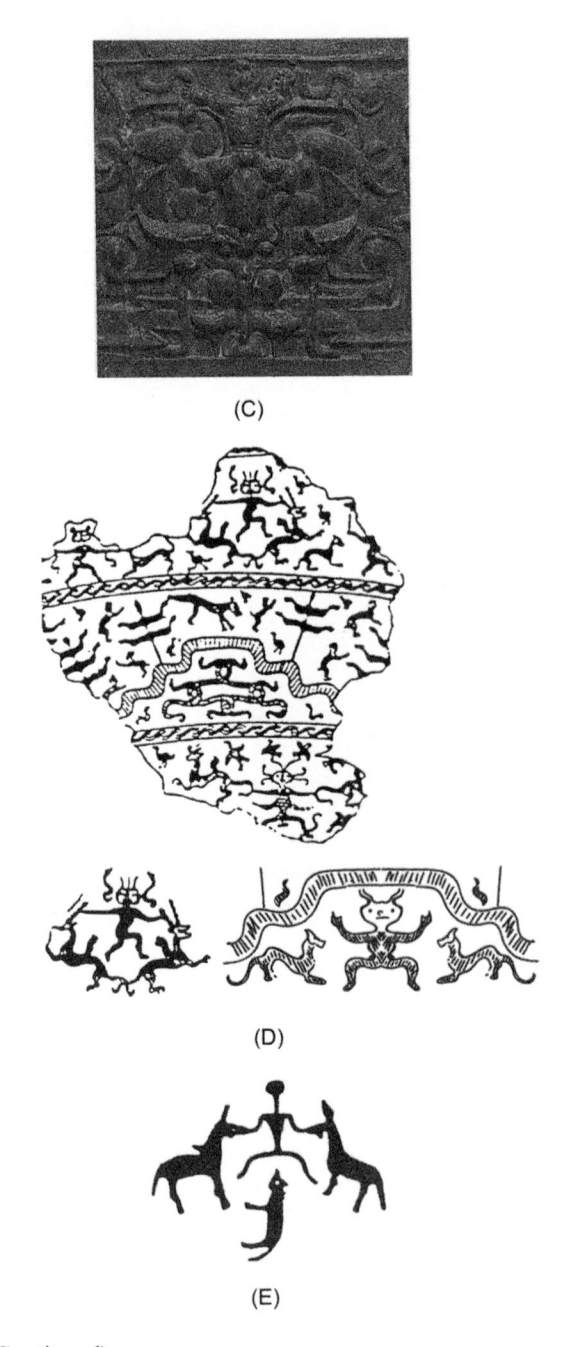

(C)

(D)

(E)

Figure 8.8 (Continued)

Chinese history and myth (Hayashi 1972). Similarly, the ten *yi* deities with varying headdress ornaments holding weapons painted on the Leigudun coffin may represent deified leaders associated with the ten suns of Shang and early Zhou times (see Figure 8.8B). As outlined earlier, metamorphic imagery may be categorized into generalized and specific, real and fantastic, earthbound or visionary modes of representation. The religious program over the long sweep of history, although naturally with variations, held onto well-worn tropes of representation.

Hybrid Deities

Variations of feline hybrids in carved wood, whether lacquered or not, are like depictions of those mythic creatures in hunting scenes on narrative bronzes; they inhabit the liminal realm of nature (Figure 8.9). The most outstanding variations of this hybrid creature are the large bronzes or carved and lacquered wooden sculptures that serve as supports for sets of chimes, bells, or drums; they may be deities who escort the deceased in the afterworld (C Cook 2006a), or actors frolicking and racing in the liminal realm of the other world. It should be no surprise that one of the monthly deities depicted on the Chu Silk Manuscript is crowned by antlers, suggesting an immediate comparison with one of the carved and lacquered hybrid Chu tomb figures (So 1980) that serve as helpers for the deceased *hun* spirit (C Cook 2006a). This comports with the whole Bronze Age tradition of controlling death through vehicles of transformation and possession.

During the Eastern Zhou, the fundamental belief in the power of spirit world and the need to protect the *hun* soul was crucial in guaranteeing safe passage on its journey in the afterlife. There is no better illustration of this theme than on the so-called "Huai style" inlaid bronze *hu* and related vessels.

The Hunt

We have witnessed variations on the spirit powers of *long* and *feng* and their transformative variations, as well as the new appearance of related hybrids in feline form with bird claws for feet and snakes for horns. Related cosmological narratives of spirit survival were assembled in 1991 by Kiyohiko Munakata in his major exhibition and catalog, *Sacred Mountains in Chinese Art*. The artworks chosen for the exhibition by Munakata included bronze and their fragments from two representative major site burials, a Chu burial near Huaiyin, Jiangsu and another at Liulige, Huixian, Henan (Figure 8.10). In addition to new treatments of bronze vessels, which could be inlaid with colorful malachite, turquoise, copper, and other precious materials, vessels began to feature narratives whose imagery was predominantly the wild and imaginary animal realm (see Figure 8.10). As interpreted by Munakata, these narratives and symbols, often without ground

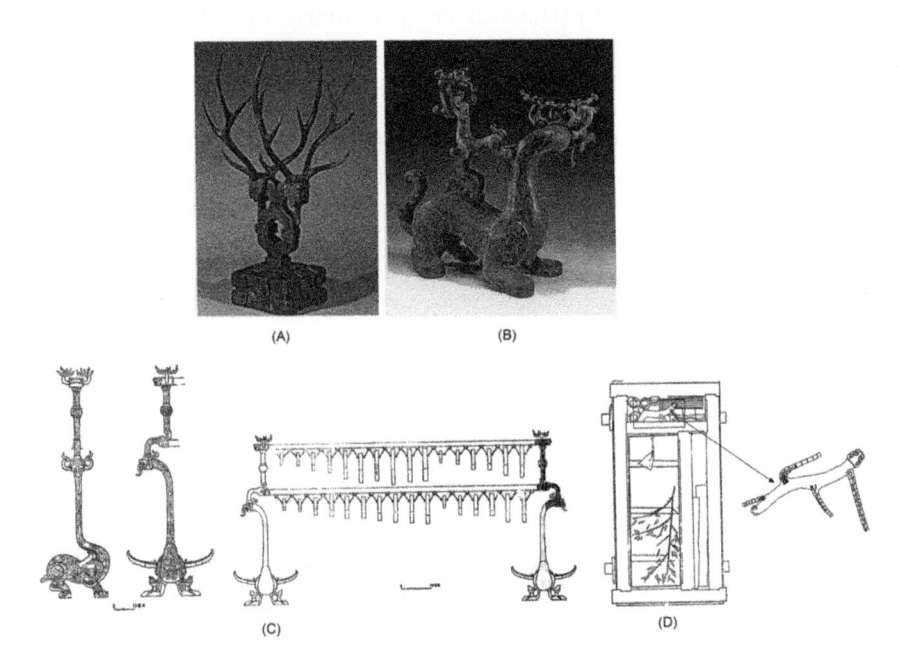

(A)   (B)

(C)   (D)

Figure 8.9 Whole and abstract variations of representative metamorphic hybrid deities as a tiger with head extensions of stag horns and as part tiger with bird wings, or as a bamboo crafted image, Spring and Autumn–Warring States periods. (A) Addorsed hybrid tiger deities, lacquered wood, Xu Jialing M9, Xichuan, Henan. Henan Provincial Institute of Archaeology and Cultural Relics, Zhengzhou, Henan. (B) Squatting bronze tiger with turquoise inlay, Xu Jialing, Xichuan, Henan. Henan Provincial Institute of Archaeology and Cultural Relics, Zhengzhou, Henan (C) Opposing pair of hybrid deities supporting four sets of 32 stone chimes, Leigudun, Hubei. (D) Ground plan of burial and context of bamboo crafted hybrid metamorphic deity. (A) After Creative Commons CC0 1.0 Universal Public Domain Dedication, Daderot, exhibited Portland Art Museum Nov. 2, 2017 DSC0851.jpg. (B) S Lee 1997: colorpl 46. (C) Hubei 1989: Figures 59, 61. (D) Wang H 2003:7.

line, portray a ritualistic vision – a shamanic experience representing the journey of the soul (*hun*) through the intermediary realm of the wilderness between heaven and earth. This experiential imagery included not only the abstract forms on the bronze vessels, but the pell-mell hunt on the so-called "hunting *hu*", and the vision painted on the walls of the coffin belonging to Marquis Yi of Zeng illustrated in Figure 8.8.

If one looks closely at the images on these vessels, one sees that they include hunted beasts such as large felines (tigers and others) and boars, as well as monkeys, tapirs, cranes, and other birds. The hunters include humans and semi-humans, some with a single head, some with a bird head,

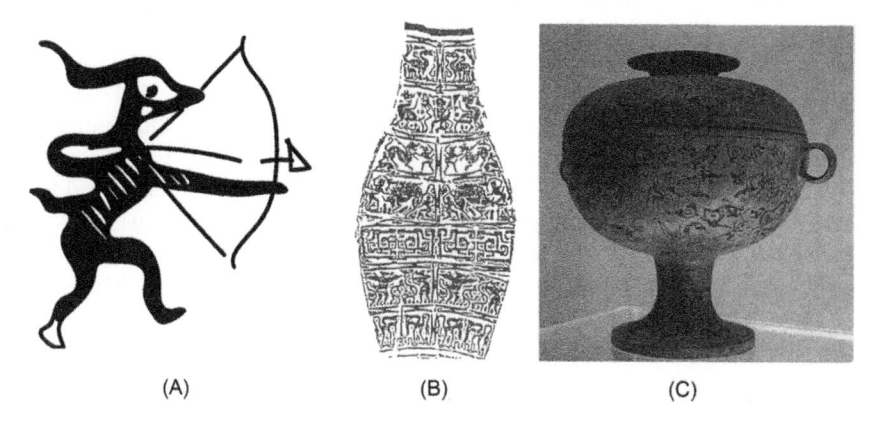

(A)   (B)   (C)

Figure 8.10 The liminal hunt as narrative featured on various vessel types, Eastern Zhou Period. (A) Detail of bird headed and winged human archer depicted as part of a hunting narrative (B) Rubbing of body of *hu* vessel, Liulige, Henan. (C) Round bronze lidded *dou* vessel with narrative of a spirit hunt, Walters Art Gallery. (A) For this detail see related images in Fig 8B for reference. (B) *Shanbiaozhen yu Liuliko*: pl 93 and Weber 1966: Figure 43A. (C) Weber 1966; Figure 52.

some in displayed frontal disposition, sometimes holding snakes or felines, as does the anthropomorphic large-scale deity sculpted in wood and painted with bright lacquer colors. Some of these otherworldly figures carry *mao* spears, others wield bows and arrows. Most of the feline animals have reverted heads, comparable to the larger-scale versions decorating bronze *hu* and their appendages. These are spirit powers, winged and endowed with the power of flight as well as the power to exorcize. Munakata interprets the hunt as a reference to spirits fighting through the realm of the wilderness, a feared journey for the wandering soul of the recently dead. The theme of hunting refers to the exorcistic ritual associated with the capture of prey (Munakata 1991) that, in Shang times, signified possession of the hunted animal's spirit. The hunt in Shang and Zhou times was a religio-political power symbol of man as king over the wild, ruler of beasts (see Figure 8.8D), as clearly explained by the prominence of hunted animals in Shang ritual imagery. The continued importance of the royal hunt accounts for the continued maintenance in Western Zhou, Springs and Autumns, and Warring States times, of the Shang practice of maintaining royal hunting grounds. The hunt continued to symbolically re-enact the Shang imagery of humans conquering the wild and purging it of demonic influences. These rituals are enacted in the intermediary realm that is lyrically portrayed in the "Summons" poems and related elegies of the *Chuci*, as analyzed above.

In some cases, the animal bodies are displayed as bifurcated – a mode used since the Jade Age, Xia, Shang, Western Zhou, and into the Springs and Autumns Period. In the narrative decor of these bronzes, mountains are abstracted and simplified to pyramidal mounds, often with trees growing from them (see Figure 8.10). This is the realm that is described in the "Dahuangjing" (Classic of the Great Wilderness), Chapters 14–17 of the *Classic of Mountains and Seas*, and that informs the visions of Qu Yuan and Shao Tuo in their exquisite testimonials about the afterlife (C Cook 2006a). As Hayashi Minao demonstrated, the antecedents of the 12 peripheral figures painted around the edges of the "Chu Silk Manuscript" were likely selected from the same primary source as were certain shamans mentioned in the *Classic of Mountains and Seas* (Hayashi 1974), some of which are also mentioned in oracle bone divinations of the Shang.

Birdmen

The half-human, half-bird image is a clear symbol of spiritual flight. This image may vary in details of bird and semi-human features, including bird wings, bird claws, bird beak, to human limbs and legs. Sometimes the legs are bent underneath the human in fetal-like position (indicating rebirth by flight), as was so commonly represented in Western Zhou metamorphic icons. Facial features are almost always mask-like and never descriptive of a human face. These half-human, half-bird images are well represented since the Jade Age and throughout the historic Shang and Zhou phases (Figure 8.11). And they signify, as do the hybrid feline sculptures, a symbol of transformative power. The small-scale fetal bird persons in high relief decorating the flat square *pan* vessel of Warring States date from the Shanghai Museum, one of the most exquisite testimonies of beauty and love for representing numinous spirit powers (Figure 8.11). The bird persons at the corner edges of the bronze look outwards towards the viewer as do the small-scale animals in relief. And, as related below, these half-bird, half-human deities commonly appear on cosmological trees, which as will become apparent are another venue for the love of representing the cosmological powers between sky and earth.

Cosmological Trees

The universal image of the cosmological tree, the well-known axis-mundi symbol, is another persistent motif of early Chinese *sifang* cosmology and belief in metamorphism. The earliest visually descriptive example is witnessed in bronze at Sanxingdui (Figure 8.12B) during the Shang period and becomes a common feature by the end of the Eastern Zhou Period. The cosmological tree is one other significant representation of the spirit orientation, underscoring belief in life after death. Mountains may be drawn simply in a pyramidal outline (Figure 8.12B) and sprout trees whose branches are filled with birds, winged persons, dancers, and deities (Figure 8.12C).

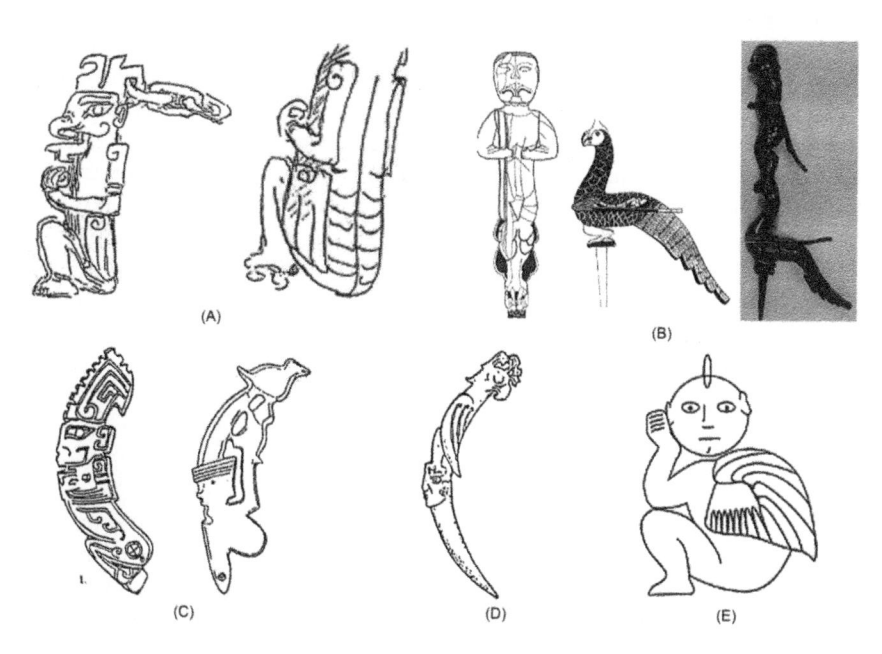

Figure 8.11 Variations of the bird person (usually a winged human in fetal position with bird head) from the Jade Age through Eastern Zhou periods, 3000–300 BCE. (A) Two views of a jade birdman from Xingan, Jiangxi, Middle Shang period. (B) Three views of bird mount plus birdman with wings in bronze, from Jingmen Tianxingguan, Hubei, Warring States period. (C) Jade birdman, Zhaolingshan, M77: 71, Liangzhu culture. (D) Two birdmen from Yinxu, Shang period. (E) Detail from rectangular bronze *pan* vessel with tiger supports and raised décor of squatting birdmen and tapirs, and a detail of the squatting bird-person looking out at the viewer. Late Springs and Autumns/Early Warring States Period, 6th–5th centuries BCE. Palace Museum Beijing. (A) Jiangxi 1997: 138, Figure 80.1; drawings courtesy of Hayashi Minao. (B) Hubei. gov.cn 08/12/2016 09:47. (C) Childs-Johnson 2009: Figure 15 H5-10. (D) IA CASS 2015:32, pl. 18. (E) Lee, ed 1998: colorpl 48 (detail); drawing by Margaret Panoti.

This shorthand symbol for hill or mountain recalls in its simplicity the similarly designed mountain emblem on Neolithic, Liangzhu, and Dawenkou ritual implements (Figure 8.12A). This similarity of religious interest of two seemingly distant periods is telling in drawing them together as a tradition of belief. The "mountain" emblem of Jade Age date is comparable with the mountain base of the bronze spirit trees and ceramic lamps. In addition, both the mountain altar emblems portrayed on Neolithic jades are furnished with the sun and moon symbols, as represented below the feet of the Eastern Zhou image of Taiyi, as well as by the traditional tropes of spirit flight, a winged bird or bird perched atop a stand of some sort. The pyramidal symbols portrayed on the Eastern Zhou vessels are "essentially animistic images of the spirit realm in an area of mountains enlivened with the activities of many animals and monstrous creatures" (Munakata 1991: 13; also see pages 2–48 for a review of mountain worship and transcendental afterlife). This mountain and tree combination, as with the cosmic tree, in Sichuan art of Shang date, is a cosmological symbol of the world axis that served the soul in its ascent from earth to the upper realm of the empyrean.

It is unclear why there appears to be a gap in the representation of the cosmological tree between Shang and Eastern Zhou Period art. The tree as

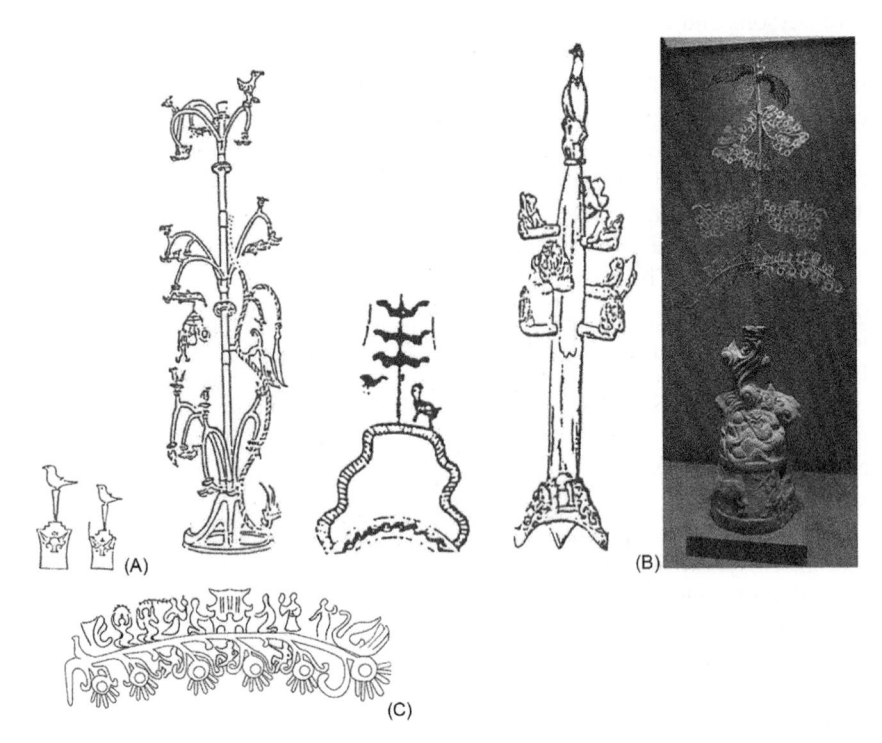

Figure 8.12 Drawings showing stepped altars or abstract mountain shapes with cosmological trees and branches filled with birds, from the Jade Age through the Warring States and Han periods, ca. 3000–300 BCE. (A) Drawings of outdoor raised altars, some with sun and moon, and bird symbols, Hemudu and Liangzhu cultures. (B) Drawings of cosmological trees emerging from an abstract mountain shape and branches with birds. (C) Bronze cosmological tree as a glazed ceramic mountain base with wild animals and bronze tree, drawings of tree branches with immortals, and detail showing replicated eyes of the peafowl feather symbolizing sun icons. (A) See this text, Ch. 3 Figure 3.1E. (B) Sichuan 1997: opposite 218: Figure 120; Munakata 1991: 14AB. (C) Hong Kong Heritage Museum. https://en.wikipedia.org/wiki/Money_tree_(myth)

world axis is common in Warring States and Han art, but it is known as early as the Shang Period in regional Sanxingdui, Sichuan. In distant Zhongshan, the Warring States state of King Cuo on the northern edge of the realm at Shijiazhuang, Hebei has a lamp in the form of a tree with branches on four axes upon which perch birds, monkeys, and other creatures of the wild (Wu Xl 2017). A dragon whose snake-like body wraps around the tree's trunk identifies this tree as imaginary, part fantastic and part real. Other cosmological trees have been identified elsewhere during later eras than the Eastern Zhou Period, as represented, for example, by a version recovered in the Three Gorges in what heretofore was identified as Sichuan (Eckholm 1998).The latter bronze tree balances *feng* birds and masked birdmen. These bird persons and multiple "sun birds" perched on branches simulating peafowl feathers clearly reference an enlightened state of existence beyond the murky wilderness fraught with danger. The artist has subtly and aesthetically expanded the *feng* theme by abstracting branches into feathery shapes of the peafowl species, with the oscillation of the feather represented as a large, pearl-shaped bud upon which the birds and masked birdmen perch. The cosmological tree of bronze sun-birds may have been associated with the later myth where the golden sun-birds, the *feng*- peafowls present the world with light. The base of the tree is in the shape of a mountain and is often filled with wild animals. It may not be fortuitous that the cosmological trees of Teothuacan and earlier Mesoamerican sites are also characterized by a symbolic base out of which rises a tree with limbs decorated with supernatural birds, and in the former case by symbolic hands issuing water-seeping flowers (see e.g. Schele 1999: no 7310). Clearly, western and eastern religious traditions find commonalty tied to aesthetics and belief systems.

It is understandable why animals, both fantastic and real, are so popular in early Chinese art and why the *long* and *feng*, feline, and hunted animal were singled out for representation. The hunted animal was a religious vehicle, invested with ancestral spirit power in Shang times and with apotropaic power in later times. The animal's frequent presence throughout pre-imperial times in China is directly tied to the Chinese belief in zooanthropy – the conviction that the ethereal human double may settle in animals and men may be transformed into beasts and vice versa. The realm of the wilderness – identified by the mountain theme and hunted animal – was honored through exorcism and invocation. Although we may identify certain of the felines and *feng* and *long* and *yi* masks with specific spirits mentioned in bone inscriptions or in the *Chuci*, the intention to represent a "ritualistic vision" and the superterrestrial realm of Di (or Tian), known since Shang times, is corroborated by both representational and literary evidence. The vessel surfaces plastered with spirits are the mystical parks of Di, the intermediary spaces between heaven and earth, that later become identified with more benign spaces of retreat in the organized faith of Han period Daoism.

Yi Metamorphic Power in the Han period and Beyond

The belief in *yi* metamorphic power was pre-eminent from the Jade Age through the Bronze Age and continued to serve as the basic substratum of faith and practice in Chinese tradition. The *yi* metamorphic power mask was the pre-eminent visual representation of this belief from its inception in the Jade Age Liangzhu culture, well into the Western Zhou. As we have demonstrated, the *yi* mask on the one hand represented the transformed soul of a deceased king, powerful and transcendent, demanding sacrifice and worship, and on the other a powerful distant royal spirit power. The *yi* mask lost its status of iconic primacy in the Springs and Autumns Period, but it did not disappear. Instead, it survived, sometimes reinterpreted as a narrative and sometimes as an apotropaic device appearing on door handles, chariot linchpins, keystones of arches, saddlebags, the solar plexus of body armor, and other vulnerable places, particularly associated with arches and openings. Long after the end of the Bronze Age, *yi* metamorphic power continued to play a fundamental role in the belief system of Chinese culture, for aeons of time to the current century (Figure 8.13).

Figure 8.13 Drawing of the bronze bell image depicting the *yi* spirit empowered deity riding a wild buffalo beast (as a frontal mask) and surrounded by curling feline and bird forms – the four standard metamorphic tropes of Bronze Age China. Leigudun, Hubei, last phase, Springs and Autumns/ early Warring States, 5th century BCE. Drawing by Margaret Panoti.

Notes

1 For studies of Springs and Autumns history see Pines 2020 and cited references in his bibliography.
2 For an in-depth study of Eastern Zhou bronze art see So 1980; 1995.
3 See comparable examples of Chu sculptures in Salmony 1954 and Demattè 1994: 353–404.
4 Fu and Chen 1992, 35, where, however the main figure is mistakenly identified as *Tubo*土伯, the Lord of the Soil. See also Lai 2017, pl 14.

9 Conclusion

In this book, we have drawn upon the methods and insights of Archaeology, Art History, History of Religion, Intellectual History, and related fields to explore and confirm our thesis that metamorphism – the ability of (some) people, such as kings both living and dead – to transform themselves into numinous beings possessing great spiritual power; and that metamorphic imagery, therefore, is the key to understanding the art and religion of ancient China and its antecedents. We show that this imagery, and the beliefs and practices that it entailed, originated in the Jade Age (the final phase of the Chinese Neolithic) and remained remarkably stable for many centuries before declining (though never disappearing) during the Eastern Zhou period. Ancestor worship, the defining characteristic of Chinese religion, was deeply rooted in belief in the phenomenon of metamorphosis and expressed in metamorphic imagery.

In tracing the long history of metamorphic belief and imagery, we adopted a chronological approach, with chapters tied to the major stages of ancient Chinese history. Within each chapter, we provided archaeological, historical, and other forms of context for our discussions of metamorphism. It is appropriate, as the book comes to a close, to review our findings.

In our Introduction (Chapter 1), we explained what we mean by metamorphism and the related terms "metamorphic image" and "metamorphic power mask." We also commented on a few other important terms, such as *yi* 異 "spiritual empowerment," which endows one with special powers and religious efficacy, and the much-debated word "shamanism." In that Introduction, we also set out what we intended to demonstrate in the book itself. Chapters 2–4 explored the three main cultural drivers of the Jade Age, namely Hongshan, Liangzhu, and Longshan.

In Chapter 2, on the Hongshan culture, we noted that in many ways it was an outlier among the various ancient cultures that, in time, coalesced to form a clear Chinese culture. Located in the far northeast of the East Asian Heartland region, it was far removed from the great river drainage basins that played a dominant role in creating the land and culture that we call China. Moreover, Hongshan customs and beliefs, from stone-lined tombs to the supposed "Goddess Temple" at Niuheliang, left almost no trace of

DOI: 10.4324/9781003341246-9

influence on later Chinese culture. What captured our interest was their skill at jade-working, the elevation of jade to the highest rank of precious and prestigious material, and the development of fanciful hybrid beings carved in jade and buried with elite persons as funerary treasure. Prominent among Hongshan jades are the so-called "pig dragons," which imply a concept of metamorphism. Significantly, examples appear in areas south of Hongshan territory, such as the Yangzi river culture of Lingjiatan and in later cultural historic phases there.

The decline of Hongshan coincided with the rise, in the lower reaches of the Yangzi River and its delta, of the Liangzhu culture, the second of the great jade-working cultures of the Jade Age. Spread over a large, populous, and resource-rich area, Liangzhu probably was divided politically into two or more city-states or proto-states. Liangzhu elites were able to command enormous mobilizations of labor to build walls, building foundations, and mortuary step pyramids. Elites were buried in the terraces of such pyramids; near their tombs were buildings that apparently were used for ongoing post-funerary rituals, an important step in the development of ancestor worship. Some individuals were buried with dozens of jade objects, including the signature Liangzhu *bi* perforated circular disks and *cong* prismatic cylinders, as well as *yue* axes and other shapes, all worked with consummate skill and a refined aesthetic sense. Essential to our argument is the appearance on many Liangzhu jades of a clearly depicted metamorphic power image, the formal characteristics of which perfectly matched and anticipated, for example, the metamorphic power masks that were ubiquitous on Shang bronzes more than a millennium later. This testifies to a larger point that religiously meaningful images can remain remarkably stable over long periods of time.

Chapter 4 took us to the last phase of the Jade Age, the Longshan culture (or, as some scholars would have it, the Longshan *cultures*, there being many local variants of the basic Longshan theme). Originating in Shandong, the Longshan culture spread widely in the East Asian Heartland Region, probably engendering a number of proto-states in that vast area. Two unmistakable cultural markers, *zhang* jade blades (probably symbols of rank or authority) and eggshell-thin blackware ceramics, track the spread of Longshan culture. The presence of large numbers of blackware goblets in elite tombs testifies to graveside funerary feasting, while buildings set aside for ritual use indicate a further development of the cult of ancestors. The metamorphic power image, with antecedents in Dawenkou and Liangzhu, was interpreted as a frontally displayed humanoid, often depicted in jade. The solar observatory at Taosi, a large and important Longshan city in Shanxi, testifies to a concern for seasonal and directional orientation as key elements of Longshan engagement with the cosmos, a trait that was passed down to Longshan's Bronze Age successors. With Longshan, the archaic Sinitic world begins to look Chinese.

Chapters 5–8 trace the theme of metamorphic belief and ancestor worship through the Bronze Age. Chapter 5 deals with the first of China's

Bronze Age cultures, centered on the ancient city at Erlitou, in the Yellow River valley. Many scholars identify Erlitou with the Xia, the first of China's three ancient dynasties as described in the received literary tradition. We cautiously largely avoided the term Xia, using "Erlitou period" and "Erlitou state" instead. By any name, it is clear that Erlitou was a dynastic state that asserted control over a substantial hinterland and engaged in long-distant trade. Bronze revolutionized the ancient Sinitic world. The rulers of Erlitou used bronze vessels (sometimes with shapes that originated in clay) to make offerings of millet ale, grain, and meat. If there was written language in the Erlitou period, no evidence of it has survived, so we cannot know the details of their ritual practices. It is clear from present evidence for large-scale ritual buildings and elite graves that ancestor worship was well established as a feature of royal authority. Images, such as the spectacular death shroud featuring a power mask and *long* dragon in turquoise inlay and comparable jade images of semi-humans and masks, document the profound belief in the power of metamorphosis.

Chapter 6 deals with the Shang dynasty, which succeeded the Erlitou state around 1600 BCE. Oracle bone inscriptions provide a detailed picture of metamorphic beliefs in practice, with the use of bronze vessels representing metamorphically transformed royal ancestors in rites of propitiation tied to the ten-day week, as well as rites directed to the High Cosmic God Di and other nature deities. Utilizing various techniques such as mask-wearing, drumming, and dancing, a Shang king would enter an altered state of consciousness called *yi*, "spiritual empowerment," that allowed him to communicate directly with the High God; we refer to this performative ritual as "institutional shamanism." The kings, or specialists acting on their behalf, employed bone-cracking or plastron-cracking divination with great frequency on a wide array of subjects. The world of Shang royalty was saturated with metamorphic beliefs and imagery. The metamorphic power mask representing deceased royal ancestors was ubiquitous on bronze vessels used in the ancestral rites, reaching a new technological and aesthetic apex in that medium. Deceased Shang kings were buried in huge cruciform tombs aligned with the polar axis and richly stocked with grave goods, including bronze ritual vessels that would enable the tomb occupant to continue to worship his own ancestors.

Recent studies of Shang cities beyond the capital make clear (overturning the conventional view) that the Shang kings ruled a substantial territory, probably including subaltern states governed by royal kinsmen. The kings' domain extended to the Four Quarters (*sifang*), territories extending in the four cardinal directions. The kings sometimes made ceremonial progressions through the realm. Of particular note were massively organized royal hunts that served to affirm the primacy of the king as well as to capture the sorts of wild animals (buffalo, deer, caprids, and tigers) whose bodily attributes were combined in the visual vocabulary of the metamorphic power mask.

These attributes – institutional shamanism, a strong concern with directional orientation, a fully developed system of royal ancestor worship, the key role of the royal hunt, and the ubiquity of metamorphic imagery including the standardized metamorphic power mask on ritual bronzes – represent the culmination of two millennia of metamorphism as the foundation of religious belief and practice in ancient China.

The Shang dynasty was overthrown by the founders of the Zhou dynasty in 1046 BCE. Zhou kings would occupy China's throne for the next nine centuries. But for much of that time, they reigned but did not rule. The kings of the Western Zhou period (1046–771 BCE), the subject of our Chapter 7, ruled a large and powerful realm, but with military defeat and a shift of their capital to a shrunken realm in the east, the house of Zhou, and its ancient religion, ultimately fell into a long-term decline. Western Zhou rule retained many aspects of Shang rule, including ongoing sacrifices to *Di* and in bronze imagery, a style that may be described as *weiyi* 畏儀, the Shang-related icon of awesome metamorphic power. There were also innovations. The Zhou had their own sky-god, Tian; the Zhou kings referred to themselves as "sons of Tian" and claimed that Tian had sanctified their hereditary rule by granting them a "mandate." Divination by stalk-casting largely replaced scapulimancy; the regular weekly worship of royal ancestors was discontinued. Bronze décor showed a continuing evolution of the metamorphic power mask, which began to feature prominently the iconic *feng* bird (the Zhou kings identified themselves with the color red, the direction south, and the *feng* bird among numinous creatures) and its counterpart, the *long* dragon. Inscriptions on bronze vessels, sometimes running to several hundred characters, provide first-hand evidence of the concerns and actions of the Zhou kings and their aristocratic supporters. Many such inscriptions record the granting of gifts to a subject; these often include a quantity of bronze to make vessels with which the grantee could worship his ancestors. This is an important change in early Chinese religion: ancestor worship was no longer the sole prerogative of kings, and royal relations New metamorphic imagery began to appear during the Western Zhou: not only the *feng*, symbolizing flight (an important theme in later Chinese conceptions of immortality), but also humanoid beings in displayed or fetal poses, engraved on jade or depicted in other media, apparently symbolizing the rebirth in an altered form of the deceased occupant of the tomb in which such images appear. But it is apparent by the end of the Western Zhou that the old metamorphic imagery was in decline. The power mask was no longer ubiquitous on bronzes, giving way to new surface décor on new vessel shapes. Bronzes themselves acquired new meanings, being treated mainly as prestigious luxury goods for display rather than as spiritually charged objects used in ancestor worship.

Chapter 8 recounted the circumstances of the defeat and decline of the royal house of Zhou in 771, the principal effect of which was to open the way for the various territorial states, supposedly subordinate to the Zhou kings, to become semi-independent kingdoms in their own right. The Springs and Autumns era (722–479 BCE), and especially the Warring States period (479–221), politically was a chaotic and dangerous time, as big states conquered and absorbed smaller states and themselves struggled to survive. Territorial monarchs competed culturally as well as on the battlefield. New virtuoso bronze-working techniques, such as the lost-wax casting method, produced new-style bronzes of stunning complexity. Some types of vessels were produced in sets of graduated sizes; the number of vessels in a set for a nobleman of a given rank were prescribed by sumptuary regulations that were often flouted. The secularization of bronze, already apparent in the late Western Zhou, was a dominant trend thereafter. The bronze metamorphic power mask devolved into a protective talisman. However, metamorphic symbolism did not disappear; it evolved in new ways in a new place: the great southern state of Chu. Culturally distinct from the central and northern states (in part, at least, because of the ethnically diverse local cultures included within its boundaries), the art and literature of Chu are replete with shamanistic images and other manifestations of metamorphic thinking. Lacquered wooden tomb guardians, bug-eyed and often crowned with antlers, are re-imagined versions of the classic metamorphic power mask. The bizarre-looking monthly gods of the Chu Silk Manuscript, or the depictions of Taiyi on a silk document from Mawangdui, and the mountain-dwelling shamans described in the *Shanhaijing* (Classic of Mountains and Seas) continue a centuries-long tradition of visualizing deities in metamorphically transformed guise. The shamanic references in the *Chuci* (Elegies of Chu) recall the ability of the kings of the ancient Shang dynasty to communicate directly with the High God without mediation. Chu culture had a strong impact on broader Chinese culture, especially during the Han dynasty, preserving metamorphic imagery and ways of understanding the cosmos and mankind's place in it.

We believe that, with this book, we have advanced by a step or two the scholarly understanding of the origins and evolution of China's ancient religion. That understanding will continue to evolve and become more complicated, as new material in the form of objects and texts emerges from China's earth. We hope that our book will stimulate younger scholars to pursue further the issues we have raised here. Potential topics for exploration are numerous, including, for example, the relevance of nomenclature – the names for winds [symbolized by bird imagery], the 12 monthly spirits of Chu, and the name of the distant ancestral deity Kui. How does this nomenclature fit with the imagery of metamorphic power? How do we explain the variations in attributions of metamorphic mask imagery and ancestral spirit powers? How did the supernatural power-flow of life and afterlife come to be invested in the concept of *qi*氣? How did the bureaucratic structure of the Zhou period effect the religion of metamorphosis? Why is the humanoid in displayed guise a mainstay of early Chinese religious art and religion? These and many similar topics await, and will reward, further research.

Works Cited and Additional Sources

Academia Sinica n.d. "先秦甲骨金文簡牘詞彙資料庫 (Lexicon of pre-Qin oracle bones, bronze inscriptions and bamboo slips)." https://inscription.sinica.edu.tw/.

Alexandridis, Annetta with Markus Wild and Lorenz Winkler-Horaček 2008. *Mensch und Tier in der Antike: Grenzziehung und Grenzüberschreitung.* Verlag: Ludwig Reischert.

Allan, Sarah 1991. *The Shape of the Turtle: Myth, Art, and Cosmos in Early China.* Albany: SUNY Press.

Allan, Sarah 2007a. "On the Identity of Shang Di and the Origin of the Concept of a Celestial Mandate (*tian ming* 天命)" *Early China* 31: 1–46.

Allan, Sarah 2007b. "Erlitou and the Formation of Chinese Civilization: Toward a New Paradigm," *Journal of Asian Studies* 66.2: 461–96.

Allan, Sarah 2016. "The Taotie Motif on Early Chinese Ritual Bronzes," in Jerome Silbergeld and Eugene Wang, eds., *The Zoomorphic Imagination in Chinese Art and Culture,* 21–66. Honolulu: University of Hawai'i Press.

Allsen, Thomas 2006. *The Royal Hunt in Eurasian History.* Philadelphia: University of Pennsylvania Press.

Anhui 2000. Anhui Sheng Wenwu Kaogu Yanjiu Suo 安徽省文物考古研究所, ed., Lingjiatan Yuqi 凌家灘玉器 (Jades of Lingjiatan). Beijing: Wenwu Chubanshe.

Anhui Daxue 安徽大學 and Anhuisheng Wenwu Kaogu Yanjiusuo 安徽省文物考古研究所 2006. 皖南商周青铜器 (Shang and Zhou Bronzes of Southern Anhui). Beijing: Wenwu Chubanshe.

Anhuisheng Wenwu Guanli Weiyuanhui 安徽省文物管理委员会, and Anhuisheng Bowuguan 安徽省博物馆 1956. 寿县蔡侯墓出土遗物 (Remains from the Tomb of Cai Hou in Shouxian). Beijing: Kexue Chubanshe.

Anhuisheng Wenwu Kaogu Yanjiusuo 安徽省文物考古研究所 and Hanshan Xian Wenwu Ju 含山县文物局 2015. "安徽含山县韦岗遗址新石器时代遗存发掘简报" (Brief Excavation Report of Weigang Site at Hanshan County, Anhui Province), *Kaogu* 考古 2015.3: 35–50.

Anhui Daxue 安徽大學Anhui Daxue, Anhuisheng Shehui Kexueyuan 安徽省社會科學院, and Anhuisheng Wenwu Kaogu Yanjiusuo 2014. 安徽省文物考古研究所, 安徽江淮地区商周青铜器 (Shang and Zhou Bronzes Unearthed in the Yangzi River and Huai River Area of Anhui). Beijing: Wenwu Chubanshe.

Back, Youngsun 2017. "Who Answered the Shang Diviner, The Nature of Shang Divination." *Journal of Confucian Philosophy and Culture* 27: 1–22.

Bagley, Robert 1987. *Shang Ritual Bronzes in the Arthur M. Sackler Collections.* Washington D.C.: Arthur M. Sackler Foundation.

Baojishi Bowuguan 宝鸡市博物馆, and Baojishi Wenhuaguan 宝鸡市文化馆 1978. "陕西宝鸡县太公庙村发现秦公钟秦公镈" (The Bo and Zhong Bells of Qin Gong Discovered at Taigongmiao Village, Baoji County, Shaanxi Province"). *Wenwu* 文物 1978.11.

Baoli/Poly Bowuguan Bianji Weiyuanhui (Poly Art Museum Editorial Committee) 保利艺术博物馆编辑委员会 eds 1999. 保利艺术博物馆精品选 (Selected Bronzes in the Collection of the Poly Art Museum). Lingnan: Meishu Chubanshe.

Barnard, Noel 1973. *The Ch'u Silk Manuscript. Translation and Commentary.* Canberra: Department of Far Eastern History, Australian National University.

Barnard, Noel with Cheung Kwong-yue 1996. *The Shan-Fu Liang Kuei and Associated Inscribed Vessels.* Taipei: SMC Publishers.

Baxter, William 1992. *A Handbook of Old Chinese Phonology.* New York: Mouton de Gruyter.

Beijing Daxue 2000. Beijing Daxue Kaogu Xuexi and Shanxisheng Kaogu Yanjiusuo 北京大学考古学系, 山西省考古研究所 2000. 天马-曲村1980–1989 (Tianma-Qucun 1980–1989). Beijing: Kexue Chubanshe.

Beijing Daxue 2007. Beijing Daxue Kaogu Wenbo Xueyuan, and Henansheng Wenwu Kaogu Yanjiusuo 北京大学考古文博学院, 河南省文物考古研究所 2007. 封王城岗考古发现与研究 2002~2005 *(Archaeological Discovery and Research on Dengcheng Wangchenggang 2002~2005).* Zhengzhou: Daxiang Chubanshe.

Beijing Daxue 2008. Zhendan (Aurora) Gudai Wenming Yanjiu Zhongxin and Zhengzhoushi Wenwu Kaogu Yanjiusuo 北京大学震旦古代文明研究中心, 郑州市文考古研究所 2008. 新密新砦-1999~2000 年田野发掘报告 (Field Report on Excavations from 1999–2000 at Xinzhai Xinmi). Beijing: Wenwu Chubanshe.

Bennet, Gwen 2007. "Context and Meaning in Late Neolithic Lithic Production in China: The Longshan Period in Southeastern Shandong Province." *Archeological Papers of the American Anthropological Association* 17.1: 52–67. DOI: 10.1525/ap3a.2007.17.1.52.

Birrell, Anne, ed and trans. 1999. *The Classic of Mountains and Seas.* London and New York: Penguin Books.

Boltz, William G. 1994. *The Origin and Early Development of the Chinese Writing System.* American Oriental Series, vol. 78. New Haven: American Oriental Society.

Borić, Dušan 2005. "Body Metamorphosis and Animality: Volatile Bodies and Boulder Artworks from Lepenski Vir," *Cambridge Archaeological Journal* 15.01: 35–69.

Boodberg, Peter A. 1940. "Chinese Zoographic Names as Chronograms," *Harvard Journal of Asiatic Studies* 5.2: 128–36.

Buck, Jeffrey. n.d. *Basic Guide on How to Make Your Very First Archery Arm Guard.* https://outdoorwarrior.com/diy-archery-arm-guard.

Cai Dewei, *et al* 2011. "Early History of Chinese Domestic Sheep Indicated by Ancient DNA Analysis of Bronze Age Individuals." *Journal of Archaeological Science* 38.4: 896–902.

Campbell, Roderick B, ed 2014. *Violence and Civilization, Studies of Social Violence in History and Prehistory.* Oxford: Joukosky Institute Publication.

Campbell, Roderick B. 2016. *Archaeology of the Chinese Bronze Age: From Erlitou to Anyang.* Los Angeles: Cotsen Institute of Archaeology Press.

Campbell, Roderick B. 2018. *Violence, Kinship and the Early Chinese State: The Shang and their World*. New York and Cambridge: Cambridge University Press.

Campbell Roderick B. 2020, "Ritualized Violence, Sovereignty, and Being: Shang Sacrifice," *Tagungen des Landesmuseums Ür Vorgeschichte Hall* 2020: 1–13.

Campbell, Roderick B. Campbell, Zhipeng Li, Yuling He, and Yuan Jing 2011. "Consumption, Exchange and Production at the Great Settlement Shang: Bone-working at Tiesanlu, Anyang." *Antiquity* 85:1279–97.

Cao Dingyun 曹定雲 1993. 殷墟婦好銘文研究(*Research on Inscriptions from the Tomb of Fu Hao [Zi] at Yin*). Tianjin: Wenjin Chubanshe.

Cao Dingyun 2004. 夏代文字的鉴定-二里头文化陶器文字研究 (Identification of Writing in the Xia Period: A Study of Pottery Glyphs in the Erlitou Culture), *Kaogu* 2004.12: 76–83, with abridged English summary in *Chinese Archaeology* 5 (2005): 183–87.

Cao Dingyun 2020. "Late Shang: Fu Zi and M5 at Xiaotun," in Elizabeth Childs-Johnson, ed., *Oxford Handbook of Early China*, 350–61. New York: Oxford University Press.

Cao Wei 曹玮 1993. "從青銅器的演化試論西周前後期之交的禮制變化周秦文化學術討論會論文集" (The Change in Ritual Regulations During the Transition of Early and Late Western Zhou as Witnessed in the Change of Bronze Artifacts). 周秦文化会议论文集 (Proceedings of the Conference on Zhou and Qin Culture). Xi'an: Shaanxi Renmin Chubanshe.

Cao Wei 2002. 周原甲骨文 (Zhouyuan Oracle Bones). Beijing: Shijie Shuju.

Cao Wei 2004. 周原遺址與西周銅器研究 (Research on the Western Zhou Remains at Zhouyuan and Their Bronzes). Beijing: Kexue Chubanshe.

Cao Wei 2005. 周原出土青铜器 (Bronzes Excavated in the Zhouyuan Region). 10 vols. Chengdu: Ba Shu Shushe.

Cao Wei 2006. 汉中出土商代青铜器 (Shang Era Bronzes Unearthed in the Mid-Han River Region). 3 vols. Chengdu: Ba Shu Shushe.

Carneiro, Robert L. 1981. "The Chiefdom as Precursor to a State." in Grant D. Jones and Robert Kautz, eds., *The Transition to Statehood in the New World*, 37–79. New York: Cambridge University Press.

Chang, K. C. [Zhang Guangzhi] 1976. *Early Chinese Civilization: Anthropological Perspectives*. Cambridge, MA: Harvard University Press.

Chang, K. C. 1981. "The Animal in Shang and Chou Bronze Art." *Harvard Journal of Asiatic Studies* 41 (2), 527–54.

Chang, K. C. 1983. *Art, Myth, and Ritual: The Path to Political Authority in Ancient China*. Cambridge, MA: Harvard University Press.

Chang, K. C. 1986. *The Archaeology of Ancient China*, 4th ed. New Haven: Yale University Press.

Chang, K. C., ed 1986. *Studies of Shang Archaeology: Selected Papers from the International Conference on Shang Civilization*. New Haven: Yale University Press.

Chang, K. C. 1990. "商代的巫与巫术" (Shang Shamans and Shamanistic Arts). *Zhongguo Qingtong Shidai*, 2nd series, 39–66. Beijing: Sanlian Press.

Chang, K. C.1993a "Shang Shamans," in Willard Peterson, ed., *Power of Culture*, 10–36. Princeton: Princeton Univ. Press.

Chang, K. C.1993b "仰韶文化的巫覡覡資料" (Data on Yangshao Culture and Shamanic Arts), *Zhongyang Yanjiuyuan Yuyan Yanjiusuo Jikan* 中央研究院语研究所集刊 64.3: 611–25.

Chang, K. C. 1993c "人類歷史上 的巫教的一個初步定義" (A Preliminary Definition of Shamanism in Human Anthropological History). *Guoli Taiwan Daxue Kaogu Renlei Xuekan* 49 (1993.12): 1–6.

Chaoyangshi Wenwuju and Liaoningsheng Wenwu Kaogu Yanjiusuo 朝陽市文物局, 辽宁省文物考古研究所 2004. 牛河梁遗址 (Niuheliang Remains). Beijing: Kexue Chubanshe.

Che Guangjin 車廣錦1995. "玉琮與寺墩遗址(Sidun Remains and the Jade Cong)," *Zhongguo Wenwu Bao* 中國文物報 1995.12.3. Reprinted in Xu Huping 徐湖平, ed 1996. *Dongfang Wenming* 東方文明之光 (The Dawn of Eastern Civilization), 良渚文化發現60周年紀念文集 (1936–1996) (*Collected Papers Commemorating the 60th Anniversary of the Discovery of the Liangzhu Culture (1936–1996)*), 371–373. Haikou: Hainan Guoji Xinwen Chubanshe and Nanjing: Nanjing Hangkong Hangtian Daxue Feida Chubanshe.

Chen De'an 陳德安1997. 四川三星堆玉章的種類源源及宗教意義 (The Typology, Development, and Religious Significance of Jade Scepters from Sanxingdui, Sichuan," in Deng Cong, ed, 南中國及鄰近地區古文化研究 (Studies in the Cultures of South China and Neighboring Regions). Hong Kong: Chinese University of Hong Kong Press.

Chen Guoliang 陈国良2008. 二里头文化铜器研究 – 中国早期青铜文 化 – 二里头文化专题研究 (Research on Erlitou Culture Bronzes, Early Bronze Culture of China – Special Study of the Erlitou Culture). Beijing: Kexue Chubanshe.

Chen Guoliang 2016. "二里头遗址铸铜遗存" (Smelting and Casting Bronze Remains Preserved at Erlitou),. *Zhongyuan Wenwu* 2016: 35–44. Beijing: Kexue Chubanshe.

Chen Mengjia 陳夢家 1956. 殷墟卜辭綜述 (A Review of Yin Divinatory Language). Beijing: Kexue Chubanshe. (Reprint Zhonghua Shuju, 1988).

Chen Peifen 陈佩芬 2004. 夏商周青铜器研 (Research on Xia, Shang, and Zhou bronzes), 6 vols. Shanghai: Shanghai Guji Chubanshe.

Chen Quanfang 陳全方1988. 周原与周文化 (Zhouyuan and Zhou Culture). Shanghai: Renmin Chubanshe.

Chen Quanfang 2003. 西周甲骨文注 (Notes on Western Zhou Oracle Bone Inscriptions). Shanghai: Renmin Chubanshe.

Chen Xiaosan 陈小三2013. "试论镶嵌绿松石牌饰的起源" (Discussion on the Origin of Turquoise-inlaid Plaques), *Kaogu yu Wenwu* 5: 91–100.

Chen Zhenyu 陳振裕 2003. 楚文化與漆器研究 (Research on Chu Culture and Lacquerware). Beijing: Kexue Chubanshe.

Childs-Johnson, Elizabeth 1995a. "The Ghost Head Mask and Metamorphic Shang Imagery." *Early China* 20: 79–92.

Childs-Johnson, Elizabeth 1995b. "Symbolic Jades of the Erlitou Period: A Xia Royal Tradition." *Archives of Asian Art* 48: 64–90.

Childs-Johnson, Elizabeth 1998a. "Metamorphic Imagery in Ancient Chinese Art: *Long*-Dragons, *Feng* Phoenixes, *Gui* Spirit-Masks, and the Spirit Journey." *Kaikodo Journal* VII : *The Power of Form* 30-51.

Childs-Johnson, Elizabeth 1998b. "The Metamorphic Image: A Predominant Theme in Shang Ritual Art." *Bulletin of the Museum of Far Eastern Antiquities* 70: 5–171.

Childs-Johnson, Elizabeth 2002a. "Jade as Confucian Ideal, Immortal Cloak, and Medium for the Metamorphic Fetal Pose," in E Childs-Johnson, *Enduring Art of Jade Age China*, 15–24. New York: Throckmorton Fine Art.

Childs-Johnson, Elizabeth 2002b. "Review of Xiaoneng Yang, *Reflections of Early China Decor, Pictographs, and Pictorial Inscriptions.*" College Art Association Reviews 9/23, 2002:1-3. http://www.caareviews.org/contents.html.

Childs-Johnson, Elizabeth 2007. "Fu Zi, the Shang Woman Warrior," in Lily Xiao Hong Lee and A. D. Stefanoska, eds., *A Biographical Dictionary of Chinese Women,* Vol. 1, *Shang through Sui Period,* 119–25. Armonk, New York: M. E. Sharpe.

Childs-Johnson, Elizabeth 2008. *The Meaning of the Graph Yi*異 *and Its Implications for Shang Belief and Art.* East Asia Journal Monograph. London: Saffron Books.

Childs-Johnson, Elizabeth 2009. "The Art of Working Jade and the Rise of Civilization in China," in E. Childs-Johnson, The Jade Age & Early Chinese Jades in American Museums玉器时代，美国博物馆 藏

Childs-Johnson, Elizabeth 2013. "Divine Authority and Legitimacy: The Monumental Tetrapod *Ding* of the Shang Period." *Asian Perspectives* 52.1: 164–220.

Childs-Johnson, Elizabeth 2016. Urban daemons of early Shang, *Archaeological Research in Asia* (2016), http://dx.doi.org/10.1016/ j.ara.2016.08.001

Childs-Johnson, Elizabeth 2019. "The Erlitou Aesthetic and State Building," 二里头美感跟建筑国家有影响), 国邦): 一个反思第二届世界古都论坛暨纪念二里头遗址科学发掘60周年学术研讨会 (The Second International Academic Conference on Ancient Capitals and Celebration of the 60th Anniversary of Excavations at Erlitou, Luoyang Symposium Papers), October 18–20, 2019.

Childs-Johnson, Elizabeth 2020a. "The Jade Age Revisited, ca. 3500-2000 BCE," in E Childs-Johnson, ed, *Oxford Handbook of Early China,* 101–18. New York: Oxford University Press.

Childs-Johnson, Elizabeth 2020b. "Shang Religion, Belief and Art," in E Childs-Johnson, ed. *Oxford Handbook of Early China,* 287–305. New York: Oxford University Press.

Childs-Johnson, Elizabeth 2020c. "Late Shang Layout and Architecture of Anyang Shang City, in Elizabeth Childs-Johnson, ed. *Oxford Handbook of Early China,* 316–52. New York: Oxford University Press.

Childs-Johnson, Elizabeth and Gu Fang 古方 2009. 玉器時代，美國博物館藏中國早期玉器 (The Jade Age and Early Chinese Jades in American Museums). Beijing: Kexue Chubanshe.

Childs-Johnson, Elizabeth and Gu Fang 2010. "Chinese Jade Types of the Shang and Western Zhou Periods." *Shang and Western Zhou Jades,* 23–43. New York: Throckmorton Fine Art.

Childs-Johnson, Elizabeth and Gu Fang 2012. "Speculations on the Significance of the *Cong* and *Bi* of the Liangzhu Culture," in E. Childs-Johnson 2012, *Liangzhu Jades,* 5–12. New York: Throckmorton Fine Art.

Cioffi-Revilla, Claudio and David Lai 1995. "War and Politics in Ancient China, 2700 BC to 722 BC." *The Journal of Conflict Resolution* 39.3: 471–72.

Cohen, David J. and Robert E. Murowchick, 2014. "Early Complex Societies in Northern China," in Colin Renfrew and Paul Bahn, eds, *The Cambridge World Prehistory,* 782–806. Cambridge, UK: Cambridge University Press.

Cook, Constance A. 1997. "Wealth and the Western Zhou," *Bulletin of the School of Oriental and African Studies* 60.2: 253–94.

Cook, Constance A. 2006a. *Death in Ancient China: The Tale of One Man's Journey.* Leiden and Boston: Brill.

Cook, Constance A. 2006b. "From Bone to Bamboo: Number Sets and Mortuary Ritual," *Journal of Oriental Studies* 41.1: 1–40.

Cook, Constance A. 2017. *Ancestors, Kings, and the Dao*. Cambridge: Harvard University Asia Center.

Cook, Constance A. and Paul R. Goldin, eds 2016. *A Source Book of Ancient Chinese Bronze Inscriptions. Early China Monograph Series*, No. 7. Berkeley: The Society for the Study of Early China.

Cook, Constance A. and John S. Major, eds 1999. *Defining Chu: Image and Reality in Ancient China*. Honolulu: University of Hawai'i Press.

Cook, Constance A., and Zhao Lu, eds and trans., 2017. *Stalk Divination: A Newly Discovered Alternative to the I Ching*. Oxford: Oxford University Press.

Cook, Scott 2012. *The Bamboo Texts of Guodian: A Study & Complete Translation*. 2 Vols. Ithaca, NY: Cornell University East Asian Series.

Dai Yingxin 戴应新1977. "陕西神木县石卯遗址调查" (Investigation of Remains at Shimao, Shaanxi Site). *Kaogu* 1977.3 154–57, 172, 217–20.

Dai Yingxin 1988. "神木县石卯龙山文化玉器" (Jades of the Longshan Culture at Shimao, Shenmuxian). *Kaogu yu wenwu* 1988.5: 6-16.

Dai Yingxin 1994a. 高家堡国墓 (The Ge State Cemetery at Gaojiaobao). Xi'an: Sanqin Chubanshe.

Dai Yingxin 1994b. "石卯牙璋与再刻 – 石卯龙山文化研究札记" (Shimao *Yazhang* and Recarving – Notes on Research on the Shimao Longshan Culture Jades), in Tang Chung ed. 南中國及鄰近地區古文化研究 (Ancient Cultures of South China and Neighbouring Regions), 79–86. Hong Kong: The Chinese University Press.

Demattè, Paola 1994. "Antler and Tongue: New Archaeological Evidence in the Study of the Chu Tomb Guardian," *East and West* 44.2–4: 353–404.

Demattè, Paola 1999a. "The Role of Writing in the Process of State Formation in Late Neolithic China," *East and West* 49.1: 241–72.

Demattè, Paola 1999b. "Longshan-era Urbanism: The Role of Cities in Predynastic China," *Asian Perspectives* 38.2: 119–53.

Demattè, Paola 2006. "The Jade Age: Between Antiquarianism and Archaeology," *Journal of Social Archaeology* 6.2: 202–226.

Demattè, Paola 2010. "The Origins of Chinese Writing: The Neolithic Evidence," *Cambridge Archaeological Journal* 20.2: 211–228.

Demattè, Paola 2022. *The Origins of Chinese Writing*. New York: Oxford University Press.

DeSantillana, Giorgio and Hertha von Dechend 1969. *Hamlet's Mill*. Boston: Gambit.

Dietler, Michael 2001. "Theorizing the Feast: Rituals of Consumption, Commensal Politics, and Power in African Contexts," in Michael Dietler and Brian Hayden, eds., *Feasts: Archaeological and Ethnographic Perspectives on Food, Politics, and Power*, 65–114. Washington: Smithsonian Institution Press.

Dietler, Michael 2011. "Feasting and Fasting," in Timothy Insoll, ed, *The Oxford Handbook of the Archaeology of Ritual and Religion*, 179–94. Oxford: Oxford University Press.

Digital Archives Bronze Taiwan. Academia Sinica Center for Digital Cultures, Taipei, n.d. http://catalog.digitalarchives.tw/item/00/0c/ c0/00.html

Dobson, W. A. C. H. 1962. *Early Archaic Chinese, A Descriptive Grammar*. Toronto: University of Toronto Press.

Drennan, Robert D., Xueming Lu and Christian E. Peterson 2017. "A Place of Pilgrimage? Niuheliang and its Role in Hongshan Society." *Antiquity* 91.355: 43–56.

Du Jinpeng 杜金鵬 2007a. 夏商周考古学研究 (Archaeological Research into the Xia, Shang, and Zhou periods). Beijing: Kexue Chubanshe.

Du Jinpeng 2007b. "师二里头遗址都邑制度研究 (Research on the Remains of Erlitou and Urbanization)," in *Xia Shang Zhou Kaoguxue Yanjiu* 夏商周考古学研究. Beijing: Kexue Chubanshe.

Du Jinpeng 2009. "周原宫廷建筑类型学及相关问题研究" (A Typological Study of the Palace Buildings at Zhouyuan and Related Issues), *Kaogu Xuebao* 2009.4: 435–68; English translation in *Chinese Archaeology* 10 (2013): 164–71.

Du Jinpeng and Xu Hong 許宏 eds 2006. 二里頭遺址與二里頭文化研究 (Research into the Remains of Erlitou and Erlitou Culture). Beijing: Kexue Chubanshe.

Du Zhengsheng 杜正勝1992. 古代社會與國家 (Ancient Society and the State). Taipei: Yunchen Wenhua.

Eckholm, Eric 1998. "Sold China 'Spirit Tree' May Have Been Stolen," *New York Times*, May 16, 1998, Section A.

Eno, Robert 2008. "Shang State Religion and the Pantheon of the Oracle Texts," in John Lagerway and Mark Kalinowsky, eds, *Early Chinese Religion, Part One: Shang through Han (1250 BC-220 AD)*, 41–102. Leiden: Brill.

Erkes, Eduard 1926. "Chinesisch-americanische mythenparallelen," *T'oung Pao* 24: 32–54.

Falkenhausen, Lothar von 2006. *Chinese Society in the Age of Confucius (1000–250 BC). The Archaeological Evidence.* Los Angeles: Cotsen Institute of Archaeology, University of California.

Fang Hui *et al*, 2008. "山东东南沿海地区居民点格局变化与社会复杂性发展研究" (A Study on the Change of Settlement Patterns and the Development of Social Complexity in Southeastern Coast Area in Shandong, China), *Dongfang Kaogu* 2008.4: 253–87.

Fang Yousheng 方酉生1965. "河南偃师二里头遗址发掘简报" (Preliminary Excavation Report on the Site of Erlitou in Yanshi, Henan), *Kaogu* 1965.5.

Feng Shi 冯时 1994. "山东丁公龙山时代文字解读" (Reading and Analysis of the Writing of Longshan Period in Dinggong, Shandong Province], *Kaogu* 1994.1: 37–54.

Feng Puren 冯普仁 2007. 吴越文化 (Wu and Yue Cultures). Beijing: Wenwu Chubanshe.

Fiskesjö, Magnus 2001a. "Rising from Blood-stained Fields: Royal Hunting and State Formation in Shang China," *Bulletin of the Museum of Far Eastern Antiquities* 73: 48–191.

Flad, Rowan 2001b. "Ritual or Structure? Analysis of Burial Elaboration at Dadianzi, Inner Mongolia," *Journal of East Asian Archaeology* 3(3–4): 23–51.

Flad, Rowan 2008a. "Divination and Power: A Multiregional View of the Development of Oracle Bone Divination in Early China," *Current Anthropology* 49.3: 403–38.

Flad, Rowan 2008b. "贞人: 关于早期中国施灼占卜起源与展的一些思考 Divine Specialists: Some Thoughts on the Origins and Development of Pyromantic Divination in Early China)," in Jing Zhichun and Ken-ichi Takashima, eds, *Proceedings of the Workshop on Early Chinese Civilization*, 85–113. Beijing: Kexue Chubanshe.

Flad, Rowan 2013. "The Sichuan Basin," in Anne P. Underhill, ed, *Companion to Chinese Archaeology*, 125–46. Malden, MA: Wiley-Blackwell.

Flad, Rowan and Pochan Chen 2013. *Ancient Central China: Centers and Peripheries Along the Yangzi River (Case Studies in Early Societies)*. Cambridge and New York: Cambridge University Press.

Flad, Rowan 2017. "Urbanism as Technology in Ancient China," *Archaeological Research in Asia* 14: 121–34.

Fong, Mary 1988–89. "The Origin of Chinese Pictorial Representation of the Human Figure," *Artibus Asiae* 49.1/2: 5–38.

Fracasso, Riccardo 1993. "Shan hai jing," in Michael Loewe, ed, *Early Chinese Texts: A Bibliographic Guide,* 357–67. Berkeley: Society for the Study of Early China.

Fracasso, Riccardo 1996. *Libro dei monti e dei mari (Shanhai jing): Cosmografia e mitologia nella Cina Antica.* Venice: Marsilio.

Fu Juyou 傅舉有 and Chen Songchang 陳松長 1992. 馬王堆漢墓文物 (The Cultural Relics Unearthed from the Han Tombs at Mawangdui). Changsha: Hunan Chupanshe.

Fu Sinian傅斯年1934, 1992. 城子崖山東歷城縣龍山鎮之黑陶文化遺址 (Chengziyai: Black Pottery Culture Remains at Longshan, Li Chengxian, Shandong). Taibei: Guoli Zhongyang Yanjiuyuan Lishi Yuyan Yanjiusuo.

Fujiansheng Bowuguan and Guangzexian Wenhuaju Wenhuaguan 福建省博物馆, 福建省光泽县 1985. "古代墓葬遺址检查与发掘" – (Investigation and Clearance of Ancient Tomb and Site Remains at Guangze County in Fujian province). *Kaogu* 1985.12: 1095–1108.

Galvany, Albert 2020. "Political, Military, and Economic Reforms: The Amy, Wars, and Military Arts [Warring States]," in E. Childs-Johnson, ed., *Oxford Handbook of Early China,* 639–58. New York: Oxford University Press.

Gan, Fuxi *et al*, 2010. "The Non-destructive Analysis of Ancient Jade Artifacts Unearthed from the Liangzhu Sites at Yuhang, Zhejiang." *Science China Technological Sciences* 53.12: 3404–419. DOI: 10.1007/s11431-010-4167-1.

Gansusheng Wenwu Kaogu Yanjiusuo 甘肃省文物考古研究所 2002. "礼县圆顶山春秋秦墓" (The Springs and Autumns Period Qin Tombs at Yuandingshan, Lixian), *Wenwu* 2002. 2.

Gansusheng Wenwu Kaogu Yanjiusuo 2005. "甘肃礼县圆顶山 98LDM2、2000LDM4 春秋秦墓" (The Springs and Autumns Period Qin Tombs 98LDM2 and 2000LDM4 at Lixian, Gansu), *Wenwu* 2005.2 4–27.

Gao Chongwen 高崇文 1983. "东周楚式鼎形态分析 (A Formal Analysis of Chu-style *Ding* Vessels of the Eastern Zhou Period), *Jianghan kaogu* 1983.1.

Gao Guangren 高广仁 and Shao Wangping 邵望平 2005. 海岱文化与齐鲁文明 (Haidai Culture and Qi-Lu Civilization). Nanjing: Jiangsu Jiaoyu Chubanshe.

Gao Ming 高明1981. "中原地区东周时代青铜礼器研究下" (Eastern Zhou Period Bronze Ritual Vessels in the Central Plain Area, Part III), *Kaogu yu Wenwu* 1981. 4: 82–91.

Gao Ming 1987. 古文字通论 (General Treatise on Ancient Written Characters). Beijing: Wenwu Chubanshe.

Gao Ming 1990. 古陶文汇编 (Collected Essays on Ancient Writing on Ceramics). Beijing: Zhonghua Shuju.

Gao Ming 1991.古陶文资政 (Materials on Ancient Writing on Ceramics). Beijing: Zhonghua Shuju.

Gao Xiangping 郜向平 2011. 商系墓葬研究 (A Study of the Shang Burial System). Beijing: Kexue Chubanshe.

Gettens, R. J. 1969. *The Freer Chinese Bronzes.* Vol. II: Technical studies. Washington, D.C.: Smithsonian Institution.

Goepper, Roger 1996. "Precursors and Early Stages of Chinese Script," in Jessica Rawson, ed., *Mysteries of Ancient China: New Discoveries from the Early Dynasties*, 273–81. New York: G. Braziller.

Green, Jean M. 1993 "Unraveling the Enigma of the *Bi*: The Spindle Whorl as the Model of the Ritual Disk," *Asian Perspectives* 32.1: 105–24.

Gu Derong顾德融and Zhu Shunlong朱顺龙 1999. 楚都紀南城复原研究 (Studies on Recovering the Chu Capital at Ji'nan). Beijing: Wenwu Chubanshe.

Gu Derong and Zhu Shunlong 2003. 春秋史 (History of the Springs and Autumns Period). Shanghai: Shanghai Renmin Chubanshe.

Guo Baojun 郭宝钧 1959. 山彪镇与琉璃阁 (Shanbiaozhen and Liulige). Beijing: Kexue Chubanshe.

Guo Baojun 1981. 商周铜器群综合研究 (Comprehensive Studies on Shang and Zhou Bronze Assemblages). Beijing: Wenwu Chubanshe.

Guo Dashun 郭大顺 and Sun Shoudao 孙守道 1997. 牛河梁紅山文化與玉器精粹 (Jade Gems and Hongshan Culture at Niuheliang). Beijing: Wenwu Chubanshe.

Guo Dashun 郭大顺 and Hong Dianxu 红殿旭, eds. 2007. 红山文化鉴赏 (A Study of Hongshan Culture Jades). Beijing: Wenwu Chubanshe.

Guo Jue 2011. "Concepts of Death and the Afterlife Reflected in Newly Discovered Tomb Objects and Texts from Han China," in Amy Olberding and Philip J. Ivanhoe, eds., *Mortality in Traditional Chinese Thought,* 85–115. Albany: SUNY Press.

Guo, Jingyun郭靜云 (Olga Gorodetskaya (Rapoport), and Zihao Fan 范莘浩2021. "中國青銅文明錫鉛銅合金技術可能自創發明於楚地" (The Probable Independent Discovery of China's Bronze Civilization Tin-Lead-Copper Alloy Technology in the Homeland of Chu), in Xu Shaohua徐少华, Taniguchi Mitsuru 谷口滿, and Lothar v. Falkenhausen, eds., 楚文化與長江中游早期開發, 國際學術討論會論文集 (Proceedings of the International Conference on Chu and the Early Development of the Middle Reaches of the Yangtze River), 22–9. Wuhan: Wuhan Daxue.

Guojia Wenwuju國家文物局 ed., 2006. 中国重要考古发现 (Major archaeological discoveries in China in 2005). Beijing: Wenwu Chubanshe.

Guojia Wenmuju 2009. 早期中国, 中华文明起源 (Early China, Origins of Chinese Culture). Beijing: Wenwu Chubanshe.

Han Guohe 韩国河 and Zhang Sunlin 张松林 eds. 2006. 中原地区文明化进程学术讨论会 (A Collection of Works from the Symposium on the Civilizations in the Central Plains). Beijing: Kexue Chubanshe.

Harrison, Robert Pogue 2003. *The Dominion of the Dead.* Chicago: University of Chicago Press.

Hayashi Minao 林巳奈夫 1961–62. "戦国時代の画像紋飾" (Warring States Pictorial Imagery). 考古学杂志 (*Journal of Archaeology*), 47. 3 (1961–62): 27–49; 47.4 (1961–62): 21–48; 47.5 (1961–62): 1–21.

Hayashi Minao 1968. "殷周時代の圖像記號" (Yin and Zhou Period Icons and Signs), *Tōhō gakuhō* 39 1969. Abridged and adapted by Alexander C. Soper (1990): "On the Chinese Neolithic Jade Tsung/Cong." *Artibus Asiae* 50.1/2: 5–22.

Hayashi Minao 1972. "The Twelve Gods of the Chan-kuo Period Silk Manuscript Excavated Ch'ang-sha, Hunan," in Barnard, ed., *Early Chinese Art and its Possible Influence in the Pacific Basin*. 3 vols. 123–86. New York: Intercultural Art Press.

Hayashi Minao 1981. "文化の玉器若干お巡って (A Few Points Concerning Jades of the Liangzhu Culture)." *Kokuritsu Hakubutsukan Bijutsushi* 國立博物館美術史 (National Museum of Art History): 360: 22–33.

Hayashi Minao 1984. "所谓饕餮文わ何象徵した物か" (What is represented by the so-called Taotie Image), *Tōhō gakuhō*东方学报 56 (1984): 1–97.

Hayashi Minao 林巳奈夫 1991.中國古代玉器 *(Research on Chinese Archaic Jade)*. Tokyo: Yoshikawa Kobunkan.

Hayashi Minao 1992. 中國古代遺物上所表示的气推昂形表現 ("The Pushing Up Effect of Life Breath (Qi) on Ancient Chinese Artifacts)," trans. by Yang Meili. *Gugong xuekan* 1992.9: 31–74.

Hayashi Mnao 1997. "中國古代的玉器琮 (The Ancient Chinese Jade *Cong*)," trans. by Yang Meili, in 中國古代玉研究 (Research on Ancient Chinese Jade), 124–69. Taibei: Fine Arts Library.

Hayashi Minao 1999. 中國古玉器總說 (Surveys of Ancient Chinese Jades). Tokyo: Yoshikawa Kobunkan, Ltd.

Hayashi Minao 2020. 中国古代の神がみ (Ancient Spirits (神) of China). Tokyo: Yoshikawa Kobunkan Co., Ltd.

He Nu 何駑 2009. "都城考古的理论与时间-从陶寺遗址和二里头遗址都城考古分析看中国早期城市化进程 (Theory and Practice of Capital Archaeology: From Perspective of Early Urbanization Process Based on Capital Archaeology of Taosi Site and Erlitou Site)," *Sandai Kaogu* 3: 3–58.

He Nu 2013. "The Longshan Period Site of Taosi in Southern Shanxi Province," in Anne P. Underhill, ed., *A Companion to Chinese Archaeology,* 255–277. New York: John Wiley & Sons.

He Nu 2015. "对于陶寺文化晚期聚落形态与社会变化的新认识" (Re-Recognizing the Changes of Settlement Pattern and Society in the Late period of Taosi), in Zhongguo Shehui Kexueyuan Kaogu Yanjiusuo, ed., 新世纪的中国考古*Chinese Archaeology in the New Century,* 158–71. Beijing: Kexue Chubanshe.

He Nu 2018. "Taosi: An Archaeological Example of Urbanization as a Political Center in Prehistoric China," *Archaeological Research in Asia* 14 (June 2018): 20–32.

Hebei 1996a. Hebeisheng Kaogu Yanjiusuo 河北省考古研究所. 燕下都 (The Later Capital of Yanxiadu). 2 vols. Beijing: Wenwu Chubanshe.

Hebei 1996b. 戰國中山國國王之墓 (The Cuo Tomb—the Royal tomb of the Warring States Period State of Zhongshan). 2 vols. Beijing: Wenwu Chubanshe.

Hebei 2005. 戰國中山國靈壽城: 1975–1993 年發掘報告. (The City of Lingshou of the Warring States Period State of Zhongshan: Report on Archaeological Excavations 1975–1993). Beijing: Wenwu Chubanshe.

Heji 1978–82. 甲骨文合集 (Jiaguwen heji) ed. by Guo Moruo郭沫若 and Hu Houxuan胡厚宣. Vols. 1–12, rubbings; vol. 13, seal script. Beijing: Zhongguo Shuju.

Henan Bowuguan 2011. 辉县琉璃阁甲乙二墓 (The Two Tombs Jia and Yi at Liulige, Huixian). Zhengzhou: Daxiang Chubanshe.

Henan Bowuyuan 河南博物院, and Taibei Guoli Lishi Bowuguan 台北国立历史博物馆 2001. 新郑郑公大墓青铜器 (Bronzes from the Grand Tomb of Duke Zheng at Xinzheng). Zhengzhou: Daxiang Chubanshe.

Henansheng Wenwu Kaogu Yanjiusuo and Wenwudui文物对与河南省考古研究所 1959. 鄭州二里岗遗址 (Zhengzhou Erligang Site). Beijing: Kexue Chubanshe.

Henansheng Wenwu Kaogu Yanjiusuo 河南省考古研究所1991. 淅川下寺春秋楚墓 (Chu Tombs of the Chunqiu Period at Xiasi, Xichuan County). Beijing: Wenwu Chubanshe.

Henansheng Wenwu Kaogu Yanjiusuo 2001. 郑州商城1953–85 考古发掘报告 (Zhengzhou Shang City 1953–85 Archaeological Excavation Reports). Beijing: Wenwu Chubanshe.

Henansheng Wenwu Kaogu Yanjiusuo 2006. 新郑郑国祭祀遗址 (The Zheng State Sacrificial Site at Xinzheng). Zhengzhou: Daxiang Chubanshe.

Henansheng Wenwu Kaogu Yanjiusuo and Samenxiashi Wenwu Gongzuodui河 南省文物考古研究所, 三门峡市文物工作队1999. 三门峡虢国墓 (Tombs of the Guo State at Sanmenxia). Beijing: Wenwu Chubanshe.

Henansheng Wenwu Yanjiusuo 河南省文物研究所 1986. 信阳楚墓 (The Chu Burial at Xinyang). Beijing: Wenwu Chubanshe.

Henan Xinyang Diqu Wenguanhui and Guangshanxian Wenguanhui河南信阳地 区文管会, 光山县文管会 1984. "春秋早期黄君孟夫妇墓发掘报告" (Report on the Excavation of Early Chunqiu Period Tombs of Meng, ruler of the Huang State, and his Wife), *Kaogu* 1984.4: 302–32, 348, 385–90.

Hong Shi 洪石 2006. 戰國秦漢漆器研究 (Research on Warring States, Qin, and Han Lacquer). Beijing: Wenwu Chubanshe.

Hou Yi 侯毅 1989. "试论太原金胜村251号墓墓主身份" (A Preliminary Discussion on the Identity of the Tomb Owner of Tomb 251 at Jinshengcun, Taiyuan), *Wenwu* 1989. 9.

Hsü, Cho-yun 1965. *Ancient China in Transition: An Analysis of Social Mobility, 722-222 BC*. Stanford: Stanford University Press.

Hsü, Cho-yun 1999. "The Spring and Autumn Period" in Michael Loewe and Edward L. Shaughnessy, eds, *The Cambridge History of Ancient China: From the Origins of Civilization to 221 BC*. Cambridge and New York: Cambridge University Press.

Hsü, Cho-yun and Katheryn M. Linduff 1988. *Western Chou Civilization*. New Haven: Yale University Press.

Hsü, Chin-hsiung 1972. *Menzies Collection of Shang Dynasty Oracle Bones: A Catalogue*. vol. 1. Englewood Cliffs NJ: Prentice Hall.

Hsü, Chin-hsiung 1977. *Menzies Collection of Shang Dynasty Oracle Bones: The Text*. vol. 2. Englewood Cliffs NJ: Prentice Hall.

Hsü, Chin-hsiung 1984. *Ancient Chinese Society: An Epigraphic and Archaeological Interpretation*, trans. by Alfred H. C. Ward. Taipei: Yee Wen Publishing Company.

Hu Houxuan 胡厚宣 1989–90. 甲骨学商史論叢 (Collected Works on Oracle Bone Studies and Shang History). Reprint, 3 vols. Taipei: Taiwan Datong Shuju.

Huang Fengchun 黄凤春 2014. *The Eastern Zhou Cemetery at Wenfengta, Suizhou, Hubei* 湖北随州文峰塔东周墓地, Beijing: Kexue Chubanshe. Also see http://www. kaogu.cn/html/cn/xueshu huodongzixun/ 2013nianquanguo shidakaoguxin faxian/2014/0411/45829.html.

Huang Xuanpei 黄宣佩, ed 2000. 福泉山 *Fuquanshan*. Beijing: Wenwu Chubanshe.

Hubeisheng Bowuguan北省博物馆 1989. 曾侯乙墓 (The Tomb of Marquis Yi of Zeng), 2 vols. Beijing: Wenwu Chubanshe.

Hubeisheng Bowuguan 1995. 曾侯乙墓文物珍赏 (An Appreciation of the Cultural Relics of the Zeng Hou Yi Tomb). Wuhan: Hubei Meishu Chubanshe.

Hubeisheng Bowuguan, Hubeisheng Wenwu Kaogu Yanjiusuo and Suizhoushi Bowuguan 随州市博物馆, 湖北省文物考古研究所, 湖北省博物馆 2013. 随州叶家 山西周早期曾国墓地 (Zeng State Cemetery of the Early Western Zhou Period at Yejiashan, Suizhou). Beijing: Wenwu Chubanshe.

Hubeisheng Jingsha Tielu Kaogudui 湖北省荆沙铁路考古队1991. *The Chu tombs at Baoshan* 包山楚墓, 2 vols. Beijing: Wenwu Chubanshe.

Hubeisheng Jingsha Tielu Kaogudui 2000a. "马王堆汉墓帛书整理小组" (The Organization of a Small Group of Silk Manuscripts from the Tomb of Mawangdui), *Wenwu* 2000.7: 85–94.

Hubeisheng Jingsha Tielu Kaogudui 2000b. 長沙楚墓 (Chu Burials at Changsha). 2 vols. Beijing: Wenwu Chubanshe.

Hwang, Ming-chorng [Huang Mingchong] 黄铭崇 1996a. "Ming-tang: Cosmology, Political Order and Monuments in Early China." Ph.D. Thesis, Department of East Asian Languages and Civilizations, Harvard University.

Hwang, Ming-chorng 1996b. "古史即"神話 – 以'大荒經'及'堯典'為中心的再檢陶討" (Ancient History as Myth? – A Critical Review Centering upon the *Dahuangjing* and the *Yaodian*)," *Xinshixue* (*New Historical Studies*) 7.3 (1996): 175–95.

Hwang, Ming-chorng 2012. "考古发现看西周墓葬的分器现象与西周时代礼器制度的类型与阶段上篇" (A Study of "*Fenqi*" or Vessel Distribution in Western Zhou Date Tombs and the Type and Phase of Western Zhou Ritual Practice (Part 1)), *Zhongyang Yanjiuyuan Lishi Yuyan Yanjiusuo Jikan* 83(4): 607–70.

Ji Kunzhang 吉琨璋 2006. "晋叔家父"器和 M93 组晋侯墓的归属" (The Bronzes Ascribed to Jin Shu Jia Fu and the Occupant of the Tomb M93 at the Jin Marquis Cemetery), *Gudai Wenming Yanjiu Tongxun* 29: 27–30.

Ji Kunzhang 2007. "再论羊舌墓地" (A Further Discussion on the Jin Marquis Cemetery at Yangshe), *Gudai Wenming Yanjiu Tongxun* 34: 43–7.

Jiangsusheng Wenwu Guanli Weiyuanhui 江苏省文物管理委员会 2017. 江苏江庄良渚文化遗址的新发现" (New Discovery of the Liangzhu Culture Site at Jiangzhuang, Jiangsu), *Kaogu* 2016.7: 19–30. Abridged English version, *Chinese Archaeology* 17 (2017): 18–31.

Jin Zhengyao *et al*, 2015. "Luminescence Study of the Initial, Pre-casting Firing Temperatures of Clay Moulds and Core Used for Bronze Casting at Yinxu (13c. BC~11c. BC)," *Quaternary Geochronology* 30: 374–80.

Jing Zhongwei 井中伟 and Wang Lixin 王立新 2014. 夏商周考古學 (Xia Shang Zhou Archaeology, 2nd ed). Beijing: Kexue Chubanshe.

Jing Zhongwei and Wang Lixin 2015. "OSL Chronology of Traditional Zinc Smelting Activity in Yunnan Province, southwest China," *Quaternary Geochronology* 30: 381.

Jingmenshi Bowuguan 荆门市博物馆 1998. 郭店楚簡 (Chu Bamboo Slips from Guodian). Beijing: Wenwu Chubanshe.

Kane, Virginia C. 1982–83. "Aspects of Western Chou Appointment Inscriptions: The Charge, the Gifts, and the Response," *Early China* 8: 14–28.

Keightley, David N. 1978. *Sources of Shang History: The Oracle-bone Inscriptions of Bronze-Age China.* Berkeley: University of California Press.

Keightley, David N. 1984 (reprint 2006). "Late Shang Divination: The Magico-Religious Legacy," in Henry Rosemont, Jr., ed., *Explorations in Early Chinese Cosmology* (*Journal of the American Academy of Religion Studies*) 50.2:11–34.

Keightley, David N. 1996. "Art, Ancestors, and the Origins of Writing in China," *Representations* 56: 68–95.

Keightley, David N. 1998. "Shamanism, Death, and the Ancestors: Religious Mediation in Neolithic and Shang China (ca. 5000–1000 BC)." *Asiatische Studien* 52.3: 763–831.

Keightley, David N. 2000. *The Ancestral Landscape: Time, Space, and Community in Late Shang China (ca.1200–1045 BC).* Berkeley: Center for Chinese Studies, Institute of East Asian Studies, University of California.

Keightley, David N. 2015. *These Bones Shall Rise Again: Selected Writings on Early China*. Albany: State University of New York Press.

Kern, Martin 2008. "Bronze Inscriptions, the *Shangshu*, and the *Shijing*: The Evolution of the Ancestral Sacrifice during the Western Zhou," in John Lagerwey and Marc Kalinowski, eds., *Early Chinese Religion Part One: Shang through Han (1250 BC–220 AD)*, vol. 1, 143–200. Leiden: Brill.

Kern, Martin 2017. "The "Harangues" (*Shi*誓) in the *Shangshu*," in Martin Kern and Dirk Meyer, eds, *The Classic of Documents and the Origins of Chinese Political Philosophy*, 281–319. Leiden: Brill.

Kesner, Ladislav 1991. "The Taotie Reconsidered: Meaning and Functions of the Shang Theriomorphic Imagery," *Artibus Asiae* 51(1–2): 29–53.

Khayutina, Maria 2008. "Western 'Capitals' of the Western Zhou Dynasty: Historical Reality and Its Reflections Until the Time of Sima Qian," *Oriens Extremus* 47: 25–65.

Kyayutina, Maria 2010. "Royal Hospitality and Geopolitical Constitution of the Western Zhou Polity (1046/5–771 BC)," *T'oung Pao* 96.1–3: 1–77.

Khayutina, Maria 2016. "The Tombs of the Rulers of Peng and Relationships Between Zhou and Northern Non-Zhou Lineages (Until the Early 9th Century BC)," in Edward L. Shaughnessy, ed., *Imprints of Kinship: Studies of Recently Discovered Bronze Inscriptions from Ancient China*, 71–132. Hong Kong: The Chinese University of Hong Kong.

Khayutina, Maria 2018. "Reflections and Uses of the Past in Chinese Bronze Inscriptions from ca. 11th–5th Centuries BC: The Memory of the Conquest of Shang and the First Kings of Zhou," in John Baines, Tim Rood, Henriette van der Blom, and Samuel Chen, eds, *Historical Consciousness and Historiography (3000 BC–600 AD)*. Sheffield: Equinox Publishing.

Khayutina, Maria 2019. *Kinship, Marriage, and Politics in the Light of Ritual Bronze Inscriptions from 11–8 Centuries* BCE. London and New York: Routledge.

Khayutina, Maria 2020. "Western Zhou Cultural and Historic Setting," in Elizabeth Childs-Johnson, ed *Oxford Handbook of Early China*, 367–402. New York: Oxford University Press.

Khayutina, Maria (Xia Yuting 夏玉婷) 2021. "商末周初江、河之间交通线上的家族政体以息邦为例" (Late Shang and Early Zhou Lineage-based Polities on Transport Routes Between the Yangze and the Yellow River: The Example of Xi), in Xu Shaohua 徐少華, Taniguchi Mitsuru 谷口滿, and Luo Tai 羅泰 (Lothar von Falkenhausen), eds., 楚文化與長江中游早期開發國際學術研討會論文集), 415–29. Wuhan: Wuhan Daxue.

Khayutina, Maria and Yuri Pines, eds 2013. *Qin: The Eternal Emperor and His Terracotta Warriors*, Chapter 1. Bern: Bernisches Historisches Museum.

Kirkland, Russell 2004. *Taoism: The Enduring Tradition*. New York and London: Routledge.

Kuhn, Dieter 1995. "Silk Weaving in Ancient China from Geometric Figures to Patterns of Pictorial Likeness," *Chinese Science* 12 (1995): 84–85.

Lai Guolong 2005. "Death and the Otherworldly Journey in Early China as Seen through Tomb Texts, Travel Paraphernalia, and Road Rituals," *Asia Major* 18.1: 1–44.

Lai, Guolong 2015. *Excavating the Afterlife: The Archaeology of Early Chinese Religion*. Seattle and London: University of Washington Press.

Lacquer, Thomas W. 1985. *Collections of Oracular Inscriptions in France*. Taipei, Paris, and Hong Kong: Ricci Institute.

Laqueur, Thomas W. 2016. *The Work of the Dead: A Cultural History of Mortal Remains*. Princeton: Princeton University Press.

Lawton, Thomas 1982. *Chinese Art of the Warring States Period: Change and Continuity, 480–222 BC*. Washington, D.C.: Published for the Freer Gallery of Art by the Smithsonian Institution Press.

Lefeuvre, Jean A. 1985. *Collections of Oracular Inscriptions in France*. Taipei : Ricci Institute.

Lefeuvre, Jean A. 2008. *Collections of Oracular Bones Inscriptions*. Taipei : Ricci Institute.

Lewis, Mark Edward 1999. *Writing and Authority in Early China*. Albany: Suny Press.

Lewis, Mark Edward 2006a. *The Construction of Space in Early China*. Albany: Suny Press.

Lewis, Mark Edward 2006b. *The Flood Myths of Early China*. Albany: Suny Press.

Li Boqian 李伯谦 2011. "中国古代文明演进的两种模式—红山、良渚、仰韶大墓随葬玉器观察随想," (Two Processing Modes of Ancient Chinese Civilization Observed on Jade Wares from the Big Tombs of Hongshan, Liangzhu, and Yangshao Culture), in Li Boqian, ed., *Collection of Research on Civilization and Three Dynasties Archaeology*). Beijing: Wenwu Chubanshe. Abridged English trans. in *Chinese Archaeology* vol. 10 (2010):136–42.

Li Boqian 李伯谦ed 2003. 商文化論集 (Collected Essays on Shang Culture). Beijing: Wenwu Chubanshe.

Li Chi (Li Ji) 1977. *Anyang*. Seattle: University of Washington University Press.

Li Feng 2003. "'Feudalism' and Western Zhou China: A Criticism." *Harvard Journal of Asiatic Studies* 63: 115–44.

Li Feng 2006. *Landscape and Power in Early China: The Crisis and Fall of the Western Zhou, 1045–771 BC*. Cambridge and New York: Cambridge University Press.

Li Feng 2008. "Transmitting Antiquity: The Origin and Paradigmization of the 'Five Ranks,'" in Dieter Kuhn and Helga Stahl, eds., *Perceptions of Antiquity in Chinese Civilization* 103–34. Heidelberg: Edition Forum.

Li Feng 2013. *Early China: A Social and Cultural History*. Cambridge and New York: Cambridge University Press.

Li Hui *et al* 2015. "Y Chromosomes of Prehistoric People Along the Yangtze River," *Human Genetics* 122: 383–8.

Li Jianmin 李健民 2001. "论新干商代大墓出土的青铜戈矛及其相关问题" (Discussion of the Ge and Mao Unearthed from the Xin'gan Large Tomb and Related Questions), *Kaogu* 2001.5: 60–9.

Li Jinchang *et al*, 2017. "Temporal-Spatial Variations of Human Settlements in Relation to Environment Change During the Longshan Culture and Xia-Shang Periods in Shanxi Province, China," *Quaternary International* 436: 129–37.

Li Ling 李零 1985. 長沙子彈庫戰國楚帛書研究 (Research on the Warring States Pictorial Silk Banner from Zidanku, Changsha). Beijing: Zhonghua Shuju.

Li Ling 2000. 中国方术考 and 中国方术续考 (Research on China *Fangshu* [Shamanistic Arts], vols. 1 and 2. Beijing: Dongfang Chubanshe.

Li Ling 2004. 入山與出塞 (Entering the Mountains and Going Abroad). Beijing: Wenwu Chubanshe.

Li Ling and Donald Harper 1995. "An Archaeological Study of Taiyi (Grand One) Worship." *Early Medieval China* 1–2: 1–39.

Li Ling and Constance A. Cook 1999. "Translation of the Chu Silk Manuscript, "in Constance A. Cook and John S. Major, eds., *Defining Chu: Image and Reality in Ancient China,* 171–76. Honolulu: University of Hawai'i Press.

Li Min 李旻 2017. "重返夏墟社會記憶與經典的發生" (The Genealogy of Yu Gong Spatial Ideology), *Kaogu Xuebao* 2017.3: 287–316.

Li Min 2018. *Social Memory and State Formation in Early China.* Cambridge: Cambridge University Press.

Li Min *et al* 2018. "When Peripheries were Centres: A Preliminary Study of the Shimao-centred Polity in the Loess Highlands, China," *Antiquity* 92 (364): 1008–1022.

Li Shaolian 李绍连1999. "关于商王国的政体问题——王国疆域的考古佐证" (On the Question of the System of Administration of the Shang Kingdom – An Archaeological Investigation of the Kingdom's Boundaries), *Zhongyuan Wenwu* 1999.2: 28–35.

Li Xueqin 李学勤 1984a 东周与秦代文明 (Eastern Zhou and Qin Civilization). Beijing: Wenwu Chubanshe.

Li Xueqin 1984b. "論仲稱父簋與神國" (On the Zhongchengfu *gui* and the Spirit Realm," *Zhongyuan wenwu* 1984.8: 31–32.

Li Xueqin 1985 "考古發現與中國文字起源" (Archaeological Discoveries and the Origins of Chinese Writing), *Zhongguo Wenhua Yanjiu Jikan* 2 (1985) 144–57.

Li Xueqin and Kwang-chih Chang 1985. *Eastern Zhou and Qin Civilizations. Early Chinese Civilizations Series.* New Haven: Yale University Press.

Li Xueqin 2005. "論豳公盨及其重要意義" (Analysis of the Duke of Sui/Bin xu inscription and it importance and significance," reprinted in Li Xueqin 中國古代文明研究 (Research on Ancient Chinese Civilization), Shanghai: Huadong Shifan Daxue, 126–136.

Li, Yung-ti 2022. *Kingly Crafts: The Archaeology of Craft Production in Late Shang China.* New York: Columbia University Press.

Li Zuozhi 李佐之2008. 骨铭文中的捐赠者签名 (Signatures of Donors in Shang Oracle Bone Inscriptions). Beijing: Kexue Chubanshe.

Lian Haiping, 廉海泙, Tan Derui 潭德睿, and Zheng Guang 郑光 2011. "二里头遗址的青铜铸造技术" (Bronze Casting Technology at the Erlitou Site), *Kaogu Xuebao* 2011.4: 561–75.

Liangzhu Bowuyuan 2015.良渚文化刻画符号 (Inscribed Symbols of the Liangzhu Culture). Shanghai: Shanghai Renmin Chubanshe.

Liaoningsheng Wenwu Kaogu Yanjiusuo 辽宁省文物考古研究所, ed 1997. 牛河梁红山文化遗址与玉器精粹 (Site Remains of the Hongshan Culture of Niuheliang and Its Jade Gems. Beijing: Wenwu Chubanshe.

Liaoningsheng Wenwu Kaogu Yanjiusuo 2013. 牛河梁: 红山文化遗址发掘报告1983–2003 (Report on the Investigation of the Hongshan Culture Site at Niuheliang, 1983–2003). Beijing: Wenwu Chubanshe.

Liaoningsheng Wenwu Kaogu Yanjiusuo with Zhongguo Renmin Daxue Lishixueyuan 中国人民大学历史学院 2015. "2014 牛河梁遗址系统性区或考古调查研究), "Report on the 2014 Investigation of the Site at Niuheliang," *Huaxia kaogu* 2015.3: 3–8, 62.

Lin Huadong 林华东 1992. 河姆渡文化初探 (Preliminary Analysis of the Hemudu culture). Hangzhou: Zhejiang Jiaoyu Chubanshe.

Lin Huadong 1996. 良渚文化研究 (Research on the Liangzhu culture). Hangzhou: Zhejiang Jiaoyu Chubanshe.

Lin Huadong 2006. 良渚文化探秘 (Analysis of the Liangzhu Culture). Beijing: Renmin Chubanshe.

Lin Yun 林沄 ed 1998. 林沄学术文集 (Collected Academic Studies by Lin Yun). Beijing: Zhongguo Dabaike Quanshu Chubanshe.

Linduff, Kathryn M. and Yan Sun, eds 2004. *Gender and Chinese Archaeology*. Walnut Creek, CA: Altamira Press.

Liu Bin 刘斌 2007. "余杭县良渚城遗址发掘报告" (Excavation on the Liangzhu City-Site in Yuhang District, Hangzhou City), *Kaogu* 2007.9: 10–18.

Liu Bin 2008. "余杭莫角山遗址1992–1993" (The Mojiaoshan Site in Yuhang, 1992–1993), *Kaogu* 2008.7: 3–10. Abridged English version, *Chinese Archaeology* 2: 104–109.

Liu Bin 2009. "良渚文化发现与研究初步" (Discovery and Preliminary Study of the Liangzhu Culture), *Kaogu* 2009.1: 19–22. Abridged English version, *Early China* 9: 19–22.

Liu Bin 2013a "寻找失落的文明：良渚古城的新发现" (Searching for a Lost Civilization: New Discoveries from the Liangzhu Ancient City), *Kaogu* 2013.8: 28.

Liu Bin 2013b. 神巫的世界 (The World of Spirits and Shamans). Hangzhou: Zhejiang Sheyi Chubanshe.

Liu Bin 2020. "Liangzhu Culture and the Ancient City of Liangzhu," in Elizabeth Childs-Johnson, ed *The Oxford Handbook of Early China*, 119–39. New York: Oxford University Press.

Liu Bin *et al*, 2017. "Earliest Hydraulic Enterprise in China, 5100 Years Ago," *Proceedings of the National Academy of Sciences of the USA* 114: 13637–42. https://doi.org/10.1073/pnas. 1710516114.

Liu Bin, Wang Ningyuan, and Chen Minghui 2016. "A Realm of Gods and Kings: The Recent Discovery of Liangzhu City and the Rise of Civilisation in South China," *Asian Archaeology* 4: 13–31.

Liu, Binhui 刘彬徽 1995. 楚系青铜器研究 (Studies on Chu Bronzes). Wuhan: Hubei Jiaoyu Chubanshe.

Liu, Jue 刘珏 2015. "Sunrise Before Time," *The World of Chinese*, 8/29/2015 digital version http://www.theworldofchinese.com/2015/08/sunrise-before-time/.

Liu Guoxiang 劉國祥 2006. "牛河梁玉器初步研究" (A Preliminary Study of the Jade Articles from the Niuheliang Site), *Wenwu* 2006.6: 74–85. Abridged English version, *Chinese Archaeology* 2 (2002): 14–17.

Liu Junshe 劉軍社 1994. "鄭家坡文化與劉家文化的分期及其性質" (The Periodization and Nature of Zhengjiapo Culture and Liu Clan Culture), *Kaogu Xuebao* 1994.1, 25–62.

Liu Junshe 劉軍社, Liu Junshe, Wang Hao, Xin Yihua, Wang Zhankui, Hao Mingke, Wang Xiaomei, and Ding Yan (Shigushan Archaeological Team) 2013. "西周墓在陝西寶雞石鼓山 (Western Zhou Tomb at Shigushan in Baoji, Shaanxi), *Kaogu yu wenwu* 2013.1: 1–24. Abridged Eng. version, *Chinese Archaeology* 14: 129–41.

Liu, Li *et al*, 2007. "The Earliest Rice Domestication in China," *Antiquity Project Gallery* 81. http://www.antiquity.ac.uk/ projgall/liu313/

Liu, Li 1996. "Mortuary Ritual and Social Hierarchy in the Longshan Culture," *Early China* 21: 10–46.

Liu, Li 2004. *The Chinese Neolithic: Trajectories to Early States.* Cambridge and New York: Cambridge University Press.

Liu, Li and Chen Xingcan 2012. *The Archaeology of China: From the Late Paleolithic to the Early Bronze Age.* Cambridge and New York: Cambridge University Press.

Li, Qingzhu 2005. "New Perspectives of Archaeological Research on Early Capital Cities in China," *Chinese Archaeology* September 2005.9: 18.

Liu Yiman 刘一曼 1995. "安陽殷墟青銅禮器逐核的幾個問題 (Pursuing some questions about Anyang Yin bronze ritual vessels), *Kaogu Xuebao* 1995.4: 395–412.

Loewe, Michael, ed 1993. *Early Chinese Texts: A Bibliographical Guide.* Berkeley: Society for the Study of Early China.

Loewe, Michael and Edward Shaughnessy, eds 1999. *The Cambridge History of Ancient China.* Cambridge and New York: Cambridge University Press.

Long, Tengwen and David Taylor 2015. "A Revised Chronology for the Archaeology of the Lower Yangtze, China, Based on Bayesian Statistical Modelling," *Journal of Archaeological Science* 63: 115.

Lu Jianfang 陆建方1995. "渚文化墓葬研究" (A Study of Liangzhu Culture Burials), *Science China Technological Sciences* 1996: 258–70.

Lu Liancheng 卢连成 and Hu Zhisheng 胡智生 1988. 寶雞魚國墓地 (*The cemetery at Baoji, state of Yu*). 2 vols. Beijing: Wenwu Chubanshe.

Lu Xiaoke *et al*, 2013. "Analysis of the Potteries from the Ancient Liangzhu City-site," Science China Technological Sciences 56: 945–51.

Luan Fengshi 栾丰实 1994. "山东钉宫龙山时代文字解读" (Analysis of Graphs from the Longshan site of Dinggong, Shandong), *Kaogu* 1994.1, 37–54.

Luan Fengshi 1997. 海岱地区考古研究 (Archaeological Research in the Haidai Region). Jinan: Shandong University Press.

Luan Fengshi 2013. "The Dawenkou Culture in the Lower Yellow River and Huai River Basin Areas," in Anne P. Underhill, ed, *A Companion to Chinese Archaeology*, 411–34. New York: John Wiley & Sons.

Luoyang, Luoyangshi Wenwu Gongzuodui 洛阳市文物工作队 2009. 洛阳王城广场东周墓 (Eastern Zhou Tombs at Wangcheng Guangchang, Luoyang). Beijing: Wenwu Chubanshe.

Ma Bing 马冰 2007. "也谈羊舌墓地M1和北赵晋侯墓地M93的墓主 (Once Again on the Occupants of M1 of Yangshe Cemetery and M93 of the Marquis of Jin Cemetery at Beizhao)," *Zhongguo wenwubao* 2.2:7.

Ma, Chengyuan 1986. *Ancient Chinese Bronzes.* Oxford and New York: Oxford University Press.

Ma Chengyuan 馬承源1988. 中國青銅器 (Chinese Bronzes). Shanghai: Guji Chubanshe.

Ma Chengyuan 1986–90. 商周青铜器铭文选 (Selected bronze Inscriptions of the Shang and Zhou Dynasties), 4 vols. Beijing: Wenwu Chubanshe.

Ma Chengyuan 1999. "关于神面纹卣" Concerning the *You* with a Spirit Face,") in *Baoli Bowuguan Bianji Weiyuanhui* 保利博物馆编辑委员会 ed (Selected Bronzes in the Collection of the Poly Art Museum), 353–6. Lingnan: Meishu Chubanshe.

Ma Chengyuan 2001–2005, 2007–2009, 2012. 上海博物館藏戰國楚竹書 (Warring States Chu Bamboo Books of the Shanghai Museum), 9 vols. Shanghai: Shanghai Shudian.

Ma Jiangbo *et al,* 2016. 陈福, "湖南宁乡县炭河里遗址出土青铜器的科学分析" (The Alloy Composition, Metallographic Structures, and Lead Isotope Ratios for Bronzes Unearthed at Ningxiangxian, Hunan), *Kaogu* 2016.7: 111–19.

Mair, Victor 2020. "Worker from the West" [interview with Victor Mair], *Archaeology Archive* 10 July 2006, http://archive.archive.org/online/interviews/mair.html (accessed 24 May 2020).

Major, John S. 1984. "The Five Phases, Magic Squares, and Schematic Cosmography," in Henry Rosemont Jr., ed, *Explorations in Early Chinese Cosmology. JAAR Thematic Studies,* 133–66. Chico: Scholar's Press.

Major, John S. 1986. "New Light on the Dark Warrior," *Journal of Chinese Religion* 13/14: 65–86.

Major, John S. 1993. *Heaven and Earth in Early Han Thought: Chapters Three, Four, and Five of the Huainanzi.* Albany: State University of New York Press.

Major, John S. 1999. "Characteristics of Late Chu Religion," *Cook and Major* 1999: 121–43.

Major, John S. and Constance A. Cook 2017. *Ancient China: A History.* New York: Routledge.

Major, John S. and Elizabeth Childs-Johnson 2020. "Chu Religion and Art," in Elizabeth Childs-Johnson, ed, *Oxford Handbook of Early China*, 713–46. New York: Oxford University Press.

Major, John S., Sarah A. Queen, Andrew Seth Meyer, and Harold D. Roth, eds and trans. 2010. *The Huainanzi: A Guide to the Theory and Practice of Government in Early Han China.* New York: Columbia University Press.

Mei Jianjun 2009. "Early Metallurgy in the Eurasian Steppe and China: Some Challenging Issues," in Jianjun Mei and Thilo Rehren, eds., *Metallurgy and Civilization: Eurasia and Beyond,* 9–16. London: Archetype.

Meyer, Andrew 2020. "Social, Intellectual, and Religious Transformations: The *shi*, Diplomats, and Urban Expansion [Warring States Period]," in Elizabeth Childs-Johnson, ed., *Oxford Handbook of Early China*, 659–73. New York: Oxford University Press.

Michael, Thomas 2015. "Shamanism Theory and the Early Chinese *Wu.*" *Journal of the American Academy of Religion* 83(3): 649–96.

Michael, Thomas 2017a. "Early Chinese Shamanism." *Numen* 64(5.6): 459–96.

Michael, Thomas 2017b. "Shamanic Eroticism and the *Jiu Ge* (Nine Songs) of Early China." *Monumenta Serica* 65/1: 1–20.

Michael, Thomas 2019. "Shamanism, Eroticism, and Death: The Ritual Structures of the *Nine Songs* in Comparative Context" *Religions* 10 (1): 1–26.

Michaelson, Carol and Jane Portal 2006. *Chinese Art in Detail.* Cambridge, MA: Harvard University Press.

Mickel, Stanley 1978. "Good and Bad Fortune in the Shang Oracle Inscriptions," paper presented at the annual meeting of the American Oriental Society, Toronto, April 12, 1978.

Munakata, Kyohiko 1991. *Sacred Mountains in Chinese Art.* Urbana: Krannert Art Museum.

Needham, Joseph 1970. *Science and Civilisation in China*, Vol. 3. Mathematics and the Sciences of the Heavens and the Earth (Section 19–25). Cambridge: Cambridge University Press.

Nelson, Sarah M., ed 1995. The *Archaeology of Northeast China: Beyond the Great Wall.* London and New York: Routledge.

Nelson, Sarah M. 1998. *Ancestors for the Pigs: Pigs in Prehistory*. Philadelphia: MASCA Papers in Science and Archaeology.

Nelson, Sarah M. 2014. *Hongshan Papers: Collected Studies on the Archaeology of Northern China*. London: BAR International Series 2618.

Nickel, Lukas 2006. "Imperfect Symmetry: Re-Thinking Bronze Casting Technology in Ancient China," *Artibus Asiae* 66.1: 5–39.

Nivison, David S. 1983. "The Dates of Western Chou," *Harvard Journal of Asiatic Studies* 43.2: 481–580.

Nivison, David S. 2009. *The Riddle of the Bamboo Annals*. Taipei: Airiti Press.

Nivison, David S. 2018. "The Nivison Annals, Selected Works of David S. Nivison on Early Chinese Chronology, Astronomy, and Historiography," in Adam C. Schwartz, ed, *Library of Sinology 1*. Berlin: De Gruyter Mouton.

Nivison, David S. and Kenneth D. Pang 1990. "Astronomical Evidence for the *Bamboo Annals*' Chronicle of Early Xia," *Early China* 15: 87–95.

Normile, Dennis 2016. "Massive Flood May Have Led to China's Earliest Empire." *Science Online* www.sciencemag.org/news/2016/ accessed August 4, 2016.

Okamura Hidenori 岡村秀典 2003. 夏王朝王權の考古學 (The Xia Dynasty: Archaeology of the Emergence of Royalty). Tokyo: Kodansha.

Owen, Steven 1996. "Foreword," in Arthur Waley, trans., *The Book of Songs*, edited with additional translations by Joseph R. Allen. New York: Grove Press.

Pankenier, David W. 1981. "Astronomical Dates in Shang and Western Zhou." *Early China* 7: 2–37.

Pankenir, David W. 1995. "The Cosmo-Political Background of Heaven's Mandate." *Early China* 20: 121–76.

Pankenir, David W. 2013. *Astrology and Cosmology in Early China: Conforming Earth to Heaven*. Cambridge: Cambridge University Press.

Peng Yushang 彭裕商 2003. 西周青銅器年代綜合研究 (Comprehensive Studies on the Dates of Western Zhou Bronzes). Chengdu: Ba Shu Shuju.

Peng Yushang 2011. 春秋青銅器年代綜合研究 (Comprehensive Studies on the Dates of Springs and Autumns Bronzes). Beijing: Zhonghua Shuju.

Peterson, Christian E., Christian E. Peterson, Lu Xueming, Robert D. Drennan, and Zhu Da 2014. *Hongshan Regional Organization in the Upper Daling Valley*. Pittsburgh: Center for Comparative Archaeology, University of Pittsburgh.

Pierce, Jessica 2018. "Do Animals Experience Grief?" *Smithsonian.com*, www/ smithsonian mag.com/science-nature/do-animals-experience-grief-180970124 (accessed August 24, 2018).

Pines, Yuri 2000. "'The One That Pervades All' in Ancient Chinese Political Thought: Origins of the 'Great Unity' Paradigm," *T'oung Pao* 86. 4–5: 280–324.

Pines, Yuri 2002a. *Foundations of Confucian Thought: Intellectual Life in the Chunqiu Period, 722–453 BCE*. Honolulu: University of Hawai'i Press.

Pines, Yuri 2002b. "Changing Views of *tianxia* in Pre-imperial Discourse," *Oriens Extremus* 43.1–2: 101–16.

Pines, Yuri 2009. *Envisioning Eternal Empire: Chinese Political Thought of the Warring States Era*. Honolulu: University of Hawai'i Press.

Pines, Yuri 2012. *The Everlasting Empire: Traditional Chinese Political Culture and Its Enduring Legacy*. Princeton: Princeton University Press.

Pines, Yuri 2020. "Historiography, Thought, and Intellectual Development," in Elizabeth Childs-Johnson, ed, *Oxford Handbook of Early China*, 514–29. Oxford: Oxford University Press.

Pines, Yuri, Lothar von Falkenhausen, Gideon Shelach and Robin D.S. Yates, eds 2014. *Birth of an Empire: The State of Qin Revisited* (*New Perspectives on Chinese Culture and Society*). Berkeley: University of California Press.

Pope, John Alexander, Rutherford John Gettens, James Cahill, and Noel Barnard, eds 1967. *The Freer Chinese Bronzes: Volume 1: Catalogue*. Washington: Smithsonian Institution Press.

Porter, Deborah Lynn 1996. *From Deluge to Discourse: Myth, History, and the Generation of Chinese Fiction*. Albany: Suny Press.

Postgate, N., Tao Wang, and T. Wilkinson 1995. "The Evidence for Early Writing: Utilitarian or Ceremonial?", *Antiquity* 69.264: 459–80.

Posthumus, Liane 2011. "Hybrid Monsters in the Classical World: The Nature and Function of Hybrid Monsters in Greek Mythology, Literature and Art." Ph.D. Thesis, University of Stellenbosch.

Powers, Martin 2006. *Pattern and Person: Ornament, Society, and Self in Classical China*. Cambridge, MA: Harvard University Asia Center.

Psarass, Sophia-Karin 1998–99. "Shared Imagery: Eastern Zhou and Shared Iconographies," *Early China* 23/24: 1–88.

Psarass, Sophia-Karin 2015. *Han Material Culture*. New York and Cambridge: Cambridge University Press.

Queen, Sarah and John S. Major, trans. 2015, *Luxuriant Gems of the Spring and Autumn, Attributed to Dong Zhongshu*. New York: Columbia University Press.

Qi Wenxin 齐文心. 2003. 婦好(子)本意試探 (Analysis of Fu Hao's [Zi's] Intentions), in Wang Yuxin 王宇信 and Song Zhenhao 宋鎮豪, eds, 紀念殷墟甲骨文發現一百周年 國際學術研究會論文集 (Collected Papers from the International Scholarly Conference Commemorating One Hundred Years of Oracle Bone Research Since the Discovery of the Wastes of Yin), 149–54. Beijing: Kexue Chubanshe.

Qin, Liu 2013. "The Liangzhu Culture," in Anne P. Underhill, ed, *A Companion to Chinese Archaeology*, 574–96. New York: John Wiley & Sons.

Qin, Xiaoli 2016. "Turquoise Ornaments and Inlay Technology in Ancient China." *Asian Perspectives* 55.2: 208–39.

Qiu, Xigui 1989. "An Examination of Whether the Charge in Shang Oracle-Bone Inscriptions Are Questions." *Early China* 14: 77–114.

Qiu Xigui 裘錫圭 2000. 文字學概論 (Chinese Writing), trans. by Gilbert L. Mattos and Jerry Norman. *Early China Special Monograph Series* No. 4. Berkeley: The Society for the Study of Early China and the Institute of East Asian Studies, University of California, Berkeley.

Qu, Feng 2017 "Anthropology and Historiography: A Deconstructive Analysis of K. C. Chang's Shamanic Approach in Chinese Archaeology," *Numen* 64 (2017): 497–544.

Rawson, Jessica 1985. "Late Western Zhou: A Break in the Shang Bronze Tradition." *Early China*, 11/12: 289–96.

Rawson, Jessica 1995. *Western Zhou Ritual Bronzes from the Arthur M. Sackler Collections*. New York: Harry N Abrams Inc.

Rawson, Jessica 2017. "Shimao and Erlitou: New Perspectives on the Origins of the Bronze Industry in Central China," *Antiquity* vol. 91, no.355, published online 2o January 2017, https://doi.org/10.15184/aqy.

Renfrew, Colin and Bin Liu 2018. "The Emergence of Complex Society in China: The Case of Liangzhu." *Antiquity* 92.364: 975–90. https://doi.org/10.15184/aqy.2018.60.

Salviati, Filippo 1994. "Bird and Bird-Related Motifs in the Iconography of the Liangzhu Culture," *Rivista Degli Studi Orientali* 68.1–2: 133–60.

Sawyer, Ralph D. 2011. *Ancient Chinese Warfare*. New York: Basic Books.

Sawyer, Ralph D. 2013. *Conquest and Domination in Early China*. Charleston, SC: Self-published.

Sena, David 2005. "Reproducing Society: Lineage and Kinship in Western Zhou China." PhD. Dissertation, University of Chicago.

Schele, Linda, Peter Matthews, Justin Kent, and McDuff Anderson 1999. *The Code of Kings: The Language of Seven Sacred Maya Temples and Tombs*. New York: Touchstone.

Serruys, Paul W. 1974. "Studies in the Language of the Shang Oracle Bone Inscriptions," *T'oung Pao* 60.1: 12–120.

Shaanxisheng Kaogu Yanjiusuo 陕西省考古研究所 1979. 陕西出土商周青銅 (Shang and Zhou bronzes Unearthed in Shaanxi), vol 1. Beijing: Wenwu Chubanshe.

Shaanxisheng Kaogu Yanjiusuo 2013. "陕西神木縣石峁遺址" (Shimao in Shenmuxian, Shaanxi), *Kaogu* 2013.7: 15–24. Abridged English version, "The Shimao Site in Shenmu County, Shaanxi," *Chinese Archaeology* 14: 18–26.

Shaanxisheng Kaogu Yanjiusuo 2016. 發現石峁古城 (The Discovery of the Ancient City of Shimao). Beijing: Wenwu Chubanshe.

Shaanxisheng Kaogu Yanjiusuo and Weinanshi Wenwu Baohu Kaogu Yanjiusuo, 陕西省考古研究所, 渭南市文物保护考古研究所 eds 2010. 梁带村芮国墓地: 2007年度发掘报告 (The Rui State Cemetery at Liangdaicun: Report on the Excavation of 2007). Beijing: Wenwu Chubanshe.

Shaanxisheng Kaogu Yanjiusuo, Yulin Municipal Office Archaeological Team, and Shenmu County Shimao City Site Administration陕西省考古研究所, 榆林市政府考古队, 石峁市+神木县工地管理局 eds 2018. 陕西省神木县石峁城址皇城台地 (The Imperial City Terrace Locality of the Shimao City Site in Shenmu County, Shaanxi Province), abridged trans. in *Chinese Archaeology* 18.1 (2018). https://doi.org/10.1515/char-2018-0003 De Gruyter: Published online, 13 Nov. 2018.

Shaanxisheng Kaogu Yanjiusuo, Yulinshi Wenwu Kaogu Kantan Gongzuodui, Shenmushi Shimao 陕西省考古研究院 榆林市文物考古勘探工作队 神木市石峁 2020a. "石峁遗址皇城台地点 2016 ~ 2019 年度考古新发现" (New Archaeological Discoveries from 2016–2019 at the Royal City Site of Shimao), *Kaogu yu wenwu* 2020.4: m3–12.

Shaanxisheng Kaogu Yanjiusuo, Yulinshi Wenwu Kaogu Kantan Gongzuodui, Shenmushi Shimao 2020b. "陕西神木市石峁遗址皇城台大台基遗迹" (Remains from the Royal Mound at Shimao in Shenmushi, Shaanxi), *Kaogu* 2020.7: 34–4.

Shaanxisheng Kaogu Yanjiusuo, Taiyuanshi Wenwu Guanli Weiyuanhui 陕西省考古研究所, 太原市文物管理委员会, 陶正刚 eds 1996. 太原晋国赵卿墓 (The Qin State Tomb of Jin State Minister Zhao at Taiyuan). Beijing: Wenwu Chubanshe.

Shaanxisheng Wenwuju 陕西省文物局 and Zhonghua Shiji Tan Yishuguan 中华世纪坛艺术馆, eds 2003. 盛世吉金–陕西宝鸡眉县青铜器窖藏 (Millennium Art Museum: The Bronze Cache of Meixian, Baoji, Shaanxi). Beijing: Wenwu Chubanshe.

Shandongsheng Wenwu Kaogu Yanjiusuo 山东文物考古研究所1982. 曲阜鲁国故城 (The Ancient Capital City of the State of Lu at Chufu). Ji'nan: Qilu Shushe.

Shandong Daxue Lishixi Kaogu Zhuanye 山東大學歷史系考古專業 1990. 泗水尹家城 (Yinjiacheng at Sishui). Beijing: Wenwu Chubanshe.

Shandongsheng Wenwu Guanliqu 山东省文物管理曲 and Ji'nanshi Bowuguan 濟南市博物館 1974. 大汶口 (Dawenkou). Beijing: Wenwu Chubanshe.

Shandongsheng Wenwu Kaogu Yanjiusuo 1982. 曲阜鲁国故城 (The Ancient Capital City of the State of Lu at Chufu). Ji'nan: Qilu Shushe.

Shandongsheng Wenwu Kaogu Yanjiusuo 2013. 临淄齐故城 (The Ancient Qi Capital at Linzi). Beijing: Wenwu Chubanshe.

Shandongsheng Wenwu Kaogu Yanjiusuo 2016. 沂水纪王国春秋墓 (The Springs and Autumns Graves of the Kingdom of Ji on the Yi River). Beijing: Wenwu Chubanshe.

Shanxisheng Kaogu Yanjiusuo 山西省考古研究所 1993. 侯马铸铜遗址 (The Bronze Foundry Site at Houma). Beijing: Wenwu Chubanshe.

Shanxisheng Kaogu Yanjiusuo 1994. 上马墓地 (Shangma Cemetery). Beijing: Wenwu Chubanshe.

Shanxisheng Kaogu Yanjiusuo 1996. 太原晋国赵卿墓 (Tomb of the Jin State Minister of the Zhao Family, Taiyuan). Beijing: Wenwu Chubanshe.

Shanxisheng Kaogu Yanjiusuo 2013. "2012 年的陶斯遗址發掘的主要收穫" (Excavation of Important Remains from Taosi Site in 2012), *Zhongguo Shehui Kexueyuan Gudai Wenming Yanjiu Zhongxin Tongxun* 24: 60–63.

Shanxi Kaogu Yanjiusuo 2015. "2013–14年山西省襄樊市陶寺的发掘" (Excavation at Taosi, Xiangfeng, Shanxi in 2013–14), *Zhongguo Shehui Kexueyuan Gudai Wenming Yanjiu Zhongxin Tongxun* 28: 64–6.

Shanxisheng Kaogu Yanjiusuo and Quwoshi Wenwuju 山西省考古研究所, 曲沃市文物局2009. "山西曲沃金侯阳社墓地"(Yangshe Cemetery of the Jin Marquis in Quwo, Shanxi), *Wenwu* 2009.1: 4–14. English translation of the original report in Chinese by Ji Kunzhang 吉琨, Su Yonghe 孙永和, Lü Xiaoming 吕小明 and Tao Xiangming 陶向明in *Chinese Archaeology* 10: 126–35.

Shanxisheng Kaogu Yanjiusuo, Yunchengshi Wenwu Gongzuozhan运城市文物工作站, Jiangxian wenwuju绛县文化局 (Song Jianzhong 宋建忠, Xie Yaoting 谢尧亭, Tian Jianwen 田建文and Ji Kunzhang 吉琨璋)1996. "山西绛县横水西周墓地" (A Western Zhou Cemetery at Hengshui in Jiangxian, Shanxi). *Kaogu* 1996.7: 16–21; English abridged version in *Chinese Archaeology* 7 (2008): 40–46.

Shanxi and Linfen, Shanxisheng Kaogu Yanjiusuo, 山西省考古研究所Zhongguo Kexueyuan Kaogu Yanjiusuo, 中國科學院考古研究所, and Linfen Wenwuju临汾文物局, eds 2004. "从陶寺寨城恢复的陶寺中文化墓" (Tombs of Middle Taosi Culture Recovered from Taosi Walled Town), *Kaogu* 7: 9–24.

Shanxisheng Kaogu Yanjiusuo 山西省考古研究所 eds 2020. 山西绛县横水西周衡水墓地M2158墓的发掘 (The Excavation of Tomb M2158 at the Hengshui Cemetery of the Western Zhou Dynasty in Jiangxian County, Shanxi Province), XXXX, Abridged English summary in *Chinese Archaeology* 20.1 (2020): 97–110.

Shanxisheng Kaogu Yanjiusuo 山西省考古研究所and Quwoxian Wenwuju曲沃县文物, eds. 2009. "山西羊舌晋侯墓地发掘简报 (Brief Report on the Excavation of the Yangshe Cemetery of the Marquises of Jin at Quwo, Shanxi), *Wenwu* 2009.1: 1–14. Abridged English summary in *Chinese Archaeology* 10 (2010): 126–35.

Shanxisheng Kaogu Yanjiusuo and Houma Gongzuozhan 侯马工作站 eds 1996. 晋都新田 (The Jin Capital of Xintian). Taiyuan: Shanxi Renmin Chubanshe.

Shao Wangping 邵望平 1998. "Reconsideration of the Shandong Culture," in Institute of Archaeology, Chinese Academy of Social Sciences, eds, *Archaeological Excavation and Research in New China*, 97–104. Beijing: Kexue Chubanshe.

Shao Wangping 2000. "初期的文明与龙山文化时期" (The Longshan Period and Incipient Chinese Civilization)," *Kaogu* 2.1: 195–226.

Shao Wangping 2013. 邵望平氏學考古學文選 (Selected Writings of Shao Wangping on Archaeology). Jinan: Shandong Daxue Chubanshe.

Shao Wangping and Gao Guangren 高广仁1984. "中华文明的发源地：海岱历史文化区" (A Birthplace of Chinese Civilization: Haidai Historic and Cultural Region), *Shiqian Yanjiu* 1: 7–14.

Shaughnessy, Edward L. 1993. "*Shang shu* 尚書 (*Shu ching* 書經)" in Michael Loewe, ed., *Early Chinese Texts: A Bibliographic Guide,* 376–89. Berkeley: Society for the Study of Early China and The Institute of East Asian Studies.

Shaughnessy, Edward L. 1997. *Before Confucius: Studies in the Creation of the Confucian Classics.* Albany: Suny Press.

Shaughnessy, Edward L. 2006. *Rewriting Early Chinese Texts.* Albany: Suny Press.

Shaughnessy, Edward L. 2009. "Chronologies of Ancient China: A Critique of the 'Xia-Shang-Zhou Chronology Project," in Clara Wing-chung Ho and Patricia Buckley Ebrey, eds., *Windows on the Chinese World: Reflections by Five Historians,* 15–28. Lanham, MD: Lexington Books.

Shaughnessy, Edward L. 2013. "The Zhou Dynasty and the Birth of the Son of Heaven," in Maria Khayutina and Yuri Pines, eds., *Qin: The Eternal Emperor and His Terracotta Warriors.* Bern: Bernisches Historisches Museum.

Shaughnessy, Edward L. 2018 "Of Trees, A Son, and Kingship: Recovering an Ancient Chinese Dream," *Journal of Asian Studies* 77: 593–609.

Shima Kunio 岛邦男 1964, 1970. 殷墟卜辭研究 (Studies on the Bone Inscriptions from Yinxu), translated by Wen Tianhe 溫天河and Li Shoulin 李壽林. Taibei: Dingwen Book Co.

Shirakawa Shizuka 白川靜1962. 金文通釋 (Explanations of Bronze Inscriptions). Kobe: Hakutsuru Museum of Art. 1972/1977. Chinese translation as 甲骨文的世界-古殷王朝的締構 (The World of Jiaguwen—The Structure of the Shang Dynasty). Taipei: Juliu Lushu Gongsi.

Smith, Jonathan and Fan Yuzhou 2020. "Shang Cultural and Historical Setting," in Elizabeth Childs-Johnson ed., *Oxford Handbook of Early China,* 227–52. Oxford and New York: Oxford University Press.

So, Jenny F. 1980. "New Departures in Eastern Zhou Bronze Designs: The Spring and Autumn Period," in Wen Fong, ed., *The Great Bronze Age of China: An Exhibition from The People's Republic of China.* New York: Metropolitan Museum of Art.

So, Jenny F. 1995. *Eastern Zhou Ritual Bronzes from the Arthur M. Sackler Collections.* Washington, DC: Arthur M. Sackler Foundation.

So, Jenny F. 2019. "Jades from Niuheliang: Answers to an Archaeological Problem?" *Zurich Studies in the History of Art* 13/14: 1–25.

Song Guoding 宋国定1993. "1985–92年郑州商城的考古研究概述，郑州商城的新发现和研究 (The Overview of Zhengzhou Shang City's Archaeological Research from 1985 to 1992, New Discoveries and Research of Zhengzhou Shang City). Zhengzhou: Zhongzhou Jingdian Chubanshe

Song, Guoding 2020. "Early and Middle Shang," in Elizabeth Childs-Johnson, ed., *Oxford Handbook of Early China,* 254–86. Oxford and New York: Oxford University Press.

Song Jian 宋健 1996. "马桥遗址" (Maqiao Site Remains), *Kexue Tongbao* 1996.2.

Song Jianzhong 宋建忠 *et al* eds. 2005."彭伯和他的妻子Tombs of Count of Peng and His Wife," in 中國重要考古發現 (Major Archaeological Discoveries in China). Beijing: Wenwu Chubanshe.

Song Lingping 宋玲平 2002. "东周青铜器叙事画像纹地域风格浅析" (A Preliminary Analysis of the Regional Styles of Narrative Pictorial Images on Eastern Zhou Bronzes), *Zhongyuan Wenwu* 2002.2.

Song Lingping 2007 晋系墓葬制度研究 (Studies of the Burial System of Jin Tombs). Beijing: Kexue Chubanshe.

Song Zhenhao 宋镇豪 2005. 夏商社會生活史 (History of Xia and Shang Social Life). 2 vols. Beijing: Zhongguo Shehui Kexue Chubanshe.

Song Zhenhao 宋镇豪 and Xiao Xianjin 肖先进 2003. 殷商文明暨纪念三星堆遗址发现七十周年 (Celebrating Yin Shang Civilization and the 70th Year of Sanxingdui Site Remains). 2 vols. Beijing: Kexue Chubanshe.

Soper, Alexander C. 1990. "On the Chinese Neolithic Jade Tsung/Cong," *Artibus Asiae* 50.1 –2: 5–22.

Stanley, Daniel Jean, Zongyuan Chen and Jian Song 1999. "Inundation, Sea-level Rise and Transition from Neolithic to Bronze Age Cultures, Yangtze Delta, China," *Geoarchaeology* 14.1: 15–26.

Steinke, Kyle and Dora C. Y. Ching, eds 2014. *Art and Archaeology of the Erligang Civilization*. Princeton, NJ: Princeton University Press.

Strassberg, Richard 2002. *A Chinese Bestiary: Strange Creatures from the Guideways Through Mountains and Seas*. Berkeley: University of California Press.

Su Bingqi 苏秉琦 1996. "太湖周围的古代文化, 城市和州"(Ancient Cultures, Cities and States around Taihu Lake), in 东方文明的曙光, 梁祝六十周年纪念文集 (Dawn of Oriental Civilisation, Essays in Commemoration of the 60th Anniversary of the Liangzhu Culture), 159–64. Haikou: Hainan Guoji Xinwen Chuban Zhongxin.

Suizhoushi Bowuguan 隨州市博物館 ed 2008. 隨州擂鼓墩二號墓 (Tomb No. 2 at Leigudun, Suizhou). Beijing: Wenwu Chubanshe.

Sukhu, Gopal 2012. *The Shaman and the Heresiarch: A New Interpretation of the Li sao*. Albany: Suny Press.

Sukhu, Gopal 2017. *The Songs of Chu: An Anthology of Ancient Chinese Poetry* by Qu Yuan and Others. New York: Columbia University Press.

Sun Bo 2007. "从大汶口文化向龙山文化过渡的探讨" (Discussion on the Transition from the Dawenkou Culture to the Longshan Culture), *Gudai Wenming Yanjiu Zhongzin Tongxun* 19: 38–45.

Sun, Bo 2013. "The Longshan Culture of Shandong," in Ann Underhill ed, *A Companion to Chinese Archaeology*, 435–58. New York: John Wiley & Sons.

Sun Qingwei 孙庆伟 2007. "试论曲沃羊舌墓地的归属问题" (A Tentative Discussion of the Attribution Issues of Yangshe Cemetery in Quwo), *Gudai Wenming Yanjiu Tongxun* 33: 33–6.

Sun Qingwei 2012. "祭祀還是盟誓:北趙和羊舌晉侯墓地祭祀坑性質新論" (Tomb Sacrifices or Oaths of Alliance Ceremonies: New Analysis of the Nature of Sacrificial Pits at the Cemetery of the Marquises of Jin at Yangshe and Beizhao), *Zhongguo Bowuguan Tongbao* 106.5.

Sun Yabing 孙亚冰 and Lin Huan 林欢 2006. 商代地理与方国 (Geography and States in the Shang Dynasty). Beijing: Kexue Chubanshe.

Sun, Yan 2003. "Bronzes, Mortuary Practices and Political Strategies during the Zhou Period," *Antiquity* 77: 761–70.

Sun, Yan 2013. "Bronzes, Mortuary Practice and Political Strategies of the Yan during the Early Western Zhou Period," *Asian Archaeology* 1: 52–72.

Sun, Zhixin 1983. "The Liangzhu Culture: Its Discovery and its Jades," *Early China* 18: 1–40.

Sun Zhouyong 孙周勇 2019. "陕西石峁遗址发现30遇见清美石雕" (The Discovery of 30 Exquisite Stone Carvings from Shimao Site in Shaanxi), *Zhongguo Wenwu Bao* 2019.1: 40.

Sun Zhouyong and Shao Jing 邵晶 2017. "石峁城: 图为河畔神秘古城分核桃死亦敌亦友" (Shimao City: Illustration of a Mysterious Ancient City on the Banks of the Yellow River), *Zhongguo Guojia Dili* 2017.10: 142.

Sun Zhouyong and Shao Jing 2020. "石峁遗址皇城台大台基出土石雕研究" (Research on Unearthed Stone Carvings from the Citadel Foundation at the Royal City of Shimao Remains), *Kaogu yu Wenwu* 2020.4: 40–63.

Sun Zhouyong 孙周勇, Shao Jing, and Zhi Nan 邸楠 2020. "石峁遗址的考古发现与研究综述" (Summary of Research and Archaeological Discoveries at Shimao Site), *Zhongyuan Wenwu* 2020.1: 39–62.

Suzhou Bowuguan 苏州博物馆1999. 真山东周墓地--吴楚贵族墓地的发掘与研究 (Eastern Zhou Cemeteries at Zhenshan—the Excavation and Study of Elite Cemeteries of the Wu and Chu States). Beijing: Wenwu Chubanshe.

Taiyuanshi Wenwu Kaogu Yanjiu Suo太原市文物考古研究所 2004. 晋国赵卿墓 (The Tomb of Jin State Minister Zhao). Beijing: Wenwu Chubanshe.

Takashima, Ken-ichi and Jiang Shaoyu, eds. 2004. *Meaning and Form: Essays in Pre-Modern Chinese Grammar*. Munchen: Lincom Europe.

Tan, Danjiong 1986. "The Mao Gong Ding," *The National Palace Museum Monthly of Chinese Art*, 127–36. Taipei: National Palace Museum.

Tang Chung [Deng Zong 登聰] 1994. "香港台湾遗址出土的商雅章初步报告" (Preliminary Report on the Shang *Yazhang* Unearthed at the Tai Wan Site, Hong Kong), *Wenwu* 1994.12. 54–63.

Tang, Chung 2017. "*Yazhang* and an Incipient Stage of the Political World Order of Early China," *Xu Gu Heng Jin –110th Anniversary of the Birth of Professor Cheng Te-k'un*, 30–3. Hong Kong: Centre for Chinese Archaeology and Art, Chinese University of Hong Kong.

Tang Chung 登聰 and Cao Jingyan 曹錦研, eds. 2015. 良渚玉工: 良渚玉器工藝來源論集 (Liangzhu Jades: Essays on Prehistoric Jade Technologies in China). Hong Kong: Centre for Chinese Archaeology and Art.

Tang Chung, Luan Fengshi 欒豐實, and Wang Qiang 王強2014. "东亚最早的牙章-评山东龙山牙章" (Earliest *yazhang* in East Asia – A Discussion of Shandong Longshan *yazhangs*), in東方玉器 (Jades in the East), 51–62. Beijing: Wenwu Chubanshe.

Tang, Chung and Wang Fang 2020. "The Spread of the Erlitou *Yazhang* to South China and the Origin and Dispersal of Early Political States," in Elizabeth Childs-Johnson, ed., *The Oxford Handbook of Early China*, 202–26. New York: Oxford University Press.

Tang Chung, Xu Hong 許紅, and Du Jinpeng 杜金鵬 2007. "二里头文化玉器及相关问题分析" (Analysis of Jade-Working and Related Questions of the Erlitou Culture), *Keji Kaogu* 科技考古2007.2: 120–32.

Tang Lan 唐蘭 1974. "關於江西吳城文化遗址与文字得出不谈说" (Preliminary Discussion of the Words and Remains from Wucheng, Jiangxi), *Wenwu* 1974.7: 72–6.

Tang Lan 1981a. "从大汶口文化的陶器文字看我国最早文化年代" (The Date of Our Country's Earliest Words on Dawenkou Ceramics). *Dawenkou Wenhua Lunwenji* 79–84.

Tang Lan 1981b. "再论大汶口文化的社会性质的大汶口陶器文字" (Again Discussing the Social System of the Dawenkou Culture, and Words on Dawenkou Ceramics), *Dawenkou Wenhua Lunwenji* 90–5.

Tang Lan 1995. "赵孟壶" (Zhao Menghu) in 唐籣先生金文编辑 (The Edited Bronze Inscription Papers of Tang Lan). Beijing: Jincheng Chubanshe.

Teng Mingyu 滕铭予2002. 秦文化:从封国到帝国的考古学观察 (Qin Culture: from Fiefdom to Empire Examined from an Archaeological Perspective). Beijing: Xueyuan Chubanshe.

Thote, Alain 2014. "Zhou Bronze Workshops and the Creative Work of Design and Decoration," *Jao Tsung-I Academy Bulletin* 2014.4: 27–54.

Thumiger, Chiara 2014. "Humans into Animals" in G. L. Campbell, ed., *Oxford Handbook of Animals in Classical Thought and Life*. New York and Oxford: Oxford University Press.

Trigger, Bruce 2006. *History of Archaeological Thought*. Cambridge: Cambridge University Press.

Trümpelman, L., ed 1980. *Reallexikon der Assyriologie und vorderasiatischen Archäology*. Berlin: de Gruyter (quoted and translated in Allsen: 1980–83: 234–38.)

Tsai Che-mao [Cai Zhemao] 1976. 殷禮總考 (Study of Yin Rituals). MA Thesis, Taiwan National University, Taipei.

Tseng, Lillian Lan-ying 2011. *Picturing Heaven in Early China*. Cambridge: Harvard University East Asia Center.

Underhill, Anne P. 1998. *An Analysis of Mortuary Ritual at the Dawenkou Site, Shandong, China*. New Haven, CT: Human Relations Area Files.

Underhill, Anne P. 2002. *Craft Production and Social Change in Northern China*. New York: Springer.

Underhill, Anne P. ed 2013. *A Companion to Chinese Archaeology*. New York: John Wiley & Sons.

Underhill, Anne P. *et al*, 2019. "Mortuary Ritual and Social Identities During the Late Dawenkou Period in China," *Antiquity* 93.368: 378–92.

University Art Museum and Art Gallery, Chinese University of Hong Kong 2018. *Animal Magic: Ancient Art from Jingzhou, Hubei Province*. Hong Kong: University Art Museum and Art Gallery.

Van Auken, Newell Ann 2011. "Who is a *ren*人? The Use of *ren* in *Spring and Autumn* Records and Its Interpretation in the *Zuo, Gongyang*, and *Gulang* Commentaries," *Journal of the American Oriental Society* 131.4: 555–90.

Valmisa, Mercedes 2013. "Formulaicity in Western Zhou Bronze Inscriptions," unpublished paper, 29 pages, Princeton University. https://www.academia.edu/11486919/ Formulaicity_in_Western_Zhou_Bronze_Inscriptions

Wang, Aihe 2000. *Cosmology and Early Political Culture in China*. New York: Cambridge University Press.

Wang Changfeng 王长丰 2015. 殷周金文族徽研究 (Research on the Clan Emblems in Bronze Inscriptions of the Shang and Zhou Dynasties), 2 vols. Shanghai: Shanghai Guji Chubanshe.

Wang, Fangkui 2004. "Cemetery Dig Yields Clues to Western Zhou," *China Daily*, May 28.

Wang, Haicheng 2015. *Writing and the Ancient State: Early China in Comparative Perspective*. New York: Cambridge University Press.

Wang Qiang 王强 2008. "试论史前玉石器镶嵌工艺" (Discussion on Prehistoric Jade Inlay Techniques), *Nanfang Wenwu* 2008.3: 85–91.

Wang Qing 王青ed. 2000. 西朱封 龙山文化大墓神徽饰纹的复原研究 (Research on the Reconstruction of the Deity Decoration Found in a Tomb of the Longshan

Culture at Xizhufeng, in山东大学考古学系, ed., 敦愿先生纪念文集 (Essays in Memory of Liu Dunyuan) 171–81. Ji'nan: Shandong daxue chubanshe.

Wang Qing 2002. 海岱地区周代墓葬研究 (Studies on Zhou Dynasty Tombs in the Haidai Region in Shandong). Jinan: Shandong Daxue Chubanshe.

Wang Qing 2004. "镶嵌铜牌饰的初步研究" (Basic Study of Inlaid Bronze Plaques"), *Wenwu* 2004. 5: 65–72.

Wang Qing 2005. "神秘的夏代遗宝: 镶嵌铜牌饰" (Mysterious Treasure from the Xia Dynasty: Inlaid Bronze Plaques), *Xungen* 寻根 02 (2005): 84–88.

Wang Qing 2007. "纽约新见两镶嵌铜 牌饰辩伪" (On the Authenticity of Two Inlaid Bronze Plaques Newly Seen in New York). *Zhongguo wenwubao* 中国文物报 February 16 (2007).

Wang Qing 2012. "镶嵌铜牌饰的寓意诸问题再研究" (A Second Study on the Implied Meaning of Inlaid Bronze Plaques), *Dongfang kaogu* 2012.9: 224.

Wang Renxiang 王仁湘 *et al*, eds. 1980. 楚皇城考古发掘. "湖北宜城楚皇城勘察简报 1" (A Brief Report on the Survey of the Chu Royal City in Yicheng, Hubei Province), *Kaogu* 1980.2: 108–113, 134, 195.

Wang Shimin 王世民, Chen Gongrou 陈公柔, and Zhang Changshou 張長壽 1999. 西周青銅器分期斷代研究 (Research on the Periodization of Western Zhou Bronzes). Beijing: Wenwu Chubanshe.

Wang Shougong 王收功 1998. "景阳冈城址刻纹陶片发现的意义" (The Significance of the Engraved Designs on Ceramics from the City Remains at Jingyanggang,) *Zhongguo Wenwu Bao* 1998.1: 14.

Wang Shuming 王书明1987. "林洋河墓地初一" (Preliminary Study of the Cemetery at Linyang), *Yenching Journal of Chinese Studies* 49–58.

Wang, Wenjing 2011. "Lingjiatan Social Organization in the Yuxi Valley, China: A Comparative Perspective." B.A thesis, Jilin University.

Wang, Yuxin 1985–87. "Once Again on the New Period of Western Zhou Oracle-Bone Research: With a Brief Description of the Zhouyuan Sacrifice Inscriptions," *Early China* 11/12 (1985–87): 164–72.

Wang Yuxin 王宇信2003. 今年殷墟甲骨文发现一百周年国际学术研讨会论文集 (Proceedings of the International Symposium on the 100th Anniversary of the Discovery of Bone Inscriptions at Yinxu). Beijing: Shehui Kexue Wenxian Chubanshe.

Wang Yuxin and Song Zhenhao 宋镇豪 1979. "试论殷墟妇好墓的年代" (Discussion of the Date of the Fu Hao Burial at Yinxu). *Z,engzhou Daxue Xuebao* 1979.2: 49.

Wang Yuxin, Zhang Yongshan 张永山, and Yang Shengnan宋镇豪 1977. "试论殷墟妇好[子]墓" (Discussion of the Fu Hao [Zi] Burial at Yinxu), *Kaogu Xuebao* 1977.2: 1–22.

Wang Zhenzhong 王震中 1994. 中国文明起源的比较研究 (Comparative Research on the Origins of Chinese Civilization). Xian: Shaanxi Renmin Chubanshe.

Wang, Zhenzhong 2018. "The Emergence of Kingship in China: With a Discussion of the Relationship Between Kingship and Composite State Structure in the Xia, Shang, and Western Zhou Dynasties," *Social Sciences in China* 39.2: 5–21.

Wu, Hung 2015. "The Invisible Miniature: Framing the Soul in Chinese Art and Architecture." *Art History*. https://doi.org/10.1111/1467-8365.12150.

Wu, Hung 2016. "Rethinking Meaning in Early Chinese Art: Animal, Ancestor, and Man," *Critical Inquiry* 43: 139–90.

Wu, Li 2014. "Holocene Environmental Change and its Impacts on Human Settlement in the Shanghai Area, East China," *Catena*. 114: 78–89.

Wu, Qinglong *et al*, 2016. "Outburst Flood at 1920 BCE Supports Historicity of China's Great Flood and the Xia Dynasty," *Science* 353: 558 and 579–80.

Wu, Xiaolong 2017. *Material Culture, Power, and Identity in Ancient China*. Cambridge: Cambridge University Press.

Wu, Xiaolong 2020. "Cultures and Styles of Art during the Springs and Autumns Period" in Elizabeth Childs-Johnson, ed., *The Oxford Handbook of Early China*, 530–82. Oxford: Oxford University Press.

Wu Zhenfeng 吴镇烽 1996. "歧周宗周和成周地区青铜器概论 (Discussion of Bronzes from Cheng Zhou Area and Zhoucong") in *Zhongguo Qingtongqi Quanji*, 1–28. Beijing: Wenwu Chubanshe.

Wu Zhenfeng 2012. 商周青銅器銘文暨圖像集成 (Shang and Zhou Bronze Images and Inscriptions). 35 vols. Shanghai: Guji Chubanshe.

Xia Shang Zhou Duandai Gongcheng Zhuanjiazu 夏商周斷代工程專家組 eds. 2000. 夏商周斷代工程1996/2000年階段成果報告:簡本 (A Simplified Version of the Report of the Results of the 1996/2000 Analysis of the Xia, Shang and Zhou Dynasties Project). Beijing: Shijie Tushu Chubanshe.

Xie, Zhidong *et al*, 2008. "New Evidence for an Impact Origin of Taihu Lake, China: Possible Trigger of the Extinction of Liangzhu Culture 4500 Years ago," https://www.researchgate.net/ publication/253443406.

Xing, Wen 2000. "The Guodian Chu Slips: The Paleographical Issues and Their Significances," *Contemporary Chinese Thought* 32.1.

Xinzheng Zheng Gong Da Mu Qingtongqi Weibianji Weiyuanhui, eds 1997. 新郑郑公大墓青铜器 (Bronzes from the Prince Zheng Tomb). Taibeishi: Bowuguan.

Xu Fengxian 徐风先 2006. 商末周基基斯普合历研究 (A Study of the Late Shang Sacrificial Rostrum). Beijing, Shanghai: Shijie Tushu Chubanshe.

Xu Hong 許宏 2000. 先秦城市考古學 (Studies on Pre-Qin Cities). Beijing: Yanshan Chubanshe.

Xu Hong 2004. 何以中国公元前2000年的中原图景 (What is China ca. 2000 BCE?). Beijing: Sanlian Shuju.

Xu Hong 2009. 最早的中國 (Earliest China). Beijing: Kexue Chubanshe.

Xu Hong 2013. 大都无城—论中国古代都城的早期形态 ("The Largest Cities Are Not Fortified: Discussing the Earliest Phase of Ancient China's Capital Cities"). *Wenwu*, 2013.10: 61–71.

Xu, Hong 2020. "Introduction to the Erlitou Culture: Definitions, Themes, and Debate" in Elizabeth Childs-Johnson, ed., *Oxford Handbook of Early China*, 161–75. Oxford: Oxford University Press.

Xu Hong, Zhao Haitao赵海涛and Li Zhipeng李志鹏2007. "二里头遗址出土的大型绿松石龙形神器" (A Large Turquoise Dragon-form Artifact Discovered at the Erlitou Site), *Kaogu* 2007.5 15–20, English translation in *Chinese Archaeology* 13 (2013).

Xu, Hong and Li Xiang 2020. "Settlements, Buildings, and Society of the Erlitou Culture," in Elizabeth Childs-Johnson, ed., *Oxford Handbook of Early China*, 176–89. New York : Oxford University Press.

Xu, Hong and Liu Yu 2020. "The Bronze Casting Revolution and the Ritual Vessel Set," in Elizabeth Childs-Johnson, ed, *Oxford Handbook of Early China*, 191–202. Oxford: Oxford University Press.

Xu Huping 徐湖平 ed 1997. 東方文明 (Eastern Civilization). Nanjing: Nanjing Bowuyuan.

Xu, Jay 1996. "The Cemetery of the Western Lords of Jin," *Artibus Asiae* 56.3/4: 193–231.

Xu Shaohua徐少华, Taniguchi Mitsuru 谷口满, and Luo Tai 羅泰 (Lothar von Falkenhausen), eds 2021. 楚文化與長江中游早期開發國際學術研討會論文集(Research Papers from the International Symposiumon Chu Culture and the Beginning of Early Period of the Yangzi River Valley). Wuhan: Wuhan Daxue Chubanshe,

Xu Xitai 1987. 周原甲骨文綜述 (A Comprehensive Study of Oracle Bone Writing from the Zhouyuan Region). Xi'an: Sanmin Chubanshe.

Xu Xitai 徐錫臺 and Jin 金 2005. "西周纵轴和成周地区青铜器概论 (An Introduction to the Bronze Wares of the Western Zhou Longitudinal and Chengzhou Areas,") *Wenwu*.

Xu Xusheng 徐旭生 1959. "1959 年夏豫西调查夏墟"的初步报告" (Preliminary Report on the 1959 Survey of the "Xia Ruins" in Western Henan), *Kaogu* 1959.11: 592–600.

Yan Wenming 严文明 2003. "稻作农业的起源与小鲁里稻谷" (The Origin of Rice Agriculture and Xiaoluli Rice), *Nongye Kaogu* 2003.3: 73–9.

Yan Wenming and Yasuda Yoshinori 安田喜宪 eds 2000. 作水稻农业陶器和都市的起源 (On the Origins of Rice Agriculture, Pottery and Cities). Beijing: Wenwu Chubanshe.

Yan Zhibin 嚴志斌 2013. 商代青铜器铭文研究 (Study of the Bronze Inscriptions of the Shang Dynasty). Shanghai: Shanghai Shiji Chubanshe and Shanghai Guji Chubanshe.

Yang Hu 楊虎, Liu Guoxiang 劉國祥and Tang Chung 登聰 2007. 玉器來源探索 (The Origin of Jades in East Asia: Jades of the Xinglongwa Culture). Hong Kong: Centre for Chinese Archaeology and Art.

Yang Kuan 杨寬1985. 中國古代陵寢制度史研究 (Studies of the Sumptuary Regulations of Ancient Chinese Royal Tombs). Shanghai: Shanghai Guji Chubanshe.

Yang Kuan1993. 中國古代都城制度史研究 (Studies of the History of Sumptuary Regulations in China's Ancient Capital Cities). Shanghai: Shanghai Guji Chubanshe.

Yang Hu, Liu Guoxiang, and Tang Chung, eds 2006. 玉器起源探索 (The Origins of Chinese Jade Culture), in 興隆洼玉器研究與圖錄 (Xinglongwa Jades Research and Catalogue). Hong Kong: Chinese University of Hong Kong Press.

Yang Shengnan 杨升南1992. 商代經濟史 (An Economic History of the Shang Era). Guizhou: Guizhou Renmin Chubanshe.

Yao Xiaosui 姚孝遂 and Xiao Ding 肖丁, eds. 1988. 殷墟甲骨文可辭摹釋總集 (The Complete Series of Rubbings and Transcriptions of Yinxu Oracle Bone Inscriptions). 3 vols. Beijing: Zhonghua Shudian.

Yi Hua 易华 2015. 齐家华夏说 (Talking about Qijia as Huaxia culture). Lanzhou: Gansu Renmin Chubanshe.

Yi Hua 2016. "齐家华夏说" (Explanation of the Qijia Huaxia), 光明日报 *Guangming Ribao* February 2, 2016: 11.

Yin Qun 印群 2001. 黃河中下游地區的東周墓葬制度 (Eastern Zhou Sumptuary Regulations for Tombs in the Middle and Lower Yellow River Region). Beijing: Shehui Kexue Chubanshe.

Yin Zhiyi 殷之彝1977. "山东益都蘇埠屯墓地和亞醜銅器" (The Yidu Sufutun Burial in Shandong and the Ya Chou Inscribed Bronzes), *Kaogu xuebao* 1997.2: 23–34.

Yu, Jiang 2004. "Ritual Practice, Status and Gender Identity: Western Zhou Tombs at Baoji" in Kathryn M. Linduff and Yan Sun, eds., *Gender and Chinese Archaeology*, 117–36.

Yu Weichao 俞伟超1985. 先秦两汉考古学论文集 (Collected Essays on Pre-Qin and Han Archaeology). Beijing: Wenwu Chubanshe.

Yu Weichao 1999. "神面卣上的人格化'天帝 "The Anthropomorphized 'Tian Di' on the Spirit Faced *You*), 349–52. Beijing: Baoli Bowuguan.

Yu Weichao and Gao Ming 高明 1978–79. "周代用鼎制度研究" (Sumptuary Regulations Concerning the Use of *ding* Vessels During the Zhou Dynasty), *Beijing Daxue Xuebao* 北京大學學報 1978.1: 84–98; 1978.2: 84–97; 1979.1: 83–96.

Zhang Changping 张昌平 2009. 曾国青铜器研究 (Studies on the Bronzes of the State of Zeng). 北京大學 震旦古代文明研究中心學術叢書 (Compilation of Studies from the Peking University Center for Research in Ancient Culture), vol. 18. Beijing: Wenwu Chubanshe.

Zhang Changshou and Yin Weizhang, eds. 2004. 商周考古學: 兩周卷 (Shang and Zhou Archaeology: [Western and Eastern] Zhou Volume). Beijing: Kexue Chubanshe.

Zhang, Chi and Hsiao-chun Hung 2008. "The Neolithic of Southern China – Origins, Development, and Dispersal," *Asian Perspectives* 47.2: 299–329. APv47n2299329.pdf

Zhang Guangli 张广立 1983. "东周青铜器刻纹" (Engraved Images on Eastern Zhou Bronzes), *Kaogu yu Wenwu* 1983.1.

Zhang, Guangyu 1999. 东周青铜器刻纹 (A Study of the Chu Bamboo Manuscripts of Guodian). Taipei: Yee Wen Publishing.

Zhang, Hai, Andrew Bevan and Dashun Guo 2013. "The Neolithic Ceremonial Complex at Niuheliang and Wider Hongshan Landscapes in Northeastern China," *Journal of World Prehistory* 26.1: 1–24.

Zhang Jingguo 张敬国 and Anhuisheng Wenwu Kaogu Yanjiusuo 安徽省文物考古研究所 2008. "安徽省马鞍山市含山县凌家滩第五次发掘新发现" (New Discoveries in the Fifth Excavation of the Lingjiatan Site in Ma'an City, Hanshan County, Anhui), *Kaogu* 2008.3: 7–17. English summary in *Chinese Archaeology* 9: 63–73.

Zhang, Liangju 2002. "A Study on the Composition and Properties of Xiuyan Jade in Liaoning Province," *Acta Mineralogica Sinica* 2002.2.

Zhang Tian'en 张天恩 2002. "天水出土的 兽面铜牌及有关问题" (Bronze Plaque with Animal Mask Unearthed at Tianshui and Its Relevant Questions), *Zhongyuan Wenwu* 2002.1: 43–6.

Zhang Weilian 张渭莲 2008. 商文明的形成 (The Layout of Shang Civilization). Beijing: Wenwu Chubanshe.

Zhang Xuehai 张学海 ed 1989. 海帶考古 (The Archaeology of the Haidai Region). Jinan: Shandong Daxue Chubanshe.

Zhang Yongshan 张永山 2001. "利簋'歲鼎'克闻補正" (The Li gui and the sui ding Inscription), *Qinghua Daxue Xuebao* 16.4: 42–4.

Zhang, X *et al*, 2015. "Radiocarbon Dating of Charcoal from the Bianjiashan Site in Hangzhou: New Evidence for the Lower Age Limit of the Liangzhu Culture," *Quaternary Geochronology* 30(A): 9–17. https://doi.org/10.1016/j.quageo.2015.07.001)

Zhang Zhongpei 1999. "New Understandings of Chinese Prehistory," in Yang Xiaoneng, ed. *The Golden Age of Chinese Archaeology*. New Haven, Connecticut: Yale University Press, 519-25.

...Zhang Zhongpei 张忠培 with J. Xu, and J. Qin 1999. 中国文物地图集: 陕西 (Collection of Archaeological Site Maps of China: Shaanxi). Xi'an: Ditu Chubanshe.

Zhang Zhichao 张智超 2010. "新石器时代至二里头文化时期镶嵌装饰与设计系统之发展" (The Development of the Inlay Design System from the Neolithic Age to the Erlitou Culture Period). Master's Thesis, Tainan National University of the Arts.

Zhao Boxiong 趙伯雄 2004. 春秋學史 (A History of Springs and Autumns Studies). Ji'nan: Shandong Jiaoyu Chubanshe.

Zhao, Chaoqing 2013. "The Longshan Culture in Central Henan Culture Province, c. 2600–1900 BC" in Anne P. Underhill, ed, *A Companion to Chinese Archaeology*, 236–54. New York: John Wiley & Sons.

Zhao Chunqing 赵春青 2009. "新砦聚落考古的实践与方法." (Practice and Methods of Settlement Archaeology at Xinzhai.) *Kaogu* 2009.2.

Zhao Ye 赵晔 2001. "1992–1993年余杭磨角山遗址" (The Mojiaoshan Site in Yuhang in 1992–1993), *Wenwu* 2001.12: 4-1, English translation in *Chinese Archaeology* 11 (2001): 104–09.

Zhao Zhiquan 赵芝荃 1991. 赵芝荃考古文集 (Collected Archaeological Papers of Zhao Zhiquan). Beijing: Kexue Chubanshe.

Zhejiang 2001. Zhejiangsheng Wenwu Kaogu Yanjiusuo 浙江省文物考古研究所 "余杭县莫角山遗址" (Yuhangxian Mojiaoshan Site Remains). *Wenwu* 2001.12: 4–19.

Zhejiang 2003a. 河姆渡 (Hemudu), 2 vols. Beijing: Wenwu Chubanshe.

Zhejiang 2003b. 瑶山 (Yaoshan). Beijing: Wenwu Chubanshe.

Zhejiang 2005. 反山 (Fanshan), 2 vols. Beijing: Wenwu Chubanshe.

Zhejiang 2016. "杭州市良渚古城周边水利控制系统概况" (Survey of the Water Control System on the Periphery of the Liangzhu Ancient City in Hangzhou), *Kaogu* 16: 106–18.

Zheng Guang 郑光1995。二里头陶器集粹 (Gems of Erlitou Ceramics). Beijing: Kexue Chubanshe.

Zhongguo 1959. Zhongguo Shehui Kexueyuan Kaogu Yanjiusuo 中国社会科学院考古洛阳发掘报告--1955–1960 洛阳涧滨考古发掘资料 (Report on the Excavations at Luoyang—Documents on the Archaeological Excavations at Jianbin, Luoyang, 1955–1960). Beijing: Yanshan Chubanshe.

Zhongguo 1994. Zhongguo Shehui Kexueyuan Kaogu Yanjiusuo 殷墟的發現與研究 (Discoveries and Research at Yin). Beijing: Kexue Chubanshe.

Zhongguo 1995. Zhongguo Shehui Kexueyuan Kaogu Yanjiusuo二里頭陶器集粹 (Cream of the Pottery from Erlitou). Beijing: Kexue Chubanshe.

Zhongguo 1998. Zhongguo Shehui Kexueyuan Kaogu Yanjiusuo大甸子--夏家店下层文化遗址与墓地发掘报告 (Dadianzi, Excavations on the Residence and Cemetery of the Lower Xiajiadian Culture). Beijing: Wenwu Chubanshe.

Zhongguo 1999a. Zhongguo Shehui Kexueyuan Kaogu Yanjiusuo 张家坡西周墓地 (The Western Zhou Cemetery at Zhangjiapo). Beijing: Zhongguo Dabaike Quanshu Chubanshe.

Zhongguo 1999b. Zhongguo Shehui Kexueyuan Kaogu Yanjiusuo and Zhongguo Shehui Kexueyuan Jiaguxue Yin Shang Shi Yanjiu Zhongxin 中国社会科学院甲骨学殷商史研究中心 ed. 胡厚宣先生紀年文集 (Collected Essays in Memory of Mr. Hu Houxuan). Beijing: Kexue Chubanshe.

Zhongguo 2001a. Zhongguo Shehui Kexueyuan Kaogu Yanjiusuo 金文集成釋文 (Transcribed Texts of Collected Shang and Zhou Bronze Inscriptions), 6 vols. Hong Kong: Xianggang Zhongwen Daxue Yanjiusuo.

Zhongguo 2001b. Zhongguo Shehui Kexueyuan Kaogu Yanjiusuo "天馬曲村遗址北趙晉侯墓地第六次發掘" (The 6th Excavation of Remains of the Jin Hou Tomb at Beizhao, Chucun Tianma), *Wenwu* 2001.8: 4–21.

Zhongguo 2002. Zhongguo Shehui Kexueyuan Kaogu Yanjiusuo 安陽小屯 (Xiaotun, Anyang). Beijing: Shijie Tushu Chuban Gongshe.

Zhongguo 2003a. Zhongguo Shehui Kexueyuan Kaogu Yanjiusuo 中國考古學夏商卷 (Chinese Archaeology: Xia and Shang Volumes). Beijing: Kexue Chubanshe.

Zhongguo 2003b. Zhongguo Shehui Kexueyuan Kaogu Yanjiusuo 中國考古: 夏 (Chinese Archeology: Xia). Beijing: Kexue Chubanshe.

Zhongguo 2004a. Zhongguo Shehui Kexueyuan Kaogu Yanjiusuo 殷墟婦好婦子墓 (The Tomb of Lady Fu Hao [Fu zi] at Yin). Beijing: Wenwu Chubanshe.

Zhongguo 2004b. Zhongguo Shehui Kexueyuan Kaogu Yanjiusuo 中国考古学: 两周卷 (Chinese Archaeology – Western Zhou and Eastern Zhou). Beijing: Kexue Chubanshe.

Zhongguo 2004c. Zhongguo Shehui Kexueyuan Kaogu Yanjiusuo 陕西竹园沟 (Zhuyuangou, Shaanxi) Beijing:Kexue Chubanshe.

Zhongguo 2014. Zhongguo Shehui Kexueyuan Kaogu Yanjiusuo 全国十大考古新发现评选活动办公室. (All-China Top Ten Archaeological Discoveries Chosen by Popular Acclaim, 2014). Beijing: China Culture.org.

Zhongguo 2017. Zhongguo Shehui Kexueyuan Kaogu Yanjiusuo "山东沂水纪王崮春秋墓葬" (The Tomb of the Spring and Autumn Period at Jiwanggu, Yishui, Shandong).

Zhongguo Qingtongqi 1996. Zhongguo Qingtongqi Quanji Bianji Weiyuanhui 中国青铜器全集编辑委员会, ed. 中國青銅器全集 (Complete Collection of Chinese Bronzes) vols. 1–6 (vol. 1 Xia-Shang; vols. 2–3 Shang; vols. 4–6 Western Zhou). Beijing: Wenwu Chubanshe.

Zhou, Nanquan 2005. *Chinese Jades of the Hongshan Culture, ca. 4700–2920 BCE.* New York: Throckmorton Fine Art.

Zhou, Ying 2007. *The Dawn of the Oriental Civilization: Liangzhu Site and Liangzhu Culture.* Beijing: China Intercontinental Press.

Zhou, Ying 2018. "How to Live a Good Life and Afterlife: Conceptions Of Post-Mortem Existence And Practices of Self-Cultivation in Early China." Ph.D. dissertation, University of Pennsylvania.

Zhouyuan Kaogudui 周原考古队 2002. "陕西扶风县云塘, 齐镇西周建 筑基址 1999–2000 年发掘简报" (Excavation of Western Zhou Building Foundations at Yuntang and Qizhen in Fufeng County, Shaanxi, in 1999–2000), *Kaogu* 2002.9: 3–26.

Zhu Fenghan 朱峰焊 2004. 商周家族形态研究 (Research on the structure of Shang and Zhou Clans). Tianjin: Tianjin Guji Chubanshe.

Zhu Xinyu 朱新予1992. 中國絲綢史 (History of Chinese Sericulture). Beijing: Fangzhi Gongye Chubanshe.

Zhu Zhao 朱超 *et al*, eds 2019. "济南市章丘区城子崖遗址2013～2015 年发掘简报" (Simplified Report on the 2013–2015 Excavation Discoveries at the Ruins of Chengziyai in Zhangqiu District, Jinan City), *Kaogu* 2019.4: 3.

Zou Heng 邹衡 1998. 夏商周考古學論文集 (Collected Essays on Xia, Shang, and Zhou Archaeology), 2 vols. Beijing: Wenwu Chubanshe.

Index